Fe

lix Dupanloup

The Papal Sovereignty

Viewed in its relations to the Catholic Religion and to the law of Europe

Fe

lix Dupanloup

The Papal Sovereignty
Viewed in its relations to the Catholic Religion and to the law of Europe

ISBN/EAN: 9783742860200

Manufactured in Europe, USA, Canada, Australia, Japa

Cover: Foto ©Lupo / pixelio.de

Manufactured and distributed by brebook publishing software (www.brebook.com)

Felix Dupanloup

The Papal Sovereignty

THE
PAPAL SOVEREIGNTY:

VIEWED IN ITS RELATIONS TO

THE CATHOLIC RELIGION,

AND TO THE

LAW OF EUROPE.

Translated

FROM THE FRENCH OF Mgr. DUPANLOUP,

Bishop of Orleans,

MEMBER OF THE FRENCH ACADEMY.

LONDON:

Catholic Publishing & Bookselling Company, Limited,

CHARLES DOLMAN, MANAGER,

61, NEW BOND STREET, & 21, PATERNOSTER ROW;
DUBLIN: J. MULLANY, 1, PARLIAMENT STREET.

1860.

CONTENTS.

INTRODUCTION ix

CHAPTER I.
THE FISHERMAN OF GALILEE 1

CHAPTER II.
THE PRESENT STATE OF THE QUESTION 15

CHAPTER III.
REASONS OF GOD'S DESIGNS IN ESTABLISHING THE TEMPORAL SOVEREIGNTY OF THE HOLY SEE.—THE POPE MUST BE INDEPENDENT OF FOREIGN POWERS 28

CHAPTER IV.
THE POPE SHOULD BE INDEPENDENT WITHIN HIS OWN STATES 42

CHAPTER V.
ORIGIN AND PROVIDENTIAL PREPARATION OF THE TEMPORAL POWER OF THE HOLY SEE 57

CHAPTER VI.
FINAL AND PROVIDENTIAL ESTABLISHMENT OF THE TEMPORAL SOVEREIGNTY OF THE HOLY SEE 73

CHAPTER VII.
GENERAL VIEW OF THE HISTORY OF THE TEMPORAL POWER 98

CHAPTER VIII.
ROME WITHOUT THE POPE 108

CHAPTER IX.
ITALY WITHOUT THE PAPACY 124

CHAPTER X.
EUROPE WITHOUT THE PAPACY 136

CHAPTER XI.
FRANCE AND THE HOLY SEE IN 1849 151

CHAPTER XII.
FRANCE AND THE HOLY SEE IN 1849.—SPEECH OF M. DE FALLOUX 159

CHAPTER XIII.
FRANCE AND THE HOLY SEE IN 1849.—M. THIERS' REPORT 167

CHAPTER XIV.
FRANCE AND THE HOLY SEE IN 1849.— SPEECH OF M. DE MONTALEMBERT... 181

CHAPTER XV.
FRANCE; 1849—1859. — WHY IS THERE STILL A ROMAN QUESTION?.. 200

CHAPTER XVI.
PIEDMONT.—FIRST PERIOD: HOSTILITY TO THE HOLY SEE—LAWS AGAINST THE CHURCH—RELIGIOUS PERSECUTION 208

CHAPTER XVII.
PIEDMONT.—SECOND PERIOD: CONGRESS OF 1850—MEMORANDUM OF COUNT CAVOUR, AND ITS CONSEQUENCES 231

CHAPTER XVIII.
PIEDMONT.—THIRD PERIOD: REVOLUTIONARY VIOLENCE...... 251

CHAPTER XIX.
ENGLAND.—MALEVOLENT PREJUDICES 281

CHAPTER XX.
ENGLAND.—HER BLINDNESS AND INJUSTICE 293

CHAPTER XXI.
ENGLAND.—RELIGIOUS PACIFICATION 324

CHAPTER XXII.
THE DISMEMBERMENT.—THE THEORY OF SPOLIATION......... 339

CHAPTER XXIII.
THE DISMEMBERMENT.—THE THEORY OF SPOLIATION—CONTINUATION OF THE SUBJECT 360

CHAPTER XXIV.

THE DISMEMBERMENT.—THE RELIGIOUS QUESTION 369

CHAPTER XXV.

THE DISMEMBERMENT.—THE EUROPEAN QUESTION 391

CHAPTER XXVI.

THE REFORMS DEMANDED FROM THE PAPAL GOVERNMENT. ARE THOSE SINCERE WHO DEMAND THEM? 416

CHAPTER XXVII.

THE REFORMS DEMANDED FROM THE PAPAL GOVERNMENT... 425

CHAPTER XXVIII.

THE REFORMS DEMANDED FROM THE PAPAL GOVERNMENT, CONTINUED.—LIBERAL GOVERNMENT 436

CHAPTER XXIX.

THE REFORMS DEMANDED FROM THE PAPAL GOVERNMENT.— THE QUESTION OF RIGHT................................... 455

INTRODUCTION.

Since the memorable day when Pope Pius IX. inaugurated his reign by setting an example of reform to the different princes of the Italian peninsula, the temporal sovereignty of that great and holy Pontiff has been twice attacked. In 1849, at Rome, by Romans and foreigners: in 1859, in the Romagna, by Piedmont.

In 1849, the government of the French republic interfered, and the French arms soon reinstated at Rome the august head of Catholicity. In undertaking this generous intervention, the French government was actuated by motives both of gratitude and of policy. Their gratitude was due to the Pontiff, whose just and immense popularity had so largely contributed to stamp a peaceful character upon the startling events of 1848, and to secure a respect but rarely displayed in revolutions, for all that was honorable and sacred. The line of policy, too, pursued by the great statesmen who then governed France, was fundamentally opposed to a dispossession, which, had it been allowed to truimph, would have established an iniquitous precedent, and endangered the liberty of conscience of all Catholics, as well as the peace of Europe. The prince president of the French republic himself declared that "the maintenance of the temporal sovereignty of the supreme head of the Church was intimately connected with the liberty and independence of Italy."

The Catholics showed themselves neither indifferent nor ungrateful; their votes testified, by millions, their approbation of this spirited policy, and, during the last ten years, the emperor, who has continued our respectful protection at Rome, has had reason to admit that the gratitude of our hearts is not unworthy of the favours we receive.

As the incessant machinations of the Italian revolution obliged France, contrary to her intention, to prolong her occupation, so, for the same reason, the Pope, though he effected extensive administrative reforms, had to adjourn some of the political changes he had inaugurated. Some may have considered our stay, as well as his scruples, too long continued: that there was at least some reason for them, no one has denied.

Such was the conduct of the government and the French Catholics, in 1849 and the succeeding years.

In 1859, when the Roman states were again threatened, not this time by their subjects, but by a neighbouring power, the French government decided not to interfere, except with its advice, which Piedmont, though under deep obligations to its ally, disregarded. It is not for me to examine or criticise here the motives which suggested such a course; but the Catholics were not blind to the peril of these attacks, less menacing at first, it is true, but really far more formidable, and maintained in 1859 the same sentiments and the same attitude which they adopted in 1849. They felt that the more pressing the danger, the more resolute should be their resistance; that the call upon their loyalty was more imperative, in proportion to the indifference shown in other quarters. Such were the sentiments of the great majority of the Catholics.

The flagrant violations of right and justice which characterized the earlier events of the Italian convulsion, at first, were not positively alarming. Honesty and good faith, indeed, could not see without indignation, a neutral, Italian, and pacific sovereign held up as the agent of the Austrians, his neutrality violated, and the war carried into his states; and a nefarious ambition masking its designs against him under the great name and cause of Italian independence,—the cause which he had so faithfully and sincerely served.

But, in the sequel, the religious faith and the dearest rights of Catholics became involved. They saw that the hostilities against the Prince must soon take the shape of attacks upon the Pontiff. When a portion of the states of the Church were invaded in the name of principles which implicated all that remained, when these principles were built up into a theory in significant publications,—publications immediately adopted as their programme by the declared enemies of the Papacy as an institution, in Italy, France, and throughout Europe—all uncertainty vanished, and to keep silence would have been to consent.

The Catholics spoke out: and I myself, a bishop, felt it my duty to protest. In so doing, I was not serving my interests, or my tranquillity: or to speak more correctly, I was securing the interests and the tranquillity of my conscience. I was certainly not consulting my taste. My taste would have been not to break my peace, that laborious peace which is the life of every bishop in his diocese.

Nor did I at first lend more than a partial attention to the rumours of the assaults which menaced the Holy See. Such was my love for peace and calmness, and so laborious my duties, that I turned with reluctance to mark the symptoms which foreboded a coming storm, though so ominous and unequivocal that they forced themselves upon my view. Not that I have ever shrunk from discussion, whether before public opinion, which sooner or later yields to truth, or even before the laws of my country, whose decision I have not shunned. Such conflicts, though tinged with bitterness, serve a great cause more effectually than silence and apathy: they feed and trim those lamps, which, as good servants, we should keep always burning. By fighting, though without success, we at least save our honour; by desertion, all is lost, and honour more surely than the rest.

Still, I did not think myself called upon to speak till roused at last by a crowning piece of audacity on the part of the enemies of the Church. My conscience would not be silenced. The words, *Tu es Petrus, et super hanc Petram ædificabo Ecclesiam meam*, again and again rose up before me. I saw but too clearly, that the peril was not subsiding, but becoming imminent. I felt that I must of necessity take my part in the toil, the turmoil, the conflict. Silence was treason. Such peace would be of the nature of that which elicited the divine malediction—*Pax et non est pax*. And then it was that I protested.

It was a consolation to me that I was not the first to enter the lists: none of us held back; the emotion was universal. Never perhaps was there a more imposing demonstration of opinion; bishops, priests, laymen, the entire Christian world, were unanimous. Not a single French bishop remained silent; and nearly three hundred pastorals show that many must have thought it their duty to lay, more than once, before their flocks, the perils of the vicar of Jesus Christ and of his Church.

The old champions of the Catholic cause showed themselves more faithful, more devoted than ever. Even laymen of but little fervour were moved. An explosion of eloquent writings burst forth in France. Spirited and conscientious political writers, with the freedom and self-possession which letters and experience give, spoke the same language as the bishops.

As the temporal power of the Holy See concerns both religion and politics, so politicians, as well as Churchmen, were among the band of its defenders. The Papacy being the greatest visible manifestation of the power of spirit, as oppposed to matter, philosophers sustained it, in the name of *spiritualism*, with all the ardour of Christians. We had on our side the spirit of man, as well as the spirit of God.

The fears of the Catholics were frankly laid before the Corps Législatif; respectful but energetic petitions were presented to the Senate, though, unhappily, they received a very inadequate consideration. Generous offerings were contributed, and humble and fervent prayers ascended to Heaven, from every point of the Catholic world. Vain prayers! it has been scoffingly said:

Providence has passed to the order of the day![1] As if man had penetrated the counsels of Heaven, and could infer from passing events the decrees of providence as to the future! As if the Divine Majesty were tied down by parliamentary forms, and disclosed in a day what had been conceived in eternity!—But let us forget this unhappy speech. Already the Holy Father has received unlooked-for aid. At his invitation, a chivalrous and illustrious soldier, one of the glories of modern France, has placed his name and renown at the service of the Pontiff. His noble heart felt that in the service of the Church it is not presumption to anticipate success, even when all seems lost.

Thus when the Father was attacked, the children resisted: *when the head was struck,* as an Irish bishop eloquently said, *the hands were instinctively raised to protect it.* God was pleased to give to those who sneer at the weakness of the Church, a new proof of her strength. These imposing manifestations created surprise, and even provoked irritation and suspicion.

Those were surprised, who, so long unused to demonstrations of public opinion in France, which were discouraged by the prevailing apathy, and thwarted by so many restrictions, least of all expected them from the Catholics. These are generally regarded as worthy people, naturally inclined to obedience, and with reason: but their conscience must not be trifled with, and it should be known that it is never far distant. They are like certain genial and easily cultivated soils, where, however, one must not dig too deep; one comes to rock.

The surprise of some took the shape of admiration, though indignation was the more general sentiment. I doubt whether we ever received such a number of passionate affronts and invectives. The injury they did us was trifling; but we were grieved for the weak minds which are dispirited by such

---

[1] M. Dupin's speech in the French Senate, 29th, March, 1860. See *Constitutionnel,* of April 7.

outrages, and for those who, already traitors at heart, only waited for a pretext to quit our ranks.

The word seems to have been passed to treat the expressions of Catholic feeling as party manœuvres. There are feelings in the heart which others may not have the happiness to share, but which delicacy at least should enjoin them to respect.

At all events, a man who has passed half a century in this world, can estimate the worth of this hacknied accusation. Of course, parties seek to turn everything they can to account,— the parties who have the upper hand, as well as as those who are on the defensive: but it would be puerile to keep silence lest we may furnish them with weapons, for they know how to make use of silence, as well as of speech. Granted that the conduct of the French Catholics meets the views of certain parties of whom they want to know nothing, has not that of the government served the purposes of parties whom it disowns? Whenever, then, duty calls, we should act, in singleness of purpose, without examining whether we are indirectly seconding or deranging the calculations of others; for otherwise nothing can be done; our scruples will issue in remorse, and, for fear of serving the truth injudiciously, we shall abandon its service altogether.

For my part, I beg to be informed of what party I have been unintentionally furthering the ends. While I respect all sincere opinions, I am a stranger to all parties, and, concerning myself exclusively with the interests of religion and the honour of my country, I acknowledge, and mean to serve, no cause but that of God, the Church, and France.

A party, indeed! what is now at stake is the keystone of the Christian world, the corner-stone of the European edifice, the Papacy. I have just gone over the whole history of the Pontifical sovereignty, and I believe that since the eighth century, no more deadly attack has been made upon the Holy See. I do not so much dread the acts of violence and usurpation, as the principles invoked against it, and the novel and perfidious form in which the question is presented. At no former period was it stated in its present form. It is not possible to reflect on the doctrines now put forward, to listen to the views of the revolutionary journals of France and Italy, and those of the greater part of the English press, without being convinced of the drift of the present controversy. There lurks a deadly design against the Catholic Church, unknown to some, but to the delight of others, under this great aggression upon the temporal power of the Pope. Yes! the circumstances are critical, the moment solemn.

I am convinced the juncture is critical, not only for the Church, but for Europe. The whole of the fourteenth and fifteenth centuries suffered by the removal of the Papacy to Avignon; that fatal event was the occasion of innumerable scandals and woes to Europe. We now see the most vital questions relating to the Church agitated by journalists, and summarily decided with a levity unequalled, unless by the greatness of the danger; and while the irreligious press discusses them, the revolutionary bandits march, and events succeed one another with frightful rapidity. I felt myself forced into polemical composition, and I have endeavoured to make my pen keep pace with events. I have had at once to accommodate myself to governmental measures, which fetter far more the freedom of speech of the bishops than the articles of newspapers, and to raise my voice, in detached and hurried publications, in compressed and incomplete arguments. But this is evidently but a part of what such a grave emergency calls for: a subject so important also needs ampler developments and more satisfactory demonstrations.

Accordingly, having published pamphlets, I felt it necessary to write a book; having taken my part in the skirmishing, I have sought, if possible, to build a rampart. Had I been a party man, I should have contented myself with the unconnected efforts I had already made; but because I am a man of conviction, I wish to furnish my proofs, and to give a warrant for my assertions. This work will have at least one merit,—it will testify to the profound sincerity of my preceding attempts.

Many reasons, indeed, dissuaded me from undertaking it. It took me away from a more grateful task,—a work upon Catechisms, which I had begun for young people, with whom I had hoped to end my life. To leave children for men, and for the disputes of men, was not an agreeable change.

There was, too, the salvation of those souls which are committed to my charge, to whom I owe the word of life, whom no interest, however elevated, can efface from my memory and my heart, and who had a paramount claim upon me,—*væ mihi si non evangelizavero!*

I was obliged, too, in preparing for such a work, to examine anew the doctrines involved, and, moreover, to undertake long historical researches, which the weakness of my eyes rendered doubly trying. I had to study afresh, in a particular point of view, eighteen centuries, and more particularly the last fifteen years, and the contemporary history of France, Italy, Piedmont, and England.

Nor was my toil uninterrupted; unexpected combats awaited me, breaches had to be repaired, more pressing than the construction of my edifice. I wrote while I fought: with one hand I built up the laborious structure of this book, while I had to repel with the other numerous assailants, and attacks continually renewed.

I will add, that the years of my life gliding away so rapidly, the labours which crowd upon me, the close of my earthly career which threatens to overtake me before I have done anything of moment for the salvation of souls, the deep and involuntary yearning for peace and calmness which haunts a life of unintermitting toil, the dispiriting sadness occasioned by the sight of the triumph of evil—of the hardened blindness and injustice of men,—other sources of affliction besides, fatal misconceptions, which it was impossible to avert and equally impossible now to dissipate,—all these things would fain have persuaded me that I was not called upon for more than my daily toil, and the desultory efforts necessitated by the hourly fluctuations of the conflict.

But profounder reflection convinced me that so great a cause should be more effectually defended than by the animated protestations which vivid faith and injured consciences might dictate; that it was worthy of more than fleeting words and ephemeral publications. I felt that interests so paramount and so enduring demanded something fuller and more elaborate,—a work, in short, which may, if it so please God, remain and speak hereafter.

I may then say with St. Hilary, "I have written because I was obliged,"—*Coactus hæc scripsi*. "I have expressed the inmost convictions of my soul,"—*Et quæ ipsæ credebam locutus sum*. I recollected, like that great doctor, that a bishop is not only the disciple, but also the witness of the truth,—*Discipulus veritatis, testis quoque veritatis*. I have fought, because I felt it was my duty to fight for the Church,—*Conscius mihi hoc me Ecclesiæ stipendium meæ militiæ debere*. I have published these pages because I owed to Christ the voice of my episcopate,—*Ut Christo per has literas episcopatûs mei vocem destinarem*.

No one can say, at least no upright mind will believe, that any human, narrow, or unworthy motive has guided my pen,—*Nemo me aliquo vitio humanæ perturbationis ad hæc scribenda arguet incitatum*. If I have brought forward so many facts, and appealed to so many principles,—if I have pronounced, freely, and I hope justly, a judgment upon so many men and things,—*si vero universa hæc manifesta esse ostendimus*,—I may also say with St. Hilary, we have not gone beyond our apostolic liberty,—*Non sumus extra libertatem apostolicam*.[1]

However, I know but too well that neither this book nor

---

[1] *S. Hilarii*, lib. contra Constantium, p. 1247; lib. de Synodis, p. 1206, edit. Benedict.

any other will set things to rights: the all-powerful hand of God alone can, and no man knows his hour. Alas! humanly speaking, we are far from having done with the Italian question. The future veils its secrets here as ever; but what we can see is far from reassuring, and the horizon remains charged with angry clouds.

Some may tell me, "Your views are too gloomy, you are shortsighted, and do not see the skilful and judicious plans by which influential parties hope shortly to unravel all difficulties; all will end well."

I do not deny that I am blind, or rather, we are all blind: as Bossuet says, "The wisest and most powerful do either more or less than they intend, and their plans, in the execution, escape from their control, and produce unforeseen effects. There is no human power which is not made, in spite of itself, to serve ends at which it does not aim. God alone can reduce everything to his will."

God has made us blind; but we are blind men who can feel their way,—who cannot see the morrow, but have light enough for the present day,—enough to avoid, if we will, wrong roads and dangerous precipices, and to walk straight for our journey's end. To-morrow belongs to God, he alone knows its secrets, and disposes of it as he pleases. Let us all do our duty to-day in truth and justice, and God, to-morrow, will do the rest.

At all events, I trust that I have avoided bitterness and rancour in this work. I pity those whom I condemn the most. It is always painful to me to speak harshly, even when it is necessary. If I have dwelt upon the unwarrantable prejudices of a great and illustrious nation, it was to offer them a fair and honourable peace. And I would particularly remark here, that though truth has compelled me to speak severely of the descendant of an ancient house, of a glorious and Christian dynasty, which I had been from childhood accustomed to revere, I have done so with heartfelt pain, and not without the tears which the prophets of old shed for those princes who forsook the God of their fathers,—*Lugebat Samuel . . . . propheta Domini.* Indeed, Samuel was so inconsolable for the prince whom he had loved, that God himself said to his prophet, "How long wilt thou mourn for Saul ?"—*Usquequo tu luges eum?* We find again in the Scriptures another touching account of the grief which the sins of princes and the sufferings of peoples cause the ministers of God. When Eliseus announced to the envoy of the king of Syria that his master was to die, and he himself to succeed him, "he was troubled so far as to blush, and the man of God wept,"—*conturbatus est, flevitque vir Dei.* Hazael said to him, "Why doth my lord weep ?"—*quare dominus meus flet?* And he said, "Because I know the evil that thou wilt do to the children of Israel,"—*quia scio quæ facturus sis filiis Israel mala.*

While writing these lines, I feel deeply moved by the recollection of a circumstance, which I do not think delicacy forbids me to record here, and which is not inapposite at the outset of the present work.

I visited, some time ago, a desert sanctuary, in a wild gorge of the Apennines, where the unfortunate Charles Albert, after the disaster of Novara, and before taking a last farewell of Italian soil, came alone and unknown, to kneel and meditate, and utter a parting prayer. He had left his attendants in the valley below, and arrived there alone, on foot, wrapped in his cloak. He heard mass there, and received the Sacraments of Penance and Communion, without being recognized by any one. Then, having prayed for a long time, and left an alms for the poor, he continued his way in silence, without again halting till he reached Oporto, where he was to die. It was not till after his departure that the monks found out who he was.

When the good religious who had heard his confession without recognizing him, related to me this trait of his chequered life, I felt myself deeply touched. I had known that unfortunate king, and seen his two young sons a very few years before; he was even pleased then to give me a striking mark of confidence, which I cannot forget. I had remained deeply attached to him. I could not picture him to myself, praying before that solitary altar, in that trying hour, without compassion. I approached the spot where he had knelt, with sympathy and with respect. What had been the reflections which there passed through his soul? What petitions had he addressed to the God of his fathers? From that mountain did he cast a glance towards Rome? Did he think of Pius IX, of his alliance and his counsels, which he had refused? What were his impressions before Heaven, of the past and the future of Italy, the destinies of his family—his son?

I prayed there for him: then, sad and silent, I left that holy spot, and slowly descended the mountain, along the narrow path which he had taken, and occupied probably with the same mournful thoughts as he; and when, from the top of the rock of *Turbie*, I looked down upon the vast and radiant waters, I imagined him there, casting a long and last look over the horizon, and beyond the Mediterranean, towards Oporto: and the grand image of Virgil occurred to me—

> "Cunctæque profundum
> Pontum aspectabant flentes."

He departed, never to return.

And I recollected with pain, the words applied in Scripture to the princes from whom Heaven seems to withdraw its light: *Effusa est contemptio super principes:* for they walk in devious and fatal paths—*et errare fecit eos in invio et non in via*. And therefore we should mourn and pray for them.

ORLEANS, *May 8th*, 1860.

PREFACE TO THE SECOND PARIS EDITION.

The First Edition of this Work has been very rapidly exhausted.

Whatever the favour of the public for its author, it is clear that it is to the nature of the subject, to the ever-present and growing interest of the most solemn question of our time, that the success of so grave and extensive a work must be attributed. Yes, the Roman question is, and continues to be, the most interesting of all topics ; and, to the honour of the French public be it said, that nothing has succeeded, as yet, in distracting attention from it. The publication of so many books and pamphlets on the subject, has not created satiety ; even the strange and lamentable events in Sicily and the East, far from causing us to forget Rome, have only enhanced our zeal and our anxiety. We feel that the end of the religious moral conflict which agitates the world, can only come through Rome ; for there is guarded the sacred deposit of the fundamental principles of order and justice, the neglect of which issues in the terrible convulsions which appal us.

If any thing more ought to be said here as to this work, written amidst so many other labours in the struggle,—in the breach, as I may say, I must attribute all its merit, if it has any, to the conscientious efforts I made to treat the question in its fulness ; to accumulate all the principles, reasons, proofs, facts, and particularly authorities, which from all the diversified regions of the political and religious world, concur with singular unanimity, in sustaining the thesis I was defending. I had proposed to raise a rampart ; it has been said that I have constructed an arsenal : I should be happy if the expression were true—if I had succeeded in storing up here all the facts and arguments of the case, and if, in writing a faithful history of the present, I had forged weapons available for the future struggle.

I have intended this work both to meet the present needs of the controversy, and to remain as a text-book. It comprises three distinct divisions:—

The first, doctrinal, in which I have laid down the essential principles of the question, the providential reasons, and the necessity, religious and political, for the Pontifical Sovereignty.

The second, historical, in which I have endeavoured to corroborate those principles by facts, and by the history of ten centuries.

The third, polemical, and adapted to present circumstances, in which I follow the contemporary policy of the revolution throughout all its phases, and demonstrate the ultimate and fatal consequences, as to Catholicism and European society, of the dismemberment of the Papal States.

Such are the contents of my book. In giving a new edition to the public, what shall I add as to the present state of events? I need, indeed, say nothing; for events speak loudly enough of themselves, and only confirm too well my arguments and anticipations. Alas! they prove more and more, that, to my deep sorrow, I was right: each day that passes adds a new chapter to my work, with a pressing, disheartening, relentless logic, which outdoes my prognostications.

Since it appeared, the clouds which overcast the horizon have grown visibly blacker and more threatening: evil has made fearful progress; the confusion, moral and social, grows daily more inextricable: men, princes themselves, and national assemblies speak a language the import of which they do not comprehend themselves, and we might aptly utter the complaint of the old Roman; *Jampridem vera rerum vocabula amisimus.* Those grand words, justice, liberty, religion, honour, seem with certain nations to have lost the sense once attributed to them, by the conscience of mankind: and conscience itself, appalled and paralyzed, seems to have been stifled from one end of Europe to the other.

Words and deeds are equally unparalleled. England and Piedmont, in particular, have so far confounded the best-defined notions of good and evil, that nothing they do can surprise us.

At Turin, at the very moment that Piedmontese bands, led by Zambianchi, are invading the Papal territory, Count Cavour, the prime minister of the Crown, dares to speak openly in Parliament, of the *Papal hordes* and of *that Lamoricière* who has *put himself* at *their head.* It is now the Pope—who has been despoiled of a part of his provinces by Piedmont, and is threatened with the loss of the remainder—who is attacking Piedmont! "The Pope," says Count Cavour, "has recourse to every means in his power to attack us."

What are we to think of this? For my part, I prefer Garibaldi. The revolutionary chief does not belie his character, when with, impious effrontery, he calls to arms the Marches, Umbria, the Roman Campagna, and Naples, *to extirpate the gangrene of the Papacy.* But how characterize the speeches of Count Cavour.

But here is another sovereign, on amicable terms with a neighbouring country, who suddenly sees his states invaded by thousands of revolutionary adventurers from that country. Garibaldi starts from Genoa, to carry fire and sword throughout Sicily: but Piedmont had no eyes to see him. Europe has heard the protestations of Count Cavour, that he was not aware of the departure of fleets equipped by Piedmontese hands, hired with Piedmontese money, and starting from Piedmontese ports, to fall, in open day and in time of peace, upon Sicily, and sustain a rebellion in the name of Piedmont; and fresh bands are daily hurrying from every corner of Piedmont, to join the former. Garibaldi constitutes himself Dictator, in the name of Victor Emmanuel; he issues his edicts in the name of Victor Emmanuel, King of Italy! Yet Piedmont is ignorant of all this! And truth and honour have still names among men! And Europe imagines that international justice and a law of nations are still in force in the civilized world!

We must add, that this novel public code makes its appearance in Europe under the auspices and the too much dreaded flag of another power, foreign to Italy, but the ally of all the revolutions which now are troubling the world. England has not done less, but perhaps more for Garibaldi than Piedmont. English vessels protect the landing of Garibaldi. The Neapolitan cruisers capture two vessels laden with arms and Garibaldian volunteers; Piedmont, backed by British agents, claims these ships, and succeeds in having them restored.

The enthusiasm for Garibaldi in England breaks forth even in Parliament. Lord Brougham declares that 999 Englishmen out of 1,000 are for him; and while money and arms are forwarded to him from the ports of the United Kingdom, and officers leave the British army to place their sword at his disposal, the government proclaim illegal the subscriptions, and recruiting for the Pope.

Soon Palermo surrenders to Garibaldi : 25,000 men capitulate to 8,000. After the capitulation blood flows—even women are slaughtered ; and then it is that M. Cavour, at last grown weary of his official denials, receives the deputies of Garibaldi, and sends him envoys in his turn : then, too, he protests the most energetically against any intervention in Sicily. It would seem that what he is doing there himself, and what England is doing, is not an intervention !

The Sardinian chambers grant him a sum of £6,000,000, on condition that he shall pursue "the militant policy which brought Piedmont to Milan, to Bologna, to Florence ; and which will conduct from Palermo to Naples, from Naples to Venice and to Rome : on condition that the jewel of Sicily be added to the Piedmontese crown, which has lost that of Nice and Savoy." Yet all this is not intervention ! The King of Naples is advised to negotiate with Piedmont ! He makes the attempt, proclaims a constitution, removes his faithful regiments, deputes envoys to Paris, London, and Turin ; meanwhile Garibaldi continues his work ; after Palermo, Messina falls, and the massacres recommence ; the Dictator calmly orders disarmed prisoners to be shot, to give "a salutary example," and to offer a guarantee for the perfect freedom of the Sicilian suffrage !

Such are the deeds which obtain for Garibaldi the title of Liberator of Italy, and the moral support of free England !

The revolution hurries onward : to-day perhaps it is at Naples—to-morrow at Rome. In the mean time it has its foot on the neck of a king, who, isolated, abandoned by all, is struggling in vain ; and Europe looks on !

And what are we to think of the news which we have just heard of an armistice concluded between the royal troops and Garibaldi ? Every honest man sees that it is not peace, but death, which is meant. Such a treaty is a worthy counterpart to that which the Druses have just concluded with the Maronites. I know not whether the events in Sicily or those in the East make the saddest impression on the soul—the massacres of Beyrout and Damascus, or the fratricidal combats of Palermo and Melazzo—the connivance of the Turks, or that of Piedmont.

One may trace at present in Italy the operation of the inexorable law which decrees that chastisement shall follow crime. I see there a revolution which abrogates justice, to be soon, most probably, followed by a reaction which will extinguish liberty—that liberty which its panegyrists are forsaking for the pursuit of a chimerical unity. When is that noble land to be delivered from this fatal circle? O generous, beneficent aspirations of Balbo, of Pellico, and of Pius IX., where are ye? When will Italy repent for having scorned you?

But while the common Father of the faithful suffers with Italy, his children are massacred in the East. Europe deliberates, and during her deliberations the extermination proceeds: the blood of Christians cries out to us; but the English cabinet is deaf to its cries, and to many others too. Read the journal of Lord Palmerston, and say if that Government is not dead to truth and justice.

But shall France, who has so often fought for an idea, do less for a duty? Her Government has not held back; and throughout France a universal cry of approbation has greeted and anticipated its initiative. Such policy may well be called national, as we have pursued it under every form of government, at all epochs, from Charles Martel to St. Louis, and from the battle of Nicopolis to the siege of Candia and the recent emancipation of Greece. Great and instructive lesson! When France, in her external policy, shows herself Catholic, the universal sentiments of the country respond; they proclaim that she is obeying her duty, her noblest interests, and appearing in her true character. However, the British Government takes exception to her generous enthusiasm. What a contrast! England makes very light of the integrity of the rights of the *venerable old man* of Rome (as he has been called); but she is jealous of any departure from precedent with regard to the *worthy Sovereign of Constantinople*, and those Turks who are an incubus on Europe. Yet perhaps we are mistaken in calling her conduct inconsistent. If in Europe she is the advocate of the violation of right and the abuse of force, of bloodshed and of the oppressors of the weak, it is not strange that she should take part with, not against, the barbarians of the East.

But enough on this lamentable subject. I am unwilling that the impression produced by my book should be one of despondency and gloom. A Christian book should always inspire hope. Let us, then, remark, before concluding, that the events which are now agitating Europe convey a profound and encouraging lesson; they teach us that no human prudence can annul the inviolable harmony established by Providence, between principles and their consequences, causes and their effects; that the seed sown must bear its natural fruit; and that it is vain for men to expect peace when they have contemned and trampled upon justice.

There is in Scripture a text of consoling and celestial force, which has often been my support in the conflicts which have fallen to my lot. *Expecto cœlum et terras ubi Justitia habitat*— I look for a heaven and earth where justice inhabits. Justice! she ought to be the queen of the earth; but too often she is an exile. It would be the honour and the happiness of men, especially of the great, to cause her to triumph upon earth; but too often they tread her under foot. There is, then, no champion to take her part but God; but then it is that he rises in her defence. At times he seems to delay. We must wait, according to another expression of the Holy Scriptures, *till justice be turned into judgment—donec convertatur justitia in judicium;* that is, till she be publicly vindicated and triumph; we must wait till God himself arise and turn judgment into victory— *donec ejiciat ad victoriam judicium;* but we shall not wait in vain. God's time will come at last; and his mighty hand will straighten the bruised reed, and kindle into flame the smoking flax; and, when we least expect it, our hearts are consoled by one of those special interpositions of Heaven which confirm, for centuries, the supremacy of truth and justice upon earth.

ORLEANS, *August 6th*, 1860.

Letter from His Holiness Pope Pius IX. to the Author of " The Papal Sovereignty."

PIUS, PP. IX.

VENERABILIS FRATER, Salutem et Apostolicam Benedictionem.

Nihil jucundius nobis contingere potest, in ea quam gerimus misero hoc et luctuoso tempore totius Christiani populi gravissima sollicitudine, quam intelligere venerabiles Fratres Episcopos, tempestate sæviente, quasi in murum æreum stare pro domo Israel, seque attentos ac vigiles in retundenda hostium Ecclesiæ pravitate jugiter exhibere. Hoc igitur solatium attulerunt nobis studia et contentiones tuæ, venerabilis Frater, qui strenue Sanctæ hujus Sedis juribus et auctoritate ac pro Ecclesiæ disciplina dimicatus, tam vera tamque præclara de civili nostro ejusdemque Sedis Apostolicæ principatu scripsisti, ut nullus qui hac nostra ætate in hujusmodi operam incubuit, videatur cum te comparandus. Opus itaque quod de civili ipso Principatu Nostro mox exarasti ac typis superiore mense in lucem publicam edidisti, perlibenti prorsus animo accepimus. Tibique propterea, qui tantam hac in re et immortalem ubique adeptus es laudem multas nos denuo agimus et habemus gratias. Deum optimum maximum et enixe precari ne desistamus ut hostium nostrorum elidat superbiam ac consilia disperdat, atque ut Ecclesiæ suæ Sanctæque huic Sedi splendidum cito tribuat triumphum. Te interim, Venerabilis Frater, præcipua in Domino Jesu Christo caritate complectimur, atque omnem animi et corporis prosperitatem ipsi tibi ab eo summis precamur votis. Hujus auspicem habeas Apostolicam benedictionem, quam ex imo corde depromptam ipsi tibi, venerabilis Frater, atque omni tuæ istius Ecclesiæ clero ac populo peramanter impertimur.

Datum Romæ apud S. Petrum, die 27 Junii, 1860.

Pontificatus nostri anno XV.

PIUS PP. IX.

[Translation.]

VENERABLE BROTHER, Health and Apostolic Benediction.

Amidst the grave cares imposed upon us by the charge of the whole Christian people, in these times of sorrow and calamity, nothing is more consoling to our heart than to see our venerable Brothers the Bishops standing up, amid the raging tempest, as a wall of brass, in the defence of the house of Israel, and ever showing themselves firm and vigilant in repelling the wicked attacks of the enemies of the Church. Your labours and efforts, venerable Brother, have afforded us this consolation—you who, after defending so energetically the rights and authority of this Holy See, and the discipline of the Church, have published such true and admirable writings upon our temporal sovereignty, that none of those who, in our time, have engaged in this laborious task, seems comparable to you. We have therefore received with joy the work which you have just completed, and published last month, upon the Pontifical Sovereignty. We, accordingly, once more express to you, who have thereby won the immortal praise of the universal Church, our heartfelt thanks. Let us not cease earnestly to pray to the great and good God, that he may bring down the pride of our enemies, and dissipate their designs, and that he may soon grant a glorious triumph to His Church and to this Holy See. In the mean time, venerable Brother, we embrace you with especial charity in the Lord Jesus Christ, and beseech Him, with all our heart, to grant you all prosperity of mind and body. Receive, as a pledge of this, the Apostolical Benediction, which, from the bottom of our heart, we impart, with the utmost love, to yourself, venerable Brother, and all the clergy and faithful of your Church of Orleans.

Given at St. Peter's, at Rome, June 27, 1860.
The fifteenth year of our Pontificate.

PIUS IX.

THE PAPAL SOVEREIGNTY.

CHAPTER I.

THE FISHERMAN OF GALILEE.

1.

ALL the works of God are characterized by wonderful grandeur and simplicity; and assuredly Jesus Christ displayed superhuman grandeur and simplicity when he chose a mortal man, ignorant and obscure, as the supreme chief of his immortal Church, the father of souls, the guide of consciences, the sovereign judge of the religious interests of humanity. He surely gave one of the most astonishing proofs of his power, when he said to that man, or rather, that grain of sand from the shores of a lake of Galilee, "Thou art Peter, and on this rock I will build my Church, and the gates of hell shall not prevail against it." *Tu es Petrus, et super hanc petram ædificabo Ecclesiam meam.*

One observes, in this singular play upon words, a touching condescension and familiarity, if I may so speak, in the language of the Almighty. Meditating upon it, and calling to mind the ages and events which the world has since seen, the expression of Fenelon occurs to me: "The words of upright men express what is; but the omnipotent words of the Son of God accomplish what they express."

So it was. It is now eighteen hundred years since that weak creature, that reed, became PETER—the rock on which is built the great Church of the Son of God, and the gates of hell have never prevailed against her.

For my part, I confess that this man, so wonderfully conceived in the purposes of God, and so fashioned by his power, the centre and foundation of the greatest of the divine counsels which has been realized in time, so preserved by an immutable Providence, throughout the course of ages, and amid so many tempests, not only excites my faith and touches my heart, but is also the continual wonder of my reason. I shall never forget my feelings when I first beheld him, at Rome, in 1831, when, for the first time, I saw the Vicar of Christ appear under the majestic dome of S. Maria Maggiore. Deeply moved at the sight of the common Father of the Faithful, and by feelings yet more powerful, I said to myself, "That, then, is the Pope—the successor of Peter—the Chief of Catholic Christendom—the mouth of the Church, *os Ecclesiæ*, everliving and open to teach the universe—the centre of Christian faith and unity—the light of truth, kindled to illuminate the world, *lux mundi*—that weak old man is the adamantine base of a divine edifice, which the powers of darkness can never shake—the corner-stone on which the city of God here below reposes. I see before me the mortal whose head is encircled by so many glorious recollections of the past, hopes of the present, and plans of the eternal future! Prince of priests, father of fathers, heir of apostles; a greater patriarch than Abraham, as St. Bernard has said—greater than Melchisedeck in priesthood, than Moses in authority, than Samuel in jurisdiction; in a word, Peter in power, Christ by unction, pastor of pastors, guide of guides, the cardinal joint of all the churches, the keystone of the Catholic arch, the impregnable citadel of the communion of the children of God."

And this marvel has lasted eighteen hundred years, on this earth, where all passes away! it lasts, not in the midst of darkness and of nations slumbering in an eternal infancy—no, but surrounded by the brilliant light of this great modern civilization shining far and wide; it lasts in the very centre of the activity of European nations, which wears out everything else; it lasts and it resists the wickedness of men, the fatality of events, the instability of things, and, more than all, the natural weakness of those in whom it is personified, who are but flesh and blood, as we are. Has God created anything greater or more strange? Is there not here manifestly a divine work, the sport, as it were, of infinite power, *ludens in orbe terrarum*, as the Scriptures say?

Now, in this work, God has eternal designs in view: it is to remain to the end of time, and its past duration is to us Catholics a warrant of the truth of the oracles which declare it to be imperishable. Let us inquire what are the means and instruments employed by Providence to accomplish its ends in this divine institution, to sustain and preserve it throughout the agitation of ages, *in medio annorum*, as the sacred text speaks.

But before thus following the Papacy throughout its long history, it is necessary to cast a closer glance upon its first origin.

II.

Modern science loves to go back to the origin of events, and with reason; to contemplate things as they first appeared throws light on their nature and their consequences, raises questions pregnant with interest and instruction, and thereby excites the attention of inquiring and reflecting minds.

The sovereign pontificate, like Christianity itself, and like most things that are divine, possesses the double attraction of the prodigious results it has produced in the world, and the mysterious humility which surrounds its origin. All modern civilization has sprung from it. It is from the first focus of Christianity that has shone, and still shines, upon humanity, the new and vivid light, whose powerful influence we now feel even in spite of ourselves, and which, however we may disdain it, is still the basis of our moral life. What then commenced in Judea was nothing less than the renewing of the old world, the conception and birth of the new.

But the beginnings of such great things were singularly little, strange, and obscure—I may almost say, surprisingly original. Nothing similar was ever seen or ever said. It is both the humblest and the greatest fact in history; and, whether one has faith or not, so lowly a preparation for the most stupendous moral revolution that ever took place must excite profound reflections in every thinking mind which seeks to account for facts.

We see these details so simple, so ordinary in appearance; yet their bearing, how comprehensive! In the background of an immense picture, vast as the world, are suddenly traced in silence a few feeble touches, imperceptible lines which insensibly swell and brighten, and soon, with an art ineffable and divine, have changed all the perspectives, illuminated the whole horizon, and we behold the picture radiant and transformed.

Does not this wonderful contrast disclose, to a discerning eye, an unseen hand which disposes all things with infinite force and sweetness? At least, we cannot seek to trace, in any more singular event, the divine action which sooner or later reveals itself in all human affairs, and which history must recognize, or be incomplete. It is upon this interesting study we are about briefly to enter.

III.

Rome had conquered the world by her arms, and governed it by her laws, from the shores of Great Britain to the Euxine Sea, from the Pillars of Hercules to the Euphrates. Her historians related with enthusiasm her humble beginnings, and the wondrous course of her progress and her conquests; her poets sang with pride of her sway reaching to the farthest confines of the known world; her name was extolled to the stars—*imperium oceano, famam qui terminet astris;* and the unshaken rock of her Capitol was an emblem of her eternal empire—*Capitoli immobile saxum.*

At peace with the universe and with herself, after so many wars and intestine troubles, she was now sitting at the feet of a master, wearied with her agitations and the very weight of her greatness; and one man, concentrating in his hands all the power of the people and of the Senate, alone representing the majesty of Rome, ruled the city and the world—*urbi et orbi.*

That man had played on the political arena a part without a parallel. Having risen by treachery, duplicity, and cruelty, he found it answer his ambition to make the second part of his life a contrast to the crimes of the first, to parade those virtues which charm a people, good faith, moderation, and clemency: all had gone well with him, good as evil; he had seen his crimes triumphant, his person adored; and adulation rising into apotheosis, he was styled a divinity, even during his lifetime.—*Præsens Divus habebitur.*[1]

The contrasts of his own life, and the constant view of so much baseness, had inspired him with a contempt for mankind, and a sarcastic and universal scepticism: and, his thoughts limited to the sphere whose centre he had been, and to the stage where he had been the sole actor, he died with these words upon his lips, accompanied with a bitter and ironical smile, " My friends, the play is over; but have I not acted my part well?"

Yet, still—what a cruel stigma on fortune and human glory—the name of Augustus, with which flattery had clothed his crimes, remains as the highest title to which earthly ambition can aspire; and his age, called by his name, is reckoned one of the four famous ages of history. So be it: such is the worth of earthly things. Those who are dissatisfied with such a decision, may trust in Providence, and believe in a future world: to those who are content with it we can only say that they are worthy of it; *talibus dominis terra erat digna,* the world was worthy of such masters, and had no right to complain of them, says, justly, St. Augustine, in his " City of God."

IV.

While, then, Augustus reigned over the world, a little boy was playing by his father's boat on the shore of a lake in Galilee, in an obscure corner of the world, the

---

[1] Horace.

meanest province[1] of a despised country. His name was Simon, son of John the fisherman. It was that child, that fisherman's son from the lake of Genesareth, who was one day to succeed Augustus, after a new manner, in the empire of Rome and of the world.

In the fifteenth year of Tiberius, the successor of Augustus, this little boy had reached the age of thirty. Then it was, Tiberius being at Capræa, where history tells us how he lived, that a strange voice was heard upon the banks of the Jordan. An extraordinary man, of austere and prophetical life, was saying, "Do penance, or you shall all perish." "Art thou the Christ?" he was asked. He answered, "No; but I come before Him; prepare His ways, make straight His paths, fill up the valleys of your corruption, bring low the mountains of your pride."

Christ was, in fact, coming: He was already among the crowd whom John was baptizing; He even came, the type of penitent and regenerate humanity, to be baptized as the rest; and as John the Baptist poured the purifying water upon His bare head and shoulders, the heavens opened, and a glory shone around Him.

Shortly after, as He was coming up from the desert, John, pointing Him out to two of His disciples, said, "Behold the Lamb of God; behold Him who taketh away the sin of the world."

Now, one of the two was called Andrew, and he was brother of Simon, the son of John, of Galilee: "We have found the Messias," said he to Simon his brother; and he brought him to Jesus. Jesus gazing upon him—*intuitus eum*—said to him, "Thou art Simon, son of Jona, thou shalt be called Peter."

Some days later, Jesus was walking by the sea of Galilee, and saw the two brothers, Simon surnamed Peter, and Andrew, casting their nets into the sea; he said to them, "Follow me, and I will make you to be FISHERS OF

---

[1] Can anything good come out of Galilee? *Numquid aliquid boni à Galilæa potest esse?* A Jewish proverb.—*St. Matt.*

men." And they immediately leaving their nets, followed Him.

Such was the first apostolic vocation, such were the first instruments of universal regeneration chosen by this man; still unknown in that world which soon was to adore Him, as He walked solitary along the lake, His thoughts dwelling on the race He had come to save, and gazing with love upon the two poor fishermen, busy catching fish, ignorant of Him and His designs.

They left all, and followed Him : and undoubtedly their courage was great, their faith generous. Julian ridicules them; but I bless them for it, or rather I admire Him whose word has such sovereign virtue to touch the soul of man, whose hand, when He pleases, is felt to be the Master's. Then comes the Sermon on the Mount, that sublime and simple code of evangelical morality, the exaltation of the poor, the compassion for those who mourn, and all the new beatitudes; and then those miracles, where, as Bossuet says, mercy is still more conspicuous than power. Peter and his brother, and all the disciples with them, feel their faith confirmed; and Peter, always the first, soon proclaims it, and receives for his glorious confession an unlooked-for reward. The circumstance is memorable, and I leave the account of it to those who were present:—

"And Jesus came into the quarters of Cesarea Philippi : and he asked His disciples, saying : Whom do men say that the Son of Man is? But they said : Some John the Baptist, and other some Elias, and others Jeremias or one of the prophets. Jesus saith to them : But whom do you say that I am? Simon Peter answered and said : Thou art Christ, the Son of the living God. And Jesus answering, said to him, Blessed art thou, Simon Bar-Jona : because flesh and blood hath not revealed it to thee, but my Father who is in heaven. And I say to thee : That thou art Peter, and upon this rock I will build my Church, and the gates of hell [1] shall not prevail against it. And I will give

---

[1] In the East the gates of cities where patriarchs, kings, and

to thee the keys of the kingdom of heaven. And whatsoever thou shalt bind upon earth shall be bound also in heaven; and whatsoever thou shalt loose on earth, it shall be loosed also in heaven."[1]

Christ's meaning is now revealed: this was the sense of the first mysterious look He cast on Peter, and of the symbolical name He substituted for his original one. He, then, is now the foundation of a divine edifice—he, mere weakness and obscurity, a poor fisherman! But he is more than this: to this poor unlettered man, who, however, believes in the love of God for men, in the kingdom of heaven, and the divinity of the Son of God, is said, "I give thee the keys of the kingdom of heaven;" those eternal keys, which by means of faith and grace, hope and charity, the exercise of spiritual sovereignty and the virtue of Christian obedience, will open and shut the gates of heaven: in short, to him is here committed all moral power, all religious authority, the direction and the tranquillizing of consciences, and all that concerns the security of the souls of men. All this is given to the humblest, the last of men. For my part, jealous of the just rights of conscience, and the true dignity of man, I must say that I far prefer to see such powers in the hands of Peter the fisherman, and in those of his poor fellow-labourers, unarmed and simple men like myself, than in those of the masters or autocrats of the world, of a Julian the Apostate, of a Peter the Great, or of an Elizabeth of England. The dignity of my conscience, the liberty of my soul, the honour of my life, and my feeble virtues, are safer and more at ease in the Church of Jesus Christ: I there find, to use the happy expression of one to whom my respect and gratitude would wish the full light which his words contain, what I most require here below—"an authority before which my soul may bow, and yet suffer no humiliation."[2]

---

judges sat in judgment, were used to signify the power. Since the East was separated from the see of Peter, the ironical term, the Sublime Porte, is the only remnant of these ancient associations.

[1] S. Mat. 16.   [2] M. Guizot.

It is better as it is, for my weakness, as well as for my dignity; and I would repeat here the words of our great Master: "I confess to Thee, O Father, Lord of heaven and earth, because Thou hast hid these from the wise and prudent, and hast revealed them to little ones."

V.

However, the fisherman of Galilee must understand that the honour imposed upon him is a burden; such a load will press upon his natural weakness; he must suffer and groan under it. He knows not this at present, but he will soon learn it. It is, indeed, but the ordinary condition which the great gifts of God carry with them; even earthly ones, as genius and glory; but far more his heavenly ones, only in them there is this consolation, that they sustain him whom they overwhelm.

About eight days after, Jesus took with him Peter, James, and John, and retired to a mountain to pray. As he prayed his face became bright as the sun, and his raiment as white as snow. Peter saith to Jesus, "Lord, it is good for us to be here; if thou wilt let us make here three tabernacles, one for thee, and one for Moses, and one for Elias." But, adds the Gospel, he knew not what he said. The great Bishop of Hippo, commenting on this, says:—O Peter, thou desiredst rest; but no, come down from the mountain and labour; have charity, preach the truth, and so thou shalt gain eternity, where thou shalt rest in peace—*Petre, in monte requiescere cupiebas: descende laborare; habere caritatem, prædica veritatem, et sic pervenies ad æternitatem, ubi invenies securitatem.*

O Roman Pontiffs, successors of St. Peter, it is not your lot either to rest upon the mountain in the splendour of your transfiguration, in the glory of the human diadem or the temporal power, which time and Providence have added to your tiara and joined to your spiritual power. Doubtless you shall be kings, no Jews shall efface that title from your cross; what is written by Providence is written; only your royal title will be read upon a cross;

your sceptre will often be a reed; with it you will sometimes be struck upon the face; your crown will often be one of thorns, your purple a derision: from time to time the kings and princes of the earth will come to mock you. So your Master would have it; He has not willed that His disciples should be treated differently from Himself.

Who knows not the mysterious details which follow? Peter walking on the water to go to Jesus, and as the wind blew strong, being afraid, and crying out, "Lord save me;" and Jesus stretching out his hand to him with these words, "O thou of little faith; why didst thou doubt?"

Another day they are on the sea; the storm rises, the boat is ready to sink. Jesus was asleep; the disciples awake Him with the cry, "Lord save us, we perish." Jesus rises, commands the sea and the winds, and there is a great calm.

Again, Jesus enters Peter's boat, and says to him, "Launch out into the deep, and let down your nets for a draught."—"Master, we have laboured all the night and have taken nothing; but at thy word I will let down the net." He casts it, and it is ready to break with the multitude of fishes. Peter, amazed, falls down at his Master's feet; "Depart from me, for I am a sinful man, O Lord." Jesus repeats what He had said before, "Fear not; from henceforth thou shalt catch men."

It was thus, by striking facts, and by simple words yet of deep meaning, that Jesus Christ formed His apostles and their chief, placing continually before their eyes prophetical images of the perils, the tempests, and the future destinies of the Church, and of the divine assistance which was never to fail her.

But Peter's most memorable lesson was to be the passion and death of his Master. On the eve of those great and sorrowful days, Peter seeing Jesus coming to wash His feet, exclaims, "Lord, dost thou wash my feet." Jesus gives this profound answer; "What I do, thou knowest not now, but thou shalt hereafter:" thou shalt know that, as supreme pastor, thou must be the servant of the servants of God, and wash the feet of all thy brethren.

Soon after: "Simon, Simon, behold Satan hath desired to have you, that he may sift you as wheat. But I have prayed for thee, that thy faith fail not; and thou, being once converted, confirm thy brethren."

Sublime promises thus always accompany the sad and solemn lessons he receives.

Afterwards, before entering the garden; "Whither I go thou canst not follow me now, but thou shalt follow me hereafter." Peter saith to Him, "Why cannot I follow Thee now? I will lay down my life for Thee."—"Wilt thou lay down thy life for me? Amen, amen, I say to thee, the cock shall not crow till thou deny me thrice."

Yet surely, remarks here St. John Chrysostom, Christ knew well whom he had chosen, and on what a frail foundation he was building His Church. He had foreseen all—weakness, prevarication, fall. Such things are inevitable here below; it is but the undiscerning and the short-sighted who are surprised at them. God, in all His plans relating to man, and particularly in the foundation of His Church, assumes as necessary conditions human weakness and human liberty; and this is the chief glory of His works. Peter is a weak man, a fisherman; his successors are like him, and must pay their tribute to human nature; Jesus Christ knows it; but what of that? Men are men, but the Lord is God. And honest minds, seeing the extreme weakness of those who bear the weight of the Church, will not say, God is not here, these are but men, as we; but, on the contrary, the men we see are but of dust, *therefore*, God is here, and the work is divine, because it lasts.

In the passion there is another secret for Peter; the salvation of the world is not to be accomplished in peace, nor amidst human joys and prosperity, but in tears, in suffering, and in blood. It is all important he should learn this; but to convince him of it will require great and terrible lessons, and, most terrible of all, the lesson of his fall. Christ himself, the Man-God, at Gethsemane, His soul, sorrowful unto death, falls prostrate on the ground, and wills to taste, in His last moments, the sorrows and anguish of humanity. At sight of the bitter chalice, in His agony, what does Christ do? He prays. And Peter? He sleeps. "Simon," said Jesus, "sleepest thou? couldst thou not watch one hour?" And soon after, during the first accusation of Christ, Peter denies Him three times, at the questions of a maid-servant. The cock then crew, and Jesus, from afar, looks upon His unfaithful disciple. At this look, Peter wept bitterly—*flevit amare*—and his tears never ceased to flow for the rest of his life; so that Christian artists have always represented him in tears.

VI.

But, wonderful to relate, notwithstanding his fall, Peter did not lose his election and the apostolic primacy; and it could not have been otherwise, according to the unanimous opinion of Christian doctors; it was necessary that he who was to be first in the Church, the sovereign pastor, should have a more profound compassion than others for human frailty: and St. Bernard says this was the reason why, in spite of his crime, and perhaps because he had fallen so grievously, he continued supreme pastor—"It was such a pastor mankind required, because mankind is a great sinner, and needs great pity."

He finds himself first the mercy he is to render to others: "Simon, son of John, lovest thou me more than these?" asks Jesus, risen from the dead. Yea, Lord, Thou knowest that I love Thee. He saith to him, Feed my lambs. Again: Simon, son of John, lovest thou me? He saith to him, Yea, Lord, Thou knowest that I love Thee. He saith to him, Feed my lambs. He saith to him the third time, Simon, son of John, lovest thou me? The Gospel adds, Peter was grieved because he said to him the third time, Lovest thou me? But it was fitting that our Lord should thus persist; it was a refinement of the Divine goodness; it was necessary, says St. Augustin, that love should generously confess thrice, what fear had denied thrice. After this, all is forgotten. "Feed my sheep—*pasce agnos, pasce oves.*" Thus Peter receives anew his divine investiture, in presence of all his brethren, and is again constituted pastor of the lambs and of the sheep, of the little ones and their mothers,—that is to say, of the whole flock of Jesus Christ.

Finally, all assembled, they heard the last words of the Saviour: All power is given to me in heaven and in earth; as my Father has sent me, I send you; going therefore teach you all nations; and behold I am with you all days, even to the consummation of the world.

"From that time," says Bossuet, " all is settled: Peter always appears the first; he is everywhere named first by the evangelists and apostles. First in his confession of faith, and first in his confession of love; he is first in the election of a successor to Judas, first in the solemn promulgation of the evangelical law, first in preaching to the Gentiles, first in the internal government and discipline of the Church, first in the council of Jerusalem. Everything, his weaknesses themselves, concurs to establish his primacy.

A strange transformation, morever, has passed upon all these men since the apostolic flame has descended upon them; Jerusalem and all Judea resound with their teaching. They soon find Judea too little; they divide the world among them: and now in this mighty movement, directed by Peter, whither is he led himself by an influence evidently from above? In what place is to reside the supreme authority with which he is invested? What is to be the seat of the spiritual sovereignty upon earth?" Bossuet thus describes the road traced for him by Providence:—

"Jesus Christ never speaks in vain. Peter is to carry about with him everywhere, while preaching the gospel, the foundation of all the churches; and the road he is to take is this. Beginning at Jerusalem, the holy city, where Christ appeared, where the Church must necessarily begin, in order to continue the succession of the people of

God, whence Peter used to visit all the churches and confirm them in the faith, whither Paul is to come to see him, to contemplate and study him, to recognize him, says St. Chrysostom, as greater than himself, as well as before him in time, so that it might be for ever settled, that, however holy and learned one may be, were one a second Paul, one must still look to Peter;—beginning with this holy city, and then passing to Antioch, the metropolis of the East, the most illustrious Church in the world, in that the name of Christian originated there; to Antioch, of which St. Paul, who had preached the faith there, regards Peter as the pastor; through these two cities, so peculiarly distinguished in the Christian Church, Peter had yet to reach a city still more illustrious—Rome, the capital of idolatry as well as of the empire, but which, being predestined to become the capital of religion and the church, is for this reason to become St. Peter's own Church; this is where he must arrive after Antioch and Jerusalem."

I have nothing to add to the grandeur, the clearness, and the depth of these words; yet, before concluding, I cannot avoid reflecting on the first obscure entry of the fisherman of Galilee into Rome;—who would have said, to see him passing unobserved, among the crowd, along the Via Sacra, surrounded by superb buildings and celebrated temples, a wooden cross under his Jewish robe, that there was the future successor of the masters of the world, and that the unknown God whom he announced, the crucified, would soon reign upon the Capitol, having dethroned the Cæsars and all the gods. Still all this was to happen. Capitoline Jupiter has fallen; the Cæsars are no more; Rome has seen the end of the eternal empire promised by her poets; and if she is still a great name upon earth, she owes it to that fisherman, who came to knock at her gates with his traveller's staff, repaying her hospitality with the cross of Calvary, and with a new empire, the immortal and universal empire of souls.

What that hospitality was, how Rome received the apostolical sovereignty, is no secret. Nero thought to cut it down at a blow, when he fastened Peter to a cross with his head downwards, at the same moment that Paul's head fell beneath the sword. But imperial cruelty concurred, in spite of itself, in the execution of the divine plan. By raising Peter upon the cross, Nero fixed for ever at Rome the sovereignty he dreaded. Rome, which Providence had made the seat of the fisherman of Galilee, which witnessed his death and received his venerable dust, acquired thereby the right to preserve his chair. That chair of Peter still exists, after so many centuries, and continues, under the divine protection, there where Peter himself had brought it, and fixed it by his death; there where he left his sacred bones, when he had given his Master the greatest of all proofs of his love.

"It is thus," to conclude in Bossuet's words, "that the eternal chair, the principal principality was elevated and fixed at Rome; the mother Church whose hand guides all other churches; the head of the episcopate, the centre of government; the one only chair in which unity is safe; it is there that Peter remains for ever in his successors, the chief of Catholic bishops and the foundation of the faithful."[1]

CHAPTER II.

THE PRESENT STATE OF THE QUESTION.

I.

EVEN those who have not the faith, and do not consider as divine the spiritual power with which the Roman Pontiff is invested, must confess that its origin is extraordinary; and that, in fact, it was the fisherman of Galilee who

---

[1] "In these words," adds Bossuet, "you hear the joint opinion of the East and the West."—*S. Aug.* epist. 43.—*S. Iren.* iii. 3.—*S. Cypr.* epist. 55.—*Theod.* ep. ad Ren. 116.—*S. Avit.* ep. ad Faust.—*S. Prosper*, Carmen de Ingr. cap. 2.

brought to Rome the apostleship of the Gospel, and the Christian faith, which has shone from thence upon the world for so many centuries. The Pope is the successor of this wondrous fisherman: and Pius IX., the reigning Pope, is really the spiritual sovereign of two hundred millions of souls, scattered over the globe, as well in the midst of the infidels as in Christian countries; among schismatical and Protestant nations as among Catholic; who all look to him as the supreme judge of their religious faith, and the guide of their conscience: such is the prodigious fact introduced into the world by Peter the fisherman.

This vast moral authority, unparalleled in the world, this spiritual and universal sovereignty exists, and it has sprung from the humble and imperceptible origin we have been tracing; so much is historical.

This power required an abode, a residence, a seat of some kind here below. The Christian Church is not a vague speculative idea; it was intended to be a living fact, a real society, having consequently at its head a real power, which speaks and governs, and therefore subject to the conditions of other human affairs, the conditions of time and space. Where is to be this abode? We have seen that the place chosen by Peter, or rather by Him who guided him unknown to himself, was the seat of that Roman sovereignty which the whole world obeyed; the centre of all the lights of ancient civilization, and of the imposing organization of the imperial power: doubtless Peter's choice, if it was his, was a singularly bold one.

The question which at first presented itself, and has done so several times since, and which is still the question at the present moment, is, what is to be, in the place of its abode, the external condition of this spiritual power? What is to be the manner of its visible, terrestrial existence? What means, what instruments will God employ to guide it to its end, to enable it to accomplish its work, to sustain and preserve it in life and activity during the whole course of time? The answer is as simple as it is indisputable: God sustains, preserves, and perpetuates it, according to His uniform mode of action, by human means co-operating with His powerful and supernatural assistance; the idea, the work, are from heaven; the instruments are, in part, of the earth: such is the secret of the divine economy.

This is, moreover, God's uniform mode of action. It may be unhesitatingly laid down as a principle, that, miracles not being the ordinary rule of the divine government, the ordinary, regular, normal means employed by God to establish the spiritual power in the world, to maintain it firm and respected, to prepare for it a due influence, and to render its action free and fruitful, will not be a continual derogation from the laws which regulate the moral world, but a visible application of those laws, joined to the invisible support of His omnipotence.

The analogy of the most remarkable of God's works, together with universal history, attest the truth of this principle.

God has wrought two works of primary importance in this world; the Creation and the Redemption. He wrought both himself by the direct intervention of His sovereign power; but to perpetuate them, He makes use of His creatures.

Thus He perpetuates the Creation by the institution of families, by the lawful and sacred union of man and woman.

So also by an organized and permanent institution, the Christian priesthood and its supreme chief, who is the guardian, the doctor, and minister of truth, of morality, and of the Catholic worship, the teaching, the sacrifice, and the benefits of redemption are continued. But God has clothed men, not angels, with this priesthood and this power; the external means He employs in this divine work are human, simple, vulgar in appearance; natural means, and not miracles.

Doubtless there is always present a secret intervention of Providence, concealed under the operation of second causes, distinct both from human means and from visible miracles; not, strictly speaking, miraculous.

If I were asked:—Humanly speaking, considering

only ordinary causes and probabilities, can the Church subsist? I should answer, no. Means human, visible, foreseen, are clearly insufficient to save her. She is saved by the unforeseen, the accidental, as men speak; that is, by the intervention, more or less secret, of Providence; by a sort of latent miracle continually renewed; but not a miracle properly so called; and it is always true that God's mode of government is not by prodigies, but by laws; laws from which He departs when He pleases, and a miracle results. But He usually governs by law, sustained by the secret action of His ordinary Providence; the law follows its course, but He incessantly superintends its working and its effects.

If God governed the world, even in the spiritual order, by constant and palpable miracles, He would destroy, in some degree, for us the merit, and for Himself the homage of our liberty. The moral world would be subjected to an impulsive force which would savour of constraint, and would resemble too closely the blind movements of the material world.

God would not have it so, and if we may dare to say it, He was right. It seems even easy to penetrate the reason of this divine arrangement. In fact, if God's action only manifested itself in a continual derogation from His own laws, there would exist no longer the beautiful calmness of order, the peace, according to St. Augustin, of the works of God and of the world—*Pax est tranquillitas ordinis.*

There would be, as St. Ambrose says, more miracles, but also less mercy. It may even be asserted, in the case we are considering, that a perpetual miracle would not reveal a greater power; for, on the one hand, in the history of the Church, the miracle of the divine assistance, though its operation be hidden, is nevertheless to be discerned by an attentive eye; and, on the other, the means employed by God are so feeble, so vulgar, so contemptible to human wisdom—*infirma, stulta, contemptibilia* [1]—that

---

[1] 1 Cor. ch. i.

the divine power receives from the very weakness of the means it uses, the glory of a perpetual miracle. Thus God employs virtue and genius in the service of His Church; but learning grows vain, genius errs, virtue often falters; still the Church remains.

Thus too, the Church was established by a bloody miracle which lasted three hundred years. Reversing the order of all human institutions, it pleased God she should enter on her royalty by martyrdom. For three centuries, suspended between heaven and earth, without human support, resting on nothing in this world, crowned with the double diadem of apostleship and sacrifice, the Roman Church sent all her first pontiffs to the confession of blood, and not one of them refused this testimony to his ministry and his see. But when by this long and terrible experience, God had shown the world that his Church neither feared nor depended upon men, he changed his plan, and allowed the Roman Church to acquire a human government and sovereignty, as a sort of temporal security and external protection against the agitations of the world.

As he chose but once to change fishermen suddenly into apostles; as there was but one Pentecost, when the spirit of God bestowed the gift of tongues; the ministers of religion having since then been forced to study diligently, and to toil and strive to sanctify themselves, and to place at the service of the Church a learning and a virtue laboriously acquired: so, after permitting for three centuries that thirty-three popes should have no dwelling but the catacombs, no throne but the scaffold, he at length chose that the chief of his Church, the pastor of pastors, the prince of all the bishops of the Catholic world, should have a house at Rome, in the centre of Europe, to shelter his spiritual crown, an independent altar at St. Peter's whereon to offer the eternal sacrifice, and a seat at the Vatican to proclaim the oracles of truth. He chose that the spiritual sovereignty, which rules so many millions of Christians, and reigns by faith over so many consciences, should have a temporal power, humble enough not to give umbrage to the great powers of the world, and yet sufficient to secure the independence necessary to the Supreme Judge of so many human beings, so many different countries and interests, necessary,—in short, to the liberty of the universal guide of souls. He chose, not only since Charlemagne, but in some degree since Constantine, that this human means should serve to accomplish and perpetuate his divine work; and nowhere does his providential intention more visibly appear. The popes, indeed, have never become unaccustomed to martyrdom; there have been popes exiled, imprisoned, martyred at all times. No; for them the Vatican has not always been a place of rest.

We consider that the liberty of Catholic conscience, and the independence of Catholic truth, have been providentially linked to the liberty and independence of the Holy See. And we are not alone here; the greatest politicians, and even the adversaries of the Holy See, have thought so too. To speak only of recent times, the first consul bore a remarkable testimony to the truth of this principle. The heir of his name and of his power has solemnly proclaimed and reiterated it. Long before them, the great bishop of Meaux had taught it with all the authority of his genius. We have seen the French republic, Protestant England, and Catholic Spain, declare it with one accord; the schismatical autocrat of all the Russias, not long ago, did homage to this truth in the person of the venerable Gregory XVI. Who knows not that even infidel princes have sent ambassadors to the Papacy? What shall we say, then, of the temerity which would contest to the temporal sovereignty of the popes, rights consecrated by so visible an interference of Providence, and recognized by such homages on earth?

Still, this is what we are condemned to witness at the present moment.

II.

Yes; at the present moment, this ancient institution, which its undoubted necessity, its providential origin, its past benefits, and its long duration, ought to render for ever sacred and venerable to the whole world, finds itself exposed, more than it ever was, to attacks, spoliations, insults, and calumnies of all sorts. One would imagine we had gone back to the worst times. Everything seems to presage for Rome and the Papacy one of the most perilous periods of their history. A plot, deeply contrived, lurking in secret for a long time, but perseveringly followed out, employing by turns subtilty and violence to beguile peoples and to overthrow sovereigns, bursts forth all at once and audaciously declares itself, pressing the most opposite factions into the service of a far-reaching ambition. Yet such is the strange excitement created by the wars and political convulsions we have witnessed that people seem scarcely to be aware of this. As storms shake and strip the tops of trees, so revolutions and the clash of arms agitate the heads of men; the strongest do not always resist such shocks, and the excitement they feel strangely disturbs at times their ideas and their best-founded convictions.

In fact we are shocked and horror-struck, not only at the schemes of the wicked, but at what we hear said at times by well-meaning men—shocked and horror-struck, but not for the Roman Church, not for the Catholic Church. The Church has grown old amid combats; nothing surprises her: persecutions, clamours, treasons, novelties, everything is impotent against her, and unruffled she sees the angry waves break at her feet. This new conflict, whatever its incidents, or its duration may be, for her will be but one victory more. But we are terrified for the loss of souls, the corruption of weak spirits, the delusions, the selfishness, the presumption of some who are entering on a wrong and fatal path, for the obstinacy, the blind prejudices, the ambition, and the hatred which ingulf and hurry them along.

The temporary sovereignty of the Holy See has opponents who attack it only from inconsistency, presumptuous temerity and blindness. I am aware of this; but it has also mortal enemies who combat it with all the tenacity, all the energy, and all the perspicacity of hatred; precisely because they feel of what importance it is, especially in the present state of society, to the dignity and the free exercise of the spiritual power.

Here, as ever, according to the sad and infallible words of our dear Master, the men of the age, "the children of this world are wiser in their generation than the children of light."

The atheists, the revolutionists, the anarchists, and demagogues of all countries, feel that to effect most surely the destruction of the Church and the ruin of Catholicism (which they justly consider as the most insurmountable obstacle to their designs), they must begin by overthrowing the temporal power of the Holy See. Indeed they make no secret of it; they have expressed themselves explicitly enough upon the point.

"The abolition of the temporal power," the most famous of them[1] has lately written, "necessarily involves, in the judgment of any one who understands the secret of the Papal authority, the emancipation of the human race from the spiritual power." Though there be in these words a grave error, they show at least what the object of these men is in attacking the temporal power of the Holy See.

Manin himself writes:—"As long as the Pope is supported at Rome by the French arms, we must not attempt an insurrection; this would be to fight against our allies; but if France should wish to overthrow the Pope, we will aid her with all our heart."

How can people help seeing too, that it is not the Papal power alone which is thus menaced, but at the same time every power, which, like his, is based upon right? Is it not clear, that if sovereign right is vanquished in its most august representative, the eternal enemies of all right and order will soon have conquered it elsewhere, and that the success of their conspiracy against the Papacy will be the

---

[1] Mazzini.

signal of a vast revolution, not only religious but social, throughout all Europe?

In its fanatic irritation against the Church, conservative and political Protestantism does not weigh this sufficiently; and this is why we see it at present take part with revolutionists and infidels in their attacks on the temporal power of the Holy See, hoping afterwards to ruin that spiritual authority which is such an eyesore to it. Frederick, a Protestant and an infidel, lets us into the secret of such conduct, in a private letter to Voltaire: "We must undertake," says he, "the easy conquest of the Pope's States, and then the *Pallium* will be ours and the curtain will fall. None of the potentates of Europe choosing to recognize as Vicar of Christ a subject of another sovereign, they will each create a patriarch for his own State. By degrees each will wander from the unity of the Church, and will end by having in his kingdom a separate religion, as well as a separate language."

The predictions of Frederick the Great trouble me but little; the crowned philosopher of Berlin is not the first false prophet of his sect; for all that he says, I feel at ease as to the immortal duration of the Church here below, and of the Papacy, which is inseparable from it. Still, these impious reveries contain a great lesson for us; for the method they point out for ruining the Church in Europe would be, humanly speaking, infallible, were God not with her, were He to let loose completely the revolutionary passions, and thus to allow an irrevocable malediction to fall upon European society.

There are others who would sacrifice the temporal sovereignty of the Pope, as well as all the sovereignties and nationalties of the Peninsula, to the great Utopia of Italian unity. They feel that the Pope would not remain as a subject in the place where he had been a sovereign; they think his sovereignty, fixed there in the centre of Italy, an obstacle to the realization of their plans, and declare that the Papacy should limit itself to the Vatican, or, still better, be banished from Italy, and even from Europe, where there is no room for it, and go—where is it to go? They see no difficulty—these great political geniuses have arranged all; the Papacy is to seek a last refuge where its cradle was, in Syria, at Jerusalem, or on the shores of the Lake of Genesareth, or, if the East and the ancient world will not have it, in the free republics of the New World, in deserts where none will dispute possession with it, at least, before it has peopled, civilized, and enlightened them.

Some of my readers may be surprised at this; but I have stated nothing but what has been proposed, written, and published. These brilliant ideas have been publicly produced; they have been discussed in French, Belgian, and Spanish journals, and to many a clever intellect they have appeared an ingenious, at least, a pacific solution of the Italian question.

The Pope exiled from Rome and from Italy! The Pope at Jerusalem, in America, or the islands of the Pacific! Ah! doubtless he would always remain the Chief of the Church, the spiritual sovereign of souls, the vicar of Jesus Christ upon earth. And if the Romans, that people so dear to St. Peter and St. Paul—if the Romans, who have already often fallen, or rather, been precipitated into anarchy—for they are almost always more weak than guilty—were ever to fall into infidelity, which, God forbid, the successor of St. Peter, then Bishop of Rome *in partibus infidelium*, would still be, on whatever shore the tempest had cast him, the common Father of the faithful. He might cross the seas, and, the Gospel and Cross in one hand, the constitutions of the Church in the the other, transport his sacred *Penates* to a town or a desert of the New World; but the Church, would voyage, would land, and would remain with him, and we should always say with St. Ambrose, "*Ubi Petrus, ibi Ecclesia.*" Like the sun, immovable in the firmament, that man might seem to change place upon the earth, but undisturbed upon his divine base, he would still illuminate the whole world; from every region of Catholicity souls would still look to him, and he would for ever have a right to say, giving to grand words a still grander sense—" Rome is no longer at Rome; it is wherever I am."

It would remain, however, to inquire what Rome would be, what Italy, what Europe, without him. We shall have to treat these questions, whose importance, in a social and religious point of view, is so strangely disregarded and ignored, even by some who consider themselves religious.

For it is not only hatred, impious prejudice, political passions, and a grasping ambition, which now menace the temporal power of the Holy See; we see also with surprise some who ought to be its natural defenders abandon it, or, at least, prepared to receive with singular resignation its entire destruction, or its curtailment and social degradation. It is only the Romagna, say they, only a province, more or less. Such rash and deplorable sentiments, prevail too extensively among the presumptuous and the unreflecting.

There are pious people who are grieved by them, perhaps, but not greatly scandalized. Some noble spirits, who have foreseen all, and whom nothing surprises, dream in their sublime zeal of a perfection for the future unknown to the Christianity of the past, and see in the troubles and temporal humiliation of the Papacy, a grand horizon of social transformation opening upon Europe and the world: if such revolutions apparently threaten the interests of the Church, they know, or think they know, that all changes will infallibly turn to the greater glory of God and the good of souls. Chivalrous adventurers of the faith, they courageously consent to the destruction of the temporal sovereignty of the Pope. By its annihilation the Church seems to them to renew her youth. Altars stripped, chalices of glass, priests begging their bread, the Vicar of Christ not having where to lay his head, a return to the night of the catacombs—all this seems to them sublime, and thrills their soul with joy. Well, I, with my vulgar, prosaic ideas, cannot consent to wish the Papacy all these grand adventures; and though I proclaim with joy it is a Cross of wood which has saved, and ever will save, the world, I cannot think it expedient for Christians to go back fifteen centuries, and for the Church to return on her steps and be born over again: I prefer to see her follow the path along which God has guided her, the course which his finger points out, and make use of the temporal conquests God has made for her to continue her spiritual conquests. I think, in short, that in the works of God, it is wiser to study his mode of acting and his intentions, and humbly to conform to them, than to impose as rules upon him our fancies, however brilliant, or to endeavour to shape his wisdom to the views of our genius.

It is, above all, where the interests of the Church are concerned, that we must beware of romantic illusions; that it is wise to return to the origin of things, and to go by facts—to consider them carefully, to catch their meaning and their force, and to penetrate the important and living lessons they convey. Of what use are reason and experience, if not to put realities before us in place of visions? I think, accordingly, that it will be useful here to call to mind the true principles of the question of the Pontifical sovereignty, and whatever may be the prevailing political and religious excitement, to study with my readers the design of God, and the way followed by his Providence, in establishing the temporal government of the Holy See.

The subject is a grand one; the materials are immense —I can but make a sketch; I will begin, however, humbly determined to employ all the powers of my soul in the service of a cause so great, so holy, and so unworthily outraged.

Never, thank God, shall human events shake our faith in the divine promises made to the Church. Never shall our confidence in Peter's bark be troubled by the agitations of the waves which carry it; humble passengers on that mysterious bark, our faith in the invisible pilot, who sometimes seems to sleep during the storm, is unchangeable. Nay, it is when we see the Roman Church, the dear and venerable Mother of the children of God, exposed to the most terrible assaults of her long career, that we feel most palpably whence her real strength proceeds, and what God can do to save her. The momentary tribulations which sadden her only serve to call our attention more

THE PRESENT STATE OF THE QUESTION. 27

pointedly to the solidity of the divine foundation on which her wonderful structure rests.

But it is no less certain that, if the Church can confidently refer to the promises of immortality she has received, we should not forget the threats uttered against ingratitude and injustice, and that we cannot sport with manifest danger: it is no less certain that the Christian faith is not irrevocably fixed to any of the places which it enlightens, and that it has often left behind it a fearful night to those who have despised the day; that if Religion has always repaired her losses by new conquests, those losses have not been the less fatal to the souls that have perished; that for us French in particular, we have been for seventy years hanging on the brink of a precipice; that the hand which has so often saved, and which still upholds us, may at last be withdrawn: in fact, to speak plainly, that all the greatest religious and social interests are at stake; that a fearful game is being played at the present moment; that to think we have nothing to fear would be to forget too rashly what we are; and that in every point of view, the case should, at the very least, be gone into radically and fully.

Now, the first principle, the first undeniably fact, which meets our view at the outset of this inquiry, is that leaving aside purely miraculous facts, on which no one has a right to count, the liberty of Christian conscience, the independence of Catholic truth, and the security of souls, have been in the designs of God, providentially united for centuries to the liberty and temporal independence of the Holy See.

This much reason and history irrefragably demonstrate, and this is the principle which I would ask my readers to examine closely, before finally entering on perilous courses, where none can be sure that in the hour of need the ground may not suddenly give way beneath his feet.

CHAPTER III.

REASONS OF GOD'S DESIGNS IN ESTABLISHING THE TEMPORAL SOVEREIGNTY OF THE HOLY SEE.
THE POPE MUST BE INDEPENDENT OF FOREIGN POWERS.

WHEN I thought it recently my duty to protest against the odious attacks which threatened, and still threaten, the Apostolic See, the following is the principle from which I started; and if I am to believe the innumerable marks of approbation I have received, I may say, that all Catholic consciences have declared with me:—

That it is necessary to the spiritual security of the Church, and to our own, that THE POPE BE FREE AND INDEPENDENT;

That this independence be SOVEREIGN;

That the Pope be free, and that HE APPEAR FREE;

The Pope must be free and independent AT HOME AS WELL AS ABROAD.

This is what the gravest reasons demonstrate irresistibly; and also what the greatest minds, even those the most opposed to what are called ecclesiastical pretensions, as well as all true politicians, have always admitted.

I.

It is highly important to recollect, that when one treats with the Church and with Catholics, with the intention to respect their conscience and their rights, one must hear them, learn what their principles are, and take into account the laws, the essential conditions of their existence.

Well, the Catholics say unanimously, the Pope is, in the spiritual order, our king; he is our father, in conscience and faith; his liberty is ours; and none of the great Catholic family, the members of the Church, bought by the sacrifice of the Cross, should ever see him, who is for them the august interpreter of the law of God, and the sovereign of souls, unworthily bending under subjection of any kind. All consciences, all souls would suffer; the faith, the moral law, all the most sacred interests would be in captivity with him. This was eloquently expressed by M. de Montalembert, always the first of the Church's champions in the breach on a day of peril, before the *Assemblée Nationale*, amidst the applause of the great majority of the representatives of the nation: "The liberty of the Pope is a condition *sine qua non* of the religious liberty of Catholics; for if the Pope, the supreme judge, the tribunal of appeal, the living organ of the law and the faith of Catholics, is not free, we cease to be so. We have, then, the right to ask from the State, from the the government which represents us, and which we have established, to guarantee to us both our personal liberty as to religion, and the liberty of him who is for us the living representative of religion."

It is in this point of view that the temporal sovereignty of the Pope is not a mere Italian institution; but, as an Italian declared before the *Assemblée Constituante*, in 1849, it is "a European, universal institution—in a word, an institution of Catholic *right*." And in this sense, the ambassador of France wrote with justice: "Rome does not belong exclusively to the Romans;" or, better, as the illustrious archbishop of Cambrai long ago expressed it—"Rome is the common country of all Christians; they are all citizens of Rome; every Catholic is a Roman." This is why—observe, no other cause can be alleged—the outrages committed against the temporal sovereignty of the Pope at present, have roused the entire world, wounded to the quick all Catholic nations, and caused us all to utter a cry of grief and indignation.

II.

But the liberty of the Pope, in order to be real and secure, must be *sovereign*.

"Why," an Englishman lately asked an Irishman,

must your Pope be a king?"—"Because," answered the Irishman, "he cannot be a subject, and there is no medium." This is clear.

No, the Pope can be no man's subject, because we might all fear to be in bondage with him. That noble head, crowned with the sacred tiara, should not bend under the yoke of any monarch. It requires an independent sovereignty. The persons least favourable to the temporal authority of the Holy See, even those in whom deplorable prejudices had obscured natural rectitude and the purity of the light of faith, have rendered homage to this truth. I do not intend here to take advantage of the admissions of Protestants and infidels on this point. I will cite at least one word of President Henault; it is well expressed: "The Pope," says he, "has to direct all those who command in the universe; consequently none of them should have the right to command him. Religion does not suffice to awe so many sovereigns, and God has justly permitted that the common Father of the faithful should maintain by his independence the respect which is due to him."

Sismondi, still more disinterested than president Henault on this point, agrees with him when he states: "The chief of religion, if not a sovereign, must be a subject . . . The administration of a state is, indeed, ill suited to a priest; but servitude becomes him still less. The pontiff-king will, at least, be independent of kings, and by his courage in censuring their faults, he will have his attention drawn to his own."

We are justified by the best authorities in asserting that the patriarchs of Constantinople became the degraded puppets of the Arian, Monothelite, Iconoclast, and Mahometan emperors,[1] and were a revolting image of what

---

[1] "It is well known that since the patriarchs of Constantinople became subjects of the sultan, Russia, under Peter the Great, would not submit to the authority of a patriarch governed by the Turks; Greece, also, after regaining its independence, would not be dependent on a patriarch of Constantinople; the different communions of

the popes, the supreme chiefs of Catholicity, might have become, or at least have appeared to become in the course of centuries, had not God preserved them by a perpetual miracle,—or rather, had He not provided by His infinite wisdom and power the plan, as simple as it is powerful, of an independent sovereignty, to secure the Church which is mother and mistress of all others.

The sentiments of Fleury naturally occur here; no one, surely, will accuse him of being too favourable to the temporalities of the Holy See: "As long as the Roman empire existed, it comprised within its vast extent nearly all Christendom. The Papacy then had a master, but he was master also of the whole world. But since Europe has been divided among several princes, if the Pope had been subject of any one of them, it would have been to be feared that the others would have had some difficulty in recognizing him as the common father, and that schisms would have become frequent. We may therefore believe that it is by a special intention of Providence that the Pope became independent and master of a state powerful enough not be easily oppressed by other sovereigns,'so as to be more free in the exercise of his spiritual power, and better able to keep all other bishops to their duty. This was the idea of a great bishop of our day."—*Fleury*, Hist. Eccl., t. xvi. 4th Disc., No 10.

III.

The great bishop whose authority is invoked by Fleury, was probably Bossuet; I shall soon have to cite his power-

---

the schismatical Church in the Austrian empire are also governed by a separate and independent patriarch. It is easy to understand the political reasons which always induce governments to exclude from their territory, as far as they can, an ecclesiastical authority which is under the rule of a foreign power. As to the Greek Church, since its separation from the common mother, it has been torn by intestine dissensions; its chief calls himself pompously *universal* (ὁ καθολικος); but this is but an empty title; a just punishment of pride and schismatical ambition."—*Mon. de Lucca*.

ful testimony upon this grave question; at present I shall content myself with relating a curious incident, and a striking expression of the Bishop of Meaux, on a subject analogous to the present. It will prove how well the so-called courtier bishops of the great century knew how to defend the dignity and rights of the Church and their own, and to maintain their freedom of speech, without disrespect for the authorities.

The Chancellor de Pontchartrain having proposed to submit the charges and pastoral letters of the bishops to the royal *censure*, Bossuet obstinately resisted the measure. " I would sooner give my head," he writes. He says, in a letter to Cardinal de Noailles, intended to be submitted to Louis XIV., "They want to tie the hands of the bishops in the most essential points of their office. I will never consent to it." Louis XIV., who did not like to be opposed, still commanded the Chancellor de Pontchartrain to yield.

It was Bossuet, too, who said to that all-powerful monarch, " Sire, you have nothing to fear, but the very excess of your power."

A similar incident has lately occurred in France, to which I do not attach a greater importance than it calls for, but which I mention because it throws light on the present discussion. It has been thought advisable to forbid the newspapers to publish the pastorals of the bishops relating to the affairs of Rome. Those journalists who are every day attacking the Holy See, have not failed to commend the exceptional measure directed against us, and while they continue to insult the Church and the Papacy, we have had to submit.

Does not this show what would happen, if the Pope, instead of being a prince, was only a bishop? Does not this show how he might be treated by the power whose subject he was? It would be said that it was all from respect to him, and to spare him the insults of the irreligious journals. Indeed! But, enough of this; let us return to first principles, and from them judge of facts.

IV.

For us Catholics, the Pope is admitted to be the universal doctor, the supreme judge of questions of Christian faith and morality, the interpreter of the holy Scriptures and the divine teachings; but to judge, to interpret, to define, to approve, and to condemn,—in a word, to be able to accomplish the essential acts of this high spiritual authority, he must be able to speak, and to speak freely; there must be some point of the globe, a centre of Catholicity, a chair from which the Pope may speak and make himself heard, may write and proclaim his decrees, and where his hand and his speech may be as free as his conscience.

Thought, doubtless, is always essentially free; but speech is not, it may be arrested on the lips of the speaker, if he be in the hands of those who are interested in silencing it, if he be dependent upon any who do not choose to hear his words, or still less to allow them to be heard.

The truth is, that, in order that the Pope may speak freely, that he may really be the tongue and the mouth of the Church,—*os Ecclesiæ*, he must have a house of his own, whence to speak; and no police, no foreign constraint, must interfere to silence his voice or to stay his hand, when he writes his apostolic letters and addresses them to all the bishops of the world; when he publishes a decree condemning such an heretical work, or such a scandalous proposition; when he pronounces one of those allocutions in which his lamentations on the woes of the Church warn all the faithful to lament and to pray with him.

Doubtless the jealous policy of governments can always raise barriers between themselves and the apostolic decrees, but at least they cannot stifle the words of the Pontiff upon the spot where they are uttered: a word once pronounced, as the Attic poet says, is a light thing; and, notwithstanding the weight it sometimes carries with it, has wings and flies through the air. This is sufficient.

For us Catholic bishops, who cannot always have full freedom of speech, it is important that the Pope be not treated like us, and that his voice be always heard: and this is important for every one, as otherwise Catholic consciences are unsettled, as they were when the Pope was a prisoner at Savona and at Fontainebleau.

I am glad to render this praise to the French government, that even when—for reasons which it is not for me to judge here—they directed an exceptional measure against the freedom of speech of the bishops, they accorded due liberty to the allocutions and letters of the Sovereign Pontiff.

I need not observe that the truth, even when captive, is always the truth. St. John Chrysostom has expressed it even better than Sophocles: "The divine word is as the rays of the sun; nothing can chain it,—*radius solis vinciri non potest.*" Truth is sovereign,—sovereign in the Mamertine prisons as in the Vatican, and three centuries of combats and victories have shown the world that Peter can be free in irons, or a king in exile. But God has not willed that this prodigy, which, if it were needed, would not be less wanting to the Church now than formerly, should enter into the regular course of her destinies, and be the ordinary condition of the peace promised her. It was an extraordinary remedy for passing and violent disorders,—disorders which had to be healed, combated, and overcome; but, as we have said above, miracles are not here below the regular and permanent order of the divine government. The regular, normal state of the Church is liberty with independence.

V.

Moreover, it is not enough that the Pope be free: his liberty must be *evident;* he must *appear free* in the eyes of all,—this must be known and believed; on this point there cannot be a doubt or a suspicion.

He might be really free; but if he seemed, I do not say oppressed, but simply a subject,—if he were under the authority of any prince—of the emperor of Austria near home, or the emperor of Brazil further off—we should all be injured and suffer from it; he would not appear to us sufficiently free. A natural distrust would certainly weaken, in some, the respect and obedience which are due to him. The action, the will, the decrees, the words, the sacred person of the chief of the Catholic Church, must be always visibly elevated above all influences and all passions, and neither jarring interests nor irritated passions should ever be able to protest against him with an appearance of justice.

Let us endeavour to penetrate here the vital part of the question, the true nature of this supernatural power, personified in the head of the Church. This power, established for the good of all, has never to decree anything which flatters the miserable interests or bad passions of men; it is the irreconcilable enemy of selfishness and pride, which unceasingly are driving them to dissensions and to revolts. Its honour and its duty, therefore, require it to be free from the shadow even of suspicion, to be always manifestly above all rival pretensions, all jealous prejudices. Neither murmuring and discontented spirits, nor those who are haughty and fiery, or weak and easily scandalized, nor great minds which go astray, and whom the Pope has to warn, nor kings who oppress their subjects, and whom he rebukes, nor peoples who revolt and whom he condemns,—no one, in short, upon earth must ever have reason to suspect the authority, the authenticity, and the perfect independence of his decrees. Now for this, sovereignty is indispensable; if the tiara were to bow beneath any sceptre whatever, would there not be reason to suspect the Pope of partiality and weakness? Accordingly there are no efforts, no sacrifices which he ought not to make to rescue his authority from such a danger. And this is confirmed by the example and the words of Pius IX., who, when flying from outrages and violence at Rome, protested solemnly in these terms; "Among the motives which have determined us to this removal, the most important is, TO HAVE FULL LIBERTY IN THE EXERCISE

OF THE SUPREME POWER OF THE HOLY SEE, WHICH THE CATHOLIC UNIVERSE MIGHT UNJUSTLY SUPPOSE WAS NO LONGER FREE IN OUR HANDS, UNDER THE PRESENT CIRCUMSTANCES."

VI.

We shall only add to this unexceptionable testimony one last consideration, — a consideration pertaining to Christian politics; we offer it confidently to those well-meaning men, who, at least, admiring the Catholic Church, if not sincere believers, do not wish to see this great moral authority, the protectress of all others, shaken or degraded, and who are alive to the real conditions essential to its dignity, independence, and successful operation. Is it not manifest to every honest mind, that if the Church is to be respected, she should be elevated above, not only private, but also above what may be called international passions? What I mean is this: since the fall of the Roman empire, as Fleury remarks, Christendom has been divided into a great number of states independent of each other,—some small and weak, others great and powerful. Now, I ask, is it not absolutely necessary that the former, as well as the latter, be assured of the complete impartiality of the common father, and be unable to suspect him of favouring any to the detriment of the rest?

It is well known that the popes of Avignon were formerly too dependent on the kings of France; and what sad and lamentable results ensued. "If the Pope had continued at Avignon," says Müller,[1] "he would have become a good almoner of France, and no country but France would have acknowledged his authority." Why, too, did Henry IV. attach so much importance to limiting Austrian influence in Italy? He had several reasons, doubtless, relating to French interests, but also one which was Catholic,—" lest the Pope," says Cardinal d'Ossat, our

---

[1] *Müller*, Hist. de la Suisse.

ambassador at Rome, " should be reduced to the condition of chaplain to Philip II."

What we demand here for the Holy See is not essential only to the interests of the Church, but also to those of society. The Protestant historian Voigt, in his work on Gregory VII., praising the great character of that Pope, says, "Even the enemies of Gregory are forced to admit that the ruling idea of this Pontiff—the independence of the Church—was indispensable to the good of the Church, *and also to the reform of society.*"

On the same grounds, one of the counsellors of Pius IX., the cardinal archbishop of Fermo, has remarked, with the most profound truth, that the sovereignty of the Pope is necessary, not only since, as Fleury says, Europe has been divided into a multitude of states, small and great, but especially since the Church has begun to carry the gospel into heathen countries, where the different European nations, Catholic, Protestant, and schismatic, vie with each other in influence. "*Since, then,*" he says, "*the subjection of the Pope to a foreign power would have necessarily been a source of political rivalry and of interminable discord.*"

And it must not be forgotten that not only is Europe divided into a multitude of states, Catholic, Protestant, and schismatical, but the different communions are everywhere mixed together. Protestant England has millions of Catholic subjects; Catholic Poland is under the schismatical autocracy of Russia; the Rhenish provinces, Westphalia, the grand-duchy of Posen and Silesia, are the subjects of Lutheran Prussia. I do not speak of the grand-duchy of Baden, whose sovereigns are Protestant; of Hanover, Switzerland, and so many other countries, where Catholics are mixed up with other communions. Imagine what the Papacy would appear in the eyes of Europe and of Catholicity, if the Pope were subject of one of these powers, small or great,—of the king of Hanover or the Federal Council of Berne, of Queen Victoria, the Emperor Alexander, or of King Frederick William, who laid hands on the archbishop of Cologne.

Again, were the Pope the subject of a Catholic nation,— as France, Austria, or Spain,—what would be his attitude, what his authority or dignity, with regard to the great heretical or schismatical powers, when defending against them the liberty of conscience of their Catholic subjects?[1]

No, we must keep to the true principles which are established by such strong arguments, and proclaimed by such great authorities. Let us repeat with M. de Haller: "The temporal independence, which is necessary to the credit of religion, to the free, secure, and impartial exercise of the spiritual power, is less advantageous to its possessor than to the world." With Montesquieu:[2] "Render sacred and inviolable the ancient and sacred domains of the Church; let them be fixed and eternal as herself." Finally, let us say with Bossuet: "God, who did not intend that this Church, the common mother of all kingdoms, should be temporally dependent on any

---

[1] M. de Sacy, in the noble letter he has published on this subject, says:—"Suppose that this power was Piedmont,—and there is nothing improbable in the idea, the Pope, the chief of Catholicity, is then a Piedmontese subject; that is, he holds the same position with regard to King Victor Emmanuel and M. de Cavour, as the archbishop of Paris does with regard to the emperor and the French ministers. The Pope, the spiritual head of 200 millions of Catholics, a subject of Piedmont! A subject of Piedmont, as bishop of Rome, invested with spiritual power over all Catholic nations! He will have to send them legates or nuncios, and receive ambassadors from them! In person, or by his representatives, he is to come among them to exercise the highest of all jurisdictions! He is to govern their consciences in matters of faith and divine worship, to institute their bishops, to conclude concordats on a footing of equality with their kings or emperors! He has the power to strike them with interdict or excommunication! Does any one imagine that the Catholic powers would long bear this, and that such a state of things would not force them into schism. . . . . Is it not clear that schism, immediate, inevitable schism, must result from this pretended separation of the spiritual from the temporal power, which must make the chief of Catholicity the subject of some power or other?"

[2] Esprit des Lois, l. xxx. c. 5.

"kingdom, and who desired that the see which was to constitute the unity of all the faithful, should finally be placed above the partialities which jarring interests and state jealousies might cause, laid the foundations of this great plan by means of Pepin and Charlemagne. It is the happy consequences of their liberality which have enabled the Church, independent, in her head, of all temporal powers, to exercise more freely for the common good, and under the common protection of Christian kings, her celestial power of directing souls; and, holding the scales even, in the midst of so many empires, often enemies to each other, to maintain unity throughout the whole body, sometimes by inflexible decrees, and sometimes by wise compromises."—(*Sermon on the Unity of the Church.*)

VII.

It is curious—and I will thus conclude the chapter—to see how far the opinion of the first consul on the sovereignty of the Pope coincides with Bossuet's. It is thus given by M. Thiers in his history:—

"The institution which maintains the unity of the faith; that is to say, the Pope, the guardian of Catholic unity, is an admirable one. It is sometimes regretted that this head is a foreign sovereign. He is a foreigner, it is true, and we should thank Heaven for it. The Pope is not at Paris, and it is well he is not; neither is he at Madrid or Vienna, and that is why we suffer his spiritual authority. At Vienna or Madrid they can say the same. Do you think if he were at Paris that the Austrians or Spaniards would consent to receive his decisions? We should thus be glad that he resides away from us, and that he does not reside with our rivals: that he lives in that old Rome, out of the reach of the emperors of Germany, or of the kings of France or Spain, holding the balance between Catholic sovereigns, always giving way a little to the strong, but soon checking himself if the strong becomes an oppressor. Ages have been necessary to arrange matters thus, and they have been well arranged. For the government of souls it is the best, and does the most good, of any institution that can be imagined. And I do not asssert this as a fervent Catholic, but as a man of sense."

These words are worthy of a great mind, which can when it pleases shake off the narrow prejudices of the times. Later, it was for not having always put in practice these principles, and for having forgot the sacred rights of religion, of liberty, and justice, that Napoleon found his power begin to totter. It was surely a memorable struggle, in which was seen the gentlest, the most tender of Pontiffs opposed to the proudest and most violent of Cæsars. But in this struggle, the peaceful combatant overcame; the rights of peace and sacred neutrality triumphed over the imperious will of the conqueror; and when Pius VII., menacingly summoned to declare war against England, replied that *being the common father of all Christians, he could not have enemies among them*—when the invincible Pope having thus spoken, rather than yield, allowed himself to be outraged, expelled, and imprisoned, and, finally, commenced the long martyrdom which England has too soon forgotten; he was both the generous victim and the triumphant defender of the wise and necessary principle, which places the Apostolic See and its temporal power in a superior region of independence and of peace.

In vain Napoleon had recourse to extreme measures of severity; the brutal force of the warrior was overcome by the unconquerable sweetness of the angelic Pontiff.

In vain, afterwards, Napoleon, attempting a theological argument, said before all the bishops, at the Tuileries, to M. Emery, superior of St. Sulpice: "I do not deny you the spiritual power of the Pope, since he received it from Jesus Christ; but Jesus Christ did not give him his temporal power. It was Charlemagne who gave him that; and I, who am Charlemagne's successor, intend to take it from him, because he does not know how to use it, and because it prevents him from exercising his spiritual functions. What do you think of that, M. Emery?"

"Sire," answered M. Emery, "your majesty knows Bossuet, and loves to quote him for us often. These words are his; I know them by heart:—'We know that the Roman pontiffs possess as legitimately as any one on earth, goods, rights, and sovereignty (*bona, jura, imperia*). We know, moreover, that these possessions, as being dedicated to God, are sacred, and that they cannot be invaded without sacrilege. The Apostolic See possesses the sovereignty of the city of Rome and the Roman states, in order to exercise its spiritual power in all the universe more freely and safely (*liberior ac tutior*). We rejoice that it does, not only for its own sake, but for the sake of the whole universal Church, and we wish with all our heart that this sacred principle may for ever remain safe and intact.' "—(*Defence of the Declaration of the French Clergy.*) Napoleon was worsted and withdrew. Some bishops, apologizing to him for the freedom of M. Emery, the emperor replied, "You are wrong; I am not angry with the Abbé Emery. He spoke like a man who was master of his subject. I like people to speak to me so." On going out, he saluted M. Emery with marked esteem and respect.

A few days after having borne this courageous testimony to the papacy in its captivity, M. Emery died at the seminary of St. Sulpice, at the age of eighty, happy in that his long and virtuous career could not terminate more gloriously for himself and his holy society, either before God or men. It was a fresh confirmation of Fenelon's dying message to Louis XIV., "Sire, I know of nothing more apostolic or more venerable than St. Sulpice." Unfortunately, M. Emery's advice had been asked too late. The Pope continued a captive, and the venerable society of St. Sulpice, dissolved by an imperial decree, was soon driven from its peaceful abode, as the reward of its inviolable devotion to the Holy See.

But let us quit this sad subject; Providence has its ways, which we do not understand. Every time has its own trials and its own remedies. Strange to say, it was the nephew of Napoleon, the president elect of the French republic, who, on the eve of his election, wrote thus to the representative of the successor of Pius VII.: "The temporal sovereignty of the venerable head of the Church is intimately connected with the glory of Catholicism, as well as with the liberty and independence of Italy."

CHAPTER IV.

THE POPE SHOULD BE INDEPENDENT WITHIN HIS OWN STATES.

IT is, then, clearly demonstrated that the Pope, in order to exercise freely and without embarrassment his spiritual power, must be free and independent of foreign powers; but he must also be independent at home, in his own states, that is, free from the control of sovereign assemblies and of factions: this remains for us to study.

I.

Common father of the faithful, and king of the great family of the children of God, he has been also appointed by Providence father and king of a people chosen among the nations of the world, of a city privileged above all other cities. Like all temporal princes, and more than any, the Pope has to study the welfare of his subjects; he is bound to dispense to them the benefits of a wise liberty, with those of a regular and paternal administration. And assuredly Pius IX. has not been wanting to these duties: when he was obliged, ten years ago, to fly from Rome before a triumphant rebellion and the bands of Garibaldi, he could, when he first touched foreign soil, have taken solemnly to witness the city from which he was flying, and the whole world with her, that he had done spontaneously, for the true happiness and liberty of his people, more than any European sovereign had then done.

But order is necessary with liberty, the free action of the supreme power must be combined with the regular working of the constitution, to secure the prosperity of the people; and respect for authority must always be the first law, if the public peace is to be maintained, and justice guarded from intimidation. This is still more necessary at Rome than elsewhere; not only the peace and welfare of the Roman people, but the most sacred interests of the Christian world, and the very maintenance of the European equilibrium, require the temporal government of the papacy to be independent of the yoke of intestine factions, as well as of the pressure of foreign powers. It is evident that if the Pope were to suffer violence within his states, if he were oppressed or intimidated by the caprices of the multitude, or the schemes of turbulent parties, at that instant the security of the Church herself would be profoundly shaken: all Christian states who do not choose, and justly so, that the Pope should belong to any power but himself, would feel their liberty injured. If triumphant rebellion is to be allowed, sword in hand, to besiege in his palace the heir of the supreme pontificate and of the principality which Providence has attached to it; if, as we have seen in our times, it is to be allowed, after having assassinated his minister, to threaten to set fire to his palace, to murder his faithful servants, and only to consent to spare their lives on the condition of his forced abdication, and the sacrifice of his inalienable rights, all would be over, not only with the government of the pontifical states, but with the security, the dignity, and the liberty of the government of the universal Church.

We should, or at least might, then see a ministry born of murder and rebellion, speak, act, and decree in the name of the sovereign pontiff; we might see covered by this sacred mantle a hypocritical usurpation of the rights inherent in the supreme authority of the Vicar of Jesus Christ; we might see ecclesiastical laws made by a lay and rebellious assembly, or rather by an anarchical and impious faction. We might also see ritual ordinances proclaimed, contrary to the ancient discipline of the sacred hierarchy and to all the rights of the Church,—bishops, priests, and religious proscribed, or else condemned to take oaths reprobated by their conscience; we might see the education of youth monopolized by systems subversive of parental and religious rights. All these things would be anywhere great evils and great scandals; but at Rome the evil and the scandal would be supreme, religion would be outraged in its most august sanctuary, the last refuge of liberty would be violated; and the reason of these calamities would be, that the Pope was no longer free, independent, and sovereign at Rome.

Doubtless the heir of Leo, of Gregory, and of Innocent, the successor of Pius VI. and Pius VII., those magnanimous pontiffs who confronted with an iron resistance the passions of princes, would in his turn encounter unappalled the passions of the multitude: we know it; martyrdom would, if necessary, maintain the independence of the Vicar of Christ, and his blood would protest against the usurping laws and the sacrileges which men have vainly hoped to impose upon him.

But what affliction for the Church, and what a scandal for Europe, if things were ever to come to this! if such excesses were even attempted in the sight of the Pontiff-king. How sad, if, embracing the crucifix, he were reduced to protest against violence; if the sovereign Pastor of souls, imprisoned, were obliged, in some solitary garden, a new Gethsemane, to drink, prostrate on the ground, the chalice of his passion even to the dregs! All this has happened; all this may again happen; but it surely suffices, at least, to show that the real independence of the sovereign is necessary at Rome more than anywhere else; not only the highest and most universal temporal interests require it, but divine interests also. It is necessary to the Catholic world that its spiritual head, its father and its king, be respected.

And, if I need add anything to such powerful arguments, does any one imagine that the liberty of the sacred congregations which the whole Catholic world has to consult, and, above all, the liberty of the election of the Sovereign Pontiff, and the independence of the conclave

which elects him, is of no consequence to the security of
the Church, or to the justifiable, imperious requirements
of all Christian nations?

Does any one imagine that we can see, unmoved, rebels
and assassins surround the Quirinal, disperse the sacred
college, cause the Pope to die of grief, and prepare him a
successor? Would it, then, be a sufficient consolation for
our souls to reflect that the papacy and the holy Catholic
Church possess the promise of immortality, and that, as
Providence always watches over them, we may set our
minds easy, and sleep in peace? No; we will humbly
confess that our faith is not so sublime, or rather not so
indifferent. We can believe, but we do not wish to tempt
God, nor to make light of the afflictions and the perils of
what is most august and holiest upon earth.

But, passing from these painful emotions and recollections, let us calmly examine yet more thoroughly the nature
of that spiritual magistracy which is called the Roman
Pontificate; entering further into details, we shall see still
more clearly how necessary is its sovereign independence.

II.

What is the Sovereign Pontificate? What is it to
govern the Catholic Church, and what are the external
conditions necessary to the full and free exercise of such
a government?

To govern the Catholic Church is to correspond with all
the churches in the world, with nearly a thousand bishops
or vicars-apostolic who govern them; it is to institute
bishops, to guard the sacred trust of faith and morals, to
maintain discipline, to define doctrine, to condemn errors,
to extirpate abuses, to labour for the propagation of the
Christian faith, to send missionaries of the Gospel and of
civilization into all climates, under all latitudes; it is to
treat with the kingdoms of the earth, to entertain peaceful
relations with all courts, to make those concordats which
concern so nearly the harmonious accord between the two
powers: and at Rome, it is to relieve the necessities of the

people, to found and develop benevolent institutions, to preserve the churches and religious buildings, to protect antiquities and the arts, to receive with affection the Catholics of all countries, and to exercise towards them the noble and generous hospitality which becomes the common father of the great Christian family; for all Christians are citizens of Rome, as Fenelon says: such are some of the vast duties which the government of the Church imposes on the papacy.

But, for the exercise of this great office, for this universal action, for these relations so extensive, so elevated, and so delicate, the Pope evidently requires not only liberty and authority, but numerous coadjutors, adequate temporal resources, and even something of splendour, I do not say for his person—what stranger has not been touched to see the extreme simplicity which surrounds him—but for the sake of his office: and these resources must be independent of every state but his own. Any dependence in this respect would necessarily subject him, even in the government of the Church, to trammels, hostilities, and vexations which our respect for so high a dignity will not allow Catholics to tolerate. Any kind of dependence, at home or abroad, will inevitably reduce him to impotence and degradation.

No, it was never well, and it would be less desirable now than ever, that the Pope should be protected or swayed by Roman factions: I do not mean only the Colonnas or the Frangipanis of old times, but the Rienzis of modern days, the Cicervacchios, the whites or the blacks, the right or the left of a national assembly. We can see but too well at present what might happen in poor weak Italy, if popular leaders became the protectors of the Popes, and the Holy See were under vassalage to them. As M. de Montalembert ably spoke before the *Assemblée Législative:*
—"Whenever the line of conduct adopted by the Holy Father even in the affairs of the Church did not give satisfaction, what would happen? The supplies would be refused him, or he would be threatened with such refusal; any Pope who would follow such or such a course in the general government of the Church would be threatened with a

refusal of the budget; who would not, for instance, condemn such or such an order; we should see some orator mount the tribune of the Roman Assembly, and prove the incompatibility of such or such a religious congregation with modern enlightenment." Nothing could be worse for the security and dignity of Catholic consciences than such an interior, domestic oppression of the papacy, than this shadow of royalty, merely nominal, justly suspected, and continually humbled and curtailed. " In fact," continues M. de Montalembert, "Catholics would not know how to act; their position would become, in some respects, more delicate, more difficult, more painful than if the Pope were the captive of some foreign power. Then, at least, the Catholics would know with whom they had to deal. But with a rival power by his side, they would be in constant uncertainty; his sovereignty would be divided,—that is, annihilated; the Pope would be nominally the king, but really the subject; he would be condemned to do the will of others in the name of his own; it would be for him, as well as for us, the most false, the most equivocal, the most terrible position." [1]

---

[1] It is worth while giving the rest of this speech, pronounced by one who is still an avowed partisan of parliamentary government:—" I wish," says M. de Montelambert, "first to establish why and in what certain liberties are incompatible with the temporal sovereignty of the Pope. It is not that liberty is in itself incompatible with that sovereignty. It has existed with it; in the middle ages very considerable liberties, local, individual, and general, coexisted in the Roman states with the temporal sovereignty of the popes, as they coexisted in other countries with the sovereignty of the kings. But in these latter times modern democracy has established a nearly complete synonymy between liberty and the sovereignty of the people. Certainly this identity is not in the nature of things, for there is very great liberty in England where there is no sovereignty of the people; there was great political liberty in France, too, under the Restoration, when the principle of the sovereignty of the people was not proclaimed. It is this principle of the sovereignty of the people, which, as General Cavaignac has ably remarked in this chamber, is absolutely incompatible with the temporal sovereignty of the Pope; and it is because people con-

I have mentioned concordats. Nothing is more important for the honour of the Church, the tranquillity of consciences, and the peace of religion. The Sovereign Pontiff has very lately concluded several most important concordats: with Russia, on August 3, 1847; with Spain, the 16th March, 1851; with Costa Rica, the 7th October, 1852; with Guatimala the same day; with Austria, the 18th August, 1855; with Wurtemburg, the 8th April, 1857; with Baden, the 28th June, 1859. But if he who made and signed these concordats with these powers were not free, if those with whom he treats might suspect that a foreign influence intervened between him and them, who would consent to treat with him?

I have also spoken of the election of the Sovereign Pontiff and of the independence of the conclave; but to what would they be reduced in the state of things we are considering, and to what evil times might we be brought back? To the saddest period of the middle ages,—the ninth and tenth centuries, when more than once the pontifical tiara, having become the plaything of tyrannical factions, was placed on unworthy brows, to the great scandal and grief of the whole

---

found liberty with the sovereignty of the people, that it has been stated and proved that certain liberties which are now in vogue are incompatible with the sovereignty of the Pope. (Cheers on the right.) The modern sense of sovereignty of the people is, not the right of a people to create its government and found its institutions, but the right of changing them at will, of upsetting everything, of reopening all questions every day, without a pretence, but wantonly, at its mere pleasure. This is what is absolutely incompatible with the Catholic idea of authority; and yet this is what is now meant by the sovereignty of the people; this is what the Romans in particular understand by the sovereignty of the people. (Murmurs on the left.) If they had chosen to content themselves with moderate liberty, they would now be enjoying all the liberties which Pius IX. had granted them. But no, they have preferred to the concessions of Pius IX. the delusions of certain demagogues, titled or untitled; they have preferred revolution to liberty, and now they are suffering for their choice; they have lost political liberty for having chosen to confound it with the arbitrary and illegitimate exercise of the sovereignty of the people." (Hear, hear.)

Church. Who does not know that the great schism of the West arose in consequence of one of these hasty elections, which was suspected not to have been independent? It is now four centuries since any division of this kind has afflicted the Church, and since the scourge of anti-popes has disappeared; thanks to what?—to the full sovereign power at last guaranteed by Europe to the papacy. This is what has liberated the pontifical election from the intestine pressure of parties, as well as from the tyrannical influence of crowns. Well, I repeat that it is of the highest importance to our consciences and to the peace of the world that this favourable state of things be maintained, and that the door remain shut against anti-popes and schisms: it is essential that no lay influence, external to the Catholic electoral college, to whom the Church has confided this sovereign function, may intrude into the election of the universal Pastor of souls; that no people nor assembly may say to the cardinals, "The Pontiff is yours, but the Prince belongs to me; it is for me to choose him."

III.

And here I will say freely, on the question of the rights of the Roman people, either the temporal sovereignty ought not to exist, and the Catholic powers in creating and upholding it were wrong, and have misunderstood the general and permanent interests of Christendom, or the cardinal interests which have necessitated this creation should here overrule all other interests, and place the Roman States in an exceptional position; glorious and advantageous to them, in my opinion, to abdicate which would be for them a political suicide, and whose continuance is conformable to all the principles of justice.

But, I may be asked, How do you reconcile this exceptional position with what are called national rights, the rights of the people? In whatever manner these rights are understood, M. Thiers, in his celebrated report on the Roman question, has pointed out the true answer to this question. These are his words:—" Catholic unity would be untenable if the Pontiff, who is its centre, were not completely independent; if in the territory which ages have assigned him, and which all nations have respected, another sovereign, whether prince or people, should rise to dictate laws to him: for the pontificate, sovereignty is the only independence. *This interest is one of a superior order, which should overrule inferior interests, as, in a state, the public interest silences individual interests.*" This principle explains everything; it may be called an elementary, fundamental principle, which is continually applied in political and international law, as well as in civil law. Let us give some instances.

The Turks cannot permit any vessel of war to pass the Dardanelles; their most faithful allies cannot pass from the Mediterranean to the Black Sea, nor from the Black Sea to the Mediterranean. Whatever the interests of the Turks may be in this, whatever their territorial and maritime right, it matters not, the interests of Europe and public law, which is the interpreter of general interests, forbid it. So also Europe has neutralized certain nations, for instance, Belgium and Switzerland. As M. de la Rosière said in his remarkable speech, they may feel a warlike enthusiasm, or religious and political leanings and inclinations, but they cannot make war, nor contract alliances; the general interests forbid it; Europe has stamped them with neutrality. So also in the United States, of all nations the most jealous of their liberties, and of the sovereignty of the people, while each state has a constitution of its own, Columbia alone has none. Why so? Because Columbia is the seat of the Federal Government. So that to secure the peace, liberty, and dignity of the deliberations of the government, the United States have reduced the territory of Columbia to political incapacity, and the inhabitants of Washington, in that free country, cannot even choose their municipal magistrates.

These analogies suffice to explain why the Roman people, whether as a member of Catholic society, or of the European family, ought not to have authority over its government; why it cannot be allowed to bias and to sway at pleasure the authority of the Sovereign Pontiff, "without which," says M. Thiers, "Catholic unity would be dissolved, Catholicism would be severed into sects, and the moral world, already so rudely shaken, would fall into a heap of ruins."

Hence, also, the right of interference always asserted by Catholic nations whenever attempts have been made against a government founded by the whole of Catholicity, and which it is bound by its dearest interests to protect. It is, in fact, clear that all nations which are daughters of the Church, and even others, are deeply interested in preserving intact the Pope's temporal power, as a security morally necessary to religious liberty; and hence they have here an exceptional right of interference.[1] Nay, it is incumbent on them to interfere, particularly when, as at present, what is chiefly required is to defend the real wishes and the liberty of the population against foreign demagogues who overawe them. The courageous and un-

---

[1] M. de la Rosière says:—"Shall I cite some examples of Catholic jurisprudence with regard to the Holy See? When, in the fourteenth century, the popes were at Avignon, after they had been there for some time, as soon as Catholicity began to perceive that they did not enjoy there the full independence requisite for the good use of their authority, as Voltaire says, all Catholic sovereigns began to communicate to each other their suspicions,—the king of Spain, the king of Hungary, the king of Aragon, the king of England, the king of Sicily; the emperor of Germany crossed the Alps to confer with Urban IV. as to his return, and when the Pope re-entered Rome, he was conducted to the mouth of the Tiber by the united galleys of Venice, Genoa, and Sicily. In the sixteenth century, when the duke of Bourbon besieges and sacks Rome, Francis I. instantly takes arms, and at the news of his preparations, Charles V. withdraws his army. In the wars of the Revolution and the Empire, the idea of a religious crusade plays a great part in political coalitions. In 1832 Austria takes possession of the Legations; the French flag is hoisted at Ancona to compel her to withdraw; and finally, at the present day, General Cavaignac too feels the spontaneous, involuntary, irresistible impulse which at all periods has urged Catholicity to interfere in the affairs of Rome, in order to protect either the Pope's government or his person."

fortunate Count Rossi boldly declared to these conspirators, in the city of Rome, "As to the pontifical throne, the matter is still more serious. The independence of the Sovereign Pontiff is under the common protection of the consciences of all Catholics. Rome, with its monuments raised by the treasures of all Europe,—Rome, the centre and head of Catholicism, belongs more intimately to the Christians than to the Romans themselves. Be assured that *we will not suffer Catholicity to be decapitated*, nor the Pope to be forced to fly to some place of refuge, which might cost him the sacrifice of his liberty."—(*Revue des Deux Mondes*, tom. xxiv. Dec. 1848, p. 1837.)

IV.

We could cite innumerable opinions and authorities in support of the principle we are maintaining, so irresistible is its truth, and so capital its importance. Notwithstanding his Protestant prejudices, a celebrated historian, M. Hurter, the uprightness of whose intentions, and the goodness of whose heart have since called down upon him the benedictions of God, wrote thus in his Life of Innocent III.: "The tranquillity of the country and the city where the Sovereign Pontiff resides, to watch over the Church in all other countries, is a condition necessary to the fulfilment of the duties of so elevated a position. How, in fact, could the Pope weigh so many different causes, give advice and assistance, decide the numberless affairs of so many churches, watch over the progress of the kingdom of God, repulse attacks against the faith, speak freely to kings and peoples, if he had not peace at home; if the plots of the wicked forced him to concentrate on his own states the glance which should embrace the world, to combat for his own safety and liberty, or to seek refuge and protection upon foreign soil?"

The English House of Lords, in spite of the anti-Catholic prejudices and hatred which prevail there, has more than once seen disinterested testimony borne to this principle: thus, on the 21st of July, 1849, in the debate upon the Roman expedition, Lord Lansdowne did not hesitate to say, in reply to Lord Aberdeen and Lord Brougham: "The state of the papal sovereignty is peculiar in this, that, while, temporally speaking, he is a monarch of the fourth or fifth class, he is, by his spiritual power, a sovereign *without an equal* upon earth. *Every country which has Catholic subjects has an interest in the condition of the Roman States, and is bound to see that the Pope be not embarrassed in the exercise of his authority by any influence capable of affecting his spiritual power.*"

"We will say frankly," to borrow the words of a politician noted for his extreme democratic views, "that the Catholic powers have a real and serious interest, founded upon their own security and preservation, in maintaining the temporal authority of the Popes in the metropolis of their spiritual sovereignty. Seeing that the deposal, as a temporal sovereign, of the head of the Church, may cause so many evils and disasters to society, and may involve the ruin of a universal institution, on whose integrity depend the tranquillity of consciences and the peace of the world, is not one prompted to ask whether a petty people, raised into a state solely by foreign hands, and still depending upon their support, may justly assert, in the name of their independence, that to them alone its sovereignty belongs to pronounce so momentous a decision?"

I am happy to be able to quote an opinion of still greater weight, expressed in the most convincing eloquence. "Why demand from the papacy," exclaims M. Villemain, "why require from it, what facts render impossible? Rome can never again become the political capital of a great state, precisely because she must ever remain the religious metropolis of the world. The day that the supreme pontificate was given her, it was settled that she was never again to see a dictatorial senate, or a forum. If for fifteen centuries no lay sovereignty could exist at Rome by the side of the tiara, if right and conquest have both failed to maintain any, if the imperial power found itself always forced to remove to Constantinople, Milan, or Ravenna, to some place where the Pope was not, neither can the modern sovereignty of popular elections enthrone itself in the place where the Pope must reign. . . . . The Sovereign Pontiff cannot establish all the machinery of representative government. . . . If any will but his could dispose of Rome, Rome would no longer be an inviolable and neutral asylum. The most ardent advocates of the indefectibility of the apostolic chair have never advanced that its temporal power is infallible; but it must be independent. If we cannot conceive it stretching to a distance, and encompassing all Italy in its dominion, still less can we conceive it subjected to the ascendancy of a national assembly. . . . . Let not a zeal for constitutional uniformity make us forget certain laws of human nature and of history. A sceptical writer of the last century observed, that, in general, the Pope, as a temporal sovereign, because of the usual conditions of his election and of his power, was free from most of the evils and defects of absolute government. All that Europe should desire for the improvement of Italy is to see durable reforms, granted by the free gift of a great pontiff, and united to his inalienable privilege of independent sovereignty. The imperishable glory of Rome, which the sword cannot prevail against, which has survived barbarian violence and civilized force, which arrested Attila and brought about the fall of Napoleon, is the chair from which the Pope addresses the world, whether in grandeur or in captivity, at the Vatican or at Fontainbleau.

"Let not the Roman people, then, ever be moved by agitators to reduce their Church to servitude. They would thus lose their most precious privileges; they would fall into that anarchy, the prey of every accident, which they felt at the beginning of the middle ages; or they would make another trial of the republican representation of 1798, which would bring them back a Cæsar, or even a foreign army without Cæsar. Rome is too great a temptation for ambition to remain long intact, if she is to cease to be sacred; and she can only be so in the person of the Pontiff, and for the good of those who venerate and reverence his power. Rome, if not the city of the Pope, free and happy in him, is a capital without an empire; or, as was said in Alaric's time, the decapitated head of the old world. It is better for her to be the soul of modern society."

V.

There still remains an important and final reason to be considered, upon which we have not yet touched.

The Pope must be free, independent, and sovereign at home and abroad; *at home, that he may be so abroad*, in the government of the Church. We have examined the convincing arguments which establish this. But he must also be independent at home, in order to maintain harmonious relations with all Christian nations, to preserve a neutrality of reconciliation during all their quarrels with each other, and to be ever upon earth the true prince of peace, as his divine office requires him to be.

Now, if anything is self-evident, it is that the Sovereign Pontiff could not hold this calm and lofty attitude, if the ascendancy of a body of representatives, if the caprices of a faction could involve him in the political struggles of his country, and substitute, in his relations with the universal Church, for the high, independent, and Catholic spirit which ought to be his, the narrow-mindedness, the petty and violent prejudices of parties: if, to speak plainly, he could be dragged into Italianism, exclusive, ambitious Italianism, perhaps even the dreams of Gioberti.

The common father must always be free to raise pure and peaceful hands upon the holy mountain, that the spirit of union and concord may descend upon Christian princes and people. "The earth," says St. Augustine, "is sometimes agitated by wars, as the sea is by tempests. The human race has its storms; the sky grows dark, and a whirlwind of universal war seems to devastate everything. May there be at least one people who escape this terrible storm! one tranquil city, whence pacification may arise!"[1]

---

[1] Voltaire writes:—"The interests of mankind demand some curb to keep sovereigns in check, and to protect the people. This

Though wars be sometimes inevitable, and may sometimes arm the purest hands in legitimate self-defence, they are, nevertheless," adds the holy doctor, "a cruel sport of evil spirits,—*ludi Dæmonum*. Those who make war sometimes do so from necessity; but the state of those who are spared the scourge of war, and who spare it to others, is confessedly the happiest."

Romans, listen to these words: do not complain of the glorious privilege conferred upon you by your pontiff-king, who emancipates you from the sad necessity of war, and secures to you that peaceful, honourable, and ever independent neutrality which you have enjoyed during the last centuries in the midst of Christian Europe, and which it depends upon yourselves to continue for ever to enjoy.

We concur, with gratitude, in the wish expressed in the *Assemblée Nationale*, by a distinguished French representative, on the question of restoring to the Sovereign Pontiff all his rights in their integrity.[1]

" Does any one consider that the Roman States, which have for capital the Eternal City, with the Catholic interests which are attached to it, are not in the world of a far different importance from Belgium? For my part, I am convinced that, after the criminal and deplorable

---

curb of religion might by general consent have been placed in the hands of the Popes. These chief Pontiffs, taking no part in temporal quarrels except to appease them, warning kings and people of their duty, reproving their crimes, and reserving excommunications for great offences only, would have been always regarded as the images of God upon earth."—*Essai sur l'Hist. Gén.* ch. 60.

"I should recommend," says Leibnitz, "to establish at Rome a tribunal (to judge of differences between princes), and to make the Pope president, as he was, in fact, formerly the umpire between Christian princes. This plan would succeed quite as well as that of the Abbé de St. Pierre (a plan for universal peace in Europe). But since people now are fond of speculations, why should we find fault with a fiction which would *restore to us the Golden Age*?"—*Œuvres de Leibnitz*, tom. v. p. 65, 2nd Letter to M. Grimaret.

[1] Baron Charles Dupin.

events which have just taken place in Italy, their interests will excite the deepest attention in all Christian nations. I am convinced that a benefit will result, which I most profoundly desire. Yes, the Christian Powers will do for the Roman States what they have done for Belgium; they will proclaim the perpetual neutrality of the states of the Holy Father, and will place them under the guardianship of all Christendom. All Catholic nations will secure to the Holy Father the permanent possession of the states which he received from France a thousand years ago. Such are my wishes, such are my hopes. I have the firm conviction that Christian nations will hear them, and that they will be realized."

We shall shortly explain, when examining what would be the condition of Rome without the Pope, what solid advantages abundantly compensate the peculiarity of the political position which the Romans occupy in the world.

CHAPTER V.

ORIGIN AND PROVIDENTIAL PREPARATION OF THE TEMPORAL POWER OF THE HOLY SEE.

WE have hitherto seen what were the designs, and, if we may dare to say so, what was the idea of God in establishing the temporal power of the Holy See. Providence has chosen, for the security of the Church and our own, that the Pope be free and independent, and that he appear so: that his independence be sovereign, in order that he be always free both at home and abroad, in the exercise of his august ministry. Such are the weighty grounds and reasons, the providential principles, as it were, of this sovereignty of the Vicar of Christ.

Let us now study the facts, in order to throw still clearer light upon the principles: let us see historically in what manner this idea, this plan of God for his Church, has been realized. Let us seek in history for the titles of this sacred royalty, and inquire if any power has risen in the world, whose origin is so pure and honourable, if any state was ever founded, in the face of day, upon more legitimate and irreproachable bases.

I.

So it seemed to the great genius of Bossuet, and his great episcopal heart felt a just and holy pride on this head, as we have seen in his words already cited. An illustrious writer of our century[1] has expressed himself in not less remarkable terms: "There is no sovereignty in Europe more justifiable, if I may so speak, than that of the sovereign pontiffs. It is like the divine law, *justificata in semetipsá*. But what is truly astonishing is, to see the Popes become sovereigns without their knowledge, and even, to speak strictly, in spite of themselves. The see of Rome seemed elevated by an invisible law, and the head of the Universal Church grew into a sovereign. From the martyrs' scaffold he ascended a throne which at first was not perceptible, but which insensibly became consolidated, like all great institutions." In fact, tracing back as far as we can the records of past ages, we find in the Papacy a sort of temporal magistracy, recognized and venerated by the faithful of Rome. Its vestiges may even be remarked in the epistles of St. Paul. This magistracy was at first located in the Catacombs. There, the Pontiff and his priests, according to the doctrine and the exhortations of the great apostle,[2] distributed justice to the first faithful; and the authority of this august and peaceful arbitration embraced all their affairs, even of a secular kind, all the disputes which might break out between them, and disturb the concord of their families. Nothing could be more humble and unobtrusive, less imposed by force, and more willingly accepted, than this power: still

---

[1] Count de Maistre.   [2] 1 Cor. vi.

Pagan Rome took offence at it. The Pope bore upon his brow the character of so eminent a priesthood, as Bossuet says, that *the Emperor, who counted among his titles that of Sovereign Pontiff, was more troubled at his presence in Rome than he would have been if, among his armies, a rival were pretending to the throne of the Cæsars.*

When the Church left the Catacombs, this magistracy, consecrated by the respect and confidence of the early Christians, and rendered more and more necessary by the difficulties of the times, remained in force to receive from princes and people the successive extensions which the Almighty reserved for it, and to grow, in the course of time, into the temporal sovereignty which we see at present, *but whose name Providence had not yet pronounced. Its rise, so gradual and imperceptible, is one of the most curious phenomena in history. Here are discovered no treaties, no battles, no intrigues, no usurpations:*[1] go back as far as we may, the most scrupulous investigation always finds a power established, as it were, of itself—a power peaceful, beneficent, and disinterested, and, soon endowed with an independent domain by the eager homage of universal Christendom, peoples as well as kings. Constantine, Theodosius—all the most Christian emperors —and, after the fall of the Empire of the West, Pepin, Charlemagne, Otho, the Countess Matilda, appear to our view, visibly chosen by God to constitute this sovereignty, so precious for the interests of the Church. But the force of events, as I have observed, had begun this great work long before Constantine, and the facts which history here reveals to us are most curious.

II.

Even at the time of the most violent persecutions, when the glorious martyrs of the Roman Church were shedding their blood in the Coliseum, she exercised her spiritual authority over the faithful, dispersed over the face of the

---

[1] De Maistre.

earth; and even then God provided for her all the temporal means necessary to the exercise of this sacred authority. The Church of Rome, mother and mistress of all churches, was even then, as was fitting, the richest in resources, the most powerful in action, and also the most generous in charity. The scattered faithful revered her as the centre of Catholicity, and offered her their goods in profusion, as well as their obedience and their love. They wished the Chief of Religion and Vicar of Christ not to be unequal to the immense calls of his spiritual administration; they wished to see the Pope able to meet all the exigencies of his universal mission— all the enormous expenses required for the guidance of so many peoples confided to his care, as well as for the evangelization of heathen nations, to whom he had to send bishops and apostolic missioners.

Hence the riches of the Roman Church, even during the persecutions; hence the considerable possessions she enjoyed long before Constantine; hence, also, her alms and liberalities. She supported, says Eusebius, a great number of clerks, widows, orphans, and of poor, while she propagated the faith and founded new churches in the most distant countries. Eusebius instances Syria and Arabia; our own records add the Gauls and Spain. This was not all: the Papacy, still hiding in the Catacombs, required apostolic notaries to keep the acts of the martyrs, and to answer the incessant consultations of all the churches; while it was covering the seas with ships loaded with its alms.

Such were, even before peace was granted to the Church, the temporal riches which the faithful lavished upon the Apostolic See, and which were so nobly devoted by the charity of the popes to the welfare of their flock.[1] We learn from records and from some remarkable facts,

---

[1] See *Alban Butler*, Lives of the Fathers; *Fleury*, Hist. Eccl. tom. ii. liv. 7, No. 39; *S. Ambrose*, De Officiis, ii. 28; *Pruden.* Hymn 2 de Coronis; *Euseb.* Hist. iv. 23, vii. 5.

that the Roman Church possessed not only rich vessels of gold and silver for the celebration of the holy mysteries,—chalices, ciboriums, and numbers of movables of the highest value,—but also considerable *landed property*. Constantine gave orders to RESTORE to the clergy, says Eusebius, "*the houses, the possessions, the fields, the gardens, and other goods of which they had been unjustly deprived.*"[1] It is indeed strange, and has not been sufficiently dwelt upon, that in the midst of paganism those rights of property were conceded to the Church, which, after eighteen centuries of Christianity, men who call themselves Catholics are found to dare to contest to her. Except in the last fury of the persecutions, the pagan emperors and magistrates not only recognized in the Christian Church these rights of property, but even sometimes defended them against violence and injustice. Lampridius, in his Life of Alexander Severus, cites a remarkable instance of this moderate conduct of certain pagan emperors, and relates in detail how Alexander Severus restored to the Christians, for their worship, a place the possession of which certain innkeepers disputed with them.[2] Eusebius, the historian, cites several facts of the same kind. The life of Aurelian, though he was one of the persecuting emperors, offers a particularly striking example. Paul of Samosata, protected by Zenobia, queen of Palmyra, was living at Antioch, and continued, notwithstanding the condemnation of a council, in the house which belonged to the Church. The Christians complained to the Em-

---

[1] " Omnia ergo quæ ad ecclesias recte visa fuerint pertinere, sive domus ac possessio sit, sive agri, sive horti, seu quæcumque alia, nullo jure quod ad dominium pertinet imminuto, sed salvis omnibus atque integris manentibus, restitui jubemus."—*Euseb*. Vita Constant. 2, 39; see also cap. 21, 36, and 41.—*Euseb*. Hist. Eccl. viii. 1, 2; x. 5.—*Fleury*, Hist. Eccl. tom. ii. liv. ix. 46; tom. iii. liv. x. 2 and 40.

[2] "Cum Christiani quemdam locum, qui publicus fuerat, occupassent, contrà popinarii dicerent sibi eum deberi, rescripsit (imperator) melius esse ut quomodocumque illic Deus colatur, quam popinariis dedatur."

peror Aurelian, and he ordered possession of the house to be given to those to whom the bishops of Italy and the Roman Pontiff addressed their letters; so notorious was it, even to the pagans, that the Christian churches had the right of possessing, and that the mark of true Christians was communion with the Church of Rome. Paul of Samosata was consequently expelled from the Church, and from the house belonging to the Church, by the secular magistrate.

This right of property was then the common and constant right of the Christian churches, and that from the very commencement of Christianity. Have we not seen the earliest of all churches, the Church of Jerusalem, governed by the Apostles themselves, and the model of all others, possessing goods intended for the support of the pastors and of the faithful, and for the relief of the poor? This right no one, whether Jew or pagan, thought of refusing them. Existence was often denied them; but whenever they were suffered to exist, the right of possessing was not denied them. Accordingly, the history of the foundation of all churches in the empire and all over the world, shows that there was not a single large Christian community which had not, and which was not obliged to have, goods more or less considerable, for the relief of the indigent, the support of the clergy, and other expenses relating to divine worship.[1] What I here lay down as a principle and a fact, will perhaps excite some surprise; but, independently of the historical proof, does not common sense show that it was then, as it is now, a simple necessity founded on the nature of things, and that the Church, as soon as she exists, may and must be

---

[1] The persecution excited in Africa by Maximian Hercules in 303 gives an idea of the riches of the African churches at that period. The acts of this persecution inform us that Paul, bishop of Cirta, in Numidia, placed in the hands of the magistrates of that town two chalices of gold, six of silver, six silver vases, a silver ewer, seven lamps of the same metal, and several other precious articles intended for the services of the Church.

a proprietor? She may, because she constitutes a real and legitimate community; and it is an elementary principle of law, that all the rights of property belong to communities, who acquire property and exercise their rights by the medium of their administrators. Is it not quite as evident that material resources are absolutely necessary to the Church in order to meet the wants of her ministers and her worship? And is not the least reflection sufficient to show it is only property which can secure to her these resources in a stable manner, without which her liberty must ever be precarious, and her existence miserably dependent? In fact, to refuse the Church the right of possessing, is to refuse her the right of existing; and the latter impious and deadly design inspires more or less all systems hostile to ecclesiastical property.

It has seemed to me necessary to the present inquiry to insist upon these fundamental principles; and I have thought it useful to examine how they had been understood and practised under the pagan and persecuting empire. The edict of Licinius and Constantine, when peace was granted to the churches, is extremely interesting to study in this point of view. In conclusion, I shall quote a few words of it:—

"We have ordered, moreover, concerning the Christians, that, if the places where they used to assemble formerly, have been bought by any, whether from our treasury or from any one else, they be *restored* to the Christians without expense, and without any delay or difficulty. Those who may have received them as a gift are also to return them immediately; and let both those who have bought and those who have been given them, apply to the governor of the province, in order that he may arrange with them for us. All these places shall be immediately delivered over *to the communities*, that is, to the churches, and not to individuals. You are to see all these things restored to *their corporations and communities*, on the conditions above expressed, without any difficulty or dispute, it being understood that such as shall have restored them without reimbursement may hope to be indemnified by us."

III.

With Constantine, a change passed over the world. He did not content himself with restoring to the Christians the possessions which belonged to them; he added other and far more important ones. Naturally generous, his munificence never shone forth more than towards the Church. One cannot read without surprise the details given on this subject by contemporary authors, and particularly Eusebius, the most ancient of any, and the most likely to be well-informed as to the facts he states. In all parts of the empire,—at Constantinople, at Jerusalem, at all the holy places, but especially at Rome, Constantine built magnificent churches, and assigned to them handsome revenues: he spared nothing, neither in the beauty of the structures, the richness of the ornaments and of the sacred vessels, nor in the payment of the clergy, and the assistance given to the different works of charity undertaken by the zeal of the pastors and the piety of the faithful.

Anastasius, the librarian, makes an astonishing calculation of the offerings of this great prince to the churches of Rome and some other churches in Italy.[1] If we add together the values of all the gold and silver ornaments mentioned by the historian, we find that they amounted to 685 lbs. of gold and 12,943 lbs. of silver, which comes to upwards of £68,000 of our money, without the workmanship. And Anastasius does not include in this sum the gold employed in gilding the roof of the Constantine Basilica, which was 500 feet long. Constantine also settled on this basilica considerable revenues in land, situated both at Rome and its environs, and in distant provinces.[2] All these lands which are enumerated by

---

[1] *Anastas.*, Vita S. Silvestri.—*Fleury*, Mœurs des Chrétiens, No. 50; Hist. Eccl. tom iii. xi. 36.
[2] *Zaccario*, De Rebus ad Hist. et Antiquit. Eccles. pertinentibus (Fulginiæ, 1781).

Anastasius furnished a revenue to the basilica of about £9,300 of our money. The emperor added an annual tribute of 150 lb. of aromatics for the divine services. Besides these offerings to the Constantine Basilica, the same prince made the most generous gifts to the churches of Rome which he had built or repaired, particularly to those of St. Peter, St. Paul, the Holy Cross of Jerusalem, St. Agnes, St. Lawrence, SS. Peter and Marcellinus. He also assigned to these churches extensive possessions in land, either in Rome and Italy, or in Africa and Asia, even in the provinces of the Euphrates. The lands belonging to the Roman churches, exclusive of the Constantine Basilica, brought in annually about £10,500 of our money.

Most of the successors of Constantine behaved not less generously than he towards the Roman Church. And it should be added that the generosity of the emperors was singularly encouraged by the personal disinterestedness of the popes and bishops, and the noble, charitable uses to which they put the gifts of the imperial munificence and those of the piety of the people. Of this I will enumerate some examples.

The Christian Church appeared, from the beginning, to have been raised up by God to teach sentiments of humanity towards the poor, and to inspire men with a spirit of compassion to which they had hitherto seemed entirely strangers. This was something quite new to the Pagans. At the sight of the tender charity which bound together all the faithful, they used to exclaim with amazement, according to Tertullian: *See how they love one another!* The Emperor Julian himself, that open enemy of Christianity, blushed for the contrast between the Pagans and the Christians in this respect. We see this particularly in his letter to Arsaces, pontiff of Galatia, in which he charges him to establish alms-houses for the relief of the poor, according to the example of the Christians, who, *besides their own poor*, says he, *support ours also, whom we leave in destitution.*[1] St. John the

---

[1] Ancient writers, who have described in detail the public build-

Almoner, patriarch of Alexandria, had in his episcopal city more than seven thousand five hundred poor, whom he supplied with daily bread. Besides these daily alms, the holy patriarch had established, in different parts of his diocese, hospitals for strangers, the aged, and the sick; the poor were there received in crowds. His charity was not confined to his diocesans, it ministered also to the wants of a multitude of churches and of poor, in all Egypt and the East. The popes and the bishops sold even the sacred vessels to feed the destitute and to redeem captives. St. Ambrose in particular did so, for the redemption of the captives carried away by the Goths, under the reigns of Valens and of Gratian. About the same time, St. Exuperius of Toulouse reduced himself in this way to such poverty, that he was obliged to place

---

ings of Rome, Constantinople, and other famous cities of antiquity, enumerate their palaces, baths, theatres, temples, ports, public granaries, prisons, and other buildings of public utility: but they mention no establishment for the sick or the destitute. The first hospitals on record, are due to the charity of the Christians. St. Gregory of Nazianzen, in his *Discourse against Julian*, in 363, shows that they had already established a number of these pious asylums before the reign of that prince, who in vain endeavoured to form similar ones. *Diversoria et hospitales domos, monasteria item et virginum cœnobia, ædificare statuebat, simulque et benignitatem erga pauperes adjungere, cum in aliis rebus tum in commendatitiis epistolis sitam, quibus eos qui inopiá premuntur, ex gente ad gentem transmittimus; quæ videlicet ille in nostris rebus præsertim admiratus fuerat. . . . Illius autem conatus inanis et irritus fuit.*—S. Greg. Naz. Orat. I. contra Julian. tom. i. p. 138, edit. Benedict.

Since then this new kind of institution multiplied rapidly in all parts of the empire, and everywhere that Christianity was diffused. St. Basil built, in his episcopal city, an hospital for the poor, about the year 372, and others in other towns of his diocese. Some years afterwards, St. Pammachus established one at Porto, near Rome, for strangers, and another at Rome, assisted by a Roman lady, named Fabiola, who devoted herself with the most tender charity to the service of the sick there. About the same time St. Augustin constructed at Hippo an almshouse for foreigners, and St. Gallican another at Ostia. Several constitutions of the Emperor Justinian

the body of our Lord in a wicker basket, and the precious blood in a chalice of glass.

But the Roman Church, above all, multiplied her alms and liberalities, in proportion as her resources increased. History teaches that the sovereign Pontiffs continually turned to the relief of the poor and the needs of divine worship, the rich offerings they received from the piety of the faithful. St. Jerome states this in particular of Pope Anastasius I., whom he calls on this account *a man rich in poverty*. We know all that St. Leo the Great did to repair the calamities which Italy suffered from the Vandals. Pope Gelasius I. voluntarily reduced himself to poverty, in order to be able to feed a multitude of poor. The pontificate of St. Gregory deserves particularly to be named as one of the most perfect models of pon-

---

show that there were in his time a number of hospitals established in the different parts of the empire, and grant great privileges to these precious establishments. Ducange, in the description of the buildings erected in the imperial city, under the Christian emperors, reckons thirty-five houses of charity intended for the relief of different classes of poor. Most of them had names which indicated their object. The infant asylum was called *Brephotrophium;* the orphan refuge, *Orphanotrophium;* the hospital for the sick, *Nosocomium; Xenodochium* for strangers; *Gerontocomium* for the aged; *Ptochotrophium,* for the poor in general. These establishments were generally under the superintendence of the bishop, who named a priest to act for him, and spared nothing in the relief of the sick and poor. However, flattering as is this picture of the virtues and charity of the clergy at the period we speak of, we are far from imagining that there were then no abuses in the use and administration of church property, or that all the members of the clergy were equally distinguished for their generosity and disinterestedness. One must be very ignorant, both of human nature and of history, to deny that even the ages which have been most fruitful in virtues have had many scandals to deplore. As long as a society is composed of men, and not of angels, we may wish, but cannot expect to find all its members constantly faithful to the severe rules of detachment and self-denial which the Gospel lays down. Still, the human defects which remain should not make us forget what evidently comes from God in the matters we have been considering. —*Gosselin*, Pouvoir du Pape.—*Fleury*, Mœurs des Chrétiens, &c.

tifical charity. This great Pope lavished the goods of the Church upon the poor with a holy prodigality, not only at Rome and in Italy, but in all parts of Christendom. We see in all his letters to the administrators or *rectors of the patrimony of* the Roman Church, which was situated in different countries, how he excited their charity to orphans, widows, the poor of every kind, particularly those who were ashamed to beg. In order to animate his clergy by his own example, he gave himself abundant alms daily at Rome, which he redoubled at certain times of the year, and particularly during the calamities brought by the barbarian invasions upon the empire of the West. There was still to be seen in the ninth century, at the Lateran Palace, a register of the poor of every age and sex whom the holy Pope was in the habit of relieving at Rome, in Italy, and other countries, and of the stated alms he gave them. There may be still seen at Rome (I have seen it myself) the great stone table on which he served every day a meal for the poor with his own hands.

Long before St. Gregory, there existed, wherever the Church of Rome possessed patrimonies, an almshouse for the poor, called Diaconia, because it was generally administered by a deacon. Not content with continuing these charitable institutions, St. Gregory often desired the rectors of the patrimonies of the Holy See to employ all the revenues which they produced in relieving the poor of the place: and he says distinctly, in one of his letters, that if he appoints clerks, and not laymen, to govern these patrimonies, it is less to prevent malversation, than that a wise administration may make them benefit a greater number of poor.

It was not, indeed, only towards the poor that he showed himself so prodigal of the goods of the Church. We shall soon see him employing them with the same liberality for the defence of the empire, then so violently attacked in Italy by the Lombards; and his generosity in this respect served as a rule and a model to all his successors during the whole duration of the Roman empire in the West.

But here a new and grand picture unrolls itself, which must be closely examined in the light of history, and for which all that precedes was but the providential preparation.

IV.

From the moment that Constantine, victorious by the Cross, was established on the imperial throne, an attentive glance might have observed that Providence was beginning to reveal its plans, and that the new destinies of the eternal city were becoming visible. One feels, one sees that a vast revolution is preparing in the Roman world, and being accomplished with wonderful force and sweetness. Constantine was the first to perceive it, and he became, as it were, the herald of Providence. In transporting the seat of the Roman power from the banks of the Tiber to the shores of the Bosphorus; in making a fisherman's village his imperial city, he also made Rome the holy city and the capital of another empire, the kingdom of God upon earth, *regnum Dei*, which was to embrace the whole universe. Did he foresee this great novelty? Was it given him from above to feel that Rome had been conquered by the Cross and by charity, that three centuries of persecutions and of blood had adequately paid for this conquest, and that henceforth human pomp was to disappear before sacred festivals, the Emperor before the Pontiff?

However that may be, he withdrew. After that, for the good of the people themselves, the Vicar of Christ had to fill the place at Rome of the absent Cæsar; or, rather, to borrow the words of Count de Maistre—"*The same precincts could not contain the Emperor and the Pontiff; Constantine yielded up Rome to the Pope.* From that time we also observe that the emperors seem no longer at home in Rome; they resemble strangers passing through and lodging there from time to time. But what is still more surprising, Odoacer, with his Heruli, puts an end to the Western empire in 575. Soon afterwards, the Heruli disappear before the Goths, and they in their turn give place to the Lombards, who take possession of the kingdom of Italy. What force was it which, for more than three centuries, prevented all these princes from fixing durably their throne at Rome? Whose was the arm which drove them to Milan, to Pavia, to Ravenna, &c. ?" He who cannot see here the finger of Providence must be blind indeed.

And yet, the Roman Pontiffs, already sovereigns of Rome, without intending it, almost without knowing it, ceased not to labour, as far as lay in them, to maintain there the authority of the emperors of Constantinople. We shall see them employing for several centuries, with an incomparable zeal, all their authority to nourish in the hearts of the people fidelity to their masters. But it was in vain; an invisible force was endowing the See of Rome with temporal sovereignty, and forming the independent patrimony of St. Peter. Under the hand of Providence everything concurred to forward the work; the East, the West, kings and peoples, great and small, vied with one another in generosity, as well as in affection and gratitude, towards the Holy See. Accordingly, from the fourth century we see the possessions and domains of the Church of Rome increasing in extent and importance.[1] In the sixth century, according to the most authentic records, the Roman Church possessed extensive territories in Italy, at Rome, Naples, and in Calabria, and in several other provinces, in Dalmatia, Sicily, Sardinia, Corsica, Spain, the Gauls, and Africa.[2] Among these possessions some

---

[1] Doubtless the rights of property of the Church of Rome are not the right of the Pope's temporal sovereignty: the grounds on which they rest are not the same. The title to the possession of lands does not confer sovereignty over people; the right of governing is different from that of administering domains. But the rights of property of the Roman Church preceded and prepared her rights of sovereignty; and it is as well not to forget these important facts, in times which have seen, and may again see, these two great rights of the Church contested.

[2] S. Gregorii Vita, per *Joan. Diac.* lib. ii. cap. 53, 55, &c.—Ejusdem Vita recens adornata (per *De Sainte-Marthe*), lib. iii. cap. 9, No. 6

were simple estates, whose revenues the Roman Church received; others were real principalities, embracing cities and entire provinces, such as the country of the Cottian Alps, including the city of Genoa, and all the coast of Liguria, as far as the frontiers of Gaul. The Lombards, having usurped this country about the end of the seventh century, *restored it* to Pope John VII. (about the year 708) *as an ancient possession of the Roman Church*.[1]

Historians remark, that the greater part of the patrimonies of the Roman Church, in Sicily and Calabria, had been given to her by the emperors, since Theodosius the Great, in exchange for those which she possessed in several provinces of the East, whose revenues it would have been difficult for her to receive, on account of the frequent incursions of the barbarians into those provinces.[2]

The temporal sovereignty of the Popes grew thus insensibly and involuntarily, by the providential agency of Catholic princes and nations. The donations of the emperors, the pious generosity of the faithful, prepared for the successors of St. Peter a royalty whose beneficent influence was soon to return them greater benefits than they had bestowed. It was the work of the faith, the respect and the love of Christian times; but it was at the same time the work of a careful Providence, which intended

---

(Oper. tom. iv.)—*Fleury*, Hist. Eccl. tom. viii. liv. 35, Nos. 15 and 45.—*Zaccaria*, ubi supra, cap. 3.—Hist. de l'Eglise Gallicane, tom. iii. p. 311.

[1] The following are Bede's own words, in his chronicle (year 708):—"Aripertus, rex Longobardorum, multas cohortes, et patrimoniam Alpium Cottiarum, quæ quondam ad jus pertinebant apostolicæ sedis, sed a Longobardis multo tempore fuerant ablata, restituit juri ejusdem sedis; et hanc donationem, aureis scriptam literis, Romam direxit." The Pope exercised in these provinces, by means of governors, all the rights of sovereignty.—*Zaccaria*, ubi supra, cap. 1.—*S. Gregor.* Epist. lib. i. epist. 44, 75; epist. 19, 99, 100, &c.—*Père Denis de Sainte-Marthe*, Vie de S. Grégoire, ubi supra.— *Père Thomassin*, Ancienne et Nouvelle Discipline, tom. iii. liv. i. ch. 27, No. 7.—*Zaccaria*, ubi sup. cap. 3, No. 13.

[2] Du Pouvoir du Pape au Moyen Âge.

soon to give a new sanction to this royalty by the unanimous wishes of the Italian people.

Besides, we must add, this addition of temporal to spiritual power in the person of the sovereign Pontiffs was not a fact exclusively proper to the Roman Church: from the time of the first Christian emperors, there was a general tendency throughout the empire, not only to confirm to the Church the right of property, which is a necessity founded on the very nature of things, but to invest the bishops and the clergy with several of the powers of the civil magistracy; and it is known with what beneficial results for the welfare of the people and the spread of civilization in Europe. Let us quote upon this important subject the lucid remarks of M. Guizot.

"From the 5th century, the Christian clergy had powerful means of influence. The bishops and clerks had become the chief municipal magistrates. The municipal system was, strictly speaking, all that remained of the Roman empire: such were the vexations of despotism, and the ruin of the cities, that the *curiales*, or members of the municipal corporations, had fallen into discouragement and apathy. The bishops, on the contrary, and the priests, full of life and zeal, naturally offered themselves to superintend and to manage everything. *It would be absurd to blame them for it, or to tax them with usurpation; the natural course of things would have it so; the clergy alone was morally alive and vigorous; it became powerful everywhere; such is the law of the universe.* This revolution is traceable in all the legislation of the emperors at this period. If you open the Theodosian or Justinian code, you will find a great number of arrangements which charge the bishops and clergy with municipal affairs.[1] And the Christian Church has powerfully contributed since that time, to the development of modern civilization.

---

[1] In support of this assertion M. Guizot cites in particular the Justinian Code. lib. i. tit. 4, De Episcopali Audientiâ, Nos. 26 and 30; tit. 55, De Defensoribus, No. 8.

"The presence of a moral influence, of a moral force, a force based wholly upon conviction, upon belief and moral sentiments, was a vast advantage in the midst of the deluge of material force which at that epoch inundated society. *If the Christian Church had not been in existence, the whole world would have been abandoned to pure material force.* The Church alone exercised a moral power. But she did more; she kept up and diffused the idea of a rule, of a law superior to all human laws; she professed the belief, essential to the safety of humanity, that there is, above all human laws, a law called, according to times and customs, sometimes *reason*, sometimes the *divine law*, but which, in all times and places, is the same law under different names."[1]

CHAPTER VI.

FINAL AND PROVIDENTIAL ESTABLISHMENT OF THE TEMPORAL SOVEREIGNTY OF THE HOLY SEE.

WE shall examine here—

1. The causes which brought about the establishment of the pontifical sovereignty.
2. The striking disinterestedness of the Popes, and their long fidelity to the emperors of Byzantium.
3. The abandonment of Rome and Italy by the emperors, and the accomplishment of the designs of God, by means of the sword of the Franks.

I.

We have now to exhibit one of the most incontestable titles of the Pope's temporal sovereignty, perhaps the

---

[1] *Guizot*, Histoire générale de la Civilisation en Europe, 2ᵉ leçon, pp. 55—58, 3ᵉ édition: Paris, 1840.

noblest of any. Not only the Popes did not impose themselves upon the people, as we have seen, but, as is demonstrated by history, and is very much to the point to notice, the people themselves, abandoned by their former masters, and reduced to despair, implored the Popes to govern them and to save them. It was a great sight, unparalleled in the annals of the world. There have existed, doubtless, more powerful royalties; but we know not one, which, like that of the Popes, derives from its singular rise, its benefits, the needs, the wishes and unanimous acclamations of its people, a juster right to call itself the royalty of Providence. We have here only to recapitulate briefly the known and undisputed facts.

The lamentable state of the Italian populations after the invasion is well known: defencelesss and exposed to the incursions of the barbarians, betrayed by their natural protectors, ravaged and desolated for two hundred years by the Huns, the Goths, the Vandals, and the Lombards, they turned with one accord towards the Popes, as their refuge and their bulwark. In the midst of these frightful and indescribable calamities, the Roman Pontiffs had become the only refuge of all the afflicted. The great Pope St. Leo alone saved twice the city of Rome and the Romans from the fury of Attila and Genseric; thus pointing out to Italy the moral power to which she must look for safety, the declining power of the emperors having ceased to be available. Soon afterwards, in 476, Odoacer, with his Heruli, put an end to the Western empire; some years later the Heruli disappear before the Goths, who in their turn give place to the Lombards. What was the force which, during these disastrous ages, protected the name and the remains of Rome? The Papacy! What were not the struggles of St. Gregory the Great, for twenty-seven years, to preserve the holy city from the sword of the Lombards? These fierce conquerors felt their rage and threats expire upon their lips, and their pride tamed, in the presence of the unarmed Pontiff of Rome, as if the angel of the Lord had appeared to them.

During the long and terrible assaults which the Eternal

City had to suffer from Alaric, Ricimer, Vitiges, and Totila, and after that fall which made St. Jerome say that *the light of the world was extinguished, and that the fall of one city had left the universe in ruins,* whither did the Romans fly when exiled from their abodes,—patricians, senators, plebeians, men, women, and children, driven before the barbarians like a flock of sheep?—to the churches, the basilicas of St. Peter and St. Paul. Procopius records the respect shown by the Goths to the apostolic churches. Totila, their chief, even entered the church of St. Peter to pray;[1] some years before, the barbarians, under Vitiges, had in like manner respected the basilica of St. Paul.[2] He says, "They so respect the sacred temples of these two apostles, that during the whole war they never profaned them in the least, and that the priests have always had full liberty to celebrate there all the sacred rites." St. Augustin, too, celebrates this unheard-of triumph of religion over barbarians, comparing the taking of Rome to that of Troy:—
"There, the spoils were carried off from the burning temples, not to restore them to the conquered, but to share them among the conquerors; here, things even seized elsewhere, if proved to belong to the holy places, were brought back with honour and pious reverence. There liberty was doomed; here it was preserved. There the inhabitants were reduced to slavery; here captivity was forbidden. There they were insulted by enemies whose property they had become; here they were set free by compassionate soldiers. There, finally, avarice and pride ravaged the temples; here the humility of the most savage barbarians respected the basilicas of Jesus Christ."

And it was not only in so desperate a moment that the Romans found a last refuge under the shadow of the apo-

---

[1] "Totila in templum Petri apostoli sese contulit precandi gratiâ."—De Bello Gotho, iii. 20.

[2] "Gothi sacram hanc Pauli ædem apostoli, itemque alteram apostoli Petri sic reverentur, ut neutram toto belli tempore ne minimum quidem violaverint, ac sacerdotibus de more sacra illic omnia procurare licuerit."—Lib. ii. 4.

stolic churches; it was not only in critical emergencies that recourse was had to the Popes; but in everything and from all quarters. Every important affair was submitted to them; nothing great was done without them. The Pope Agapitus, in the sixth century, negotiated a peace for the Italian people between Theodatus, king of the Goths, and the Emperor Justinian. Athalaric and Theodatus having made important donations to the Romans, Pope Vigilius travelled to Constantinople, and obtained from Justinian an imperial constitution, the principal object of which was to confirm these donations. About the same time, Cassiodorus, a Roman senator, prefect of the Prætorium, wrote to John II.: " You are the chief of the Christian people; under your name of Father, you direct everything. The security of the people depends upon your fame and your power. We have minor responsibilities in the administration of affairs, but the supreme authority is yours. Your principal care, no doubt, is the spiritual direction of your flock; but you cannot neglect their temporal interests; as man has a double nature, it is the duty of a good father to watch over both our temporal and eternal welfare."[1] Such language from a prefect of the Prætorium, one of the first officers of the empire, would surprise us, if we did not know that Italy, in her distress, was continually imploring in vain the assistance of the emperors. The people were perishing of hunger and misery; the towns were burnt down, the country devastated, the inhabitants, dispersed and exiled, were wandering here and there at the mercy of the barbarians. In so deplorable a situation, the only

---

[1] "Vos enim speculatores Christiano populo præsidetis, vos Patris nomine omnia dirigitis. Securitas ergo plebis ad vestram respicit famam, cui divinitus est commissa custodia. Quapropter nos decet custodire aliqua, sed vos omnia. Pascitis quidem spiritualiter commissum vobis gregem; tamen nec ista potestis negligere, quæ corporis videntur substantiam continere; nam sicut homo constat ex dualitate, ita boni patris est utrumque refovere."—*Cassiodor* Epist. lib. xi. ep. 2, Opera, tom. i.

resource of Italy was the authority of the Holy See and the charity of the Popes.

Such were, in the fifth and sixth centuries, the necessity and the benefits of the pontifical intervention; such was the origin of the temporal power of the Holy See. The rise of the Lombard monarchy in 568, and the calamities which followed from it, strengthened this necessity. From the time that these new barbarians, encamped in Northern Italy, became, as it were, a standing menace of invasion to the whole peninsula, the increasing weakness of the empire, and the isolation of all its provinces, rendered still more indispensable the public intervention of the Popes. Their protection was necessary, not only to the poor inhabitants, but to the exarchs themselves, who continually were imploring it from Ravenna, now to aid the expenses of administration in the provinces, now to appease the excited population, and again to negotiate with the Lombards. In a word, the Popes had become, by the mere force of circumstances, by the pressing demands upon them and their authority, the centre of government and public affairs in Italy. It was an involuntary but real and necessary sovereignty.

The modern writers who are least favourable to the Church, cannot help, in spite of their prejudices, rendering homage upon this point to the Holy See, and recognizing the supreme legitimacy of this new greatness, as well as the providential nature of the circumstances which by degrees elevated the temporal sovereignty of the Popes upon the ruins of the imperial power.

"Another cause," says one of them, "brought about and even justified the revolution which was about to deprive the Greek emperors of Italy. They had almost completely abandoned, for two hundred years, their provinces in that country. They did not keep up a garrison in Rome; and the city, continually threatened by the Lombards, invoked more than once, through its dukes or its pontiffs, the care of the exarch and the power of the emperor . . . . . Deserted by their masters, the Romans clung to their Pontiffs, then generally Romans, and worthy of their confidence. Fathers and defenders of the people, mediators between the great, chiefs of religion, in the Popes were united the different grounds of influence which are afforded by riches, benefits, virtues, and the supreme priesthood."[1]

Sismondi, whom no one can suspect of partiality to the Popes, holds the same language:[2] "The more the Romans saw themselves neglected by the Emperors, the more they clung to the Popes, who, during this period, were almost all Romans by birth, and whom their virtues have, for the most part, enrolled in the catalogue of Saints. The Popes, to protect the churches and convents from the profanations of the barbarians, lavished the ecclesiastical riches at their disposal, as well as the alms they received from the piety of the Western faithful, *so that the increasing power of these Pontiffs in the city of Rome was founded on the most respectable of all titles, virtues and benefits.*"

Gibbon, who is as free from the suspicion of partiality as Sismondi, declares that the temporal dominion of the Popes was founded upon a thousand years of veneration, and that their grandest title to sovereignty was the free choice of a people delivered by them from servitude.

St. Gregory the Great was the most remarkable personification, the most noble and impressive type of this singular sovereignty, which only afforded him a wider field for his benevolence and love for men.[3] We find this

---

[1] *M. Daunou*, Essai Hist. tom. i. pp. 29, 30.

[2] *Sismondi*, Hist. des Républ. Ital. tom i. ch. 3. p. 122.

[3] About the same time (590—604) the Papacy attained its full power in the person of St. Gregory the Great, an heroic priest, who had been reserved for the dangers of those evil times. While the walls of Rome, shaken by constant assaults, were threatening to fall on him, his thoughts were at the extremities of the world; in the East, to withstand the Byzantine court; in the North, to convert the Anglo-Saxons; in the West, where he succeeded in crushing Arianism among the Visigoths of Spain. His exhortations on the emancipation of slaves, his reform of religious psalmody, and his writings, still one of the great bases of theological instruction, had done enough for future ages.—*Ozanam*.

holy Pope continually discharging the offices of a temporal ruler, almost of a sovereign. He administers provinces; he provides for the defence of towns; he deputes governors, with injunctions to the people to obey them as they would himself. "We have charged Leontius with the care and the government of your town," he writes to the citizens of Nepi, "that he may superintend everything, and make what regulations he thinks necessary for your good and that of the state. Whosoever resists his orders, resists our authority."[1] He sends military officers to command the garrisons of towns, menaced by the enemies of the empire. He writes to the Neapolitans: "You have received as you ought our letter, by which we have deputed the noble tribune Constantine to the command of your city, and we rejoice that he has found among you the faithful obedience of military devotion."[2] We see him even, in several of his letters, excite the bishops to vigilance and zeal for the defence of towns, and to repair and provision fortresses. He gives orders to the chiefs of the army. He treats for peace with the Lombards in person, and facilitates the success of negotiations, at one time by his largesses, at another by his repeated entreaties addressed to the emperors, the exarchs, and the Lombards themselves. In short, to repeat again the words of a learned writer[3] from whom we borrow these details,

---

[1] "Leontio curam, sollicitudinem civitatis Nepæsinæ injunximus, ut in cunctis invigilans, quæ ad utilitatem vestram vel reipublicæ pertinere dignoscat, ipse disponat . . . quisquis congruæ ejus ordinationi restiterit, nostræ resultare dispositioni cognoscetur."— *S. Gregor*. Epist. lib. ii. epist. 2, alias 8.

[2] "Devotio vestra, sicut etn unc didicimus, epistolis nostris, quibus magnificum virum Constantinum tribunum custodiæ civitatis deputavimus præesse, paruit, et congruam militaris devotionis obedientiam demonstravit."—*S. Gregor*. Epist. lib. ii. epist. 31, alias 24.

[3] I mean the Abbé Gosselin, director of the Seminary of St. Sulpice, in his work "Du Pouvoir du Pape au Moyen Age," a pious and modest scholar, whose learning would have rendered his name illustrious, had not his humility studied, during his life, to prevent

his authority, equally respected by princes and subjects, by Romans and barbarians, is the centre of government and of political affairs in Italy.

This great and holy Pope was so compelled by the wants and sufferings of his people, and by the charity which oppressed his heart, to busy himself with public affairs, that he says himself his life was divided between the offices of pastor and of temporal prince.[1] He writes to the Empress Constantina, wife of the Emperor Maurice: "We have now been living twenty-seven years in this city, in the midst of the swords of the Lombards. But to live with them, I cannot tell you what sums the Roman Church has to pay them daily . . . As the emperor names a treasurer in the province of Ravenna, charged to provide for the daily wants of the troops of his Italian army, so I am the emperor's treasurer at Rome, to provide for the wants of that city, always harassed by the Lombards." One may judge of the sad state of Italy and of the services of the papacy at this period, by the following passage from a letter to the bishop of Nomentum from St. Gregory: "The impious fury of the enemy has so ravaged the churches of different cities, that there is no hope of repairing them, because the people have almost disappeared. We are therefore bound to watch with greater care over the few who remain, their priests being dead, and they being without a pastor."[2]

But to form a just idea of these frightful calamities,

---

it. We recommend strongly to all Catholics to peruse this remarkable work under the present circumstances.

[1] "Hoc in loco quisquis Pastor dicitur, curis exterioribus graviter occupatur, ita ut sæpe incertum sit utrum pastoris officium an terreni proceris agat."—Lib. i. epist. 25.

[2] "Postquam hostilis impietas diversarum civitatum, ita peccatis facientibus, desolavit ecclesias, ut reparandi eas spes nulla, populo deficiente, remanserit, majori valde curâ constringimur, ne defunctis earum sacerdotibus, reliquiæ plebis, nullo pastoris moderamine gubernante, per devia fidei hostis callidi, quod absit, rapiantur insidiis."—Epist. xx. lib. ii.

one should read the homily of St. Gregory on Ezechiel; it is the grandest funeral sermon that ever was, on Rome, Italy, and the whole empire. "If we look around us, we see nothing but mourning; if we listen, we hear but groans on all sides. The towns are destroyed, the castles are overturned, the fields are wasted, the earth has become a solitude . . . .[1] There are no longer any inhabitants in the country, and scarcely any in the towns, yet still the remnant of the human race is being struck down daily, and without intermission: some are dragged into captivity, some perish on the scaffold, others are massacred; such is the spectacle our eyes are forced to look upon. What have we then left, my brethren, to charm us in this life? If we continue to love the world in its present state, it is not pleasures but woes that we shall love. Rome herself, the queen of the world, we see all that remains of her; she is overwhelmed under manifold and immense woes, by the desolation of her citizens, the marks of the ravages of her enemies, and the abundance of her ruins.[2] Where is the Senate? Where is the people?

"Her bones are dried up, her flesh is wasted away, all her worldly pomp and glory have departed.[3] And we, the few who survive, live amidst alarms; innumerable tribulations sweep over us; our sighs and tears are renewed every day; Rome is waste—a wilderness in flames. Her inhabitants have vanished; her edifices are in ruins.[4] Once more, where are they who prided themselves in the monuments of her glory? Where is their pomp? Where is their pride? Where are the vain pleasures which revelled within her precincts? What the prophet says of Judæa'

---

[1] "Destructæ urbes, eversa sunt castra, depopulati agri, in solitudinem terra redacta est."—Hom. in Ezech. vi. lib. ii.

[2] "Immensis doloribus multipliciter attrita, desolatione civium, impressione hostium, frequentia ruinarum."

[3] "Ubi enim senatus? ubi jam populus? contabuerunt ossa, consumptæ sunt carnes, omnis in ea secularium dignitatum fastus extinctus est."

"Postquam defecerunt homines, parietes cadunt."

has happened to her: Thou shalt be bald as an eagle. She is bald as an eagle, for she has lost her feathers; that is, her people. Her feathers have fallen from her wings, with which she used to dart upon her prey; her valiant sons are no more, who formerly covered her with foreign spoils.[1] The desolation of Rome, too, is but a picture of the desolation of all our other cities. Let us then turn our hearts from the present world, now but a bleak wilderness; let us bury our worldly desires, at least, in the tomb of the world itself."[2]

The successors of St. Gregory inherited his afflictions, his charity, and his power; and it is to be remarked that the emperors of Byzantium, far from being offended by the conduct of the Popes, or by the involuntary increase of their temporal power, kept up habitually the most cordial relations with them.

II.

WONDERFUL DISINTERESTEDNESS OF THE POPES, AND THEIR LONG FIDELITY TO THE EMPERORS OF BYZANTIUM.

The establishment of the temporal sovereignty of the Holy See was not, then, one of those sudden and unforeseen revolutions which astonish the world by the rapidity of their course. An attentive perusal of history convinces us, on the contrary, that it was insensibly brought about by a concurrence of circumstances altogether independent of the will of the Sovereign Pontiffs, circumstances whose influence they would in vain have endeavoured to stay, and whose natural result they could not even have pre-

---

[1] "Calvitium ergo suum sicut aquila dilatat, quia plumas perdidit quæ populum amisit. Alarum quoque pennæ ceciderunt, cum quibus volare ad prædam consueverat: quia omnes potentes ejus extincti sunt, per quos aliena rapiebat."

[2] "Despiciamus ergo ex toto animo præsens seculum vel extinctum: finiamus mundi desideria saltem cum mundi fine."

vented without compromising the interests both of religion and society.[1]

We seek in vain in history for what the emperors then did for Italy; we find the Popes alone acting for her, taking up her cause, negotiating effectually with the barbarians, and putting the towns into a proper state of defence. The emperor Maurice so relied upon the Popes and the bishops for the defence of the Italian cities, that he earnestly requested from the Pope the removal of a bishop whom his infirmities prevented from superintending, with the necessary energy, the arrangements for the defence of his episcopal city. St. Gregory, not thinking fit to depose a bishop for such a reason, assigned him a coadjutor, qualified to provide for the defence of the town, in case of attack. Several letters of the same pontiff tend to excite the bishops zealously to fulfil this duty, to look diligently after the guard of the ramparts, the repairs and provisioning of the fortresses, and other such matters, which in ordinary times were the duty of civil magistrates and military governors.

Very often, the Popes arrested the invading march of the barbarians by their pacific interference, and sometimes even made them restore their conquests. Thus it was that John VI. preserved Rome from an invasion; and, under Gregory II., the king Luitprand, touched by the virtues of the successor of St. Peter, laid at the Apostle's tomb a silver cross, his belt, his sword, and crown. The same Gregory II. writes to the emperor Leo: "All the West turns its eyes towards our humility . . . . It regards us as the moderator and arbitrator of public tranquillity." Gregory III., his successor, sends ambassadors to Charles Martel, and treats with him as one power with another. Zachary, who filled the pontifical throne from 741 to 752, treats with like manner Rachis, king of the Lombards, and stipulates with him a peace of several years, which tranquillized all Italy.

---

[1] *Gosselin*, Pouvoir des Papes.

But what is most admirable in these great pontiffs, and should for ever silence the faintest accusation against them and the origin of their power, is their generous disinterestedness in circumstances most favourable to a justifiable ambition, and their constant, unshaken fidelity to the imperial power which so miserably abandoned them. This power, by its wretched and feeble policy, was deposing itself: not content with abandoning the defence of its people, its inefficiency was accompanied by intolerable oppression: a vexatious and tyrannical administration kept pace in Italy with the notorious and increasing degradation of the imperial power; still the Popes persisted obstinately in observing themselves, and in inculcating on the people, loyalty to the emperors.

The Popes were so far from wishing to transform themselves into temporal princes, that they deplore bitterly and unceasingly this inevitable transformation. Their authority imposes itself upon them against their will; they submit to it, and it increases according as the perils of Italy, and as the weakness of the imperial power becomes more obvious. *It would be wrong to reproach them with it, or to tax them with usurpation,* as M. Guizot says; *so the natural course of things would have it: the clergy alone was morally alive and vigorous; it gained power everywhere: such is the law of the universe.*

And, what is most remarkable, at no period was the doctrine of the Church as to the distinction of the two powers, the independence of the spiritual power in religious matters, and submission in temporals, more universally professed. We will cite the famous letter of the great Pope Gelasius to the emperor Anastasius, the protector of the Eutychian heresy: "This world, august emperor, is ruled by two powers, that of her pontiffs and that of kings; of these, the charge of priests is so much the heavier, in that they shall have to answer before the tribunal of God for the souls of kings. You know, beloved son, that, though you are above other men in dignity, yet you humble yourself before the bishops who preside over sacred things, and you apply to them for everything that concerns your salvation; and in the reception and administration of the divine sacraments, you are bound to obey them, instead of commanding. You know, I say, that in all these things you are dependent upon them, and that they cannot be subjected to your will. For if, *in temporal things, the ministers of religion obey your laws, knowing that you have received your power from above,* how dutifully, I ask, ought you not to obey those who are charged with dispensing the august mysteries?" [1]

Conformably to these principles, the Popes struggle intrepidly against the perpetual and intolerable pretensions of the Byzantine court, which claims to interfere in questions of doctrine, and supports heresies; whilst they cease not to recognize and recommend with all their influence to the people the temporal authority by which they are oppressed. It is both curious and sad to study this short-sighted and oppressive policy of the emperors. Not only the independence, but the safety and even the life of the Roman Pontiffs was often endangered in their relations with the emperors of Constantinople. St. Martin, persecuted by Heraclius Constans, perished on the shores of the Black Sea. Others, though they did not die in exile, suffered long persecutions, as Pope Vigilius, under

---

[1] " Duo sunt, imperator auguste, quibus principaliter mundus hic regitur, auctoritas sacra pontificum, et regalis potestas; in quibus tanto gravius est pondus sacerdotum, quanto etiam pro ipsis regibus in divino reddituri sunt examine rationem. Nosti enim, fili clementissime, quod, licet præsidens humano generi, dignitate, rerum tamen præsulibus divinarum devotus colla submittis atque ab eis causas tuæ salutis expetis; inque sumendis cœlestibus sacramentis, eisque, ut competit, disponendis, subdite debere cognoscis, religionis ordine, potius quam præesse. Nosti itaque inter hæc ex illorum te pendere judicio, non illos ad tuam velle redigi voluntatem. Si enim, quantam ad ordinem pertinet publicæ disciplinæ, cognoscentes imperium tibi superna dispositione collatum, legibus tuis ipsi quoque parent religionis antistiter, quo, rogo, decet affectu eis obedire, qui pro erogandis venerabilibus sunt attributi mysteriis?"
—*S. Gelas.* Pap. Epist. ad Anast. Aug.; *Labbe,* Concil. tom. iv. p. 1182; *Fleury,* Hist. Eccl. tom. vii. liv. xxx. No. 31; *Bossuet,* Defens. Declar. lib. i. sect. 2 cap. 33.

the reign of Justinian. Need we recall the forced journeys of the Popes to Byzantium, as of Agapitus and Constantine? Or the intrigues against Sergius, John VI., and Gregory II., of Monothelite or Iconoclast emperors? Still the Sovereign Pontiffs of whom we speak never took advantage of the disaffection towards the imperial power produced by such vexatious tyranny, still more odious because of the evident weakness of the princes, nor of the disgust of the people and their impatience of the Byzantine yoke, to emancipate themselves from its thraldom: they alone, on the contrary, maintained it in Italy, both against the barbarian invasions and the revolts of a discontented and indignant people.

St. Gregory the Great affords a remarkable proof of the truth of this assertion. He had sufficient reason to complain of the representatives of the imperial power. "I cannot tell you," he writes to a bishop, "all we have to suffer here from the exarch. I will say, in one word, that his tyranny does us more injury than the arms of the Lombards; we almost prefer the enemies who kill us to the officers of the empire who consume us by their frauds and extortions." Such was the conduct of the exarchs. Well, how does St. Gregory behave towards Constantinople? A law having been imposed upon him by the emperor Maurice, which appeared to him disadvantageous to the interests of the Church, he remonstrates with the prince, with all the liberty of a pontiff, but with all the loyalty of a subject. "Obeying your jurisdiction, I have forwarded your law to the different parts of the world; thus discharging my *double duty*, on the one hand, of *obeying the emperor*, on the other remonstrating with you on what concerns the honour of God."[1]

All the successors of St. Gregory imitated his loyalty

---

[1] "Ego quidem jussioni subjectus, legem per diversas orbis partes transmitti feci, et ecce per suggestionis meæ paginam serenissimis Dominis nuntiavi, utrobique ergo quæ debui exsolvi, qui et imperatori obedientiam præbui et pro Deo quod sensi minime tacui."— Ep. iii. 65.

and devotedness. Thus under Popes Sergius and John VI. their authority alone saved the envoys of the emperor, in the seditions excited by their intrigues against the Pope.[1] A remarkable incident occurred during the pontificate of Constantine, in 713, when the Romans rose against the emperor Philippicus, who had openly protected the heresy of the Monothelites. This prince having sent the duke Peter to Rome to take the government of the city, the people refused to recognize him, and even determined to repulse him by force of arms; a combat took place before the duke's palace, and would have had the most serious consequences, had not the Pope sent bishops with the gospels and crosses to appease the sedition. "The prospects of the governor were desperate, and his life was in extreme danger; but the Catholics withdrew on the Pope's order, so that the heretical party of Peter prevailed, as if they had defeated their adversaries."[2] Gregory II. himself, whose life was threatened three different times by Leo the Isaurian, continued, notwithstanding the sharp contests he had to sustain against that prince, to display, in most critical circumstances, the traditional fidelity of the Pontiffs to the imperial power. Thus, when Italy, irritated by the iconoclast fury of Leo, proposed to elect another emperor in his place, Gregory opposed it.[3] The king of the Lombards occupies Ravenna during this state of anarchy; the exarch had taken refuge in the infant city of Venice; the duke, or doge of Venice, Ursus, or Orso, as the Italians call his name, had received the exarch, but showed little

---

[1] *Anastas.* Vita Joannis VI. p. 1290.—*Fleury,* Hist. Eccl. tom. ix. liv. xl. No. 54.

[2] "Pars Petri ita angustiata (erat), ut nulla illi casset spes vivendi; rerum ad Pontificis jussionem pars alia, quæ et Christiana vocabatur, recessit; sicque defensoris hæretici pars valuit Petri, ac si illa attrita recederet."—*Anastas.* ubi supra.

[3] "Omnis quoque exercitus Ravennæ vel Venetiarum talibus jussis unanimiter restiterunt, et nisi eos prohibuisset Pontifex, imperatorem super se constituere fuissent agressi."—*Paul Diac.* De Gestis Longob.

anxiety to encounter the Lombards. Gregory II. wrote a pressing letter to the doge, and prevailed on him to equip a fleet, which retook Ravenna, and restored that imperial city to the exarch. Again, towards the end of his reign, the excitement continuing in Italy, a usurper appears in Tuscany, and is supported by numerous adherents; Gregory II. supports the exarch in quelling this rising sedition. A writer, whom we have already cited, and who is anything but partial to the Popes, M. Daunou, cannot help praising this generous conduct of Gregory II.:[1]—" At a most critical juncture, when, on the one hand, heresy, armed with the imperial power, was forcing its way into Italy, and on the other, Italy saw no way of repelling heresy but revolt against her sovereign, Pope Gregory II. found means to observe the two obligations which appeared incompatible. The intrepid head of the Church firmly opposed the execution of an edict which was contrary to the prescriptions of Christianity; he made every effort to dissuade the emperor from his impious purpose; he confirmed the people in the resolution to refuse commands which they could not obey without betraying their religion; but, at the same time, as a loyal subject, he continued to obey his prince, and animated his people to a due submission; he stifled the spirit of rebellion; and, in spite of the infamous plots against his life, planned by the prince himself, this true apostolic prelate, superior both to sentiments of vengeance and of fear, was generous enough to preserve Italy to the crown, which was on the point of losing it."

Such was the conduct, respectively, of the Emperors and the Popes. This rapid historical glance suffices to establish incontrovertibly that not only was the Byzantine despotism a standing menace to the spiritual independence and even the life of the Sovereign Pontiffs of Rome, but that the incapacity of the emperors, combined with their

---

[1] *Daunou*, Essai Historique sur la Puissance Temporelle des Papes. —*Lebeau*, Hist. de Bas-Empire, tom. xiii. liv. lxiii. No. 54; Annales du Moyen Age, tom. vi. liv. xxiii. pp. 391, 413, &c.

oppression and the rapaciousness of their officers, rendered it more and more urgent for perishing Italy to look for aid elsewhere.

One last excess of the insane policy of the despots of Byzantium brought the despair of the people to the crowning point, and severed the last bonds which united Italy to Constantinople. In 741, Luitprand, king of the Lombards, besieges the eternal city, and reduces it to the last extremity. What succour does the emperor of Constantinople send? It is with profound indignation and disgust that we read the following details in the contemporary historians:—" The emperor sent a considerable fleet to Italy, to sack Rome and several other cities, as a punishment for their continuing to venerate images. The commander of the fleet had orders to seize the Pope himself, and bring him bound hand and foot to Constantinople. The execution of this project was only prevented by the destruction of the fleet, which was dispersed near Ravenna by a furious tempest. To revenge himself, the emperor loads Italy with new taxes, and seizes the patrimonies of the Roman Church in Sicily and Calabria." It was then, in 741, that Gregory III. resolved to write to Charles Martel, and to send him a solemn embassy.

III.

ACCOMPLISHMENT OF THE DESIGNS OF GOD BY MEANS OF THE SWORD OF THE FRANKS.

It is extremely important to observe here, in order fully to comprehend the immense services rendered by the Papacy, at this gloomy period, to European civilization, that not only Rome and Italy had now to be defended against the Lombards, but the whole of the West to be protected from the invasions of the Mussulman barbarians. To understand how great the danger was, we need only state that in 712 Spain was invaded and conquered by the Mussulmans; in 719 they passed the Pyrenees, and entered ancient Gaul. About the same time the Arabs had besieged Constantinople for the third time, under Soliman I.; and the capital owed its deliverance to the effects of the Greek fire. The provinces of Gaul, then under the Carlovingian dynasty, were hemmed in between the Mussulmans of Septimania and the Pagan barbarians from beyond the Rhine.[1]

The reasons, then, are but too clear which forced the Popes and Italy, abandoned by the emperors, to turn to the Franks. The necessity was urgent, not only in order to save Italy, but the whole of Western Europe; and it was these two urgent and united necessities which decided the Popes upon the important resolution which they formed in order to insure the safety of Italy, the independence of the West, and the preservation of the whole of Christendom. The kings of the Franks, too, seemed providentially designed to assist the Popes: in the critical state of Rome, abandoned by its natural protectors, and menaced by the Lombards as well as of the West in general, assaulted by Islamism, the Popes, thoroughly acquainted with the material and moral resources of their time, saw of what powerful avail would be the bravest soldier then in Europe, Charles Martel, who was then keeping in check, with rare courage, the pagans of Germany on the north, while on the south he was presenting a formidable barrier to the irruptions of the Mussulmans, whom he had already encountered and crushed upon the plains of Tours (732).

---

[1] The attacks of the Saracens upon the coasts of Italy were incessant during the succeeding centuries. "Pope Leo IV., taking on himself in this crisis an authority which the generals of the emperor Lotharius seemed unwilling to assume, showed himself worthy, by his defence of Rome, to rule there as sovereign. He had employed the riches of the Church in repairing the walls, raising towers, and stretching chains across the Tiber. He armed the militia, he visited all the ports himself, and received the Saracens on their approach not in warlike array, but as a pontiff who was encouraging a Christian people, and as a king watching over the safety of his subjects. He had been born a Roman: the courage of the first ages of the republic reappeared in him, in a period of cowardice and corruption, like one of the grand monuments of ancient Rome appearing among the ruins of later structures."— *Voltaire.*

Moreover, in this crisis, the Popes and the Romans acted in accordance with the most universally recognized principles of law and justice. "Every one admits," says Puffendorf,[1] "that the subjects of a monarch, when on the point of perishing, and having no succour to hope for from their sovereign, may make their submission to another prince."—"No part of a state," says Grotius,[2] "has a right to detach itself from the body politic; unless that not to do so would expose it to manifest danger of perishing; for all human institutions seem to be subject to the tacit exception of a case of extreme necessity, when the natural law only can be considered." On this Grotius quotes St. Augustin, who is not less formal: "Among all nations," says the holy doctor, "it has been considered a better course to submit to the yoke of a conqueror than to suffer the last horrors of war and be exterminated; such is, as it were, the voice of nature."[3]

The ambassadors sent by Gregory III. to Charles Martel were commissioned to offer him in the name of the Pope, and the Román Senate and the people, the dignity of patrician. Charles Martel received the Pope's request favourably, and was preparing to cross the mountains, when death prevented him. The deaths of the Pope and the emperor in the same year (741) suspended the negotiations opened with France; but Pope Zachary, the successor of Gregory III., succeeded, by his tact and influence, in retrieving the affairs of the empire in Italy. He obtained from the king of the Lombards the restitution of the cities and territories of the exarchate which they had seized, re-established the authority of the exarch, and thereby that of the emperor whom he represented; yet,

---

[1] De Jure Nat. et Gent. lib. vii. cap. 7, sec. 4.

[2] *Grotius*, De Jure Belli et Pacis, ii. 6, sec. 5.

[3] "In omnibus fere gentibus, quodam modo vox naturæ ista personuit, ut subjugari victoribus mallent; quibus contigit vinci, quam bellicâ omnifariâ vastatione deleri."—*S. Aug.* De Civitate Dei, xviii. 2, 1.

singular to say, it was to himself alone, and not to the emperor, that the barbarian had made the restitution;[1] so notorious was it to every one, that the Popes, by the necessity and the force of circumstances, were, in point of fact, real sovereigns in Italy, even before the French kings had recognized and founded upon positive titles their temporal sovereignty. But not only the barbarians in the West, but the emperors of the East themselves paid an involuntary homage to this evident fact. Indeed, when Constantine Copronymus, notwithstanding his attachment to the Iconoclast heresy, made donations to Pope Zachary of new domains in the provinces which still remained to the empire,[2] did he not seem to approve implicitly the sovereign authority which it was known that the Pope, after the example of his predecessors, exercised *de facto* in those provinces, and to express openly his satisfaction at it?

Zachary dies; and, as if he had been the only barrier which kept back the Lombards, as soon as he is no more, they invade the imperial possessions, and seize upon the Pentapolis and the exarchate. The exarch flies to Naples,

---

[1] The following are the expressions of Anastasius on the restitution of the four towns of the duchy of Rome:—" (Zachariæ) piis eloquiis flexus (Longobardorum rex) . . . . . prædictas quatuor civitates *eidem sancto viro*, cum eorum habitatoribus, *redonavit* ; . . (quas) per donationis titulum, ipsi beato Petro apostolorum principi reconcessit."

The same author makes use of similar expressions when speaking of the restitution of the cities and territories of the exarchate:— "Ab eodem rege nimis honorifice susceptus (Zacharias), salutaribus monitis eum allocutus est, obsecrans. . . . . ut ablatas Ravennatum urbes sibi redonaret. Qui prædictus rex, post multam duritiam inclinatus est . . . . et duas partes territorii Cesenæ Castri ad partem reipublicæ restituit, &c.—*Labbe*, Concil. ib.

[2] "Post hæc, requirens (Constantinus princeps) missum Apostolicæ Sedis, cui ibidem (Constantinopolim) in tempore perturbationis contigerat advenisse, eumque repertum ad sedem absolvit (*i. e.* dimisit) apostolicam ; et juxta quod beatissimus pontifex postulaverat, donationem in scriptis de duabus massis (*i. e.* fundis seu prædiis) quæ Nymphas et Normias appellantur, juris existentes publici, eidem sanctissimo ac beatissimo Papæ sanctæ Romanæ Ecclesiæ, jure perpetuo, direxit possidendas."—*Anast.* ubi supra, p. 1472.

and thus terminates the exarchate, which lasted one hundred and eighty-four years. Astolphus then falls upon Rome, a prey so often and so ardently coveted. What did, what could the emperor do for its defence? He so feels his weakness, that he sends ambassadors, not to the barbarians, but to Pope Stephen II., the successor of Zachary, who, of his own accord, had already opened negotiations with the Lombards, and implores him to take in hand the cause of Italy and her despairing people. In this emergency, the Pope, after having in vain again solicited aid from the emperor, seeing no hope left for himself and his people but to implore, like his predecessors, Gregory III. and Zachary, the interference of the Franks, resolved to proceed in person to the court of Pepin.[1]

"When Pope Stephen arrived in France," says De Maistre, "Pepin and all his family came to meet him, and paid him royal honours. It is evident that the Popes were sovereigns *de facto*, and, to speak with perfect accuracy, sovereigns by compulsion, before any of the Carlovingian liberality; and yet they never ceased, up to Constantine Copronymus, to date their acts by the year of the emperors: they unceasingly exhorted them to protect Italy, to respect the opinions of the people, and to leave their consciences in peace; but the emperors would

---

[1] "Tunc præfatus sanctissimus vir, agnito maligni regis (Aistulphi) consilio, misit in regiam urbem (Constantinopolim) suos missos ... deprecans imperialem clementiam, ut juxta quod ei sæpius scripserat, cum exercitu ad tuendas has Italiæ partes, modis omnibus adveniret, et de iniquitatis filii morsibus Romanam hanc urbem, vel cunctam Italiæ provinciam liberaret. . . . . Cernens præterea et ab imperiali potentiâ nullum esse subveniendi auxilium; tunc quemadmodum prædecessores ejus beatæ memoriæ, Gregorius, et Gregorius alius, et Dominus Zacharias, beatissimi Pontifices, Carolo excellentissimæ memoriæ regi Francorum direxerunt, petentes sibi subveniri propter oppressiones ac invasiones quas et ipsi, in hâc Romanorum provinciâ, a nefandâ Longobardorum gente perpessi sunt; ita modo et ipse venerabilis pater (Stephanus), divinâ gratiâ inspirante, clam per quendam peregrinum suas misit litteras Pippino regi Francorum, nimio dolore huic provinciæ adhærenti conscriptat."
—*Anastas. ib.* pp. 1621, 1622.

listen to nothing, and the hour of doom was coming. The people of Italy consulted for their own safety; deserted by their emperors, and harassed by the barbarians, they chose themselves chiefs, and gave themselves laws. The Popes, dukes of Rome *de facto* and *de jure*, finding it impossible to resist the people, who rushed into their arms, and not knowing how to defend them against the barbarians, cast their eyes at last upon the French princes."

It is curious to hear Bossuet also upon the same subject. He says: " During the fall of the empire, while the Cæsars found it scarcely possible to defend the East, to which they confined their attention, Rome, abandoned for two hundred years to the fury of the Lombards, and forced to beg protection from the French, was obliged to break with the emperors. She endured much before coming to this extremity; she waited till the capital of the empire was thrown off and abandoned by its emperors as a prey to the enemy."

The hour had come, foreordained by Providence, when the great institution of the temporal power of the Popes was to be solemnly confirmed and proclaimed, its justice to be publicly recognized, and its high rank fixed among the new monarchies of the West, which took the place of the political unity of the ancient world,—a rank which, without giving umbrage to other sovereignties, sufficed for the designs of God upon His Church.

Pepin and Charlemagne were destined to accomplish this great work. Italy was in a critical position, as we have seen: Astolphus, king of the Lombards, was besieging Rome, which could not long resist; Stephen had been himself to the court of France, to implore aid from Pepin. In a general assembly of the lords of the kingdom, at Quiercy, Pepin solemnly binds himself by a formal act of donation, signed by himself and his sons, *to have restored* to the Holy See all cities and territories seized upon by the Lombards. He then enters Italy; Astolphus, besieged and hard-pressed in his capital, engages to restore, without delay, Ravenna and the other towns to the Church and the Roman republic (*Sanctæ Dei Ecclesiæ*).[1] But scarcely has Pepin recrossed the mountains, when the faithless Lombard returns and renews the siege of Rome. Pepin hastens back to Italy, and this time imposes upon Astolphus, defeated in a pitched battle and closely blockaded in Pavia, harder conditions than before. He adds the town and district of Comachio to those which the Lombard king had undertaken the year before to return to the Pope.[2] To insure the execution of this treaty, Fulrad, abbot of St. Denis, was to visit in Pepin's

---

[1] " Sub terribili et fortissimo sacramento, atque in eodem pacti fœdere per scriptam paginam affirmavit, se illico redditurum civitatem Ravennatum, cum aliis diversis civitatibus."—*Anast*. p. 1624.

[2] It is a common impression that the Popes were indebted for everything to the Carlovingians. Nothing, however, can be more ungrounded than this idea. The idea of the papal sovereignty, anterior to the Carlovingian donations, was so universal and undisputed, that Pepin, before attacking Astolphus, sent him several ambassadors to induce him to re-establish peace and *restore* the possessions of the holy Church of God and the Roman republic. *Ut pacifice sine ullâ sanguinis effusione, propria S. Dei Ecclesiæ et Reip. Rom. reddant jura.*—(*Anastasius.*) And in the famous charter *Ego Ludovicus*, Louis le Débonnaire declares that Pepin and Charlemagne had long before, by an act of donation, *restored* the exarchate to the blessed apostle and to the Popes. *Exarchatum quem.* . . . . *Pippinus rex et genitor noster Carolus, imperator, B. Petro et prædecessoribus jamdudum restituerunt.*—(Du Pape, *M. de Maistre,* p. 250.) Charlemagne and his envoys, when claiming from Desiderius the provinces he had taken from the Holy See, or delayed to restore, always speaks of them as a *restitution* due to the Pope and the Romans. The expressions used by Anastasius, in the life of Adrian I. are:—" Ipsi Francorum missi, properantes cum Apostolicæ Sedis missis, declinaverunt ad Desiderium, qui et constanter eum deprecantes adhortati sunt, sicut illis a suo rege præceptum extitit, ut antefatas, quas abstulerat civitates pacifice beato Petro redderet." And it is not only Anastasius, the historian of the Popes, who speaks thus; Eginhard himself, so zealous for the glory of Pepin and Charlemagne, and consequently indisposed to depreciate the value of their donations to the Holy See, says in the life of Charlemagne:—" Finis belli fuit subacta Italia, et res a Longobardorum rege *ereptæ*, Adriano Romanæ Ecclesiæ rectori *restitutæ*."

name all the towns surrendered or restored to the Church of Rome. He received their keys, which he afterwards laid down religiously on the tomb of St. Peter, along with the act by which the king of the Lombards ceded and gave them up for ever to the Holy See. These towns were twenty-two in number; they formed the greater part of the exarchate of Ravenna, and most were situated along the coast of the Adriatic, within a space of about forty leagues.[1] In vain did the emperor of Constantinople send ambassadors to Pepin to claim for himself the conquered provinces. Pepin treated his claim with contempt, and answered that the Franks had shed their blood, not for the Greeks, but for St. Peter. From this time the Popes, in all their proceedings and in all their letters, speak as sovereigns.[2] But their sovereignty was continually menaced by the proximity and the ambition of the Lombards; it was Charlemagne, of immortal memory, who finally delivered them from this danger, continuing and gloriously completing his father's work.

A few facts will suffice to illustrate the manner in which the providence of God made use of the hand of man to complete his designs. Charlemagne did not content himself with recognizing and respecting the sovereignty of the Pope in Italy; he extended and consolidated it by his victories over the Lombards, and by the complete destruction of their monarchy in 773. The year before, Adrian I. more closely pressed than ever by Desiderius, had invoked the aid of the king of France, of whose devotion to the interests of religion and of the

---

[1] The exarchate of Ravenna comprised twenty-two towns: Ravenna, Rimini, Pesaro, Fano, Cesena, Sinigaglia, Jesi, Forlimpopoli, Forli, Castrocaro, Montefeltro, Acerragio, Montelucari, Serravalla, San-Marigni, Bobio, Urbino, Caglio, Luccoli, Eugubio, Comarchio, and Narni. Of these Rimini, Pesaro, Fano, Sinigaglia, and Ancona were called the Pentapolis.

[2] "Nostras civitates. . . Nostram Senogalliam (in Pentapoli) . . nostrum castrum Valentis (in Campania)."—Cod. Carol. epist. 38, 39, 40.

Holy See he was aware. Charlemagne, having in vain employed diplomacy to force the king of the Lombards to give satisfaction to the Pope, crosses the Alps, besieges Desiderius in Pavia, takes him prisoner, sends him to France to the monastery of Corbie, and thus puts an end to the kingdom of the Lombards, which had lasted two hundred years, and adds their crown to his own.

But the conduct of Charlemagne towards the Roman Church reflected more glory upon him than the conquest of this new diadem. Not content with confirming all the donations of his father Pepin, he repaired to Rome, gave the Pope the most touching marks of his respect, made his chaplain Etherius draw up a far more ample act of donation, by which he secured for ever to the Holy See the exarchate of Ravenna, the island of Corsica, the provinces of Parma, Mantua, Venice, and Istria, with the duchies of Spoleto and Beneventum. The king signed this donation with his own hand, and caused it to be signed also by the bishops, abbots, dukes, and counts who accompanied him; after which he laid it on the altar of St. Peter, and, with all the French chiefs, took an oath to preserve to the Holy See the states which he had solemnly *restored* to it. Thus Providence consummated the establishment of the temporal sovereignty of the Holy See: we have seen what instruments it used for this work during a long succession of centuries.

Such was the providential order followed by events in Italy; such was the method chosen by God in establishing the sovereignty of the Holy See. We have carefully distinguished the periods:—

1. *Before Constantine*, in the first ages, the Roman Church had neither sovereignty nor any temporal jurisdiction, but only very considerable properties, which she received from the liberality of Christians, and which were necessary to the exercise of her spiritual sovereignty.

2. *From Constantine to Gregory II.* the Popes possessed numerous patrimonies, several of which were really *principalities*. They had, too, particularly after the pontificate of St. Gregory the Great, an immense influence in temporal

affairs, founded upon the respect and confidence of both princes and subjects, but not as yet any *sovereignty* properly so called.

3. *From Gregory II. to Charlemagne* a *real sovereignty* existed; the learned have called it a *provisional* sovereignty; but, whatever its designation, it was real: it existed *de facto* and *de jure;* it had grown with time, and was based upon long custom and the gratitude of the people; it was contested by none, and it received involuntary and glorious homage even from the East. Rome and Italy were but expecting the hour of Providence.

4. At last this hour arrives, and Charlemagne receives the glorious mission of founding definitively the temporal sovereignty of the Holy See.

CHAPTER VII.

GENERAL VIEW OF THE HISTORY OF THE TEMPORAL POWER.

THERE remain other remarkable lessons to be learned from history besides those we have been reviewing in the preceding pages, which, confirming the fact, throw light also upon the present, and the difficulties which it proposes to us.

When a great institution has lasted for ages, and has experienced the most various fortunes, it has undergone, so to speak, the ordeal of men and times, and, by the light of so protracted an experience, its interests, its needs, and its rights, may be equitably appreciated. Accordingly, after an attentive study of the above facts, we think we are justified in pronouncing, that the temporal sovereignty of the Pope, as at present constituted and recognized by Europe, places him, as regards the full and free exercise of his spiritual authority, and the peace of our consciences which depends upon it, in a better position than he was at any period of history; better than under the pagan and persecuting emperors; better than under the Cæsars of Byzantium,—protectors, indeed, but too often oppressors also; better even, or, at least less exposed to violence and outrage, than at the time of his greatest political influence in the middle ages.

We can here but cast a rapid glance over the different phases through which the Papacy has passed; but the events we have to review are important and luminous enough to show that the changes in human affairs have, notwithstanding the evident and never-failing protection of Providence, been the occasions of continual perils and great injuries to the Holy See, from which the position created for it by the modern principles of public and international law which prevail in Europe, seems eminently calculated to preserve it. And this is why we ask that this position may continue, and may be, more than ever, confirmed and placed under the safeguard of all the Catholic powers in the world.

The Papacy, as was fitting, appeared at first in the world invested with the essential powers, and all the rights which it held from Jesus Christ. The position immediately created for it by the wickedness of men, namely, persecution, was evidently unjust and anomalous; but the providential reason for it is obvious:—" The Church," as Bossuet says, " begins by the cross and martyrdom; daughter of heaven, she must prove beyond dispute that she is born essentially free and independent, and that she does not owe her origin to men." Under these abnormal and unjust circumstances, the Papacy maintained its rights and saved its independence by the extraordinary means of martyrdom, and by the transitory, exceptional assistance of miracles. It was the heroic age of the Church, the most glorious epoch in her history: yet, who would wish to bring us back to it? Who shall presume to say that the Church of God is for ever to continue an alien and an outcast here below, or that she has been placed upon earth only to confess the truth before tyrants, and to die?

After she had thus conquered earthly power, and acquired a free existence in the world, a new era opened upon her: Constantine and the new Cæsars sheltered under their imperial purple Christianity so long proscribed, and the Papacy sees peace, and sometimes triumph, succeed to scaffolds and persecutions. "When, after three hundred years of persecutions, the Church has proved by her vigorous growth, unaided by man for so many years, that she depends not upon man, appear now, O Cæsars,—it is time!" So Bossuet greets the entry of the princes into the Church, and the peaceful and honourable existence they procured for her; so does he celebrate this harmony between the priesthood and the empire, "which gives free course to the Gospel, more immediate force to the canons, and maintains discipline more visibly."

However, was this alliance with human powers a benefit which called for unreserved congratulation? Does it involve no peril for the Church? The state being all-powerful, and master of the Church, does she run no risk of often paying with her independence for her too close connection with the Cæsars? He who protects may enslave. So it was, in fact, more than once. When we read the history of the Lower Empire, and observe the fatal, and as it were irresistible, propensity of the Byzantine Cæsars to consider themselves the heirs of the emperor-pontiffs, and to extend their absolute power into the sacred domain of conscience, we are tempted to ask if the Church has been a great gainer, and if the protection of the imperial diadem profits her more than the halo of martyrdom?

This unfortunate interference of the secular power in church matters begins already under the successor of Constantine, even under Constantine himself, and continues ever after with incredible pertinacity. All heresies seem sure of a favourable reception at the court of the emperors: they depose bishops, attempt to bias councils, and even draw up articles of faith; some of the popes they send to die in exile, as Heraclius did St. Martin I., others they retain captive at Constantinople, to make them the tools of their unhappy policy, as Justinian did Pope Vigilius: the Monothelite and Iconoclast errors have no warmer supporters than the imperial theologians of Byzantium. They seem resolved, at any price, to be the judges of doctrine and the dictators of consciences. Though the absurd pretensions of the Byzantine despotism were resisted, though the temporal power did not, owing to the firmness of the popes, absorb the spiritual, do not these lasting conflicts between the powers, these perpetual struggles against a vexatious tyranny, exemplify but too clearly the dangers which must result to the Church from a state of dependence upon the protection of an irresistible power? And would our consciences be now as tranquil as they are, were universal empire to be resuscitated in Europe, necessarily exposing us to the same perils?

The destruction of the Western Empire, which put an end to the political unity of the ancient world, and the appearance of the barbarian races, whence the various nationalities of modern Europe were to spring, rendered a change necessary in the external state, in the temporal constitution of the Holy See; and Providence brought it to pass. The popes, at the fall of the Roman empire, found themselves placed in a new and elevated position. The great moral power with which they were invested gave them an immense *prestige* in the eyes of the barbarians, and enabled them to arrest more than once, at the gates of Rome, these scourges of God. From the confidence of princes, and the needs of the times, resulted then a new species of power, which gave the Papacy, not only a temporal and independent, though limited sovereignty, but the supreme arbitration between princes and people: the power of the Roman pontiffs increased immensely, not in its essential and divine rights, which can neither increase nor diminish, but in its political and social influence upon the world and civilization; and the advantage to Europe and humanity was very great, whatever complaints and objections may have been brought against details. Light has been at last thrown upon the history of those middle ages, so long decried; vain declamation has been silenced; and the greatness of that moral power is now generally felt, which, in those troubled times, alone opposed a successful barrier to the torrent of material force, pointing out to those barbarian sovereigns who only appealed to the sword, another right than that of force. " It is felt that its development at this period arose from circumstances and not from ambition; that such development was favourable to Europe and to humanity; and that, in fact, in guarding the liberty of their own election, the sanctity of marriage, ecclesiastical celibacy, and the integrity of the hierarchy, the popes were defending the cause of justice and civilization."—(*Père Lacordaire*, Conférences, tom. i.) It is felt that they were, to borrow the expression of De Maistre, the *constituting genii* of Europe.

But, what is strange and most worthy of remark, this power, which at that time influences all others, which awes the passions of kings, which conquers spiritual liberty for the Church, which summons all Europe to the crusades, and hurls it upon Asia, finds its own existence continually menaced: it is for ever exposed to the outrages of superior strength; oppressed or exiled, now by the emperors of Germany, now by the republican passions which agitated Rome and the other cities of Italy during the middle ages. More than once, at that stormy period, the work of Charlemagne was in danger of perishing; the political position of the Papacy was most insecure, its temporal sovereignty was often threatened and sometimes overthrown: and comparing times with times, we shall find that the evils which then afflicted the Holy See have been spared it, since its temporal sovereignty and independence have been secured to it, and the Pontifical States placed under the common protection of the European powers.

A double enemy continually threatened the temporal sovereignty of the Popes in the middle ages: the pretensions to suzerainty of the emperors of Germany, who would persist in considering Rome as a fief of the empire, and, at Rome, the ambition of certain great families, and the turbulence of factions. To revive the republic at Rome, and to re-establish her ancient supremacy in the West, was frequently, during the middle ages, the dearest wish and the most fantastic vision of the Romans. In the tenth century, a cabal attempted to make use of the influence of the Papacy as an instrument to further this ambitious design. The nobles had built castles, or converted the triumphal arches and the tombs of the ancient Romans into fortresses. Secure within their ramparts, they issued thence to superintend the elections of the Pontiffs, and to secure the Holy See for their creatures. The castle of St. Angelo is famous in the long history of the violence done to the Papacy in the middle ages. It was there, in the beginning of the tenth century, that the too famous Marozia took up her abode; it was there that she caused John X. to be strangled: John XIII. was incarcerated there previous to his exile in Campania: Benedict VI. was strangled there; there Crescentius starved John XIV. to death, and from thence he oppressed the Sovereign Pontiffs and Rome till the emperor Otho put an end to his tyranny in 998. In 1069, an anti-pope installed himself in this fort, and held out there for two years. St. Gregory VII. was besieged there, in his turn, by the emperor Henry IV. in 1084, and delivered by the Norman Robert Guiscard.

The absence of any temporal guarantee to the Papal independence, and these odious tyrannies, were the causes of the disreputable elections which afflicted the Church at this period. "The divinity of religion was never more clearly proved; that it should have survived the crimes of its own ministers is as great a miracle as its establishment all over the world." Such is the conclusion drawn by a learned historian from these scandals of the tenth century. But how far preferable for the Church would have been a really independent political position, which would have averted these evils!

In the twelfth century, the old chimera of a republic is

revived in the Roman cities, by the doctrines of Arnauld of Brescia; the names of citizens, of Comitia, of the Forum, are re-established—patricians and a senate are created.

Rienzi, in the fourteenth century, again renews these insane ideas; but seeing the liberty of the Holy See for ever menaced at home, by these republican aspirations, by the passions of Guelphs and Ghibellines, by the rivalry of the great families, the Colonnas, the Orsinis, the Frangipanis, the Gaetanis, the Contis; abroad, the quarrels of the Empire with the Church, which are continually bringing German armies to Rome, the Popes flying from their capital, or the prisoners of the emperors—the scandal of anti-popes; I would ask, are all these troubles and perils a state of things greatly to be envied to the middle ages, greatly preferable for the welfare of the Church and the Holy See, and with which Catholic consciences would now declare themselves satisfied? How much better is the position of the chief of the Catholic Church in modern days, when his full independence, though nothing more, has been secured to him by the provisions of the most solemn treaties; since his temporal sovereignty, guaranteed by the public consent of Europe, has never been contested, except at moments of universal confusion. True, he no longer exercises that immense influence over temporal powers which public opinion had conferred upon him in the middle ages; but this sort of jurisdiction over crowns, which rendered such real services to Europe, is not essential to the Papacy; and the reaction which stripped him of it, strengthened him in other ways.

Two vast advantages result from this settled and clearly-defined arrangement. On the one hand, the Papacy is the sole master of its temporal dominions; it is no longer umpire, as formerly, between other powers; but, emancipated from the menaces of the imperial suzerainty, from the dangers of war, and from republican schemes, it is enabled by its state of proper independence to exercise untrammelled all its spiritual prerogatives, and to give full play to its powerful and fruitful religious agency. On the other hand, its action being visibly confined to the sphere of the venerable powers which have been confided to it for the salvation of the world, other states no longer attempt to sway or to subjugate it, as they so often did in the middle ages. The great quarrels of former times, such as that on the subject of investitures, have died away, the distrusts and umbrages of the past have disappeared, peace on both sides has been the fruit of the separation of the two powers, between which the teaching and the practice of the greatest Popes had drawn so clear a distinction; the liberty of the election of the Sovereign Pontiffs has been respected; due independence and mutual harmony are now the wise foundation of the relations of Church and State, and the true principles of liberty for the Church, which should be cherished by the present generation. It is thus that the peaceful possession of its terrestrial sovereignty has placed the Papacy in a due position in Europe, for 300 years, and enabled it to exercise freely its august ministry.

See what great things, during these three centuries of peace (for which the Papacy was evidently indebted to the principle of its independent sovereignty) it has done for the propagation of the Gospel and of Christian civilization, for the development of sacred learning, for arts and letters, for the discipline and government of churches. What magnificent impulses given to distant missions!—missions to Mexico (1524), missions to the Indies (1541), missions to Japan (1549), missions to Ethiopia and Brazil (1554), missions to China (1580), missions to Paraguay (1602), missions to Canada (1613), missions to the Levant (1616). Besides, how learning is advanced, what magnificent historical, archæological, linguistic researches are undertaken, under the protection of the Papacy, by those orders which are founded or regenerated by its powerful impulse, the Jesuits, the Oratory, the Benedictines of St. Maur, and others! Consider, too, all the concordats concluded between the Holy See and the different powers: in 1516, without going higher, between Leo X. and Francis I.; in 1753, with Spain; in 1757, with the duchy of Milan;

in 1770, with Sardinia; in 1791, with the kingdom of Naples; in 1801, with France; not to mention the concordats of our own time which I have before enumerated. Would the Popes have enjoyed the same liberty of action and of government, would they have been on equally harmonious terms with all the Catholic powers, and even with some who, not having the happiness of being Catholic themselves, possess Catholic subjects, had they been the subjects of a prince or a republic, had they only enjoyed, as in the middle ages, a precarious sovereignty, for ever insulted and menaced by emperors or tribunes?

The new state of things, doubtless, was not perfect nor entirely secure; but, at least, the Pope was at peace with all the rulers of the world, in virtue of the recognition of his sovereignty and his neutrality—as Voltaire says, "Though Rome is no longer powerful enough to make war, her weakness is a blessing. She is the only state which has enjoyed peace for three centuries."—*Cour de Rome, Dict. Phil.*

If, then, the Papacy has lost its political preponderance, if it is no longer the centre of the political intrigues of Europe, it continues, with as great lustre as ever, and with greater liberty and independence, the supreme tribunal of consciences, the highest moral authority in the world. Its dignity and the freedom of its religious and civilizing action are nobly sheltered by a temporal crown, sufficiently imposing for the needs of its earthly mission, but not for its ambition, if it were so tempted, and in no way threatening to any other sovereignty. Fixed in an honourable neutrality by the respect of all, and by formal guarantees, enjoying a spiritual supremacy as complete and unquestioned as ever, its independence has been felt and recognized as necessary to the balance of power in Europe, and to the peace of the world; and Rome has become a sacred spot of territory, which the ambition of conquerors must respect, the inviolable asylum of the Sovereign Pontiff. So have died away in modern generations the unhappy collisions between the two powers, which so long and so often desolated the Lower Empire and the middle ages; so has an independent existence been created in Catholicism, and in Catholicism only, for the two orders, temporal and spiritual; so have Catholic consciences escaped from the tyranny which has everywhere else absorbed or subjugated the spiritual power, in the East as in the West, at London as at St. Petersburg and Constantinople. At the same time, sovereigns need no longer mistrust or dread a superior political influence; the concord so long sought has been realized in a due independence; the spiritual power, limited to its own sphere, has freely pronounced its oracles, and is not less deeply revered by the faithful; it has proclaimed before kings and peoples the great truths of the moral order, those immutable principles on which social tranquillity and national prosperity must ever rest. The Pontiffs on their throne, and princes on theirs, the modern world has reposed under the shadow of their concord; souls submit willingly to this authority, which does not force the truth upon them, but proclaims it in the name of God, and asks only for the free assent of the conscience; nor do even self-willed and restless spirits take offence at the authoritity of the old man who sits in the Vatican, unarmed though revered.

Men of comprehensive mind have often felt, that to subjugate the Roman Pontiff would be to enslave the general freedom of opinion, and that it is well to have an independent spiritual power upon earth, whose unappalled firmness may raise at least one free voice, one independent protest, at the moments of greatest danger for human liberty. France felt the advantage of this at the beginning of the present century; and if the Muscovite and Greek patriarchates had not altogether lost this liberty, I do not know that Christianity and liberty of opinion in Russia and Turkey would not have reason to congratulate themselves. At all events, all the Catholics of Europe now bless God for an institution which has visibly been the laborious and glorious work of ages and of Providence.

Why, then, seek to undo it? Why eradicate from the soil of Italy and of Europe a venerable institution, which has cast such deep roots there these fifteen hundred years? Is it that peace, tranquillity, and order are an eyesore to the spirits of our time? Are people no longer to be allowed to sit down and to repose under the shadow of the time-honoured traditions of the past? The edifice of the Pope's temporal power has been constructed by the hand of God to protect the liberty of mankind, and to assure the independence of their faith. Woe, then, to the sacrilegious temerity which dares to touch the work of Divine Wisdom, and, in the language of the faith of other days, *to lay its hands upon the patrimony of St. Peter!*

It is vain to make a hypocritical parade of good intentions; those cannot be sincere who dare lightly and presumptuously to speculate where such solemn interests are at stake: it is unsafe to make experiments here; it would be perilous to test a crude and random political theory upon such sacred matters, which should be approached with reverence; or, to borrow an expression of St. Paul, with fear and trembling. He who hastily broaches and presumptuously resolves such questions, runs a greater risk than he is aware, of a collision with that corner-stone, of which it is written: *Whosoever shall fall upon that stone shall be bruised: and upon whomsoever it shall fall, it will grind him to powder.* The patrimony of St. Peter is the common property of the great Catholic family: those unnatural children who have sought to usurp or appropriate it to themselves, have never prospered; it is a spoil which has ever proved the ruin of all plunderers who have endeavoured to lay hands upon it.

CHAPTER VIII.

ROME WITHOUT THE POPE.

ALTHOUGH the arguments already discussed most conclusively demonstrate the thesis we are maintaining, we shall add some important considerations of a particular nature, which will confirm and complete our proof.

And, first, as the dreams of revolutionary impiety have gone so far, and as the idea has been so often broached, and is now more loudly proclaimed than ever, let us see what Rome, Italy, and Europe would be without the Pope, and let us commence by carefully examining what the Papacy has done, and still does, for Rome.

It has been said with truth that Rome with the Papacy is neither a great centre of political action, nor a great industrial city, nor a great commercial emporium. Yes, but if Rome loses the Papacy, will she thereby become a great political, commercial, or manufacturing city, or if not, what will she gain? Rome, with the Papacy, was a city which stood alone in the world; great without earthly power, brilliant without luxury, strikingly tranquil, yet full of life; a city which rallied around her, from the extremities of Europe, whatever was great and noble: artists, scholars, bishops, kings, pilgrims, and travellers of every profession, of every rank, of every nation, I may even add, of every faith.

What would Rome be without the Papacy? A town effaced from among the number of European capitals, the fourth or fifth at most in revolutionary Italy; smaller than Naples, less graceful than Florence, less curious than Venice; the chief town of the fourth or fifth state in the Italian confederation (if such confederation be possible without the Pope); the residence of some grand-duke, if the confederation is to be monarchical; or else the capital of some puny, abortive republic, only the more ridiculous for having borrowed the great name of Roman Republic.

The revolutionary admirers of classical Rome, who doubtless far prefer their Pagan to their Christian ancestors, ought at least to feel that they have not among them Cæsars, Scipios, or consuls; it would be difficult for the Rome of Garibaldi and Mazzini to believe itself the Rome of Fabricius and Cato, or to consider the unworthy successors of the exiled Papacy as true inheritors of the majesty of the people-king.

But Rome without the Pope is a contradiction in terms: an historical, religious, and social contradiction. The imagination cannot lend itself to the idea: monuments, arts, sciences, politics themselves, religion, history, the memories of the past and the hopes of the future, exclaim and protest against the outrage done to their immemorial, their necessary protector, and declare that Rome without the Pope would be a city depopulated, a body without a soul, a place without honour and without life; *non tenebat ornatum suum civitas*, her ancient orator would have said.—(*Cic. De Repub.*) What a sudden collapse, when the imagination endeavours to portray Rome as no longer the city of the popes, the centre of Christianity, the metropolis of the Catholic world! Rome a profane and vulgar city! What surprising littleness succeeds at once to her departed grandeur! Nothing of what makes Rome herself, of what gives her that peculiar aspect, that mysterious beauty, that incommunicable charm, would remain to her new existence: we might seek for Rome at Rome, and not find her. Her stones even would complain and cry out. Yes, for the stones, the ruins of Rome, speak a language proper to themselves alone. In other places, these relics of ages which are no more, these mute but expressive witnesses to the instability of all human things, touch the soul of the beholder with deep and unmitigated sadness; but at Rome other voices issue from the wreck of the past, and sweet consolations redeem the melancholy which it inspires. At Rome, there are ruins and death, but there is also resurrection and life, a glorious transformation rather than a destruction; through the dust of the fallen monuments of antiquity, we can always distinguish a new Rome, whose youth is continually renewed in all the freshness of infancy, and all the majesty of immortality: and so the holy city is called also the Eternal City.

So a Catholic orator spoke in 1849, before the Legislative Assembly, celebrating the greatness of Christian Rome:—" What is our object? It is to restore to Rome the place which she has held for so many ages, the name which she so gloriously bears, the name of Eternal City, the name which you still give her, inconsistently, while you are depriving her of all that creates her title to it. Paris is the capital of intellect and of the arts, as we always say; yet who ever thought of calling Paris the Eternal City? London is the capital of the world in maritime and commercial affairs; yet who ever thought of calling London the Eternal City? Why then does Rome continue to bear this grand title, which none disputes with her? Because she is the capital, the ancient capital of the Christian republic, not of some thousands of chimerical republicans; because she is the second country of all Catholics, where their minds, their hearts, their faith, and their sympathies find themselves at home; to her, for eighteen hundred years, pilgrims from all regions of the world have been bringing their tributes and their respect; her very dust is venerable, impregnated as it is with the blood of the saints and martyrs. This is why Rome is called the Eternal City."—*M. de Falloux.*

It is not only Catholic orators, like M. de Falloux, who pay this homage to the Eternal City and the Papacy: the most illustrious Protestants have held the same language. To cite the words of Lord Macaulay, the great historian, whose premature end is still deplored by England:—" We see no sign which indicates that the term of her long dominion is approaching. She saw the commencement of all the governments and of all the ecclesiastical establishments that now exist in the world; and we feel no assurance that she is not destined to see the end of them all. She was great and respected before the Saxon had set foot in Britain, before the Frank had passed the Rhine, when Grecian eloquence still flourished in Antioch, when idols were still worshipped in the temple of Mecca. And she may still exist in undiminished vigour when some traveller from New Zealand shall, in the midst of a vast solitude, take his stand on a broken arch of London Bridge, to sketch the ruins of St. Paul's."

What constitutes the sovereignty of Rome and her supreme dignity is, that she is the residence of the Church which is the mother and mistress of all churches, the centre and the focus of all Christian light. This august character is everywhere stamped upon Rome: we see it in her monuments, her ruins, on the front of her palaces or temples, on her glittering domes, on her walls, even in her soil. So Dante said of old.[1] In this consists the poetry, the grandeur, the life of Rome. Once stripped of this glory, of this crown, the imagination fails to recognize her: the disconcerted pilgrim or artist, wandering over her sullied precincts, asks himself, Where is the city that was solitary upon earth, consecrated by the blood of the heroes of Christianity,

Veuve d'un peuple roi, mais reine encore du monde?

Where is that majesty of religion which hung over her, grander than the majesty of the empire? Where is the voice of the Pontiff, blessing the city and the world?

---

[1] "No further proof is needed to see that a special divine design has presided over the birth and the greatness of this holy city; and I firmly believe that the stones of her walls are worthy of respect, and that the very ground on which she rests is worthy of veneration beyond what can be imagined or expressed."—(*Dante*.) Long before the Florentine poet, the early fathers of the Church had celebrated this mysterious glory of ancient Rome in being transformed into Catholic Rome:—" What was Pagan Rome?" asks St. Jerome: "an accursed city, whose people filled the entire universe, but where vice received the palm which should belong to honour; where everything pure and sacred was defiled. But now, the holy Church reigns there; there are the trophies of the apostles and martyrs; there the true faith of Jesus Christ is preserved, and the pure doctrine of the Evangelists is preached; there the glory of the Christian name for ever shines over the ruins of gentility."—*S. Hier.* Epist. Fam. iii. 9, ad Principiam; id. ii. 17, ad Marcellam.

"Those who formerly neither knew nor loved her," says Tertullian, "when they have come to know her, have loved her." Alas! Rome has at the present time enemies to whom we may add with Tertullian,—" As for you, you love to remain ignorant of what others have rejoiced to know. You prefer not to know, because you hate, as if you were sure of losing your hatred with your ignorance."—*Tertullian*, adversus Gentes, tom. i.

Where is the reign of Christ, proclaimed by her obelisks, her churches, and her basilicas? What has become of the living splendour of Catholicism, which once attracted to her the men of the North, of the South, of the East, and of the West, in those days when she was the heart of Christendom, and a common home to all nations? Such was Rome: such was the sublime perspective which she presented to the imagination and to faith: that perspective has now been swept from our view; a cloud has lowered over Rome, her lustre is obscured, her glory turned into mourning.

Rome without the Pope, to speak plainly, would be a desert; for, who will visit it? Who will fill it? Who is there to do its honours? There are already deserts enough at Rome: permit me, Romans who would wish to give us a Rome without a Pope (if there be any such), to argue with and question you directly. You want, then, to multiply these deserts. The Palatine, the Aventine, the Viminal, the Forum, your most important quarters, are deserted! You would add to them the Quirinal, the Vatican, the entire city! In particular, what will you do with the seven basilicas? What will you do with 365 churches, answering and representing all the necessities, all the recollections, all the vows, all the pilgrimages of the Catholic world? We would all visit them one day, priests and faithful, if only in the longings of our heart; but ah! if the Pope be absent, who would set out on such a pilgrimage? What would your great solemnities be then; or rather, would a single one of your hundred feasts be possible without him? Above all, what will you do with St. Peter's, with such immensity, such light, such magnificence? The universal Pontiff of Catholicity alone can fill it. St. Peter's has been evidently made so vast, in order that the common Father of the great Catholic family may assemble there all his children and bless them! The revolutionists would labour under a sad delusion, were they to imagine that St. Peter's is only the largest parish church in the diocese of Rome: no; it is for itself that Catholicity built it, and lavished

I

upon it its treasures. St. Peter's is the august temple of Catholicity; Rome is but the vestibule and the porch; its life, its soul, its glory, is the Pope.

Rome without the Pope! But at Easter, the great feast of Christians, who shall raise his hand, to give to the city and the world, *urbi et orbi*, the solemn benediction of the Vicar of Christ? Surely there will remain some lingering echoes of that great and paternal voice, which, amidst the sublime silence of earth and sky, is heard upon the air, by the entire universe, as the voice of God himself! I have seen there the most unbelieving fall upon their knees, overcome by a superior and divine force; I have seen them, as docile children, bend respectfully under the hand of the common Father of the great Christian family; I have seen lost sheep receive with emotion and with love the benediction of the sovereign pastor of souls! Romans, Italians, Germans, French, Protestants, schismatics, Greeks, English, Russians, Poles, Americans, we were all there, of every tongue, of every tribe, of every nation, prostrate on the ground, and hanging on the lips of the Supreme Pontiff! It was the most beautiful, the most touching sight; human language fails to give expression to it. When we arose, tears were in all eyes, indefinable yearnings filled all hearts; there was there, then, but one fold and one shepherd. We all formed but one heart and one soul. You have seen all this as I have, and you would do away with this beauty and this glory! You would deprive yourselves of it as well as us— you wish Rome to have no Pope! Or you imagine some hypocritical and impious plan to humiliate and degrade him, and force him to regret the Catacombs!

It has been often said, that Rome, even with the Pope, gives us the impression of sadness and loneliness. True, but it is only a first impression: on a longer acquaintance one begins to appreciate and to love this solitude; one finds in it a singular attraction, a repose which one feels unwilling to leave. There is in it a solemnity, a profound peace, a mysterious interest, which silently captivate the soul. It possesses an inexpressible but irresistible charm. It is of Rome, in better and happier days,—of Rome with her Pope, of Rome the holy city,—that we may repeat the lines of a poet, whose name, alas! is an affliction for whom we mourn, though we never will say without hope :[1]—

> " Ici viennent mourir les derniers bruits du monde !
> Nautonniers sans étoile, abordez ; c'est le port !
> Ici l'âme se plonge en une paix profonde,
>   Et cette paix n'est point la mort ! "

But, without the Pope, the loneliness of Rome would be that of the grave! her repose would be the stillness of death! People go to Naples for the sun; but to Rome for the Pope. It is the Pope and the gentle light which surrounds him, the light of peace and grace, of faith and paternal tenderness, which rests weary eyes, which heals weak ones, which gives eyes to see to those who have them not, which is loved often by those who fear it, which captivates those who would fly from it, and sometimes gains them for ever.

In vain do the Italians or revolutionary pamphlets say the Pope might remain at Rome, and inhabit the palace and basilica of St. John Lateran, as under Constantine: he might be both mere bishop of Rome and head of Catholicity : spiritually, he would reign ; as to temporals, the Roman authorities would supply them to him. I have already said what I think of this absurd and odious hypocrisy. No; this could never be. You yourselves would soon find it was impossible. If you are serious in proposing such a dream, I tell you it would soon be dissipated. The Pope, the supreme chief of Catholicity, the universal Pontiff, at St. John Lateran! Whoever you are, senator, consul, municipal authorities, ruler under whatever title, you could not remain one day beside him. He would be to you an unceasing cause of umbrage and difficulty. The Pope would be too great for you; the

---

[1] *Lamartine*, Médit. sur la Roche-Guyon.

weight of his dignity would crush you in spite of him, in spite of yourselves; you could not suffer him; you would soon hide yourselves in despair and shame.

And what would you do with the Vatican and a hundred other wonders, which, without the Pope, would be vain and meaningless? Do you not see that if he leaves you, you would wander like shadows over those immense, void spaces, that you would appear like pigmies at the foot of such gigantic monuments, raised for a greatness which is not yours? The more I reflect on it, the more I am amazed. You, to reign at Rome, beside the Pope, above the Pope! But again, as we have already told you, the Pope cannot be your subject. Catholicity cannot tolerate it; we must have a Pope who is independent and sovereign; our consciences demand it, and also that he appear so evidently. But, did the Pope even yield to your wishes for an instant, the force of things would elevate him above you in spite of himself, and you could not hold your ground: greater men than you have failed to do so. Constantine, Theodosius, those emperors of glorious memory, placed by Providence at the head of an empire which knew no limits but those of the universe, felt that they could not remain at Rome beside the Pope, and removed to Byzantium, to Milan, to Treves, to the East or to the West. The world would not at present offer you such grand abodes, it is true: but whether you will or no, one of two things must take place; either you will expel the Pontiff from Rome, and his departure will leave you amazed and stupefied at your solitude; or you will restore him to his place, and descend to your own; and your happiness, your honour, and the peace of the world will benefit by it.

But you may say, "This matchless grandeur gone, this majesty of religion sacrificed, this Christian stamp effaced, we shall make up for them by political advantages and a better government;—in a word, we will make changes suited to modern times, to the real wants, to the material prosperity of the Roman people."

Do not imagine it: having profaned and vulgarized this

august city,—having made of it the chief town of some Piedmontese department, or the capital of some ephemeral republic, or the seat of a municipal corporation, which is to govern in the Pope's place; having banished Catholicism and extinguished the Papacy, its humiliation will be but the prelude to its ruin. The past greatness of Rome would then only serve to bring out more clearly its shame and its decay; its ruin would speedily follow. Consuls, town-councillors, and great recollections alone will not sustain life; and Rome lives, even in the most material sense of the word, by the Papacy, which does her the honour to dwell within her walls. The popes and religion have never once quitted Rome, that the town has not been impoverished and the population diminished. These variations were remarkably perceptible when the popes were at Avignon; they were so even during the absence of Pius VII., which, however, did not last five years. When, after its long residence at Avignon, the Papacy returned at last to the Eternal City, the population had diminished by more than half of what it was under Innocent III. During this sad interval, which Rome called the captivity of Babylon, no new building had embellished her; and it is for this reason that Gothic architecture, so flourishing at that period, has left no trace at Rome. When, on the departure of Pius VII., Rome became merely the chief town of the department of the Tiber, the population gradually decreased, and in 1813 was only 117,000. The Pope having returned, it increased immediately, and, under Gregory XVI., was 170,000; a difference, in a few years, of more than 50,000 inhabitants.

The revolutionists ought not to forget this. As to their complaints against the government, I would ask, Do not the people of Rome enjoy all that is wanting to the real happiness of a population? Do not all foreigners admit that they are under the most gentle of governments? One sees even the galley-slaves pass quietly along the thoroughfares of Rome, and their keepers asking them with kindness to sweep the streets. Everything bespeaks a paternal government,—perhaps even too paternal. What is wanting to you? Is it the first rank in the cultivation of the arts?' In this respect, what city can be compared to yours? Under the influence of the popes, what country has been more enriched by genius? Perhaps you desire the honour and the rewards of industry? But what prevents you from having them? You may work. Is it agriculture? Labour in your fields; Heaven has given you a privileged soil,—*terra parens frugum*. Is it commerce? Cross the seas,—all ports are open to you. You are at peace with the whole earth; what the ancient poet sung, has been realized by the pacific influence of new Rome:—

"Hæ tibi erunt artes, pacisque imponere morem!"

Voltaire himself says, "the Romans now are no longer conquerors, but they are happy." But if hitherto you have been too much attached to ease and indolence, do not blame the Papacy for the faults of your disposition and your own weaknesses: to lay their indolence to the charge of their government, *e la colpa del governo*, would be really too convenient for a people.

But you claim also other rights, or at least those who want to have you themselves, pretend that you do. They repeat that you are deprived of what are called political rights. Ah! I could say much upon the vanity of these rights among certain nations who appear to enjoy them, and have found but deep and bitter disappointment! But Pius IX., while reserving to himself, as was due to the Papacy itself, the principle of sovereign authority, which indeed it was fitting that the Pope should maintain amid the rude shocks which European civilization had undergone, Pius IX. had granted you extensive political rights, more than you were able to bear. Not a sovereign in the world has done so much for his people as Pius IX. had done for you; like the ancient Cæsar,[1] the Christian Cæsar has been so

---

[1] Pliny, vii. 25.

generous that he has been obliged to repent of it. You showed then, but too clearly, that true liberty is not in the tumult of republican assemblies, nor in the unbridled license of the press. Your jealous caprice called for laymen in public offices; he appointed numbers. "*Still,*" said he, with his incomparable goodness, "*if good is done by ecclesiastics, it is nevertheless good.*" And, in fact, when laymen and Mazzini had everything in their hands, had you fewer troubles, fewer disputes, less corruption, less taxes, fewer murders?

What immense and peculiar advantages you owe to the Pope, even temporally and politically, advantages which no monarch upon earth could ever offer to his people. Observe that you are not subjects of a family, but of an elective prince, chosen not from an aristocratic body, but in at once the noblest and the most democratic assembly than can be conceived; the cardinals, sprung from all ranks among the people, who are the people itself! The election of the Pope, the college of electors who nominate him, the Pope himself,—is not this all that is most illustrious and all that is most popular? Not a Roman, not a shepherd's boy of the Campagna or the Abruzzi,—not a citizen of the Corso, but may become Cardinal, Grand Elector, and Pope. Do the ordinary age of the popes, the maturity of their judgment, the character of their government, even the shortness of their reign, offer no security for liberty? Assuredly, at least, many of the seeds of despotism are absent here: the youth of the sovereign, military force, duration of reigns, dynastic passions, whose effects are felt elsewhere. The celebrated Addison, though a Protestant, observed that the Pope is usually a man of learning and virtue, mature in years and experience, and seldom having vanity or pleasures to be gratified at the expense of his people. The families at Rome which are called Papal are known to be only distinguished by their liberality to the poor and their encouragement of art; their name is only a just tribute to the past, and confers upon them no rights for the future.

Have the Romans ever reflected, also, that in giving

themselves a sovereign, by means of their cardinals, almost always chosen from among themselves, they also give one to all the Catholics upon earth? Is this nothing? Is it not something grand to be able to say that they have a sovereign who reigns over two hundred millions of men, who commands the respect of the universe? that they are his peculiar people, and have a right to him above all others? We should not be so jealous of his independence, were he nothing but the sovereign of Rome. But the sovereign of Rome, and because of him, Rome and the Romans, reign over the whole world. All Catholic nations accept this; but on one condition, that Rome and the Romans respect his sovereignty. At this price they partake of it themselves. The cardinals, the princes of the Church, the sacred congregations, the legates, the apostolic nuncios, are, in fact, nearly all children of Rome and of Italy, and participate in the Roman sovereignty; it is ever the *imperium sine fine*. Under one form or another, the Romans have possessed this empire for three thousand years,—*Romanos rerum dominos*, without even altering the last words of the poet,—*gentemque togatam*.

This thought, the pride of the poets and historians of Pagan Rome,[1] has assumed greater proportions with the destinies of Christian Rome; according to the eloquent tribute to her universal royalty of one of our great doctors, thirteen centuries ago :—

> "Sedes Roma Petri, quæ pastoralis honoris
> Facta caput mundo; quidquid non possidet armis,
> Relligione tenet." *S. Prosper.*

The Prince of the Apostles, the founder of Christian Rome, might have said from the beginning, with more reason than

---

[1] "Illa inclyta Roma
Imperium terris, animos æquabit Olympo."
Virg.

"Fatis debebatur tantæ origo urbis."—*Livy.*

her original founder, *Nuntia Romanis, cœlestes ita velle, ut mea Roma caput orbis terrarum sit.* And your immortal and apostolic ancestors, St. Peter and St. Paul, have raised you still higher than human poetry contemplated; you are, more than other Christian nations, *a chosen nation, a royal priesthood—populus acquisitionis, regale sacerdotium.*

It is to be noted here, that Rome is not indebted for these advantages to politics or human passions. "No," says a philosophical traveller, "Christian Rome owes nothing to policy; if she has extended her power to regions enveloped in thick darkness; if she has reduced under her sway nations who had resisted the arms, and never had acknowledged the empire of the greatest conquerors; if savage hordes, who have never pronounced the names of Alexander or of Cæsar, have listened with respect to the voice of her pontiffs, and received their instructions as oracles; if pacific Rome has made conquests which the Rome of warriors would have envied,—these prodigies were not the work of human passions; human passions only served to render them more conspicuous, by leaguing themselves to oppose the greatest obstacles to the execution of projects which they were deeply interested in defeating."[1]

The Roman people without the Pope means nothing, is nothing! with the Pope, it is ever the people-king, *populum late regem,* in the eyes of foreigners and its own. Leave to Rome her Pope, and foreigners will treat the Roman people with respect; with the Pope, the Romans appear to the other Catholic nations what the tribe of Levi, the

---

[1] Discours sur l'Histoire, le Governement, etc., par *Le Comte d'Albon.* This passage of a modern author resembles another far more ancient:—"Ut civitas sacerdotalis et regia, per sacram beati Petri sedem, caput orbis effecta, latius præsideres religione divinâ, quam dominatione terrenâ. Quamvis enim, multis aucta victoriis, jus imperii tui terrâ marique protuleris, minus tamen est quod tibi bellicus labor subdidit, quam quod pax Christiana subjecit."—*Leo M.* Serm. I. in Nat. Apost. Petri et Pauli.

family of Aaron, seemed to the other tribes of Israel;—with the Pope, Rome is, as it were, the holy tribe, and every Roman seems related to the family of the high-priest, to the royal priesthood. And it is this, perhaps, which sometimes puffs up and leads astray, unknown to themselves, this privileged and indocile people, this spoiled child of Providence, when they rebel against the hand which loads them with benefits; thus renouncing all gratitude and all dignity, and miserably dishonouring the royal and sovereign blood, which seems to have flowed in their veins for more than twenty centuries!

Yes, take from Rome her Pope, and put in his place a grand-duke, a consul, a prefect, a president, a regent—anything you please—and this people will lose in their own and in foreign eyes, all greatness and all respect; there will exist no more a Roman people; Rome will become what Athens became. Now what was Athens during long centuries? what is she now, in spite of the efforts made in her behalf? Where are now the Athenians or the old Greeks? I would almost say, the Romans without the Pope will soon be mere guardians of a large, badly-kept museum, which will soon be bought up and carried away by connoisseurs.

With the Pope, Rome is always Rome; she is the capital of the universe, the centre of the highest and greatest affairs; the peaceful rendezvous of the civilized world; the asylum of fallen kings, of greatness in misfortune, however ungrateful it may afterwards show itself to the hospitality which harboured it: with the Pope, Rome sees every year a hundred thousand strangers come to bring her their homage and their treasures. Romans, who hearken so easily to-day to revolutionary sophists, would you see all this, if you had not the Pope as your guest and your king? Learn, then, from the respect and admiration of the entire world for your city, that you are a people who stand alone, and that vulgar low outbreaks and revolutions are not suited to you.

Without leaving your own walls, it should suffice to glance at the monuments which encompass you, to understand what it is which constitutes your high dignity. When you see the Prince of Apostles, with the keys of the kingdom of heaven in his hand, raised upon the pillar of Trajan, and St. Paul armed with the sword of faith, upon that of Antoninus, cannot you feel that your own glory is embodied in them? When you look from the Capitol to the Vatican, and go over in your memory all the history and the fortunes of these two hills, do you not see the design of God? When you pass from the Coliseum and the Mamertine prisons to St. Peter's, and read upon the glittering dome of the immortal basilica, *Thou art Peter, and upon this rock I will build my Church, and the gates of hell shall not prevail against her*, do you not understand that you are the eternal city, only because you are the city of the king of souls? When in Nero's gardens you contemplate the obelisk of Christ victorious, and the radiant cross which crowns it, and these glowing words, *Christus vincit, regnat, imperat*,—how not recognize that you are a sacred and providential people; that in the inscrutable counsels of Providence, Rome has been chosen as the seat of the most legitimate, the most beneficent, and the most august sovereignty in Europe, or the world; and that to revolt against it is to incur the united anathemas of heaven and earth?

Let us hope that the masters of error and deceit, who are now abusing the ephemeral power which has fallen into their hands, will see their fatal credit give way when misfortunes have prepared the way for reason and good sense. Them it is, far more than Bologna and the people of the Romagna, whom we denounce! It is against them, above all, that we protest before all civilized and Christian nations! As to Bologna, Ferrara, and Ravenna, now so fatally misled, we cannot bring ourselves to despair of them; we do not forget the love with which, not so long ago, they welcomed Pius IX., when he entered within their walls. It is with delight that we look forward to a day when the reconciliation of these children with their Father shall renew the following consoling scene, related by an ancient historian:—" It happened then," says Otto de Frisingue, speaking of Eugene III., "by the mercy of God, that a great joy burst forth through the whole city at the news of the unexpected return of the Pontiff. An innumerable multitude ran to meet him with green branches in their hands. They prostrated themselves before him, they kissed his footprints, they overwhelmed him with embraces. Banners floated; officers and judges advanced in crowds. The Jews were not absent from this great rejoicing, bearing on their shoulders the law of Moses. All, like a choir of musicians, sung in unison these words, *Blessed is he who cometh in the name of the Lord.*"

CHAPTER IX.

ITALY WITHOUT THE PAPACY.

WHAT St. Peter's is to Rome, Rome is to Italy: Italy in her degree shares with the eternal city the respect and love of Christian nations; and the injury the Romans would do themselves, or that others would do them, in expelling the Pope, or in keeping him among them as the captive of some Roman government, would not be confined to them: its effects would be felt far beyond the walls of Rome. The whole of Catholicity would suffer; but, above all, Italy. Rome and the Pope are the head of Italy; without Rome and without the Pope, Italy would be decapitated.

What would Italy have been, what would she still be, without the Pope? "I am an Italian," said M. Rossi, "and for that reason I am devoted to the Pope: *the Papacy is the sole living grandeur of Italy.*" Even the revolutionary Italians have felt this: one of their ideas was to make the Pope, whether he would or no, the chief of some Italian league or republic; thus involuntarily testifying that the Italian nation cannot do without the Papacy.

The popes have, in fact, always generously, though peacefully, laboured for the welfare and the nationality of Italy. We have already seen all that they did for her in the 5th, 6th, 7th, 8th, and 9th centuries, and how they saved her from total ruin during the barbarian invasions. But it is worthy of remark, that Rome, papal Rome, is the only state which has always continued Italian. Invasions have never seized upon her but for a moment. She never was Norman like Naples, nor Spanish or German like Milan. The Heruli or the Lombards never mastered her; she has always been since Romulus, what she is to-day,—an independent city. The Gauls took her, but they could not hold her; nor has any barbarian since, now for nearly 2,500 years. Princes of Savoy are at Turin, princes of German extraction at Florence, Bourbons at Naples: at Rome there have never been but the popes, and generally Italian popes; never foreign conquerors. The Pope is, then, the sole really Italian potentate in Italy. And this might have been said even when the Pope was an Englishman or Frenchman, because he never brought with him dynasty, army, party, or anything, in short, from England or France. As temporal prince, he was an Italian, far more so than the princes of Lorraine at Florence, or the princes of Savoy at Turin. Nay, it is during the last three hundred years, when there was not one other Italian prince in Italy, that the Papacy has been exclusively Italian. Many have even complained of this, but certainly no Italian could. The last foreign Pope was Adrian VI., the tutor of Charles V.

History shows, then, that Rome, Papal Rome, is the true centre and sanctuary of Italian nationality. Rome, if a purely temporal state, would not have been more privileged than Naples or Florence; it would have been exposed, like them, to conquests, and foreign dynasties would have been imposed upon it by force, or by the law of succession. So that I do not hesitate to assert, that it is the Pope, in his double character of prince and pontiff, who has preserved whatever is living and immortal in Italian nationality.

Absolute political unity has been long an impossibility in Italy, and probably will long remain so. It never existed, strictly speaking, even under the Romans. As long, then, as she continues divided into different states and sovereignties,—and even her warmest partisans admit that such must continue to be her state,[1]—what can be more desirable for her independence and for the sort of unity she is capable of, than to see one of her sovereigns invested with a sacred and august character, which places him, without rivalry or ambition, above the others, and makes him morally the chief of Italy? To the popes Italy owes whatever nationality and unity it was possible for her to have. At the fall of the Western Empire, the popes, the providential chiefs of Italy, saved her from a complete invasion by the barbarians. Italy became neither Frank, like Gaul, nor Gothic and Moorish, like Spain. Why so? Because, in the fifth and sixth centuries, she had a head, when the other countries had not. All this is matter of history. At no period has Italy been able to oppose a military resistance to her enemies. At Rome alone there was an element of resistance, of a different sort, but invincible. Rome was respected; and but for her, nothing would have been respected in Italy,— it would have been utterly ravaged.

---

[1] "Can Italy be made one kingdom? History and nature herself condemn this solution. Italian unity could only be realized, after many efforts, by military influence or by revolutionary tyranny. From the Alps to Sicily, the Italian peninsula exhibits essential varieties, not less perceptible for the family resemblance which pervades them. Beside these evident differences, we perceive a community of language, of habits, and of interests, which have always produced a tendency to confederation, but never to fusion. We may say that the absolute unity under the sceptre of Rome was only an accident. The Romans were obliged, in order to master and unify the peninsula, to move entire populations. They were as long in accomplishing this conquest as in subduing the world. They had to do violence to Italy, as they did violence to the world."
—*Napoléon III. et l'Italie.*

In all the quarrels of the popes with the emperors, the chief question, doubtless, was the religious one. De Maistre, by the way, does not acknowledge this fully enough : but the independence of Italy also played a great part.

The constant ambition of the emperors of Germany during the middle ages, was to rule despotically over Rome and Italy; and all would have been over with Italian liberty, if the Papacy had not maintained at Rome a centre of resistance to the claims of the invaders. The holy Roman empire, of which it is sad to repeat with Voltaire, that it was neither *holy* nor an *empire*, nor Roman, and which was the constant enemy of the Holy See, was equally the enemy of Italian liberty; and the terrible ravages of the imperial armies in that lovely country are well known. Unfortunate Italy being then parcelled out into a number of petty principalities and rival republics, the partisans of the emperor and those of liberty were mixed everywhere together. Here a Guelph city, there a Ghibelline, and quarrels everywhere. In the midst of these intestine broils and contests, the Papacy constantly adhered to the policy of the Guelphs, and all its struggles with the imperial power benefitted Italian liberty. Voltaire himself acknowledges that the cause of the Papacy and that of Italian liberty were one and the same :—" It seems clear that Otho the Great and Frederick II. wanted to reign over Italy without control and without rivals : this is the secret of all their quarrels with the popes. The Guelphs, the partisans of the Papacy, and still more, of liberty, counterbalanced the power of the Ghibellines, the partisans of the empire."

The independence of Italy was finally achieved under the great Pope Alexander III., doubtless by force of arms, but, above all, by the sacred and universally admitted authority of the Papal power. The Lombard cities sided with St. Peter's chair, and the victory of the Papacy, followed by a generous peace, established the relations of Italy and Germany, of the Holy See and the Empire, on the most just and honourable footing. The successors of

Alexander III. energetically continued the struggle against Frederick II., which he had undertaken against Frederick Barbarossa on behalf of Italian liberty. " The temporal power of the popes," says Count Balbo, " was the cause and the beginning of Italian independence, and of the liberties of the municipal bodies." This is sufficiently proved by the history of the society of Venice, of the diet of Roncaglia, of the Lombard league, of the battle of Legnano, and the peace of Constance, which gave a legal existence to the republics of Italy.

As to the thirteenth century, M. Gaillardin, in his " Histoire du Moyen Age," has shown that the struggle between the Papacy and the Empire had, in freeing the Church, emancipated Italy. Rodolph of Hapsburg, who had, by the constitution of 1279, recognized the Ecclesiastical State, also refused to cross the Alps in order to impose his authority upon the cities which were hostile to the emperor. And in succeeding times, while the popes forced the emperors to forego even their pretensions to suzerainty over the State of the Church, the rest of Italy disengaged itself with like success from the foreign rule established by Otho, and resumed its nationality.

Italy, however, did not gain its liberty. In place of foreign tyrants, Italian tyrants arose; for Italy was then widowed of her popes : such is the forcible term used by herself to express the indissoluble union which binds her destinies to the greatness of the Papacy, and also to testify what grief a separation caused her. She has also called this period the captivity of Babylon. Then it was that the municipal independence of the cities disappeared : dynasties of petty tyrants established themselves in all the Italian republics, without strengthening the Empire which had raised them up, and which was expiring itself, because the Empire, too, had need of the Papacy, and because all Europe was suffering from the temporal degradation and exile of the popes. Hence the rage of the Italians, carried even too far, against the popes of Avignon, the disorders of their court, &c. In all the taunts of Petrarch and others, we can trace their irritation at having lost what was then, as now, the *sole living greatness of Italy*.

After this, the Papacy returns to Rome, politically weakened: it undergoes the trial of the great schism: its political authority over the Christian world disappears: Italy, too, declines and becomes more and more enthralled. The reign of the *condottieri* commences. Then come the wars, in which French, Italians, Spaniards, and Germans contend for it as a prey. The heroic but unsuccessful efforts of Julius II. and his Italian patriotism are well known.

I pause here, as the succeeding ages are too well known; and I will only add, that no nation can continue *one* without a capital. Now, for Italy, there can be no capital but Rome, and Rome can only be the capital of Italy through the Holy See. The historical recollections and municipal traditions which have illustrated the Italian cities in the middle ages, will never allow them, I am convinced, to accept any other supremacy. Florence, Naples, Milan, Venice, not to mention Bologna and Genoa, will never cede their rival pretensions to another city or another title: the constant bickerings of Genoa against Turin are notorious; and at the present moment the preponderance of Turin over Milan is far from being quietly accepted—the future will tell the rest.

In this, the author of the famous pamphlet " Napoléon III. et l'Italie" is of my opinion:—" The precedence of Rome over the other cities of the peninsula has been sanctioned by time, by fame, by the veneration and the piety of all nations. The precedence of the Pope results from his title of Pontiff: he represents the eternal sovereignty of God, and this august character permits the greatest kings to bow before him. He is not a master,—he is a father! Turin, Naples, Florence, Milan, and Venice have each a history, an importance, a greatness, which might give them equal claims and justify their rivalry; but their rights fade away before the Eternal City. None of these capitals would be degraded by recognizing as the head of the confederation a city which was the capital of the world."

But, even in the state of languor and disunion which has prevailed for three hundred years in Italy, has not Rome, at least in part, fulfilled the duties of a capital? Without being, in that disunited country, a political and military centre, still she is a national centre, because she is a religious one. Why have the Milanese not become either Spanish or German? Why did Venice, in the days of her power, neither become a Greek or Dalmatian, nor a Slavonic power, though she had more possessions on the other, than on this side of the Adriatic? Why has not Piedmont become French, with its princes of French extraction? Why has Naples, so often conquered, grown neither Norman, nor Saracen, nor Spanish? Why do Sicily, which has passed through so many hands, and Corsica, now a French island, remain so Italian as they are, notwithstanding the sea which separates them from Italy? Is it not partly that religion gives them a powerful centre at Rome,—that at Rome they meet brethren in blood and language, who prevent them from forgetting the name and the traditions of Italy?

The exaggeration of this idea forms a part of the pretensions even of modern Italianism. The "Primato" of Gioberti makes of the Pope, and even of Catholicism, an instrument in maintaining the domination of Italy over the rest of the world. Of course this would not be: Italy and Catholicism would deeply suffer if religion were made the tool of politics: the Church would never lend herself to such a scheme. It is, doubtless, glorious for Italy that the first and the most Italian of her sovereigns is also he to whom, in his sacred office, all nations owe respect and love. Italy gives a spiritual chief to the world in the Pope; she should content herself with this glory, and forego the ambition of pretending to rule all the Latin races. But even this folly serves to show us how much Italy needs to retain the Papacy. The wild ambition of Italy now desires to make the Papacy an instrument in acquiring a chimerical preponderance, because in past times the Papacy has been for Italy an anchor in dangers, a last remnant of cohesion which has saved her from dissolution, a bond which preserved to her some degree of union. The day that the Papacy abandons Italy would be a day of mourning for the Church; but for Italy it would most probably be a day of doom, and in the long catastrophes which would follow it, we might bid farewell to all hope of Italian nationality. What might we not add, were we to prosecute further our researches upon this vast subject, which seems to open wider and wider horizons to our view? In particular, where would be the glorious sceptre of letters, arts, and sciences which Italy has held so long, and for which she was indebted to Rome and the Papal influence? We can now appreciate the profound political and historical meaning of the words of the president of the French republic already cited: *The maintenance of the temporal sovereignty of the venerable Head of the Church is intimately connected with the liberty and independence of Italy.*

Ten years ago, in a providential concurrence of circumstances, Italy saw for a moment, through Pius IX., a way to terminate her humiliations. Why she did not succeed, history will declare. Pius IX. felt the military weakness of Italy; and desired that the change should be a peaceful one. Above all, he intended that the great mediator should remain neutral in the dispute, in order the more easily to bring about an honourable compromise. If his plan had been followed, upper Italy would probably be to-day a vigorous and gloriously independent branch of the Austrian empire, and the rest would form a powerful confederation of sovereigns independent of foreign influence, under the presidency of the Holy See. Such was the hope of Pius IX., and the most enlightened statesmen of Europe had shared it for an instant. As to Italian independence, the Pontiff assuredly was not then unfaithful either to the traditionary policy of the Papacy, or to the aspirations of the common country; but he did not wish to arrive at his end by either of the two means which ruined everything in 1848—war or revolution. War, and, above all, revolution, were the two evils of that period, the two great mistakes then made by Italy, or, in the expressive language of M. Thiers, " by a licentious faction, which, setting more value on the gratification of its passions than on the real interest of its cause, seized upon Italy and fatally compromised her. They stirred up the people everywhere to demand institutions *unfitted to the habits and sentiments of the time*. They did more; by provoking the untimely war of independence, they committed a most fatal and ruinous mistake; and this done, they added *the still graver one of turning against the governments of Italy the arms of the Italian people*."

The consequences of these mistakes are notorious. Well, has Italy, or what is called Italy, profited by these lessons? Alas! no; she has re-entered on her ill-advised course. The war of independence has partially succeeded, because France has thrown her sword into the scale; but the designs of the revolution have arrested the conqueror himself in his triumphal march; and at the present moment, the complications of Italian politics, or rather the violence of the licentious faction which M. Thiers alludes to, are on the point of again hurrying Italy into ruin, if Europe does not interfere. What ingratitude, and what a fatal error it is to rise against and to attack a peaceful power, to whom the Italians owe whatever liberty and nationality they enjoy, and whose interests, now as ever, are identified, by the nature of things, with the cause they have espoused! Were the Papacy even less necessary to Italy than it is, and ever has been, this ungrateful injustice to it would still be mean and cowardly. Ever since the battle of Novara, this sad policy has been followed out with the most deplorable obstinacy, as we shall soon have occasion to show; at present we would but point out the dangerous path which Italy is taking, and which is even compromising the victories which have been gained. Victory and force are not enough to constitute a nation, still less foreign force, and victories gained by foreigners.

In accomplishing a great work, too, the precedents of Providence, and the eternal laws of morality, which forbid to do evil that good may come, must be taken into account. We should also study carefully the nature, the condition, and the interests of the various parts of the complicated machine we are pretending to put in order; and, for my part, I am firmly convinced that Italy will exhaust, perhaps ruin herself in sterile agitation, unless she retracts her misguided policy, unless she arrests the torrent of revolutionary passions, unless she seeks unity in her centre, and unless she learns at last the lesson which her history teaches, and which, providentially for her, is in the very nature of things; namely, that *the liberty and independence of Italy are intimately connected with the maintenance of the temporal sovereignty of the supreme Head of the Church.*

Whatever may be my respect for Italy, and my heartfelt affection for so holy a country, for so dear and illustrious a nation, whatever my wishes for her glory and prosperity, perhaps it is not for me to offer to instruct her. But she will permit me to repeat the opinions and the advice of her own children, her most generous and devoted citizens: "Italians," says Count Cæsar Balbo, "devote courageously to your moral regeneration the time during which God chooses to delay your political. Let there be no more secret societies, no more cruel passions, no more daggers whetted in the dark; but manly habits, study, and energetic labour; these alone will conquer and secure a great position for a great nation. Europe will, sooner or later, have to remodel the distribution of her territory: Islamism is falling to pieces; Austria, our ancient enemy, will be invited to its funeral, and have a part in its spoils; and thus, her grasping ambition being satisfied in other ways, our deliverance, by general consent, will follow: the pacification of Europe will coincide with the victory and the development of Christianity over the whole world. This is the day we should abide and prepare for!" Silvio Pellico, in his turn, a liberal, but of a noble heart,—liberal, but anti-revolutionary, incapable of servility, but profoundly sensible of the necessity of virtues to the regeneration of a people, exclaims: "All forms of government have their weak points; in all, honesty may find a place, and in all, hypocrisy, intrigue, and corruption."

And, speaking of the Italians, for whom he had suffered so much: "How much evil have they done hitherto! They give themselves the airs of heroes, and they are mere children. They fancy themselves *Pelasgi*; but for this something more is necessary than satires and rhodomontade: learning and virtue are indispensable."

"Italy, Italy," exclaims on his side, one of the Protestant writers of England, who at present enjoys the most immense popularity, "while I write, your skies are over me—your seas flow beneath my feet; listen not to the blind policy which would unite all your crested cities, mourning for their republics, into one empire: false, pernicious delusion! your only hope of regeneration is in division. Florence, Milan, Venice, Genoa, may be free once more, if each is free. But dream not of freedom for the whole while you enslave the parts; the heart must be the centre of the system, the blood must circulate freely everywhere; and in vast communities you behold but a bloated and feeble giant, whose brain is imbecile, whose limbs are dead, and who pays in disease and weakness the penalty of transcending the natural proportions of health and vigour."—*Sir E. Bulwer-Lytton.*

I shall conclude these warnings and counsels by the words of an Italian, whose patriotism is well known:—
"To precipitate his country into revolution," says Signor d'Azeglio, "is a solemn step, the most solemn that a man can take: for the impulse once given, it becomes difficult, if not impossible, to distinguish clearly what is just or unjust, useful or pernicious. One may be led to the greatest and most generous actions, or hurried into the most fatal errors. One may become the occasion of immense good or evil; meet with glory or infamy; become the cause of the salvation or the ruin of a whole people ..... To throw oneself of one's own accord into such an undertaking, to put one's hand to it and set it going, may be the height of courage, of rashness, or of insanity; but, in all cases, it is an act to be dreaded by any man who values justice, the good of his country, the lot of others, his own reputation, and that of his country. To

attempt a revolution is to constitute oneself the sovereign arbiter of the will, the property, and the life of an indefinite number of one's fellows. In most cases, those who thus decide to employ, for their own ends, the most precious possessions and the most sacred rights of their fellow-citizens, *do so without their consent*, without any right, without having been authorized or chosen. Whether they be one or many, does not affect the question: the responsibility only becomes common instead of individual. It is easy to proclaim monarchies, republics, and constitutions; but no one has the power to render a population monarchical, constitutional, or republican, if their habits and opinions are opposed to it. All the terrors of the French revolution were unable to make republicans of those who were not republican. The imitations of foreign constitutions, which were introduced into Italy in 1821, have not made the Italians constitutional, who then were not so. . . . . The art of maturing our plans, and making the calculations necessary to this success,—the art of constructing the edifice stone by stone, beginning where we must begin, by the foundation, is an art which we Italians are ignorant of; and yet, without it nothing can be done; and so we have learned, to our cost. Hitherto we have resembled an inexperienced master of fiery and impetuous steeds, who, not giving himself time to harness them properly, not taking the trouble to look to the reins and the traces, whips them forward madly, and has scarcely started before he is upset, and breaks his neck. . . . . . "

Alas, alas! How is it with poor Italy now? . . . . O Italy, Italy,—*Terra parens magna virûm!* what are they doing with thee? . . . . Illustrious, unhappy nation, whither will they bring thee, those who have fixed their grasp upon thee? . . . . Shall no mighty and generous arm be stretched out to save thee?

CHAPTER X.

EUROPE WITHOUT THE PAPACY.

It remains for us to inquire, not only what Rome and Italy, but what Europe would have been, and what she would be, without the Papacy.

We have said that there are diseased and excited minds who would recklessly sacrifice the most solemn interests of Rome, of Italy, and of Europe, to the reveries of their inconsiderate imagination, and would see, without much regret, the Roman Church quit European soil, embark with the Pope, cross the seas, and settle in America, for instance, or at Jerusalem, or in China. I repeat that I have not invented these ideas; they have been imagined, expressed, and published even by respectable people, of superior minds, who, one would have thought, were inaccessible to the weaknesses and the apprehensions which too often bias minds of a more vulgar stamp.

"*Europe without the Pope is a puzzle to me,*" said one day, in our presence, a distinguished man, whose political sagacity is renowned. There is vast good sense in this expression. In fact, we cannot well understand or picture to ourselves how things would be in a state so different from the present and from what ages and Providence have established.

Europe without the Papacy, is Europe without a centre of light and of Christian civilization: this Rome has been to Europe for ages, this Rome is still to her. Europe without the Papacy, is Europe without an immemorial and venerable bond of union for her nations, without any common centre of agreement and social harmony, as well as of faith and religion. Europe without the Papacy, is Europe without the most august personification of those two great things, which are now so pressingly necessary to her—I mean, *Authority and Respect*. Europe without the Papacy, would be a revolution in religion and society: it would be probably the final doom of the European continent. And, for my part, I have always thought that if God, one day, were to determine to curse Europe, and to pour out upon us the most terrible of his judgments—that is, to take from us the light of faith and civilization, He would begin by taking away from us the Papacy, and transporting it elsewhere.

I.

We have already cited the opinions of Leibnitz and Voltaire; we will here cite, in his turn, Chateaubriand, who has expressed himself upon our present subject with his usual felicity:—" Christian Rome has been, to the modern world, what Pagan Rome was to the ancient—a universal bond of union. This capital of the nations has justified her right to the title of Eternal City. A time, perhaps, will come when people will acknowledge that the Papal throne was a grand idea, a magnificent institution. The spiritual Father, placed at the centre of the nations, united the different parts of Christendom. We still feel every day the influence of the immense and inestimable benefits which former ages owed to the court of Rome."— " Do you think," wrote, some time ago, a politician, whose authority is free from the suspicion of partiality, " that the annihilation of a power, which is now the sole bond of union of the various scattered nationalities of the world, was a great boon? Are there not, then, in the world elements enough of disunion and discord? Can any one fancy that the old trunk of Jesse has cast into the earth, during eighteen centuries of life and bloom, such frail and shallow roots, that it is easy to tear it up without disturbing and agitating the earth around it? Ah! be sure that it will not fall without shaking society to its centre, and, perhaps, not without carrying it along with it in its fall!"

Good policy and good sense here speak the same language; but the spirit of revolution speaks a different one.

The Papacy is the common bond and centre of peace and harmony in Europe, the embodiment of authority and respect: and it is just this which marks it out for the attacks of revolution; and here—strange contradiction!—a monarchy, blinded by ambition, makes itself the accomplice and the tool of the revolutionists; and it is at a congress that Piedmontese diplomacy has dared to ask the sovereigns of Europe to assist in breaking this sacred bond, to overturn this august personification, and preside at its destruction! Whilst the decay of institutions, whilst selfishness and passion, are evoking throughout Europe the spirit of insubordination, ought the plenipotentiaries of the powers which are thus menaced, solemnly to ignore the principle, that European society is deeply interested in maintaining in its bosom this providential sovereignty, which upholds as doctrines the principles of authority and respect, which puts them in practice with unyielding firmness, though, at the same time, with the most touching condescension to human weakness?

One who has played a considerable part in political affairs has said, with justice, " No, it never was more necessary to have in Europe an authority felt and accepted as a right, without requiring to have recourse to force; a power before which man may bow without lowering his dignity, and which speaks from on high with the authority, not of constraint, and yet of necessity." [1]

But if you expel the Pope from Europe, or if you unworthily degrade him, you at the same time destroy the most striking living expression of authority and of right; you take away from men's consciences the holiest motive for submission to the powers that be; you realize the audacious desires of the agitators of empires: having broken the bond which united men, you break the bridle which restrained their impetuous pride, and you let loose all the

---

[1] M. Guizot adds:—" Such is true authority: wherever it is absent, whatever be the force or the preponderance of numbers which support the ruler, obedience is always either mean or precarious, bordering either on servility or rebellion."

fury of anarchy on the world. Europe has had some lessons already; and what she has learnt is nothing to what the countless demagogues she owns would still teach her, all of whom demand, with hungry clamour, the fall of this great sovereignty, because they descry from afar its formidable and inevitable consequences. Once more, in the wreck of authority and respect which alarms us, never was it more necessary to Europe that the Pope should still preserve some fragments of them at Rome; and that he should continue to offer to sovereigns and people, in himself the embodiment and model of authority, and in his people an abiding and salutary example of obedience and respect. Here is a work all should labour at; here is a work for a European congress. As to the labours of anarchy, whose audacious and persevering progress we have been watching in Italy these ten years, as to this organized conspiracy of all ambitious and revolutionary passions against the Papacy, all should unite to stigmatize and reprobate them.

Such would be the advice of the wise: "But," as Bossuet said long ago, "are the wise believed in these times of excitement, and are not their prophecies mocked at? But what a judicious foresight could not impress upon men, a more imperious mistress will force them to believe .... Kings will suffer by it .... but it will have been their own doing."

II.

There is another order of services rendered to Europe by the Papacy, which the heart of a Catholic and of a priest cannot help recognizing with gratitude. Yes, a Christian is proud to proclaim, that if Europe rules the entire world, she is clearly indebted for it to the Church and the Gospel. Europe has been a source of light to the whole universe, because Rome has been a centre of light to the whole of Europe.

During the long ages, "when our fathers were mere barbarians, who had to be taught everything, not only to read, to speak, and to clothe themselves, but to plough their fields, and to obtain food . . . . the Papacy always showed itself to be in advance of its age. It had ideas of legislation and of jurisprudence; it was acquainted with the fine arts, with the sciences; it was polite, when all else was buried in the darkness of Gothic institutions. Nor did it hide its light; it diffused it everywhere; it broke down the barriers created by prejudice between nations; it strove to soften our manners, to deliver us from our ignorance, to break us of our coarse or ferocious customs. The Popes were among our ancestors as missionaries of the arts sent to barbarians, as legislators among savages. *The reign of Charlemagne only, says Voltaire, saw a glimmer of politeness which probably was the fruit of his journey to Rome. It is a thing generally admitted that Europe owes its civilization to the Holy See, as well as part of its best laws, and nearly all its arts and sciences.*"[1] Hume, a Protestant and sceptical historian, allows that the union of all the Western churches under a Sovereign Pontiff, facilitated the intercourse between nations, and tended to make Europe one vast republic; that the pomp and splendour of worship contributed to the progress of the fine arts, and began to diffuse a general elegance of taste, by identifying it with religion. Have not the missions of Rome, to use the expression of *Buffon* (Hist. Nat. tom. iii.), turned more savages into men than all the armies of the princes who have conquered whole barbarian nations?

The Church, in truth, has been the instructress of mankind; she has really educated, enlightened, and ennobled it: self-willed as a child in its cradle, in its youth violent, wild, and untamable, the Church has softened, civilized, and polished it, and brought it up to the age of manhood: she has been, I repeat, its instructress and its mother. Yet now there are those who think it generous to revolt against her!

Is it not strange with what supercilious ingratitude we enjoy all the benefits of the Church? The light of the Gospel, that kindly light whose beams she for ever diffuses

---

[1] Chateaubriand.

upon the world, encircles us on all sides; it has penetrated insensibly into our laws, our manners, and even our most ordinary habits, as well as into our science and literature; everywhere, in short. Yet we disdain and insult this heritage, by which we live, though we may not be aware of it.[1] We forget that religion has still, and will ever have, to teach us the most important secrets of this life, and all those of eternity—eternity, before which we are never more than children, than infants; we forget that the Gospel alone has a resource for every need of humanity, consolation for all its sorrows, lessons for all its fortunes, and infallible secrets for the security of the world. Is there not in this scorning of the Church, that venerable instructress of nations, an ingratitude and an injustice calculated to bring chastisements upon us? Ah! were the lights of the Gospel suddenly to fail us; were all its dispersed rays, which fill the atmosphere which surrounds us, extinguished, we should be appalled at our darkness! For all that men have said or done, the holy Catholic Church still holds the key of all the mysterious and vital problems of society and nature. Even now, in spite of its pride and its disdain, the civilized world reposes only under the shadow of the cross. If the cross and the Gospel were suddenly to fail, we, who even now agree so badly, would soon devour one another. And if the Pope and the Catholic bishops, shaking off the dust from their feet, were to leave an ungrateful world, closing the sacred books, and carrying them with them into the desert, the broken gleams of Christian truth they might leave behind would soon be dissipated, and chaos would not be far distant. Like the impious ages of paganism, the nations would then tremble at the mighty ruin hovering over them, which they had themselves evoked, and in their despair would dread the approach of an eternal night:—

"Impiaque æternam timuerunt secula noctem!"

---

[1] "I know not why any should attribute to philosophy the grand morality of our books. . . . That morality was Christian before it was philosophical. . . . It was all in the Gospel before it was in our books."—*J.-J. Rousseau.*

It is strictly possible (God avert the omen, I say such things with fear and trembling) that God has determined to send the Pope and the Roman Church to the New World, to transfer to it our inheritance, to crown its fortunes, and to give it, if I may so express myself, its letters patent of civilization and nobility. It is quite possible that one day the Old World may become a missionary country, as America now is with regard to Europe: that missionaries may come to us from the Rocky Mountains, and that one day it may be our turn to say, *How beautiful upon the mountains are the feet of him that bringeth good tidings, and that preacheth peace*, which we had lost.

Such mournful transformations have been seen before now in the world: the faith had risen, like the sun in the East; but now the school and the Church of Alexandria, Judæa, and Jerusalem the holy city, are in barbarism! and we are sending missionaries to them! Europe would be to the United States what China and the South-Sea Islands now are to us. The supposition is frightful; but the faith is fixed to none of the places which possess it, if they show themselves unfaithful to it; and if we will not have him who bears in Europe, in one hand the sceptre of paternal authority, in the other the torch of the Gospel, we should tremble lest we may lose, with the vicar of Jesus Christ, all true light, all respect for authority, and all union among European nations. Yes, if the Pope were to leave Europe; if Italy, Rome, France, Spain, Belgium, Ireland, and Catholic Germany lost their father; were he to carry the tabernacle of St. Peter and the keys of the kingdom of heaven to some shore of the New World, I should tremble, not as a Catholic, but as a Frenchman, as a child of the European family. It would seem to me that God had withdrawn from among us; and from the midst of the European chaos, as formerly from the midst of Jerusalem cast off by God, I should imagine I heard mysterious voices crying, *Come out of her, come out of her!*

If I be accused of exaggeration, I would say, If you will not believe my word, at least believe in facts. Consider what has been the fate of those who, after having known the Gospel, have ceased to revere it, and have lost the faith. Cast a glance upon these countries, formerly so brilliant, of the East, which contained the famous cities of Ephesus, Antioch, Cæsarea, and Nicomedia, where, with Christianity, the arts and sciences, letters, and a pure morality prevailed, which were adorned by the eloquence, the genius, and the virtues of Basil, of Gregory, and of Chrysostom. See, on the confines of Europe and Asia, what now is that Byzantium, which was once so splendid, so polished, and so learned, which was long considered a second Rome, a new Athens. Then turn your eyes towards Africa, the home of Athanasius, of Cyril, and Tertullian, where the famous school of Alexandria flourished under Origen and Clement: where Cyprian and Augustine illustrated the cities of Carthage and of Hippo. Compare the present state of these populations with their past; see how they are wrapt in the thickest darkness of ignorance, how they bend under the yoke of a brutal despotism, how degraded their morals, how gross their superstition; they have gone back, in short, from their past glory, to the infancy of society.——But I am wrong; the feebleness of that age contains within it the latent elements of growth; but here is the incurable impotence of decrepitude. Their life is gone: with the true religion they have manifestly lost their enlightenment, their liberty, their happiness, and their civilization.

I will even make a striking but irrefutable assertion:— I defy any one to name a single country where the torch of the Gospel was extinguished, which did not immediately fall into barbarism. It was just, in fact, that it should be so; that national apostasy should meet with its punishment here below, as well as individual; so that, seeing the life of those unhappy nations die out, we might learn what it was that had supported it; and that it might be said to each of them, Know and see that it is always evil and bitter to forsake the law of God, and to disregard the appointments and warnings of His Providence.—*Scito et vide quia malum et amarum est reliquisse te Deum tuum.*

III.

I know that some fertile imaginations have foreseen incalculable resources for Europe, in a new empire, a universal monarchy, or at least supremacy: civilization is to be secured by the potent unity and cohesion created by this new political order; this supreme power is to reside at St. Petersburg, Constantinople, Vienna, or Paris.

In fifty years Europe will be either republican or Cossack, said once the greatest potentate of the present century, after having vainly attempted himself to remodel the history and geography of Europe after another fashion.

I will put but one question to the excitable imaginations whom so imposing an idea may fascinate: What is to be the prime mover and the regulator of this vast machine? Force? Then you will have but slavery on a great scale. Mind? But where shall a mind great enough be found? Human intellects are rarely equal to such a task. Who shall preserve it from decay? Who shall establish its authority? Above all, who shall insure its moderation? In a word, whence shall come the *quid divinum*, without which any human organization is null? Who upon earth shall take upon him to say, with the boldness of Bossuet, to this universal monarch, *You have nothing to fear but the excess of your own power*. But what am I saying! knowing what the insolence of unresisted pride and the cringing meanness of men are capable of, we cannot conceive a Bossuet or a true Catholic episcopate in this empire of servility, with the Papacy banished or degraded. It has been malevolently stated that Bossuet was antagonistic to the Papal authority; for my part, I think that any real antagonism which existed was trifling, and that at bottom, Bossuet was as Roman as Fénélon. But however that may be, I maintain, that if the Papacy had not been in Europe when Bossuet spoke thus to Louis XIV., Bossuet would have been less firm, and would not have dared to speak so.

But this idea is not new. Aristides, the rhetorician, in his time, celebrated in flattering terms the progressive development of the various parts of the universe, by means of the universal equality, and the social tranquillity springing from the concentration of all power in the hands of a sole master: "Small and great, rich and poor, nobles and plebeians, are equal before the majesty of Cæsar, whence all power springs, and by which all rights are sanctioned. What Cæsar is to all powers, Rome is to all powers. Rome, the common forum and universal centre, receives the citizens of the world, as the ocean confounds all rivers in its bosom. The majesty of the city soars over the universe, and the nations unite to ask from the gods the eternity of such an empire." The gods, however, were deaf to such applications, and they were right.

In fact, a better arrangement was practicable; and it was realized in Christian Europe. Instead of nations crushed and degraded into a miserable equality, she saw liberty, energy, and national spirit distinguish her illustrious family of powerful nations; each, doubtless, having its own peculiarities and defects, but each accountable only to itself: mutual goodwill and respect prevailed, under an independent spiritual authority, which lowers the dignity and infringes on the true liberty of none,—neither the petty and weak, nor the proud and powerful: under that authority, of which it was so well said, as I have already quoted, "before which men may bow without lowering their dignity, and which speaks from on high with the authority, not of constraint, and yet of necessity." We may sometimes murmur against this authority, when it condemns us; but I maintain that even when it reproves it is guarding the true liberties of the human mind and conscience. Those who do not agree with me may consult Tacitus, and the Rome of his day, for past ages, and, for the present time, may look at China.

Yes, I assert that Protestants, Freethinkers, and Catholics have all a common interest here: yes, it concerns all that there may continue for ever here below a moral authority which has never yielded, a living protest and counter-poise against the supremacy of the Czar, or of a tyrannical parliament, 'against the fatal, inevitable servility of the patriarchs of Moscow and the archbishops of Canterbury. On this condition, human dignity will be safe, at least in one important respect. But if, as it was eloquently said the other day, the last bulwark of spiritual independence is forced, if the Papacy falls under the yoke of a multitude, or into the grasp of a despot, if no point of resistance to force remains but the random and impotent efforts of a few rare and isolated individuals, who does not foresee the sweeping and deadly catastrophe which would strike the liberty of the human conscience? [1]

This was clearly the sentiment of a celebrated philosopher, confessedly of powerful mind, M. Cousin, when he addressed to me, on leaving the academy the other day, in the presence of several of our fellow-academicians, on the staircase of the institute, the following remarkable words, which I give as they were uttered:—" Materialist and atheistical philosophy may be indifferent; nay, it is right in applauding the curtailment and degradation of the Papacy; for it does not require the Papacy when proving to men that the soul is a result of the body, and that there is no God but the world. But the philosophy of spiritualists looks with a different eye on the events which are going on. If it be not blinded by the most preposterous pride, it ought to see that outside the schools, among mankind, spiritualism is, as it were, represented by Christianity,

---

[1] M. Foisset, Annales Catholiques de Genève.—In his remarkable article, M. Foisset also said:—" M. de Presseusé ought to know this better than any one, claiming incessantly, as he does, independence for Protestantism; he is a minister of a private church, which does not allow that it is accountable to any authority but itself; a church which does not accept any interference of the civil power between God and man. I am sorry that his mind is not unprejudiced enough to see that, at bottom, the Pope's cause is his own, as it is the cause of all who do not admit the omnipotence of Cæsar in the things of God."

that Christianity itself is excellently represented by the Catholic Church, and that thus the holy Father is the representative of the whole moral and intellectual order. I consider that this chain of propositions is impregnable, and would undertake to maintain them against any opponent whatever, provided only that he admits the existence of God, that is of a real God, who possesses understanding, liberty, and love. So that, monseigneur, if you will excuse my familiar language, I want for mankind a Papacy strong enough to be independent, and to exercise efficaciously its sacred ministry.... I wish it to be strong, even though your humble servant may sometimes suffer a little for it. Yes, Rome may put in the *Index* my book, *Du Vrai, du Beau, et du Bien*; no matter; I shall remain faithful to her, and defend her in my own way, in the name of philosophy itself. What if I were to speak to you as a liberal, which I have always shown myself? or if I were to speak as an old and tried friend of Italy? But I will not detain you on this staircase; I only beg, that if you are writing to Rome, you will present my respects to the Holy Father, and inform him that, with all my unworthiness, I take the liberty, in these deplorable circumstances, to range myself among his warmest supporters."

I have mentioned the Protestants; it would be a great mistake, though a very common one, to imagine that Protestants can do perfectly well without the Papacy. I maintain that it is the Papacy which preserves to them, in spite of themselves, whatever Christianity they have not lost. If there were not the Catholic Church in the world, whose chief and bond of unity is the Pope; if this Church did not exist, the emporium and the guardian of true and unmutilated Christianity, with her faith, her discipline, her hierarchy, and her worship, Christianity itself, modified, travestied, and torn by so many hands, would soon totally disappear; it is clear that the separated sects have no sufficient means of preserving it. The Bible alone cannot resist false and strained interpretations. These sects, having no internal authority to guard what they possess of Christianity, and no longer having Catholicism outside them, where the sacred deposit of revealed truth is safely kept, and may always be had recourse to, these sects, I say, already so numerous, would split still farther; the fragments again would break up, and be frittered away into dust, as we see even now in America, and as is deplored by many sincere Protestants: there would cease to exist any form of belief, and even the semblance of a religious society. Christianity would utterly perish, and with it many other things of which we are justly proud, and which we would be as unable to preserve without Christianity as we were to procure them without her. The truth is, that human civilization owes everything to Christianity. Open the map of the civilized world: we see that religion and civilization have there the same boundaries; whatever is far from Christ is in the dark, whatever is near Him is in the light: the world, as well as history, is divided into two by the Cross. The Church is the guardian of the faith of Catholics: it is from her that Protestants have received the notion of a Redeemer, and it is she who preserves it to them; moreover, it is to her that Deists owe the idea of a God and a Creator. And such is the moral power against whom war is now declared!

But I must conclude. It seems to me unlikely that we shall see Europe republican in ten years: as to the threat of the Cossacks, and the danger of a schismatical and imperial Papacy, as a Catholic, I am easy; God will preserve His Church: but will He preserve Europe? I cannot say. But, certainly, I cannot think of her future without dismay, if she effaces from her soil the temporal sovereignty of the popes. I am convinced of this, that into the gulf which must inevitably open in her midst when the Papacy and Catholicism have departed, the revolutionary torrent would sweep with a headlong violence and fury as yet unknown in history, and to which it is hard to see what barrier could be opposed.

We have seen Romans, Italians, Europeans, Protestants themselves, political writers, philosophers, statesmen, as well as the most humble Christians, all testifying to the truth of the principles we have laid down, namely:—

That the temporal sovereignty of the Holy See is intimately united, in the designs of God, with its spiritual sovereignty.

That the liberty of conscience and the independence of Catholic truth are providentially united to the liberty and independence of the Pope.

That, for the security of the whole Church, it is necessary that the Pope *be free and independent.*

That this independence be *sovereign.*

That the Pope *be free, and that he appear free.*

That the Pope be free and independent *at home as well as abroad.*

Nor must these great principles be practically nullified by any hypocritical scheme, or any degrading compromise.

We have also seen the wonderful ways in which God established this temporal sovereignty. And, finally, what Rome, Italy, and Europe would be without the Pope.

We would now add, that it has given us deep pain to see worthy persons, and even some Christians, led astray by sad delusions on these points, settle these great questions with a stroke of their pen, throw out for the discussion of the ignorant, and give a most dangerous publicity to the rashest suggestions, and sacrifice, with inconceivable presumption, interests and principles, which bishops assembled in council would only enter on with trembling, and which, as the pillars of the temple, they would shrink from touching!

Assuredly, the Roman Church could remain suspended between heaven and earth, depending on nothing but the invisible hand which supports her: the Vicar of Jesus Christ could, assuredly, like Jesus Christ himself, become an apostolic pilgrim, not having where to lay his head, while the foxes have holes, and the birds of the air nests! And such a state would be certainly preferable to that proposed in a certain too well-known publication. But let our brothers in the faith, who have entertained such ideas, permit me to say that they have come to their conclusion with too philosophical an indifference. Sure to have assistance in their last moments, and a priest to give them a parting benediction, they have forgotten what great, what immense, interests would be compromised by such calamities, they have failed to see 'that conscience and charity can permit no one so coolly to accept the disastrous prospects which the humiliation of the Roman Church would open upon Rome, Italy, and the whole of Europe.

No; experiments are unsafe here. Let us all learn at least to profit by the lessons which Providence has given us, and let the thunders which roar in the distance awaken us from our dreams. When the earth trembles under our feet, it is time to abandon our wild and hazardous speculations, and to return to true principles, to the eternal laws of order, and the essential conditions of society, which can never be violated with impunity. We must admit, that, even for the interests of the people, sovereignty has rights which are the safeguard and the life of nations; that authority is entitled to respect; that there are duties towards it; that there are apostolic precepts which command obedience and respect; that the apostles are not vain speculators and declaimers; that there was a St. Paul who said: *Let every soul be subject to higher powers—Omnis anima potestatibus sublimioribus subdita sit;* that there was a prince of apostles who forbids to use liberty as a hypocritical veil to cover malice—*velamen habentes malitiæ libertatem;* that there was a St. Jude who has condemned those perverse men who despise authority and blaspheme majesty—*dominationem spernunt, majestatem blasphemant;* and, finally, that there is a Son of God, who has commanded to render to Cæsar the things that are Cæsar's, and to God the things which are God's.

It must be confessed that these principles have been strangely ignored of late. To dissipate the fatal doctrines current throughout Europe, those appalling shocks and convulsions were perhaps necessary (terrible *oportet!* as Bossuet says) which have agitated our time for more than sixty years. Are these principles to be again violated in the person of their most august representative, of the gentlest and most paternal of sovereigns? After such great and terrible lessons, let us not clap our hands, in the name of a spurious Christianity, at each new revolution which shakes European soil; let us not pursue with our anathemas the powers which dare to defend themselves, and to resist wrong and disorder; for so we should render ourselves guilty, at the very least, of infinite temerity; guilty of a sad forgetfulness of the evangelical precepts, guilty, and the real accomplices, of those odious sentiments which look behind all revolutionary passions! May Heaven breathe a new calm into the minds of men after so many tempests; may the eternal majesty of truth be henceforth the safeguard of their reason and their hearts; may such great woes not be without their fruits; may they be redeemed by a return to wisdom, order, and peace, with liberty and justice!

CHAPTER XI.
FRANCE AND THE HOLY SEE IN 1849.

NOTHING of what we have written is new: all has been felt and proclaimed on every occasion when, during its long existence, the temporal sovereignty of the popes has been called in question; it has been proclaimed, and it has triumphed, and never more gloriously than in France, in the great crisis of 1849. After the laborious discussions of the foregoing chapters, it will be a pleasure to review what France then so nobly accomplished for a cause which is now, as ever, dearer to us in proportion to the unjust outrages which are heaped upon it.

I.

I must own that, personally, I have no taste for republican institutions, nor has the fresh trial France made of them in 1848 succeeded in reconciling me to them. Still I must admit that, under the republic, two great things were done, and in accomplishing them great courage and noble qualities were displayed; I mean, what was then done for the liberty of education, and the Roman expedition. Parental rights proclaimed and secured in their most sacred province, the education of children; religious bodies freed from several of their disabilities, and enabled freely to exercise their self-denying zeal in the pious education of youth; the Roman Church delivered, and the independence of the Universal Church secured in that of her supreme head: such are the great things which will remain the eternal honour of those who accomplished them, and will shine in the eyes of posterity as a ray of light upon a sombre horizon.

To speak here only of the Roman expedition, I know of nothing, in the parliamentary annals of any nation, grander than the debate it occasioned. Looking back upon those memorable days, and the great victories then gained by reason and justice, it seems to me that never did the power of human eloquence show more gloriously; never did political orators more nobly combat in the defence of a more august cause. The difficulties of that terrible period, when social order was so deeply shaken throughout all Europe; the unlooked-for union of eminent men of different parties under the same standard; the hallowed cause which was defended, the paramount interests which were rescued; the intrepidity of the defenders, the determination of the assailants; the fury of the multitude, the energy of the good, closing into a compact phalanx both within and without the Assembly, supporting their combatants in the struggle by the moral force of their powerful union; and, lastly, their success, that consummation so desirable, though often wanting to just causes: everything in those memorable debates was grand; their memory can never perish. I do not hesitate to say, that an example was there given—a salutary and seasonable example — how the good in all countries should act, in the face of the perils of revolution; of the stern resistance with which the torrent of violence must be met, in the name of reason and justice, and of the blessing God accords to a society which deserves it by its efforts to save itself. This great cause, too, was nobly supported under the walls of Rome by our army, so worthy of the French name; its courage and discipline, its consideration during the struggle, and its moderation after the victory, were, as M. Thiers says, a real consolation to the country.

One of the things which most jars upon my feelings is, to hear the enemies of the Holy Seee attack us, as they do at present, in the name of liberty! They cry: "You are a superannuated institution, made for other times, and incompatible with the liberal ideas of our day. Stragglers from another age, drags upon modern civilization, you know nothing of the wants of our time; you are supporters of theocracy and the divine right: we know you, and all liberals disclaim you."

Well, I know what you are too! I know your pretended love for liberty; I know your works and the means you employ, and your detestable principle of the *sovereignty of the end*; and I know that you use a generous name to cover an odious thing. And, therefore, it seems to me very seasonable here to recall to you, and to those whom you are leading astray, what was then done and said by liberals of somewhat more sincerity, who have stood severer tests than you; what was then sanctioned by the great assemblies of republican France, by men sent to power by the most democratic and freest universal suffrage that ever was; at a time when the entire press said what it thought fit, when religion was attacked, but also defended, with perfect liberty. You want to oppose liberalism to the Papacy! Well, you shall be answered by liberals, genuine liberals, who still live, and whose liberalism has been proof against temptations and ordeals which few have been able to resist.

I shall now endeavour briefly to expose the political circumstances of the Holy See at that period.

II.

A fortnight after the death of Gregory XVI.,—on the 16th of June, 1846, the day after the opening of the

Conclave,—Pius IX. ascends the Pontifical throne; on the 21st, he is solemnly crowned at St. Peter's. His election is received with welcome in Italy, and the whole Catholic world. The virtues of the new Pope, his zeal for all that is good, and his love for his people, are known; people look towards him with hope and confidence.

A decisive act soon declares to the world what his policy will be. On the 16th July, the most wide and complete amnesty is granted. It is received with a chorus of acclamations; Rome makes holiday for three days; when Pius IX. passes in the streets, the horses are taken from his carriage, and he is drawn along by the people. Every day the popular enthusiasm for the kind and holy Pontiff increases. The concessions he has made only reveal the bold ideas and the new benefits which he is meditating. The amnesty is but the prelude to the rest. Of his own accord he plans great and beneficial concessions to his people; not one of his words or actions but shows the most liberal intentions on his part. The enthusiasm of the Italians spreads to the whole of Europe; in France, more particularly, the friends of liberty applaud this noble example; all hearts are touched by the confidence of the Pontiff in his people; the fears of some timid and cautious spirits are not listened to; everything is hoped for from this good understanding between the ruler and his subjects. The princes of the peninsula, moved by his example, prepare to imitate it. From the French Chamber, M. Thiers cries to Pius IX., "Courage, Holy Father, courage!" This movement of admiration even reaches the Sultan, who sends ambassadors to the Roman Pontiff. Facts soon justify this universal confidence.

On the 19th April, a *Consulta* of state, or representative of the provinces, is created.

The 5th of July, a civic guard.

The 1st of October, a senate and municipal council at Rome.

The 14th October, the *Consulta* is organized, and it is opened in state on the 15th of November.

Pleased with these benevolent institutions, and confident in the gratitude of his people, Pius IX. thus speaks, at the opening of the Consulta: "Three millions of my subjects are witnesses—the whole of Europe is a witness—of what I have done to draw my people closer to me. .... I am confident of their fidelity and their gratitude; I know that their hearts sympathize with mine." On the 21st of November the Consulta answers him: " The institution of the Consulta is the greatest of the boons which your Holiness has granted to your people. By it you have given laymen a share in the administration of public affairs, and have given one of those solid guarantees which in no way compromise the essential conditions of the Pontifical Government. We are gratified by the confidence with which you have honoured us, and will strive to show ourselves worthy of it." Having thanked the Pope for the reforms accorded, they add: "But to complete so great and difficult a work requires mature deliberation, *much time, and profound peace*. We are assured that your people will wait with patience for the salutary fruits of the seeds which you are now casting with a generous hand. The world has too often seen reforms extorted by a menacing populace, and costing many tears and much blood. With us, Holy Father, it is the sovereign himself who guides us with gentle and measured steps towards what should be the final object of a people—the reign of justice and truth upon earth."

On the 29th of December, the *motu proprio* is published, which organizes the council of his Holiness upon a new plan, changing considerably the ministerial departments; laymen are rendered eligible to it. The enthusiasm is at its climax.

While the Pontiff is generously pursuing the course of his reforms, while his name is honoured everywhere, all of a sudden alarming symptoms show themselves in his dominions; the presence of a malignant influence, of the genius of evil, of the spirit of revolution is felt: the men of the revolution mingle their hypocritical acclamations with the hearty applauses of the friends of liberty, and plot how they may turn the benefits of Pius IX. against himself. The 24th of February, 1848, arrives; the Republic is proclaimed in France; Italy and the whole of Europe vibrates to the shock. Soon the movement which Pius IX. was directing is violently diverted from it course: Pius IX., grieved, but not discouraged, perseveres, and strives to complete his work. The 14th of March, he publishes the fundamental statute: Rome has a parliamentary government, and a press. The Pontiff went so far; but it was too far for the people, better fitted to desire liberty than to bear it. The measure of benefits heaped up, the measure of ingratitude and of trials commences. The demonstrations of loved are changed into demonstrations of discontent. The 1st of May, violence forces him to change his ministry. The new ministry attempts to control the Pontiff: Pius IX. nobly resists, and calls to power M. Rossi, the late ambassador of France, a genuine liberal, assuredly, but a liberal who loved liberty and not anarchy.

The revolution throws off the mask, and calls the dagger into requisition. On the 15th of November, the intrepid minister of Pius IX. is murdered upon the very steps of the Chamber of Deputies, which has been just opened. The assembly coolly passes to business, and continues its sitting; and the civic guard quietly stands with arms grounded, while the murderers proceed in triumph through the streets of Rome, shouting, "The democratic dagger for ever!"

The rest is known. The next day the Quirinal is invested and besieged by the civic guard and the populace; cannon is pointed against the Pope's palace: one of his friends is killed a few steps from him; an hour is given to Pius IX. to accept a ministry. The Duke d'Harcourt, the French ambassador, writes to Paris: " The Pope is only a sovereign in name: none of his acts can be free." Finally, imprisoned in his palace under the tyranny of the rebels, Pius IX. leaves Rome on the 24th of November, and takes refuge upon the rock of Gaëta; the ambassadors of Europe follow him there respectfully.

The news of this catastrophe rouses the whole of Europe: at Paris the old name of Eldest Daughter of the Church, of which France has always been so proud, occurs to the government of the republic; and General Cavaignac, the head of the executive, instantly, not even waiting to consult the sovereign Assembly, moved only by the immemorial traditions of the country of Charlemagne, and by all that was noble within his own bosom, offers to the Sovereign Pontiff the sword of France, and immediately orders the march of a body of troops, despatching also an envoy extraordinary, M. de Corcelles, with instructions to protect the liberty of the Holy Father, and to offer him, if necessary, the hospitality of the republic. Soon afterwards a solemn declaration was addressed at Paris to the Apostolic Nuncio. " The maintenance of the temporal sovereignty of the revered head of the Catholic Church has a necessary connection with the honour of Catholicism, as well as with the liberty and independence of Italy." A few days after, the suffrages of 7,000,000 Frenchmen raised to the presidency of the republic the prince whose hand had traced these lines, and had offered this pledge to the votes of Catholic France.

Widowed of her Pontiff, in the grasp of Mazzini and Garibaldi, Rome suffers all the violence and outrages of the demagogues who oppress her, as well as numbers of cosmopolite revolutionists, attracted from all quarters towards her walls, as towards a prey. The supreme junta being dissolved, a constituent assembly succeeds, which crowns the work of iniquity, and votes the dethronement of the Pope, and a Roman republic. Pius IX., however, is king at Gaëta as at Rome, and sees around him the representatives of the Great Powers; but, while diplomatists are negotiating, the war is continued in Upper Italy: Novara soon justifies the sad forebodings of Pius IX.; the time of negotiations is over; the Catholic powers are preparing to interfere—Austria, Naples, Spain, and France. France hastens to appropriate to herself this great honour. A French army lands in Italy:

the heir of one the military celebrities of the Empire, General Oudinot, is at its head.

The incidents of this glorious expedition are known; the vote of blame in the National Assembly on the 7th of May; the noble letter of Louis Napoleon to comfort and encourage the general, the very day after this unhappy vote; that memorable siege; the storms which it excited in the new legislative Assembly; the appeal to arms made by the Mountain on the 12th of June; the insurrection the next day, in order to avenge what was called the violation of the constitution; the Roman republic overcome on the 13th of June at Paris, and soon after at Rome, and, finally, Rome delivered and restored to Pius IX.

But the ministry which had besieged Rome and restored the Pope, is again summoned to the bar of the Assembly to account for their glorious conduct; several questions are announced for the 6th of August. Never was there a more angry excitement,—never was the Mountain more threatening; but never did the revolution receive such a check. M. Jules Favre occupies the tribune, on the 6th and 7th of August, for more than five hours, and hurls against a ministry which had deluded the country, as he said, violated the constitution, and placed the sword of France in the hands of Austria, all the virulent invectives and unsparing accusations that anger and rancour could suggest.

On the 7th of August, M. de Falloux ascends the tribune to reply to M. Jules Favre: it is he, one of the principal promoters of the expedition, he who, on the 24th of May, like a warrior (as the *Démocratie Pacifique* said) upon a bridge, alone keeping his assailants at bay, crushed with his eloquence the same men who are there again before him, on the 7th of August, upon the benches of the Mountain,—these men whose ears still ring with the invective of the intrepid minister against revolutionists who are *capable of anything and capable of nothing,*—it is he who is to reply to them upon the Roman expedition. On the ministerial benches are observed MM. Odilon-

Barrot, De Tocqueville, and Dufaure. M. Dupin is president.

I cannot think of what I saw that day without profound emotion. What a debate! what a conflict! What principles and actions were on their trial! and before what a tribunal!

CHAPTER XII.

FRANCE AND THE HOLY SEE IN 1849.—SPEECH OF M. DE FALLOUX.

THE question before the assembly is whether the victory gained by France is an honour or a disgrace; a deliverance or a crime against liberty and the law of nations; a noble vindication of the rights of Catholics and of society, or an odious act of violence.

M. de Falloux showed himself equal to the greatness of his subject; rarely did the eloquence of a statesman more powerfully influence an assembly. He begins his triumphant apology by chastising the abusive language used by his opponent.

"Insults follow the physical law of falling bodies—this the honourable M. Favre perhaps is not aware of, and as he seems partial to such a mode of argument, he will doubtless be glad to learn—and only acquire force in proportion to the height from which they fall." (Continued cheering on the right. Murmurs on the left.)

Before entering upon the essential part of the question the speaker, wishing to dissipate the false accusation of want of patriotism, exclaims with generous indignation:

"We have been taunted with treachery to what this country is most keenly alive to; I mean its military honour. It has been said that we have placed the sword of France in the hands of Austria. No, we have not done this; we have refused the sword of France to Mazzini. We thought that the sword of France should not be wielded by hands which have held or sanctioned the dagger." (Violent murmurs on the left.)

Several voices.—" It's an infamous accusation."

Other voices.—" It's a Jesuitical calumny."

The PRESIDENT.—" The minister is defending France and the army, and you are defending their enemies." (Marked approbation on the right. Murmurs on the left.)

A member on the left, in the midst of the tumult.—" You have placed the sword of France in incompetent hands."

M. DE FALLOUX.—" No, the sword of France was never in the hands of more gallant and able Frenchmen, and all Europe has admired them; Europe has recognized in them the chivalrous and generous qualities which distinguish the true French soldier; they have been misjudged by none, except the honourable speaker who has preceded me." (Applause on the right.)

Entering then into the vital part of the question, the speaker directly attacks the objection:—"You have crushed liberty at Rome! you have trampled under foot the aspirations and the rights of a people!"

" No, we went to Rome as liberators; we went to Rome because we felt that this interposition was looked for from us, and that it was our duty; we felt so, and we have not been deceived. . . . M. de Tocqueville read to you yesterday some despatches of one of our colleagues, whose veracity and scrupulous accuracy will not be questioned by any in this assembly."

M. de Falloux then rapidly read some despatches of M. de Corcelles; despatches pregnant with meaning, and which would now again amply repay a perusal; for it was the same individuals who then were firing upon our soldiers, and from whom our soldiers rescued Rome and Italy, whom we now again find oppressing the Romagna, plotting the ruin of Italy and of Europe, if Europe does not resist them—the same leaders, the same soldiers:—

"On the 12th of June, 1849, having scarcely touched Italian soil, M. de Corcelles wrote to the French government:—

"' It seems clear that the resistance of the besieged is only kept up by the energy and the despair of a great number of foreign refugees who are now in Rome. No later than yesterday, a band of 3,000 men, under Masi, found means to throw themselves into the city. I am able to add to this hasty despatch, that nearly all the prisoners are Lombards, Genoese, &c. All here are convinced that this resistance is in no way favoured by far the greater majority of the Roman population. We have to do here with the scum of all the Polish and Italian revolutionists; with the refugees of all nations, who consider Rome as their last stronghold.' "

M. de Falloux next read the following letter from M. de Corcelles to the chancellor of our consulate at Rome, which well defines the great object which was then pursued; and the work which ought now again to be undertaken:—

"'*Head Quarters, Santucci, June* 13, 1849.

"' France has but one end in view in this painful conflict :—*the liberty of the revered Head of the Church, the liberty of the Roman States, and the peace of the world.* The nature of my mission is essentially *liberal, and tends to protect a population which has been reduced to such an extremity by external agency*.'

"M. de Corcelles added (June 15) :—

"' The patriotism of our brave soldiers is above all praise. The letter of the President of the Republic to General Oudinot, and which has been placed by him in the order of the day, has produced an excellent effect. It is very necessary thus to give moral support to our troops in their arduous task. On arriving at Civita Vecchia, I found the message of the 6th of June, which will tend to preserve the army from the despondency which certain bad citizens are endeavouring to create, by a number of publications and manœuvres, whose authors evidently act in concert at Rome and Paris. The Italian question is admirably stated in the message.'

"The message," resumed M. de Falloux, "is a document which the honourable M. Favre seems to have quite forgotten, when he accuses us of having kept our policy secret from the assemblies and the country."

In fact, no one could have expressed himself more clearly and frankly than the President of the republic in this message, upon the motives and the end of the Italian expedition. Prince Louis Napoleon thus speaks of Pius IX. :—

" People had seen, for two years, a Pontiff in the

Holy See voluntarily introducing admirable reforms, his name celebrated in songs of gratitude, from one end of Italy to the other, as the symbol and the hope of liberty, when all at once we were taken by surprise to hear that this sovereign, so lately the idol of his people, had been forced to fly in disguise from his capital. And Europe naturally concluded that the acts of aggression which obliged Pius IX. to quit Rome, were *the work of a conspiracy*, not the movement of a people who could not have passed in a moment from such lively enthusiasm to such base ingratitude."

The President of the Republic also stated in this message, according to the pledge he had given to the French Catholics in his letter to the nuncio, that the result aimed at in the French expedition to Rome was *to guarantee* to Pope Pius IX. *the integrity of his territory*. M. de Corcelles then, the worthy representative of France and of the president, very properly called attention to this important message in his despatches; and he gave the true account of the Roman revolution in the following words, which M. de Falloux read amid profound silence:

" ' The enemy is principally composed of about 20,000 foreigners, who do not care what injuries are done to the city, and would feel a malevolent satisfaction in being able to impute them to us. Up to this neither negotiation nor any intimidation from without can have any effect upon the Romans, who are under the immediate terrorism of the foreign adventurers who have successively accumulated within this unfortunate city. There may possibly be some thousands of Romans who zealously support them; but you may rest assured that the chief enemy is not Roman, but socialist. They reckon upon a general war . . . . . they reckon upon the violent co-operation of their friends and brother-conspirators in all other countries; and, far from really representing the city of Rome, they are sacrificing it as a holocaust to their furious passions.' "

These official documents crushed the violence of the opposition by the irresistible logic of facts; and they still contain all that requires to be known about the new revolution. The conspirators are the same men; it is the same individual who, in 1849, directed the defence of Rome against our troops, that now, with the same bands of men, threatens the pontifical troops at Ravenna and Rimini, oppresses the loyal inhabitants, and who only quits the struggle for a moment to issue incendiary proclamations, to seek everywhere for munitions of war, and to arm, if he can, a million of hands with *a million of muskets* against Rome, and very probably against Europe.

"Rome then has been delivered by us," exclaims M. de Falloux, "and she has blessed the day of her deliverance! I say she has blessed the day of her deliverance, and I should have been greatly surprised if she had not. For, permit me to point out to you the difference between her position, as you would have it, and that which we have formed for her. You called for a Roman republic, isolated among states which either do not recognize it, or formally rejected it; you would place it among all the opposing influences of the Italian states, between Tuscany, Piedmont, and Naples; you would leave isolated, before Austria, a republic menaced on all hands, and scarcely equal to the third-rate states of Europe. Such is the grand part you would have Rome to play.

"Well, what is the part we would assign to her, which she has now accepted, and which has ever been hers? It is not that of a Roman republic, the folly, the peril, and the emptiness of which she well understands. No, it is the part which she has played in the world for eighteen centuries, and which we have restored to her; it is that of capital of the universal Christian republic. (Groans on the left. On the right, 'Hear, hear.') It is that of the first city in the world!"

The speaker then proceeded to repel and demolish without mercy the pitiful accusations which certain deputies had ventured to utter. M. Arnault had mentioned the word *slavery*, when speaking of the restoration of the Pope; M. Jules Favre had said *ignorance, degradation.*

"Slavery!" exclaims M. de Falloux, "but what do the Romans themselves, in their eloquent and religious language, call the slavery, the captivity of Babylon? The time when Rome was without her Popes. When one walks about Rome, among monuments of all epochs, among those great historical personages as they style the monuments of Rome, one often asks,—'How is it that here are no monuments of the middle age among all these superb masterpieces of paganism, and those of the *renaissance?*' The

Roman, the genuine Roman, will answer you mournfully,—' Ah! that was the time of our captivity; the Pope was then at Avignon!' Rome had pined away; not a trace, not a token of greatness, no architecture, no sculpture, marks the period when the Popes were absent; nothing but ruin and desolation. (Loud applause.) Another reproach has been addressed to us, not by M. Arnault, but by M. Favre; he said that to restore the former government of Rome was to condemn the country to ignorance and degradation. I wonder that in using this hackneyed argument he did not also name Spain, and other peculiarly Catholic nations, as is usually done. I will do so for him; what he means is that Catholicism abases and degrades a people!"

A Member.—" Not Catholicism, but the temporal power."

M. DE FALLOUX.—" I hear a correction,—it is not Catholicism, but the temporal power. Yes, but up to this, though distinct, they have been designedly confounded, and I shall reply to the real meaning of the taunt we have received. I would ask you to look back to the origin of Catholicism, and to note the period when its unity was severed into two; see on one hand the unfaithful empire of Constantinople and of Moscow, on the other the orthodox empire of Charlemagne; on which side is the abasement, and on which the civilization, the enlightenment, and the liberty? (Hear, hear.) Say on which side is the ignorance and the slavery: these two great parallel lines are easy to follow, they stand out in eloquent and clear relief.

" And as to the inhabitants of Italy, would you have them mistake themselves for what they are not? Do you think they can regard themselves as a degraded population, when Italy is the mother of all sciences and all arts? And was she not most brilliant at the period when she was most Catholic? Have Catholicism and the temporal power degraded Dante and Tasso? Did not all the great geniuses of Italy flourish under the temporal power of the Popes? Are Manzoni and Pellico, in our own times, men of degenerate mind?"

We might now repeat these arguments to our present opponents. Not only did great geniuses and great works appear under the temporal rule of the papacy, but it was the Popes who encouraged and patronized, we may even say, produced them. Who called to Rome Michael Angelo and Raphael? Who built St. Peter's? Who created the library of the Vatican? Who has preserved and restored so many masterpieces of art? Who founded all the Italian universities? Yet this is what is branded as ignorance and debasement!

Looking at the question, then, from a still higher point of view, M. de Falloux continues:—

"We had, then, a great end in view, and we have attained it; a Catholic end, to restore to the Holy See the independence of which all Catholics stand in need; and to use the sword of France to accomplish this great and European design. We had, furthermore, another end; to lend the protection of France to the people of Rome, not, indeed, against their father, Pius IX., the author and promoter of all liberal movements that have taken place in Italy for the last two years; against him, whom you saluted with so many acclamations; him against whom you seem to have devised the *conspiracy of ovations;* whom you led from one triumph to another till the day when you overthrew him. (Repeated cheering on the right.) Yes, he who had nothing to defend him but the majesty of his office, no barrier to arrest his enemies but the rampart—alas! too feeble—of his benefits, was extolled and eulogized by you, in recurring demonstrations of gratitude and exultation, till your day came, and the dagger and the torch flashed upon the threshold of his palace!"

Alluding to the crime which was the first step towards the establishment of the Roman republic, M. de Falloux remarks, with equal truth and eloquence, that this crime itself proves the minority and the weakness of the revolutionary faction of Rome: those who are strong do not require to use the dagger.

May I be permitted here to pause for a moment, and to remark, that real eloquence is in facts; when abused by evil men, eloquence is a deadly weapon, and has produced the most ruinous effects; but when employed by noble lips in the service of justice and of right, when it faithfully expresses the sentiments of the heart, and disinterestedly asserts the eternal principles of order; when it speaks in a great assembly, at a great crisis, to point out the true course or discover an unseen precipice; it is then a noble and sacred power, one of the most sublime upon earth. History records, and religiously transmits it to future generations. And such, I am happy to say, was the eloquence so gloriously displayed by the champions of religion and society in the French Assembly during the years 1848, 1849, and 1850.

"A crime in morals," exclaims M. de Falloux, "is to violate the law; but in politics it is also a confession that one is weak, unpopular, in the minority. If the men who struck that blow had felt behind them a whole population in ferment, ripe for the institutions they wanted to give them, panting to enter on the venturesome career that was opened for them, they would not have stained their history and their institutions with so abominable a crime. They would not have contaminated at their source the blessings they could soon have won in an honourable way, with the consent of the people and the sanction of the majority. I repeat, that crime in politics is a confession of weakness. Had we no indication but this of the real sentiments of the people, I should say that we were justified in concluding that the Pope has been the object of a shameless and ungrateful conspiracy, which has nothing in common with the genuine and justifiable desires of the people." (Hear, hear.)

Having thus stigmatized the odious manœuvres of the revolution, M. de Falloux reveals its real and ultimate aims, and directly attacks the infatuated dream of a forced unity among different peoples, to which socialists and revolutionists would immolate everything else; whose impossible realization they would pursue at any price, and in spite of any obstacles; then, opposing immutable laws to wild chimeras, and showing what must be the sanguinary and inevitable issue of such a desperate conflict with the nature of men and things, he concludes his speech in these eloquent words, which the modern partisans of Italian *unitarism* would do well to study:—

"Is unity always a guarantee for peace? Unity has been seen before now in Europe; for several centuries it was entirely feudal; yet more blood was never shed than then. Was not Europe entirely monarchical in the time of Louis XIV? Did not monarchical unity prevail there for several centuries? and were those centuries free from battles and bloodshed? No, such a universal peace has never existed, and never will exist, because for this we should have to abrogate the fundamental laws of the human race. Such is the rock upon which your policy must always strike. . . .

"In foreign affairs your policy involves the same contradictions, the same impossibilities. . . . I repeat, you are not attacking such or such a political system, monarchical or republican government; you are attacking, and fruitlessly, the primordial laws of the human species and the human heart. (Murmurs on the left. Approbation on the right.) Yes, since you oblige me to insist upon an argument which I had thought so evident and so commonplace, since you contest what I say;—yes, till you have abolished all commercial and international interests, till you have reversed the course of passions and of rivers, till you have stopped the Scheldt from rolling in one direction its waters and the interests they carry, and the Danube from rolling in the opposite; till you have here removed the obstacle of a mountain, and there the convenience of a river, distributed unevenly among men, and impeding or facilitating their undertakings; till you have stopped the sun from imprinting here a more, there a less manly character upon nations; — yes, till you have modified the configuration of the globe, changed the conflicting interests of nations, and the advantages which they envy one another, till you have changed the laws of climates and of races, your system of unity must remain without effect. (Hear, hear on the right and centre.) This is just the course upon which we are determined not to enter. Yes, we desire to improve what is; to extract from our alliances and our institutions all the benefits, the liberty, and the improvements they can yield; but as to this superhuman struggle against the traditions and the nature of the countries which surround us, against the customs and traditions of our own, we have not undertaken and will never undertake it. (Acclamations.) We will not undertake it, because it has been the ruin of all who have ever entered on it." (*Continued applause on the benches of the majority. A crowd of representatives press around and congratulate the speaker.*)

After this speech, the order of the day was voted by the large majority of 428 against 176. The parliamentary annals of France registered another masterpiece; and what was more important, good sense, justice, and honour received a new and brilliant triumph.

CHAPTER XIII.

FRANCE AND THE HOLY SEE IN 1849.—M. THIERS' REPORT.

REVOLUTIONS, by agitating society, by stirring up and bringing to the surface what had long been slumbering at the bottom, and by disclosing unlooked-for perils, sometimes awaken us from a false security, and teach sad but salutary lessons. From these political storms the lightning flashes upon precipices which lay across our path; a sinister light gleams upon what before we could not see; by its glare we discover prospects hitherto wrapped in night; Providence reveals, in these great social commotions, lessons which are never entirely unfruitful.

Thus the great revolution of February was the means of enlightening many a great mind in France and the rest of Europe, manifested more clearly to all the real foundations of social peace and order, the necessity to society of the great principles of religion, and caused a happy revival of Christianity, which would have been still more general than it was, had not the passions of men again interfered to check it.

At all events, history will proclaim, that after the earthquake of 1848, which shook society to its centre, a rare and grand sight was seen in our assemblies and in the country: a sudden and striking union took place, which could little have been anticipated a few months previously, amid the stirring conflicts of the period: the sincere and the good of all parties nobly united, forgetting their old quarrels, to struggle in concert against one of the most violent outbreaks of anarchical passions the world has ever seen; France rallied around her all her most generous sons to face the common danger; she put forth all her vital strength, and succeeded in extricating herself by one of those supreme efforts which call for the blessings of Providence, and save a nation. It was then felt that there was a necessary ally, without whose aid the struggle must have been hopeless. Mere political measures were evidently inadequate; moral causes having chiefly originated the social war, moral force was indispensable to secure a peace. The war against religion ceased; peace was made with the Church; and France was saved.

M. Thiers was certainly in the first rank of the defenders of society, and of the new and eminent allies whom the Church then acquired. No one gave a more energetic and honest support to M. de Montalembert, M. de Falloux, and the Catholic cause: and, for my part, I shall never forget that the three greatest measures of that time,—the liberty of education, the liberty of religious congregations, and the Roman expedition, were heartily espoused and defended by M. Thiers.

The expedition to Rome had already given M. Thiers a new opportunity of proving the rare superiority of his mind, how readily he can grasp and master a great subject, and with what moral courage he strikes out his course, and inflexibly pursues it. The Roman cause, which M. de Falloux had so brilliantly gained, was, however, to be again brought forward, and to provoke a fresh conflict, which ended likewise in a complete victory for the defenders of the Roman expedition. We were at Rome: but what were we to do there? What was the Pope to do when we had restored him? What were to be his relations with France? What were to be the results of the expedition? Such were the questions asked in the assembly.

The government, at the first meeting of the assembly after the recess (1st October, 1849), spontaneously anticipated these demands; presented a bill to provide for the expenses of the Roman expedition; and appointed a committee to discuss anew that expedition under every point of view, moral, religious, and political: the committee consisted of—M. Molé, president; MM. de Broglie, de Montalembert, d'Hautpoul, Beugnot, Casabianca, Janvier, de la Moskowa, Chapot, Huber de l'Isle, de Lagrénée, Thuriot de la Rosière, Thiers, and Victor Hugo. M. Thiers was reporter, and his report, which we shall shortly proceed to analyze, was a masterpiece of clearness, logic, good sense, and political wisdom.

In the committee, M. Thiers eloquently defended the cause of the Pope. He replied to M. Victor Hugo in these terms:—

"You are a republican; you call for a republic. Well, I say the Papal government is one, and of the best! Yes, the best; for it is the most ancient, the most genuine, the most beneficent, and the most inoffensive. The most ancient; it is eighteen hundred years old! Do you know of any which has lasted so long, either in antiquity or in modern times? Name one, if you can, among the most potent, the most flourishing: take not only Pisa or Florence, but Genoa and Venice; those great sovereigns of the seas, where are they now? Yet Rome and its Pope remain. Whence comes this wondrous vitality?

"It is, besides, the most genuine republic. How are its sovereigns appointed? By election, and that the best kind of election, the electors being really qualified to make a choice. Among whom are they chosen? Among everybody—the people, the middle class, the nobility: sons of shepherds and of artisans have been popes. You accuse them of nepotism. Religion may blame them for it, but you cannot. What is the nepotism of the popes? It is the elevation of democracy. When the Pope is a man of the people, a plebeian family rises with him, and enters the ranks of the Roman aristocracy, itself the daughter of democracy. What has been the origin of the families of the Roman princes?—frequently the elevation of a humble family by the Papacy. But you democrats, when you rise to power, how do you act? You act like the popes, whenever it is in your power. What father, who rises in the world, does not raise his family? It is human nature. The popes have done like you, they have elevated their nephews. Again, I say, religion may desire to see them more sublimely disinterested, but you cannot reproach them. Besides, they have had, and elevated, other nephews, the glory of the human race; Michael Angelo, Raphael, and many other such, were the *protégées* of the popes: would you blame them for this?

"It is, again, the most beneficent republic. There are a few popes whom we give up to you . . . . but how many, out of two hundred and seventy-five? It was the Papacy that saved Rome in the barbarian invasions; that saved civilization in the middle ages; that inspired Charlemagne with a taste for letters; that has had manuscripts copied; that has preserved for us the classics, the arts, and sciences. You know this, yet you choose to forget and to ignore it . . . .

"It is also the most inoffensive republic. The Pope cannot, and ought not to make war. He is the common father of the faithful. By choice, as well as by necessity, he is pacific and friendly: for he is a priest. Who is he interested in attacking? and how could he attack any one? He cannot even defend himself. What is most wanting to him, whether in his foreign or domestic affairs, is force. I mean material force; for he has a force, which you have not, his moral force; he is enthroned in the consciences of 200,000,000 of Christians; and this force you cannot take from him. But he has yet another force which also defies you. Suppose, now that we are at Rome, you were to wish us to do violence to the Pope, you could not seriously propose it. If he were strong, you might; but he is weak, and you cannot. You see his weakness is a force; it is an invincible weakness. Were you to do violence to the Pope, you would not only be like a soldier beating a priest, which is vile and cowardly, but like a man beating a woman, an indignity which has not a name."

M. de Montalembert was present when these noble words were pronounced: his oratorical mind must have been struck by them: he treasured them up; and we shall see, when we refer to his speech, with what emphasis he expressed them at the tribune.

On the 13th of October, M. Thiers read his report to the National Assembly. Let us first quote the just homage, which he pays to the holy Father, and the sage counsels he gives to Italy :—

" When, three years ago, a noble Pontiff, who has since been so cruelly repaid for his generous intentions, gave from the Vatican the signal for political and social reform to the princes of Italy, all great men hoped to see Italy enter with prudence upon the path traced for her by Pius IX., and walk in it with steady and measured steps; they trusted she would not again compromise her prospects by reckless precipitation; that, in certain of her states, she would content herself with administrative reforms, as a means of arriving at political; that, in the most liberal, she would not think of passing the bounds of representative monarchy, which was as much as she could bear; that in all, she would cultivate union and concord, so as to insure the advantages of a powerful confederation, as it was not in her power to create an absolute unity; and, above all, that she would not rashly risk a war of independence, which must be premature and hopeless, unless Europe should have the misfortune to be engaged in a general war.

" Such were, we have said, the hopes of enlightened minds, friends of true liberty, and of that fair and ancient Italy, in which they saw a second country. And they were expressed at the time; they were not the fruits of a prudence which comes too late, and only forms its unprofitable reflections after the events: no, they were uttered in this house, in the presence of a throne which has ceased to exist, when we were all sanguine as to the results of a general movement, extending from Naples to Berlin and Vienna, which, unfortunately, instead of the benefits it promised, has yielded but convulsions. (Applause on the right.)

" An intemperate faction, which thought more of the gratification of its passions than of the true interests of its cause, has possessed itself of Italy, and hurried it into ruin. It has urged the people to demand institutions unsuited to the habits and ideas of the country; it has pressed into republicanism, populations who were unfitted for more than municipal and provincial liberty. But this is not all; it has committed a fatal and ruinous mistake, in provoking prematurely the war of independence; and having done this, it has added the still more fatal error of turning against Italian governments the arms of the Italian people.

"You are aware of the consequences of these mistakes. Austria, using the unquestionable rights of war, has reconquered Lombardy, invaded Piedmont, the duchies of Parma and Modena, Tuscany, and a part of the Roman states. The independence of Italy, so far from making progress, has retrograded, and her liberty has retrograded as well as her independence." (Dissent on the left; on the right, "It is matter of history.")

In fact, Pius IX. was at Gaëta, solely because he had always resisted the policy thus reprobated by M. Thiers; because he proposed to realize the independence of Italy by the union of all the Italian governments and populations, that is, by just means instead of by revolution; because he[1] negotiated for the independence of Italy, while his devoted minister, Count Rossi, fell under the democratic steel, on the steps of the parliament founded at Rome by the Pontiff. Having thus referred to the origin of the troubles of Italy, M. Thiers had no difficulty in proving that the interposition of France was necessary and justifiable.

"It was the triple interest of France, Christendom, and Italian liberty, that it should be so."

The acute mind of M. Thiers clearly distinguished the two sides of the question—the political and the religious:—

"In a political point of view, an interposition was imperatively called for by the interests of Italy and Italian liberty; for the Pope would have been restored without us, and that by Austria. Austria, using the unquestionable rights of war, had reconquered Lombardy, invaded Piedmont, the duchies of Parma and Modena, Tuscany, and a part of the Roman states. The governments, having met with an ill return for the concessions they had made, were not disposed to renew them: the enemies of liberal reforms found a powerful argument in the excesses which had been committed; sensible persons were discouraged, and the masses, after so much dangerous excitement, were reduced to submission by the pressure of physical force.

---

[1] I shall soon have occasion to cite the letter of Pius IX. to the emperor of Austria.

" " Still, in the midst of this vast wreck, was there no resource but despair? Were no fragments of the hopes conceived in 1847 to be saved? Were all efforts useless to found in Italy an equilibrium, to be watched over by all the powers, and which had been broken, to the advantage of one of them, by the fault of those who had attacked her? France did not think so, and such was the origin and the reason of her expedition to Rome; to judge of which aright, one should examine the circumstances under which it took place. An Austrian army being on the point of marching on Rome, the question was whether France should suffer Austria to push her invasion as far as Rome, and thus to become, both morally and materially, the mistress of almost the whole of Italy. To prevent this, there were but two courses to follow—war, or the occupation of Rome by a French army. War was a means which our government was unwilling to employ, even at the time of its greatest zeal for the independence of Italy, and when success was probable, as the Austrians had been driven beyond the Adige. It would have been insane to enter upon war now, when the favourable moment was past; when a juster estimate of the real interests of France had cooled the dangerous excitement of men's minds. War, then, being out of the question, one course, and only one, remained—that France should enter Italy too.

" Italian liberty was interested in her doing so; for, without pausing to inquire what is the measure of liberty desirable or suitable for the Italians—a grave question, but which here would be out of place,—no one will question but such measure would have been more restricted under Austrian than under French influence.

" Whether, then, I consider French, Catholic, or liberal interests, it seems to me that we could not have held back, and that it was better that an interposition, which the fatal mistakes of Italy had necessitated, should be effected by the arms of France than by those of Austria."

However great the force and good sense of this reasoning, religious considerations had a still more vital connection with the question than political. And we shall now see with what acuteness M. Thiers seizes, and with what courage he proclaims the real solution of the difficulty, the true argument which disperses the two great objections brought against the Roman expedition, namely, the apparent injustice of one people interfering in the affairs of another, and the strangeness of one republic going to overthrow another:—

" The Catholic powers had assembled at Gaeta, to plan the reestablishment of an authority which is necessary to the Christian universe. In truth, without the authority of the Sovereign Pontiff, Catholic unity would be dissolved; Catholicism would be severed into sects, and perish; and the moral world, already so rudely shaken, would fall into universal ruin. (Hear, hear, on the right. Murmurs on the left.)

".... But Catholic unity, requiring a certain spiritual submission from Christian nations, would be inadmissible, if the Pontiff, in whom it is embodied, were not perfectly independent; if, upon the territory which ages have assigned to him, and which all nations nave respected, another sovereign, whether prince or people, were to rise to dictate laws to him. For the Papacy, there can be no other independence but sovereignty. We have here an interest of a paramount nature, which is rightly made to overrule the private interests of nations, just as, in a state, the public interest overrules what is individual; and it fully justified the Catholic powers in reestablishing Pius IX. upon the pontifical throne."

The whole question is summed up in these few words. No one could state more clearly and correctly what it is which causes and justifies this exceptional position of the Roman States, which puzzles certain minds, who look at it from a wrong point of view. M. Thiers took the true view of it; as a politician, he casts his eye over Europe; he sees there, as living facts, the Catholic Church, and the Catholic nations, one of which is the Roman state; and, having learnt what the supreme and common interest of all these nations requires, he pronounces fearlessly, and, in accordance with all writers on the law of nations, that this interest should take precedence of the others: though, in fact, as we have shown, and will shortly have occasion to repeat, the real interests of the Roman people are in no way injured. As to that paltry policy that only looks to forms and appearances, M. Thiers demolishes it with a word:—

"Our constitution would be contrary to common sense, if it meant that such or such a form of government should render a neighbouring state either odious or sacred to us. We should be friendly or unfriendly to governments, not because of their form, but for their conduct."

This is practical common sense. M. Thiers has reason to conclude that—

"Thus political, moral, and religious considerations concurred in calling upon France to interfere at Rome. She sent an army there. The faction which has held the destinies of Italy for the last two years, instead of accepting France as an umpire, violently resisted her. Our soldiers, ever worthy of themselves, have carried every obstacle, as they did of old at Lodi and Arcola: but, more orderly and disciplined than ever, they have been the admiration of Europe for the forbearance and humanity of their conduct. (Hear.) And had we gained nothing by our expedition but this new manifestation of the military virtues of our army, we ought not to regret it; for, among the painful spectacles we are now forced to witness, the conduct of our troops is a real consolation." (Hear, hear, on the benches of the majority.)

So ends the first part of M. Thiers' report, relating to the reasons of the expedition. The second discusses its consequences, and this part has, even now, lost none of its importance, for the same question is being put at this moment:—

"Are these consequences good, honourable, and conformable to the end laid down? And what remains to be done, to attain all that was contemplated in sending an expedition which involved certain military difficulties, and very serious political ones?"

Such is the question. But M. Thiers very properly places one consideration before and above all others,—respect for the liberty of the Holy Father:—

"France, once present at Rome by her army, could not be guilty of the inconsistency of doing violence to the holy Father, whom she had delivered from the violence of a faction. Her business was to restore to him his throne and his liberty, his full and unrestricted liberty. But the circumstances of the case invested her with a right, a very uncommon right, that of giving advice. If, in ordinary cases, one sovereign were to venture to say to another, 'You are behaving wrong, you should adopt such or such a course,' he would be guilty of an impropriety, and a sort of usurpation. But a sovereign who has come to restore another, maintaining thereby the common interests of order, of religion, and of political tranquillity, receives from the gravity of the motives which have brought him, and the magnitude of the service rendered, the right to offer his advice."

The advice alluded to here by M. Thiers refers to the improvements and reforms which might be possible and desirable in the Roman States. But let us see how he means these improvements to be proposed to the Holy Father:—

"This should be accomplished by an influence brought to bear with patience, with gentleness, and with respect (hear),—an influence which, I repeat, would be an inadmissible pretension, had not extraordinary circumstances, as it were, forced it upon us; but which, confined within due limits is perfectly compatible with the independence and dignity of the Holy See." (Hear, hear.)

M. Thiers, moreover, renders a twofold justice to the Holy Father; he admits how enduring were his good and liberal dispositions, and he makes allowance, as was just, for the new and vast difficulties the revolution had accumulated before him. Many now lose sight of this, or do not choose to see it; M. Thiers was fairer:—

"France did not find the holy Father less generous or less liberal than he was in 1847; but circumstances are unhappily changed."

What was the change which now so embarrassed the Holy Father's progress as a reformer, and necessitated such prudence on his part?—

"Those who made use of his benefits to convulse Italy, and to drive liberal princes from their capitals, have been the means of deepening the prejudices of all the enemies of Italian liberty, whose reluctance Pius IX. had braved at the outset of his reign. Not to suffer the source to be reopened whence so many evils had flowed, has become almost the exclusive anxiety of all who have part in the Roman government. The difficulties in the way of Roman liberty, though considerable at the commencement, have singularly increased, through the use made of that liberty during the last two years."

Such difficulties, and many more, had been bequeathed to Pius IX. by the revolution which had undone his work. And if M. Thiers is too much of a liberal not to encourage the generous intentions that still animate the Pontiff, he has, nevertheless, too much sense to urge him blindfold upon a dangerous course, where precipices have now opened before his feet, or to require from him reforms which have become for the time being impossible. Still, Pius IX. had begun to act, in the measure which was allowed him; the Roman expedition was already bearing fruit, and M. Thiers was enabled to say :—

"The results already obtained render it impossible for us to regret that our troops are at the Vatican, as they occupy a place there which otherwise would be filled by Austrian troops; as they have behaved with so much gallantry and humanity; and, finally, as it is evident that they are the means of preserving to the people the chief benefits which Pius IX. had so liberally dispensed to them on his accession."

What were the results which had been obtained, which satisfied alike M. Thiers, the committee, and the Assembly itself, as it declared by a large majority? What were these results, the value of which could not be denied, as M. Thiers says, unless by *unjust prejudice?* They were contained in the *motu proprio* of the 12th of September, on which M. Thiers comments as follows :—

"This act gives all desirable municipal and provincial liberties. As to political liberty, that of regulating the affairs of a country, in one or two assemblies, in concert with the executive power, as in England, for instance, it is true that the *motu proprio* grants none— at least, it only grants the first rudiments, in the shape of a private *consulta*, with the power of deliberation. The question is, whether the Roman states are capable of the constitution which England has at length formed for herself after two centuries of exertions and experience. It is a question of profound importance, which it was for the holy Father to resolve, and which demanded from him the utmost caution, as the interests of the whole Christian world were involved. If he has preferred the more prudent course; if, after the experiments he has made, he has thought it wiser not to reopen the career of political agitation to a people which showed itself so unfit for it, we do not arrogate to ourselves the right to censure him, nor do we see that he deserves it.

"Municipal and provincial liberties are a sort of education, through which it is well that a people should pass; and it is dangerous to introduce them violently and prematurely into the turmoil of political liberty.

"Furthermore, the important act styled the *motu proprio* supposes a code of laws which will reform civil legislation, insure the equity of the courts, share public offices evenly among the various classes of citizens, and, in short, procure for the Romans the advantages of a prudently liberal government. These measures are promised, and the word of Pius IX. suffices to dissipate all doubts."

Such was the celebrated report of M. Thiers. The closeness of his reasoning, the clearness of his diction, his practised eloquence, his capacious, statesmanlike views, so free from all narrowness and prejudice,—everything, in short, rendered this speech worthy of the great cause which M. Thiers was defending, and of the acclamations of the great majority of the assembly in which he spoke. All the great principles of the question which still occupies Europe were there defined and proclaimed; all homage rendered to the cause of truth and justice, to the virtue and the generosity of Pius IX.; useful lessons and advice given to reformers; to the too precipitate as well as the too backward; to the ingratitude and passions of the revolution; to princes and people; and the resolutions of the sovereign assemblies of republican France ratified this wise and noble policy.

It would, however, be a mistake to suppose that such triumphs were gained by justice, good sense, and eloquence, at such a period, and in such an assembly, without occasionally causing fearful conflicts; but such struggles were an honour to the generous courage which did not shrink from meeting them. The excitement of men's minds, and the fury of the passions of that unhappy time, caused the parliamentary debates to present the most agitated and tumultuous spectacle; the representative assembly was an arena where the struggle between good and evil was violent and unremitting. The good fought with unflinching courage, for they were defending the most grand and sacred interests—those of religion and society; they were fighting *pro aris et focis*. The champions were there face to face, with menacing look, voice, and gesture. Murmurs, interruptions, clamour, loud and ironical laughter, fell thick like missiles in a combat: that angry and troubled multitude of men waved and vibrated to the voice of the speaker. Sometimes, in that part of the Assembly which, from a sinister association, was called the " Mountain," certain telling expressions of the great orators of the party of order would call forth, as it were, an eruption of a volcano; the representatives on the left would start up and gesticulate from their seats; they seemed ready to rush upon the other side of the Assembly; but honour, the liberty of speech, and the rights of attack and defence, succeded, like an invisible barrier, in repressing their fury. The Roman question was one of those which most irritated certain parties, and excited the most disturbance. From such tumults one may judge of the difficulties which had to be overcome, and of the merit of those whose energy overcame them. In order rightly to estimate the character of the struggle, and to render to every one his due, it is necessary to take into account the tempestuous scenes amid which the speeches of the party of order were delivered.

M. Thiers was admirable, while delivering his report. In vain did the "Mountain" struggle to swamp that telling report; so much so, that some members even of the right, wearied out and disgusted, called to him, "Put down the report, M. Thiers; such conduct is really too scandalous." M. Thiers persisted; he said, turning towards the left :—

"Gentlemen, if I were debating, I could reply to your interruptions; but I am only authorized to read my report to you, and my report cannot answer you, so you must only hear me out." (Hear, hear, on the right.)

And the left had to hear the report to the end. Soon, however, new interruptions are heard: "Loyola!" cries one from the "Mountain." M. Thiers replies :—

"Gentlemen, I have already told you that I will soon argue the point with you. You know, by experience, that your objections do not silence me so easily, and that I can sometimes make a reply; why not wait for a day when I may do so?"

The left kept quiet for a few minutes, but soon a new disturbance arose. M. Thiers had employed a respectful expression, when speaking of the relations of France with the Holy See, which immediately produced the most indecent interruptions, and words like the offensive ones which the revolutionary press is now again uttering against Pius IX.: he had said, " France had a right to beg of the Holy Father."—" *Beg upon her knees*," cried a member from the left.—" That's the Capuchin style," said another; " M. de Montalambert ought to be pleased." M. Thiers, turning, and looking full at the interrupters, said :—

" I am supprised at the interruption; yes, I am surprised that any one should have so little delicacy as not to understand the propriety of respectful expression towards a power which has not 500,000 soldiers." (Hear, hear. Confusion on the left.)

M. Dupin, the President of the Assembly, boldly fulfilling his part, then addresses himself to the extreme left, with the mingled causticity and energy which were peculiar to his manner :—

" What do these interruptions mean?—what purpose do they serve? You ought to listen to the speaker; silence compromises nobody, but an imprudent word often does." (Laughter on the right. Uproar on the left.)

A voice.—" The maxim is a wise one!"

M. Dupin.—" Sometimes there is an intolerable succession of interruptions; it is my duty to notice them publicly, and call attention to them; it is a reparation which I owe to the Assembly. (Hear, hear.) You cannot restrain yourselves a moment!"

M. Antony Thouret.—" That's not an easy matter."

M. Dupin.—" I beg your pardon, it is easy."

M. Thiers.—" Do you think you never put our patience to a severe trial?" (Oh, oh! New cries on the extreme left.)

M. Dupin.—" Come! allow people to speak. You think yourselves bound to interrupt; but it leads to nothing. Do you imagine it would compromise you to listen? (Laughter. New confusion on the extreme left.) In former assemblies, a report has never been interrupted!"

At last M. Dupin went so far as to say to the interrupters :—

" Those are public-house expressions it would be better not to indulge in. Such things really have but one name; and I am happy not to know the name of the person who uttered such a shameful expression : it is really indecent!"

We thought it would not be uninteresting to give here some idea of these stormy scenes; while they give some insight into the peculiar features of these great debates, they also furnish the opportunity of rendering a piece of justice which has been well merited : I think it right, then, to state, that a most important and necessary part, in these great discussions on which the fate of France depended, was most ably discharged; I mean, that of President of that agitated Assembly, whose difficult duty it was to maintain the order and dignity of the proceedings, to see that the speakers had a fair hearing, to put down interruptions, and make the Assembly respected. It gives me pleasure to pay this homage to M. Dupin, whose answers were celebrated at the time, and who, by his courageous impartiality, his firmness, his replies, full of good sense, and even eloquence, though so sharp and laconic, rendered services which were appreciated by the country, and which, for my part, I am unwilling to forget.

CHAPTER XIV.

FRANCE AND THE HOLY SEE IN 1849.—SPEECH OF M. DE MONTALEMBERT.

Such, then, were the assemblies, such the difficulties of the speakers. But the most violent tumults, the most obstinate interruption of any was provoked by the opening of the famous speech of M. de Montalembert, at the sitting of October 19th, a speech which has been read throughout all Europe, and will remain as one of the most illustrious specimens of parliamentary eloquence, defending the grandest and holiest of causes. M. de Montalembert was replying to M. Victor Hugo, who, it must be said, had passed all bounds in his attacks upon the Pope. Ascending the tribune under the immediate impression of this speech, and carried away too much, perhaps, by his emotion, M. de Montalembert had begun by strongly expressing his indignation: " Gentlemen," said he, " the speech you have just heard has already received the chastisement it deserved, in the applause which followed it."

I shall not attempt to describe the scene of disorder that broke out at these words; the firm attitude of M. Dupin, and the word *recompense* substituted for *chastisement*. I come at once to the speech itself; and shall first extract the following words, addressed to M. Hugo, and which the latter must have felt as a bitter reproach, though there is nothing in them of insult. Now that M. Hugo is an exile, that he has experienced those disappointments and reverses of politics, which M. de Montalembert then alluded to, with emotion rather than anger, these words must touch him deeply; and probably he could not peruse them now without some regret, and without looking with a more favourable eye upon that hospitable Rome, the city of refuge of all misfortunes:—

" I wish to observe to the honourable speaker who has preceded me, that perhaps he will go himself one day to Rome, to that unrivalled city, to seek there peace, repose, dignity in retirement, and all the advantages secured to that Eternal City, by that very clerical government which he has just now insulted from this tribune. One day, perhaps, it will be his lot to seek these benefits there: he will find them, and then he will bless Heaven for having inspired Christian nations with the idea of maintaining in Europe at least one such precious asylum, sheltered from the storms, the calumnies, the disappointments, and the agitations of political life, in which his inexperience would now seem to place the supreme good of nations and individuals. Well, then he will repent of the speech he has now pronounced, and his repentance will be his punishment. I wish him no other. (Murmurs on the left.)

" He will then repent of having given utterance to affronts and, permit me to add, calumnies against the revered head of the Church, the living oracle of our hearts and of our consciences. Yes, calumnies. It is to calumniate France to attribute to her the instincts and the desires of which he has been the mouthpiece at this tribune. And, moreover, it is to calumniate the Pope to suppose him capable of the injustice with which that speech reproached him." (Approbation on the right. Murmurs on the left.)

The speakers of the " Mountain," as at present the revolutionary press (for in France, as well as in Italy, we are continuing the struggle against the same foes), had not shrunk from insulting Pius IX. after his benefits ; worse again, after his misfortunes, after all that generous Pope had suffered for having attempted to set an example of reform to the Italian princes, and to regenerate his country. Such baseness revolted M. de Montalembert; he exclaims :—

"Gentlemen, Bossuet has spoken of a certain finishing grace which suffering lends to virtue. Pius IX. has received it ; he has known suffering, and he has known, too, the most cutting and bitter of misfortunes—ingratitude. Still, I cannot say I pity him ; I honour him, nay, I would almost say I envy him for this. It is not every one who can suffer ingratitude ; to do so, one must have done good to one's fellow-creatures, one must have attempted great things for humanity. Blessed, then, are they who render others ungrateful; but woe to those who are ungrateful, and to those who make themselves the mouthpieces, the orators, of ingratitude ! (Warm applause on the right.)

"He met with ingratitude not only at Rome, not only in Italy, but in Europe, and in this Assembly ! For it is sovereign ingratitude towards the Sovereign Pontiff to ignore his services and his virtues, as has been done here. It is ingratitude towards him, to requite his conduct and the whole tenor of his life by the virulent attacks of the last speaker, and by the coarse insults which were the other day stigmatized with proper severity by our president, and which the *Moniteur* will hand down to the indignation of posterity. (Cheers on the right.) Well, allow me here to oppose to such ingratitude, whose cause has been so deplorably advocated from this very tribune, the solemn tribute of my admiration, my gratitude, and my love." (Hear, hear, on the right.)

People had presumed to speak, as they are again speaking now, and as a Piedmontese minister, too, had presumed to speak, of the cruelty and proscriptions of the Papal government; they cast doubts upon the amnesty granted by Pius IX. But what had Pius IX. done then?

What had he done the very day after his election? M. de Montalembert answers:—

"You know well that the Pope always pardons; he is obliged to pardon. And it is for this very reason that he has been obliged, in the amnesty which you have slanderously styled a proscription, not to deliver up such and such individuals, whom he has excepted from it, to the executioner, or even to the prisons, but simply to exclude them from the dominions you have just reconquered for him, in order to prevent them from again seeking to render his government an impossibility. And he acts thus because he cannot punish them as other powers can, and as has been done even in France. He is obliged to resort to the preventive system, because the repressive one is more difficult and more impracticable for him than any one else."[1] (Cheers on the right.)

The speaker next enters on an important point of the question, the extent of the liberties and reforms granted by the *motu proprio*, which was, so to speak, the programme of Pius IX.; and this part of his speech is so much the more interesting to us, as it is the same pretext which now is alleged against the Pope:—

"This act gives four principal guarantees: first, the reform of civil legislation; secondly, that of the tribunals; thirdly, extensive provincial and municipal liberties; liberties greater, as the president of the council seemed to say yesterday, than what we have had, and even have now, in France; so great, that you have not ventured, up to this, to grant them to the city of Paris itself: and you are quite right. (Laughter on the right.) Fourthly, the *motu proprio* establishes the secularization of the administration, in this sense, that ecclesiastics are not excluded, but laymen admitted. It is well to remark, too, that this admission of laymen, under Pius IX., has already become so general, that, in a statistical return of all the offices of the Roman states, lately published at Naples, there are holding legal, administrative, and political employments, in all 109

---

[1] *The Pope always pardons; he is obliged to pardon.* We cannot help quoting, in connection with this fine expression, another, not less happy nor less true, of Cardinal Consalvi, prime minister of Pius VII.: "Falsehood is the habitual rule of courts. But one falsehood at Rome would at once be the ruin of a whole reign: it would make another Pope necessary."—*Artaud*, Histoire de Léon XII. tom. i. p. 167.

ecclesiastics only, and 5,059 laymen. Such is the present proportion."

A member of the committee.—" There are 243 ecclesiastics."

M. DE MONTALEMBERT.—" Yes; but that number includes 143 chaplains of prisons. Now, it seems to me that no one can think of excluding ecclesiastics from the small number of elevated positions they hold at present; I say elevated, because the sovereign himself being an ecclesiastic—unless, perhaps, you want the Pope to be a layman (laughter on the right)—he must necessarily have about him, as his chief ministers, ecclesiastics like himself. In fact, to propose that the Pope should be obliged to exclude ecclesiastics from the high offices of his states, would be something like compelling the emperor of Russia, who is essentially a military sovereign, to govern exclusively by lawyers. (Laughter on the right.) Instead of that, how does the emperor of Russia manage? He always has at the head of his principal civil departments military men like himself; he has had for a long time a general of infantry as minister of finance, and I believe his finances have not suffered by it." (Exclamations and laughter.)

A voice on the left.—" He had not the title of general."

M. DE MONTALEMBERT.—" He had—General Cancrine. Observe, too, that the *motu proprio* leaves room for the development and for manifold applications of the principles, the concessions, and the liberties which are contained in it, in embryo, as the Minister of Foreign Affairs has remarked."

But political liberties, and parliamentary institutions properly so called, were not in the *motu proprio*. Are all such institutions compatible with the peculiar character of the Papal sovereignty? And was it advisable that such even as are, and which Pius IX. had formerly accorded, should be now fully renewed and kept up? The question was an important one, and has not yet been decided. M. de Montalembert replies to it :—

"I would first clearly state why, and in what, certain liberties are incompatible with the Pope's temporal sovereignty. It is not that liberty in itself is incompatible with it. This was clearly shown in the middle ages; very extensive liberties—local, individual, and general—then co-existed in the Roman states with the temporal sovereignty of the popes, as in other states they co-existed with the sovereignty of kings. But a change has taken place in later days. Modern democracy considers liberty as almost completely synonymous with sovereignty of the people. This synonymy is certainly not founded in the nature of things, for there exists very great liberty in England without the sovereignty of the people; and there was great political liberty in France under the Restoration, though the principle of the sovereignty of the people was not recognized. It is this principle of the sovereignty of the people which, as General Cavaignac has ably proved at this tribune, is absolutely incompatible with the temporal sovereignty of the Pope: and it is because liberty is constantly confounded with the sovereignty of the people that men have been able to assert and to prove that certain liberties, now so much in vogue, are incompatible with the authority of the Pope." (Approbation on the right.)

But who were those who demanded, and who still demand, these parliamentary institutions, and this political liberty for the Romans?

"There are two classes of men who call for these institutions; the first are those who have abolished them in France. How can they call for institutions in Italy which they have destroyed in France? (Laughter on the right.) I suppose the explanation of such inconsistency is to be found in the following extract from a republican journal of the 12th September, 1849, the same date as the *motu proprio*:—

"'Whatever measures Pius IX. may adopt, the Roman people will not contentedly accept the new liberties he may grant them: they will only use them to overturn the prince who thought fit to grant them, and to rid themselves of his authority.'" (Oh, oh! Prolonged laughter on the right.)

But is not this what the revolutionary press is now again declaring? so true is it that the same struggle is still going on, and the same end aimed at. It is the very existence of the Papacy that is menaced. The real question is not to impose upon it liberties and reforms: no, but total dispossession, degradation, annihilation!

M. DE MONTALEMBERT.—" Such men, in my opinion, speak very logically. I would even say that they show most acute judgment in the matter. Only, I think, the conclusion they arrive at renders their advice somewhat suspicious, and the Pope and his counsellors must be very blind, if their eyes are not opened by such frank and logical avowals. So much for the first class of those who call for parliamentary government in Italy.

"However, there is another; and they belong to that numerous body who had no hand in overturning parliamentary government in France, but who, on the contrary, loved, served, and carried it into practice. I have done so myself. I loved that government, and I did more than love it, I believed in it. I honestly believed in it, and if I am to say what I think, I still believe in it."

M. de Montalembert proceeds to show, that if many of these partisans of liberty do not now call upon Pius IX. to renew institutions which they had loved, served, and believed in, it is that a trial has been made, which has shaken their faith, and that by Pius IX. himself:—

"Had he not given to his country, as I said just now, all the liberties now demanded, and even more? He had given it the liberty of the press, and a civic guard. He had given it two chambers, and a constitutional *statute*. Well, what return did he receive? The press had morally dethroned him before he was dethroned, in fact. The civic guard besieged him in his palace of the Quirinal. The two chambers remained dumb and unmoved when his minister was assassinated; and it was the leader of the constitutional party, Mamiani, that became the successor of the murdered minister, and the gaoler of the holy Father. Such was the Pope's experience of constitutional government." (Assent on the right. Clamours on the left.)

Has the Pope changed? or was he mistaken? The Speaker replies:—

"Neither the one nor the other; but he has had a lesson from experience. Pius IX. has neither changed nor erred; he was not mistaken, nor is he transformed.

"He was not mistaken in attempting to endow his country and Italy with liberty; in inviting, not, indeed, as has been said, the Church to become reconciled to liberty, but modern liberty to become reconciled to the Church, which it had too long slighted. If he had not made this trial, this noble experiment, and that with incomparable sincerity and straightforwardness, his magnanimity might have been suspected: some might have thought, some narrow minds might have concluded, that the Papal power was systematically antagonistic to progress, civilization, and liberty. But now, after the trial that he has made, it is unquestionable, that if liberty has not struck its roots at Rome, it is not through the fault of Pius IX., but of those to whom he had accorded that liberty. (Marked approbation on the right.) He was not, then, mistaken in undertaking the noble and great work which will immortalize him, and on which, for my part, I still congratulate him.

"Nor has he changed: I am convinced that he is by no means disposed to sacrifice liberty; that he has no wish to see true liberty superseded by the reign of physical force; but he has seen, he has been enlightened, his eyes have been opened; he has profited by the lesson which God intended him to learn from events; and he would be inexcusable had he not done so."

Such reflections are equally to the purpose at present, when Pius IX. is censured for his delay in resuming a course which, as experience has taught him, necessitates greater precautions against the wickedness of men than his heart had at first anticipated. Moreover, experience has given this lesson not only to Pius IX., not only to Rome and Italy, but also to us, and to all Europe. Accordingly, we now find many whose love for liberty, though not weakened, has grown more cautious and reserved. What! is it for you to approach us with too feeble a love for liberty, you whose sole endeavour seems to be to render it odious by your profanations, and impossible, by degrading it into licentiousness?

The speech of M. de Montalembert here still grows more animated; the orator seems to outdo himself, and these passages will bear a comparison with the grandest and most touching models of parliamentary eloquence:—

"Allusion was made yesterday to the apostasy of the great liberal party. Well, gentlemen, do you forget all that has happened in the world during the last few years? Can you fancy that men of sense, of humanity, and of conscience, still love and believe in liberty, and hope for an indefinite progress in civilisation, as they did two or three years ago? (Agitation.) Do you think that, in France and in Europe, men's hearts and feelings have received no shock? Do you imagine that a ghastly light has not broken upon many an intelligence and many a conscience? (Applause on the right.)

"And, if you doubt the competence and impartiality of us public men, if you think that we are spent, and our judgments warped by the routine of political life, I would say to you,—Go and sound the heart of nations, enter any humble dwelling and question any obscure but honest and patriotic citizen; ask men who meddle not with politics, who have ever lived remote from the turmoil and the vexations of public life; knock at the door of their heart, sound their conscience, and ask them if they now feel the same love for liberty and progress they once did; or, if they still love them, ask whether they have the same faith and confidence in them as before. You will not find one in a hundred, no, not one in a thousand, to answer 'Yes.' (Repeated applause on the right. Dissent and murmurs on the left.)

"Ah! it is sad, but it is the truth; I can conceive the grief it causes you, and I share it myself; but it is the truth, and I challenge any one to deny it. Make the inquiries which I propose to you; sound the opinions of the people, and you will not find one in a hundred, not one in a thousand, of those who were ardent liberals, who now feel the zeal and the confidence they did two years ago. (Hear, hear. No, no.) But you admitted it yesterday. One of your speakers, whom we listened to with the silence of respect, if not with that of sympathy, admitted it himself yesterday at this tribune; he called attention to it, dwelt upon it, and designated it as the apostasy of the great liberal party,—I rise to endeavour to account to you for this phenomenon, and you interrupt me!—you look upon it as an affront! But I have not done with this subject: I say that the phenomenon is universal, and I am now going to tell you what has caused it. Why such a sudden change? Because the name and the standard of liberty have been usurped by foul and incorrigible demagogues who have profaned it, and have only used it as a sanction for their crimes. (Violent exclamations on the left. Marked approbation on the right.)

"Why, gentlemen (the speaker turns towards the left), take to yourselves what I have said? (Laughter on the right.) Why will you not listen to me?—I am stating an historical fact.

"I say that the cause of liberty has been everywhere profaned by foul and incorrigible demagogues. (Fresh interruption on the left. *A voice.*—" By the Jesuits.")

"I say that everywhere—at the foot of the Capitol at Rome, as at the barrier of Fontainebleau; in the suburbs of Frankfort, as on the bridge of Pesth—the cause of liberty has been defiled by the foul aid of the democratic dagger." (New and louder applause on the right. Strong marks of disapprobation on the left.)

And, notwithstanding the contradictions of the left, could not M. de Montalembert add, if he were speaking now:—" At Naples, at Parma, at Vienna, and again at Parma, and at Paris, on the 14th of January, 1858."

M. Dupin replied to the interrupters:—

"Allow people, at least, to speak against assassination!"

M. DE MONTALEMBERT.—" Would you learn what it is that extinguishes in men's hearts the vital and glowing flame of liberty? It is not the fetters of the tyrant. Look at Poland: has this flame of liberty been quenched there yet, in spite of the threefold oppression which has weighed upon her for three-quarters of a century? No; would you know what does extinguish it? It is they!—they, those demagogues of whom I spoke just now,—those anarchists (Long-continued applause on the right. Dissent on the left)—those men who declare an unholy and implacable war against human nature, against the fundamental conditions of society, against the eternal principles of truth, of justice, and of law. It is they who quench the love of liberty! (Applause.)

" Look, I entreat, at the state of Europe three years ago. Liberty was gradually extending her empire in all directions; kings were coming, by turns—with a bad grace, if you will,—but they were all coming to lay, in some sort, their crowns at the feet of liberty, to sue from her for a new sanction, a new investiture. The Pope himself, the living symbol of authority, the incarnation of the most ancient and august power . . . ." (Ironical laughter at the extreme left.)

M. DUPIN.—" It is my duty to call attention to the fact, with whoever the blame may lie, that to attack demagogues, assassination, and anarchy, has excited displeasure and contradiction, but that to pay honour to what is respectable has been a signal for laughter and derision! (Loud cheers on all the benches at the right. Murmurs on the extreme left.) You shock all the feelings of the country." (Renewed cheers.)

M. DE MONTALEMBERT.—" Pius IX. himself, the representative of the most august and ancient authority upon earth, thought that he might borrow another jewel for his tiara from liberty, democracy, and the modern ideas. Has he succeeded? You have put a stop to all that; you have arrested, obstructed, diverted from its course, the current which inspired us old liberals, as you say, with such confidence and admiration. That current has ceased to flow. It is true, you have dethroned a few kings, but you have far more effectually dethroned liberty. (Cheers on the right.) The kings are again upon their thrones, but liberty has not returned to hers. She has not been reinstated upon the throne which she had possessed in our hearts. Oh! I am well aware that you write up her name everywhere, in all your laws, on every wall, on every ceiling. (The speaker points to the roof of the chamber. Long merriment and applause on the right.) But in our hearts her name is blotted out. Yes, the lovely, the pure, the hallowed, the noble liberty that we have so loved, so cherished, so long served . . . . (Violent murmurs on the left.) Yes, served, before you, longer than you, better than you (Renewed clamours); that liberty is not dead, I hope, but she is stifled, crushed, ravaged, trampled down!"

Fresh disturbances were just then heard upon the left, but they were soon lulled. One felt that these energetic words were telling upon the enemy; under the invectives of the orator, they looked like wounded lions, struggling in vain to shake off the terrible steel which had struck too deep.

"Yes, crushed between what one of you has dared to call the sovereignty of the end—that is, the sovereignty of evil—and the necessary revival of the severities of authority, to which you forced human nature, society, and the human heart, appalled at your excesses. (Approbation and renewed applause from the benches of the majority.)

"And the same change which I have pointed out, which you admit and point out yourselves, in the political world, the same change has taken place in the Church and that Catholic world, the destinies of which at present occupy us.

"When Pius IX. ascended the throne, and when, seeing before him modern liberty and democracy, he embraced them as his daughters, and called himself their father; from that day a difference of opinion sprang up within the Catholic Church. Some—and they were the minority—cautious, timid, somewhat diplomatic spirits, people generally of years and experience, said,—The Pope is risking a very dangerous experiment, which may turn out very badly for him. Others—and they were the great majority, and I was of the number myself, gentlemen; yes, I and my friends, who were then called the Catholic party—received with delight and enthusiasm this initiative of the Pope. Well, we are obliged to say that we have received a cruel disappointment. The issue of the experiment has turned, not against Pius IX. or us, but against liberty. (Hear, hear, on the right.) Would that I had here before me all those demagogues, those firebrands, of whom I spoke just now; I would say the truth to them once for all. (Approbation on the right. Murmurs on the left. On the right, "Go on, go on!")

"Here is the truth I would tell them, if I had them all together here: I would ask them,—Do you know what is the greatest of your crimes against the human race? It is not only the innocent blood you have shed, though it is crying to Heaven for vengeance against you; it is not only that you have sown broad-cast ruin over Europe, though that is the most formidable argument against your doctrines: no; it is that you have disenchanted the world with liberty! (Cheers on the right. Hear, hear.) It is that you have taught men to curse what they had loved! It is that you have compromised, or shaken, or extinguished, the noblest aspiration of all generous hearts! It is that you have dashed back upon itself the torrent of the destinies of mankind!" (Enthusiastic cheering on the benches of the majority.)

It is surely superfluous to point out to my readers the force and conclusiveness of this language; or to remind them at what epoch it was uttered from the tribune of the

French parliament; just after those ill-omened days, which had stained Paris with blood, and horrified the world; when the earth had scarcely ceased from shaking under men's feet; and just before those new convulsions, which were destined to transfer France, in her despair, from the arms of the republic to the hands of the imperial power. The speaker continues:—

"I cherish the belief that Pius IX. does not yet feel himself reduced to the deplorable alternative which I have alluded to; I am confident he feels that there is a middle course, between that sovereignty of evil which a false liberty demands, and a complete and aggravated return to despotism. But do you, at least, faithful friends of genuine and suffering liberty, the perils and the woes of which I have been delineating, *aid him in his task; do not embarrass, do not discourage him; his position is already sufficiently arduous and painful, take care not to multiply its complications:* lend him the support of your sympathy and your respect, concur with his pure intentions and his conscientious zeal, in tracing out that middle course for which we long—all we whose faith in liberty has not been even yet annihilated." (Loud cheers on the right.)

Alas! I cannot but pause here to ask, with grief—forgetting for a moment the time when such grand sentiments were proclaimed amid the acclamations of France, and my attention being painfully recalled to our own day—has all this been done? I ask those who have been for ten years unremittingly provoking a revolt in the Roman States, who have never ceased to menace the Pontiff with their conspiracies,—I ask them, have they *aided the Pope in his task?* Or have they not rather striven *to multiply the complications of his position, already arduous and painful enough?* Far from *lending him the support of their sympathy and respect,* have they not been ever renewing their outrages against him? Far from *concurring with his pure intentions and his conscientious zeal to trace out that middle course which the true friends of liberty longed to see,* have they not laid snares for his feet, and done all that depended on them to render his Government impossible? All this we shall soon have occasion to examine in the fullest detail. But to return to M. de Montalembert.

A great and final question remained. There were those who had said, *the Pope must be coerced.* Such was the odious, the ungenerous proposal, which remained to be held up to reprobation: and here the soul of the speaker kindles: his faith, his love, and devotion to the Church, his inmost and liveliest emotions, break forth into words. The counsels he gives, too, are those of profound and enlightened polity; and statesmen, kings, and the congress, if one is ever to assemble, would do well to weigh these passages of M. de Montalembert's speech:—

"Let us see first, how you would set about coercing him, for it would be folly to enter, as has been often done of late, upon a vague, undefined course, without examining whither it leads, or anticipating its inevitable consequences. I am convinced that there is not one here present who would propose to employ personal violence. As to the government, it is clear, from the generous language used yesterday by the minister of foreign affairs, that it does not contemplate for an instant a recourse to constraint or violence. Nay, I am convinced that no one here, whether in the majority, or even the minority, entertains such an idea. Do not tell me I am wrong, I would implore of you." (Interruptions.)

A voice on the left.—"Ah! comme c'est gentilhomme!"

M. DE MONTALEMBERT.—" I say that no one here, on either side, would deliberately propose to employ personal violence against the Holy Father. (On the left, 'No!') We are then agreed.

"Well then, since you disclaim, without exception, the intention of renewing against Pius IX. the violent measures which have been used towards Boniface VIII., and so many other popes, avoid entering upon a road which may conduct you to the violence you have disavowed beforehand. Allow me to ask you whether you imagine that they who ended by laying violent hands upon the Holy See, and upon the sovereign Pontiffs themselves, commenced their strife with the Holy See with such an intention? Do you think they said to themselves on starting, I will make the Pope prisoner, I will proceed to extremities against him? I am convinced that it was not so: but that they drifted into it, as you would do yourselves, through vexation, through impatience, or through wounded pride, urging them to carry out threats which had been uttered lightly and imprudently, and which had had no effect. It was in this way they were led on to violence. (Sensation.)

"Do you think that, at the outset of the struggle between Napoleon and Pius VII., the former foresaw the necessity in which he would, as he considered, ultimately be placed, of dragging the Pope prisoner to Savona and Fontainebleau? I am convinced of the contrary: and as I have cited these names and incidents, which have been already brought forward in this debate by General Cavaignac, I shall pause a moment. I know that this defeat of Napoleon by Pius VII. is one of the commonplaces of history; but it conveys great lessons: and first of all the following, which seems very generally overlooked:—people say, after all, our difference with the Holy See concerns only a temporal question, in no way connected with spiritual authority or dogmatic truth. Yes; but was it a spiritual or dogmatic object which actuated Napoleon in his controversy with Pius VII.? Far from it: it was purely and simply a temporal object, relating to police regulations and declarations of war. Pius VII. would not shut his ports against the English, and refused to declare war against them, just like Pius IX., who has been dethroned by his subjects because he would not make war upon the Austrians. Still, for all that, the world has seen in Pius VII. a martyr of the rights of the Church!

"And what has been the result of this conflict between Napoleon and Pius VII.? To the great emperor it resulted in discredit and loss of influence, and finally, in a complete defeat. For,—and this is most important to remark, and should strike even the most prejudiced minds, even those who least share the predilections which you probably imagine are now predominant in me,—it is not only discredit and loss of influence which sooner or later attach to those who combat the Holy See, but defeat too! Yes, nothing is more certain than their failure!

"And why is failure certain? Ah! because—note this carefully —the odds are not equal between the Holy See and you, or any others who would contend against it. And learn that these odds are not for you, but against you. You have 500,000 bayonets, artillery, fleets, and all the resources which physical force can supply. True; and the Pope has none; but he has what you have not: a moral force, an empire over men's souls and consciences, to which you can never pretend, and that empire is immortal!" (Dissent on the left. Marked cheers on the right.)

All who were present on that memorable day can remember the irritation here displayed by the "Mountain;" still their empty clamour could not altogether conceal their shame and vexation, and their presentiment of a defeat; they were evidently cowed. The speaker continued, returning to a happy comparison of M. Thiers:—

"You deny moral force, you deny faith, you deny the empire of the Papal power over souls, that power before which the proudest emperors have bowed. Yes, but one thing you cannot deny—the weakness of the Holy See. Now, know that this weakness gives it an invincible force against you. Yes, there is not in the history of the world a grander or more consoling sight than the perplexities of force when it enters the lists against weakness. (Applause on the right.)

"Allow me a familiar comparison: when a man comes to contend with a woman, if she be not the most degraded of beings, she can brave him with impunity: she says, 'Strike, you only dishonour yourself, and you do not conquer me.' (Hear, hear.) Well! the Church is more than a woman: she is a mother!" (Hear, hear.— A triple round of applause is called forth by this expression of the speaker.)

This put an end to the contest; the admiration of the Assembly extended even to the extreme left; some of the "Mountain," carried away by the general enthusiasm, were seen to applaud and clap. The victory was complete. It only remained for M. de Montalembert, in conclusion, to attack the vain pretensions of his adversaries to elevate ideas to the place of dogmas; and to pay a well-merited tribute to the French army.

"You are perhaps aware, gentlemen, that the Church has an old text, *non possumus*, in an old book called the Acts of the Apostles; that text was first used by an old Pope named St. Peter. (General laughter and approbation.) And, rely on it, with that phrase she will go on to the end of the world without yielding. (Clamour on the left.)

"I feel that it is time to conclude, still I should wish to say one word more in reply to M. Victor Hugo, and to denounce his principle that ideas are as invincible and durable as dogmas. To create ideas, and to attribute to them the eternity and immutability of dogmas, is indeed, nowadays, a right too generally asserted. Well, allow me to say that it is a chimerical pretension. (Murmurs on the left.) Yes, chimerical. There is no idea which can resist cannon and physical force so firmly as M. Victor Hugo supposes; and that for three reasons: first, because ideas are variable, and dogmas are immutable. (Hear, hear.) Secondly, because ideas are cut out by you or me,—we know in what laboratories they are compounded. (General laughter, and cheers on the right.) Dogmas, on the contrary, have a mysterious and supernatural origin. (Oh! oh! on the left. Hear, hear, on the right.) And, lastly, the reign of ideas is temporary; and they only reign over the imagination, or at most, over the passions and the reason: while dogmas reign over the conscience. Such is their difference. (Long cheering on the right.) When M. Victor Hugo finds me an idea which has lasted eighteen centuries, and which numbers a hundred millions of devotees, I am ready to recognize in his idea the rights I am now claiming for the Church. (Laughter on the right.)

"I cannot conclude without noticing a taunt which I have felt as deeply as any here: it has been said that the honour of our flag has been compromised by the expedition against Rome, intended to destroy the Roman republic and restore the authority of the Pope. (Hear, hear, on the left.) As I have said, every one here ought to be alive to such a reproach, and to repudiate it with me. No, the honour of our flag has not been compromised; the colours of France never waved over a more glorious enterprise. (Dissent on the left. Cheers on the right.) History will decide. I appeal with confidence to her decision. (So do we! on the left.) So do you; well, let us all appeal to her. If I am not mistaken, history will cast a veil over all those indecisions, those tergiversations, and those disputes, which you pointed out so bitterly and so eagerly, in the hope of creating dissensions amongst us (hear); she will cast a veil over all these, or will record them only to magnify the enterprise by the number and the nature of the difficulties which had been overcome. (Renewed cheers on the right.)

"But history will say that a thousand years after Charlemagne, and fifty after Napoleon—a thousand years from the epoch when Charlemagne immortalized himself by restoring the Papal power, and fifty from that, when Napoleon, at the zenith of his glory, fell for having attempted to undo the work of his immortal predecessor, France was true to her traditions, and deaf to the odious suggestions made to her. She will say, that 30,000 Frenchmen, commanded by the worthy heir of one of the giant names of our imperial glory (loud cheers on the right), left the shores of their country to restore, at Rome, in the person of the Pope, law, equity, and the interests of France and of Europe. (Cheers on the right. Murmurs on the left.) She will say that which Pius IX. himself said in his letter of thanks to General Oudinot: 'The victory won by the French arms has been won against the enemies of human society.' Yes, such will be the sentence of history, and it will be one of her brightest pages.

"Who would now dim, tarnish, or attenuate such glory, and precipitate us into a maze of complications, contradictions, and inextricable inconsistencies? Would you know what would for ever stain the glory of the French flag? To raise it against the Cross, against the tiara which it has just set free; to transform the French soldier from the Pope's protector into his oppressor; in short, to prefer a poor imitation of Garibaldi to the mission and the glory of Charlemagne." (Loud and long applause on the right.)

This speech, says the *Journal des Debats,* was followed by applause such as no one ever remembers to have heard in the deliberative Assemblies.

I must conclude; but I would first add, to the honour of M. de Montalembert and of those in our two National Assemblies who fought by his side in that great and memorable conflict, that, if never speeches were more applauded, never did any better deserve it. Never was enthusiasm better justified, never was human oratory more nobly used. People might well exclaim, honour, all honour to such eloquence, and to the efficacy which God at times accords to it, in the conflict of good and evil, in the struggle of conscience against evil passions! Honour to the men who place such eloquence at the service of a noble and holy cause! It is consoling and glorious to think that arms are not the only rampart of human society, and that speech can, at times, combat and conquer as effectually. It was generally felt indeed at that epoch, that the success of such speeches was not an idle oratorical triumph; that it was the victory of society; that order in Europe was deeply interested in the signal defeat of the revolutionary principle in our National Assembly, as well as in its defeat at Rome by our soldiers. And it was for this reason that these successes were echoed throughout Paris, throughout France, and the whole world. The good rejoiced. I can still remember how people congratulated each other on leaving the Assembly; they spoke without being acquainted, or rather they felt as if they knew each other, as if they were united by common sentiments of admiration, of joy, and of confidence: they felt a new strength, they foresaw better days in the future; their souls seemed to expand with hope.

And they were right; for France had done great things; she had both spoken and acted gloriously. She had shown herself courageously true to her history, her ancient traditions, and her providential vocation; and by her hands, chivalrous as in other days, a new and grand page had been added to the *Gesta Dei per Francos*.

Providence, in fact, chooses the noblest peoples here below to execute its divine counsels; or rather Providence raises up noble peoples and great races, and prepares them for the great missions it has destined for them. "The Son of God," a Pope has written, "whose commands the universe obeys, has constituted the different empires; according to the distinctions of tongues and races, He has raised up the different peoples, to be the ministers of His heavenly will; and as the tribe of Juda received a special benediction above the other sons of the patriarch, so the kingdom of France has been distinguished by the Lord with a peculiar prerogative of honour and favour."[1] And what is this prerogative, this mission of France? It is easy to see that her great mission upon earth has always been to serve as sword and shield to the Church, and thereby to European civilization.

In the eighth century the popes had recognized and signified to the Frank kings this great choice of Providence: "Consider, O my son," wrote Pope Stephen to Pepin the Short,—"consider and reflect carefully, I conjure you in the name of the living God: reflect that, after God and the Prince of His Apostles, our future and that of the Roman people principally depends upon you, whom Providence has so favoured, and upon the French nation." The triumphs of Pepin soon justified the confidence of the Pontiff; and Stephen II., gloriously restored to the eternal city by the Franks, again wrote to his deliverer:— "Our tongue, beloved son, cannot express the consolation which your actions and your courage have afforded us. We have, in fact, seen the Divine Omnipotence work miracles by you, and deliver the Roman Church. May we be permitted to exclaim with the angels of the Lord:— *Glory to God in the highest; and on earth peace to men of*

---

[1] "Dei filius cujus imperiis totus orbis obsequitur, cujus beneplacitis coelestis exercitûs agmina famulantur, secundum divisiones linguarum et gentium signum divinæ potentiæ diversa regna constituit, diversa populorum regimina in ministerium mandatorum coelestium ordinavit: inter quæ sicut tribus Juda inter ceteros filios patriarchæ ad specialis benedictionis dona suscipitur, sic regnum Franciæ ceteris terrarum populis a Domino prærogativâ honoris et gratiæ insignitur."

good will. For but one year ago, at this season, surrounded as we are by our enemies, we were mourning in sadness, we were defenceless against their attacks; but now your powerful aid has delivered us from the dangers which threatened us, and we feel a boundless joy; we bless the Lord, and cry with the Psalmist: *This is the Lord's doing; and it is wonderful in our eyes.*"[1]

Pius IX. himself repeated to General Oudinot, after our victorious expedition of 1849, the touching language addressed by Stephen II. to Pepin: and it was glorious for our country to hear the successor of Stephen II., ten centuries after Pepin and Charlemagne, recall these ancient and grand reminiscences, and address the same language to the chief of our gallant army.

"The children of France are a chosen generation! and we shall never cease to proclaim the praises of your name throughout the world. What thanks shall we render to your army? No language could do justice to your deserts; but there is in heaven a just judge, the Lord our God, who will reward you according to your works. Yes, you have raised the name of your country above the name and glory of many nations, and the honour of the kingdom of the Franks shines with a grateful light in the eyes of the Lord." Thus to thank and to honour France, Pius IX. had only to recall her ancient deeds, and to borrow the language of his predecessors, protected and liberated, as himself, by France. Like Leo III. addressing Charlemagne, Pius IX. adds these words, to the undying honour of the French name:—"There is in heaven a God who sounds the hearts and reins, and knows the love we bear you; it delights me to convey to you those sentiments of my paternal affection, and to tell you of the prayers which I unceasingly offer to the Lord for the army and the government of France, and for the whole nation. For the victory of the French arms has been won against the foes of

---

[1] Letter VI. of Pope Stephen to Pepin the Short, SS. Concil. Coll. tom. xii.

human society, and for this reason it ought ever to excite the grateful feelings of every honest man in Europe and throughout the world."

May France never be false to these grand memories of her past, which so eloquently lay down for her her duty, as regard both the present and the future! If she ever departs from them, she will inevitably incur the retribution which, as history declares, awaits such nations as are traitors to their mission. If she but continue herself, she will preserve inviolate the noblest and purest glory that has ever graced a people's brow.

CHAPTER XV.

FRANCE; 1849–1859.

WHY IS THERE STILL A ROMAN QUESTION?

WE have assuredly a right to ask, after the events detailed in the preceding chapters, Why should there be still a Roman question? Why is the question of the temporal sovereignty of the Holy See argued among us still? How is it that 1859 has rekindled a controversy that 1849 had settled amid the applauses of assembled France?

As we have seen and felt, *it was indubitably the heart of France that beat in 1849, and her voice that pronounced*, as the Bishop of Arras has expressed it. Can the heart of France have changed since then?

I can understand that the honour and independence of the Church should be for ever contested by her eternal enemies; but that the temporal sovereignty of the Pope should still be an open question with us, Catholic French, with any man of honour and good faith, with true statesmen, or with European governments — that after the noble solution which it received from France and Europe in 1849, we should now seem about to solve it in a directly opposite sense, is to me an enigma which I confess I cannot decipher.

Are we to understand that the principles on which France then acted, in vindicating the rights of the Holy See, by her sword, by the discerning policy of her statesmen, and by the eloquence of her orators, were the miserable ones of political expediency, which every breath can alter? Or were they the eternal, immutable principles of reason, of honour, and of right? Is it not true that the great religious and social interests which were at issue in those memorable debates, all those grand principles of justice, of Catholic and European law, which then merged all differences, drew together all the sections of the great party of order, and impelled republican France, in spite of formidable difficulties, to vindicate the rights of the Holy See, that all these reasons still remain unchanged, and now command us, as imperatively as then, to respect the Papal sovereignty?

I repeat, why is there still a Roman question to resolve?

After having done such great things, why must we quietly see them undone? Why should the France of 1859, more powerful, more united than she then was, having defeated Austria, her camps still pitched in Italy, renounce, with miserable inconsistency, the glory she had acquired at the expense of such magnanimous exertions, and in less propitious times? Is the "Mountain," whose fury was then foiled by the energy of reason, honour, justice, and eloquence, to win to-day, to the amazement and dismay of the Catholic world, a triumph for which it struggled in vain in its most palmy days? And are the pernicious ideas, the subversive theories, so solemnly disavowed by republican France, as contrary to her traditionary policy, to her patriotism, her sincerity, and her religious faith, now to rise from their ashes and to reign in Italy, under the eyes of our army?

No; however may be appearances, what is now doing cannot be the definitive solution of the difficulty: it cannot be, that after having delivered Pius IX. from his afflictions with the sword of Charlemagne, as M. de Montalembert said amid the cheers of the Assembly, we are now to swell the triumph of Garibaldi. It is written in our annals and in those of the Church, that, ten years ago, thirty thousand Frenchmen left their country in order to restore, at Rome, and in the person of one of the most holy pontiffs of his age, the law, the equity, and the interests of Europe. As Pius IX. wrote to General Oudinot, that triumph of the French arms will be recorded by history as a glory of France and the nineteenth century. I can understand that those who were then conquered should wish to efface this glory of the French flag; that the irreconcilable foes of the Holy See should return to their old conspiracies, and send Garibaldi in arms to threaten the Roman States; that they should presume to speak of dismembering them, though in the presence of our camps and our sword; all this I can conceive; but what I never will admit is, that we, the restorers of the Pope, the champions, too, of the true liberty of Italy, are in any way to be associated with such odious schemes, or that any one is to pretend, directly or indirectly, to represent us as accomplices in a policy and a usurpation which justice condemns and history will reprobate.

What ought we to demand, what do we demand, at so sad a juncture—we Catholic French?

We require that no one shall lay his hand upon the pontifical sovereignty, that ambition shall be prevented from dispossessing the Church of her states, that our national glory remain inviolate, that it be not betrayed or curtailed by any; in a word, that we continue the work and mission of Charlemagne. We ask that France turn, as in 1849, a deaf ear to the odious suggestions made to her, and remain true to herself, and to the real interests of Italy, of Europe, and of Catholicism.

Such were the lofty considerations which, in the parliamentary conflicts of 1849, and in the counsels of the governments of France and other countries, frustrated the narrow, revolutionary, and irreligious policy represented by the " Mountain," which, having paralyzed the Constituent, and even extorted from the Assembly a vote of blame against our army, broke out into menacing invectives and furious interruptions, in the journals and the Assembly; thus evidently showing that the enemies of public order fully appreciated the anti-revolutionary import of the Roman expedition, and felt that a reaction against disorder in France and the rest of Europe would inevitably be inaugurated by the triumph of our army.

And, we would ask, has any one argument which triumphed in 1849 now lost its cogency, and have the sophisms, then exposed by the speakers on the side of order, suddenly grown into logical truths? Has the essence of the things changed? Have the immutable principles of right varied? Has not the Papal sovereignty still the same origin, the same nature, the same necessity, both political and religious? Is the Pope no longer the Pope? Is Pius IX. no longer Pius IX.? Has the revolution ceased to be the revolution? Is what the Prince President of the French Republic proclaimed, what his ministers and ambassadors said of Pius IX., of his generous initiative, of his efforts to give liberty to his subjects, and hopes of a better lot to Italy,—and what they added as to the ingratitude of which he was, and is, the victim,— is all this no longer historical, no longer true? Is not he the Pontiff, then so insulted, and still so calumniated, who, as M. Thiers said, gave from the Vatican the signal of reforms to the Italian princes? Was he not the author and promoter of the whole liberal movement in Italy for the two years after his accession? as M. de Falloux said; he whom they saluted with such acclamations; he—to continue that orator's description—against whom they invented the conspiracy of ovations, and whom they conducted from one triumph to another, till the day when the dagger and torch flashed upon the threshold of his palace.

Are we now asking for anything that was not then asked for? We went to Italy to guard the interests of Catholicism, and in them those of France; so it was proclaimed in the National and Legislative Assemblies, in spite of passions, violence, and tergiversation. It was said: "The Papacy is not an Italian institution, but an institution of public, universal law, the maintenance of which is intimately connected with that of order and the creed of the West." We say so still, and with equal truth. It was said again: "The question is not Italian, nor French, nor even European, only, but Catholic,—that is, the most vast and elevated one that can be put: it regards the spiritual sovereign of two hundred millions of souls, and the state which is the centre of that sovereignty; it regards the liberty of the Catholic idea, of the Catholic conscience." Such were the sentiments then expressed; we now repeat them, and they will for ever compel assent. It was then proposed that France "should impose a debt of admiration and gratitude upon the hearts and consciences of two hundred millions of men, scattered over the face of the whole earth." Well, we ask that France continue to merit such an honour.

As a right due to Catholics, people then demanded the maintenance of the rights, liberty, and sovereignty of the Pope. They said: "The liberty of the Pope is an essential condition, *sine qua non*, of the religious liberty of Catholics; for if the Pope, the supreme judge, the living organ, of the law and the faith of Catholics, is not free, we cease to be so ourselves." It was well explained, and well understood, that we were going to Rome to defend the independence and inviolability of the Pope's temporal power; to uphold that noble and sacred cause, according to the traditional policy of France for more than a thousand years! and all this we now but repeat.

The noble letter to General Oudinot, the commander-in-chief of the Roman expedition, the very day after a hostile vote (7th of May) associated Prince Louis Napoleon with this religious and truly French policy. The message of the President of the Republic, as his plenipotentiary at Rome, M. de Corcelles, remarked, clearly stated the Italian question, and accurately specified the object which France had pursued in Italy. "In fact," runs the message, "our presence resulted in the return of Pius IX., and that sovereign, true to himself, brought back with him liberty and reconciliation; once at Rome, we secured the integrity of the territory of the Holy See, and the re-establishment of the Papal authority in the towns which had thrown it off." What more do we wish or ask for at present?

It was shown, in fine, with overwhelming eloquence and sagacious political discernment, that the Roman States, the States of the Church, have, as their very name indicates, received from Providence, from history, from Catholic Christianity, a special destination, whence result for them special, exceptional, inviolable rights; and also —with some drawbacks, it is true, as everything human has—a greatness without a parallel and without a rival.

Let us recapitulate, and again inquire: How is it that there is still a Roman question?

It is easy to see that Mazzini and Garibaldi will not consider the Roman question settled as long as the Pope is at the Vatican. We know what they want. Europe is aware of what their ends are; and till they gain them, the Roman question, and others too, will be regarded by them as still open. They failed in 1849: well, they have returned to the charge in 1859; no power, of course, can settle the question for them, if not in their own way. But the case should be somewhat different as regards France and Europe. Why does a question which was examined, discussed, and decided in 1849, recur in 1859? In the great councils of international polity, is there never to be an end to suits, is the law never to be, once for all, laid down? Why should the Roman question receive now a solution directly opposed to that which it so recently received?

Once more, what is it that has changed during this short interval of ten years? Is it principles? Is it facts?

It is not principles: reasons based upon fundamental principles and the very nature of things cannot change so readily.

Is it facts? All the changes in facts that have come about, so far from controverting the solution of 1849, speak in its favour, and render such a solution of the difficulty easier and not less necessary in 1860.

What are these changes? The insurrection in the Romagna? But in 1849 insurrection had triumphed at Rome and in all the Papal States. Affairs were in a far worse state; greater obstacles were in the way. The power of the Holy Father has now only to be upheld; then it had to be restored. The Pope is now at Rome, but in 1849 he was a fugitive at Gaeta.

The political changes in France? France was then a republic. It was republican hands which were asked to demolish the Roman republic and restore the Pope. Now she is an empire: her government is active, vigorous, and concentrated. It has no assembly to combat; no "Mountain" to overawe.

The general state of Europe? In 1849 Europe was on fire, over a volcano, shaken by endless revolutions. At present it is incomparably calmer. The cause of order, though still threatened, has gained considerable stability; the friends of order are more numerous, its enemies much weaker. We have gained some grounds—at least one would hope so—in ten years; and why should we spontaneously yield what we have gained? Are we tired of the little order and peace that we have recovered? We are, then, to begin over again every ten years: the revolutionary principle was overpowered yesterday, only to be let loose upon Europe again to-day! And it is idle to say: Why, Piedmont is a monarchy,—it is not the revolution. I shall soon have occasion to study this momentous point: for the present I shall merely say, that it cannot be denied that the principle of revolution is triumphing, and that therefore France and Europe are in peril.

England, indeed, may be indifferent to continental revolutions, which have seemed hitherto not to touch her: let us leave her to admire them, to second them, or seek to turn them to account, if she will. But is it desirable for us,

a great continental power,—who have suffered so much
ourselves, and been the cause of such suffering to others,
by our revolutions for the last sixty years, and who have
still within our bosom so many revolutionary elements,—
that the conflagration should burst out again at our doors,
when we are so inflammable within? It was an act of
prudence, in 1849, to go to extinguish it at Rome: let us
not be so infatuated as to rekindle it in 1860.

No; neither the principles put forward in 1849, which
are unchanged, nor the facts, which now are more in our
favour, justify a reconsideration of the Roman question.
The cause has been heard, and the judgment executed.
France cannot, after a lapse of ten years, stultify herself,
and undo what she has done.

What, then, can be the cause that has again started
the Roman question? Why are we reconsidering the
final decision we had come to? The cause is not in the
things themselves; it is not at Rome, nor even in France:
it must be looked for elsewhere. I will state what it is.
There is still a Roman question, and the interests of
religion and society are suffering in Italy, because there
is a great revolutionary ambition in Piedmont.

Nor is this my private opinion only; the famous pamphlet, "Napoléon III. et l'Italie," has already said most
truly: "The interests of religion suffer in Piedmont: it
is urgent, for many reasons, to put a stop, in a Catholic
country, to a rupture with the court of Rome, which is
an encouragement to revolutionary passions, an affliction
and a trouble *to consciences, and a real danger to governments.*"

Indeed, religious schism and social revolution must
necessarily result from such a state of things; and, as the
pamphlet we cite from continues, "it was pregnant with
dangers, not only to Piedmont, but to the whole of Italy
and to Europe, which it would be the height of political
folly to overlook."

The celebrated pamphlet also called attention to the
danger of rousing " the revolutionary element, of letting
loose subversive theories and indomitable passions, alike

incompatible with *European order, the laws of civilization, religious interests, and the political independence of the Papacy."*

No one could speak more admirably than this; for my part, I can but commend such counsels; and in entering upon the historical details which follow, I recur to them with feelings of gratitude. But I do so with sadness too, because they have been unfruitful, and because, in spite of them, a great revolutionary ambition has broken out in Italy, which is alike incompatible *with European order,* the laws of civilization, *and the independence of the Papacy:* and this is why there is still a Roman question!

CHAPTER XVI.

PIEDMONT.

FIRST PERIOD: HOSTILITY TO THE HOLY SEE—LAWS AGAINST THE CHURCH—RELIGIOUS PERSECUTION.

IN this long task, nothing has been so painful to me as what I am now entering on.

Hitherto it has been a consolation to me, though engaged in a painful controversy, to pay homage to, and to feel myself supported by, illustrious men, noble characters, and great actions. In this way, the contest was not without its consolations. But now I must deny myself everything that is cheering, and follow my adversaries into regions unknown to honour, to dignity, and to justice. I have now to discuss degrading actions, to unmask subterfuges, to reveal the cravings of ambition, and to denounce violence and outrage.

I shall endeavour to render this sad task as short as possible, and confine myself to the duties of a mere historian. I shall cite facts and dates, without comments; acts and words, neither more nor less; in short, I shall record the policy of the Piedmontese ministry for the last ten years—all that it has done against the Church, against France, against all the principles of equity which are recognised in Europe.

It may, perhaps, appear surprising that a French bishop, and a native of Savoy, should write these pages upon Piedmont; I have, however, some right to do so, and perhaps am not doing more than my duty. France is my country. I owe her much, and she is dear to me. Piedmont has not done honour to her alliance, nor kept faith with her. I love and esteem Savoy; Piedmont has been disquieting it for the last ten years, and has succeeded in alienating it from the noble and ancient house, whose cradle was in Savoy, which bears its name, and was so long an honour to it. I have a second, and still holier country, the Church; Piedmont is an affliction to her. Eminent men have said, as we have seen in the preceding pages, that Italy is a hallowed land, where every one feels himself the most at home, after his own country, in faith, in sympathies, and feelings. Even the pamphlet, "Napoleon III. et l'Italie," says,—" Italy represents in history something greater than a nationality: it represents civilization. From this chosen land have sprung the immortal principles and the glorious examples which have formed men and peoples." Well, I am deeply grieved to see that irreligious and anarchical passions are on the point of again causing the ruin of Italy.

Whatever, then, has been touched by the blighting influence of Piedmontese policy has suffered. Savoy, France, Italy, the Church; all that is most delicate and most sacred, faith and conscience, bear its traces. There was a Pope of whom it was said, " Italian patriotism in him is united to all the virtues of a Christian; he was worthy to regenerate Italy. Such was his first idea after his accession: his name was the symbol of liberty, and a warrant for every hope."[1] Well, it is against this Pope

---

[1] Napoleon III. et l'Italie.

that the policy of Piedmont has pronounced and has conspired. Yet he was the Pope who " addressed the Emperor of Austria while the Austrians were carrying on, against the Lombardo-Venetians, a conflict so painful to his patriotism as an Italian prince, and to his heart as a pontiff; and who laid down in these terms the duties and the vocation of Germany:—'We trust that the German people, who feel such a noble pride in their own nationality, will not think that their honour obliges them to sanguinary assaults upon the Italian nation; but will rather feel it becoming to recognise her nobly as a sister; and that both our daughters, each so dear to our heart, will agree each to inhabit her own territory, where they shall live a life honourable and blessed of the Lord.'"[1] All this has been shamelessly forgotten to the gentle and great pontiff, and the future of Italy abandoned to the hazards of the revolutionary tempest.

Why has this been so? Who is the evil genius of Piedmont and of Italy? Who has been the real promoter of this deplorable series of attacks upon religion, upon justice, upon all the feelings that are dear to a Christian heart? Who is he of whom it was just to say, that when he disappears from the scene, the good begin to hope, and the wicked are dismayed; and that, when the current of revolution wafts him back to it, the good tremble, and the men of anarchy exult? Facts will supply the answers to these questions; not hidden facts and private documents, but facts and documents of public notoriety, chronicled in all the journals of Europe, but yet which seem strangely overlooked: in them may nevertheless be traced, in unmistakable characters, the workings of a deep and nefarious plot; and, to use an expression which is not new, but which indicated an acute perception of the real state of things, they demonstrated that *all the acts of aggression against Pius IX. are not the movement of a people, but the work of a conspiracy.*[2]

---

[1] Napoleon III. et l'Italie.
[2] Message of Prince Louis Napoleon, in 1849.

In what I am going to review here, as to the policy pursued by Piedmont during the last twelve years, I shall distinguish three periods:—

In the first, this policy is concealed, but is being organized; in the second, it unmasks itself; in the third, it explodes. Will Europe sanction the result at which it has arrived? . . . . .

However that may be, by the following plain and faithful statement of facts, I shall have defended a sacred and innocent cause; I shall have proved to the least intelligent whether the invasion of the Papal States by an ambitious neighbour dates only from the insurrection in the Romagna, and who are the true authors of that insurrection; whether everything has not been done to stir up impious and anarchical passions in Italy, under the pretence of quieting them by concessions; whether it is not those who exclaim at the state of things in the Papal dominions who have themselves created and maintained it; whether they have not arrested, by incessant agitation, the reforms and improvements which were, and are still, contemplated and desired by the Pope; in a word, whether any efforts have been spared to swell a few malcontents into a nation of rebels, to change a tranquil and contented people into a revolutionary populace. And I would repeat, I am going now to write history; so that, if any find that it condemns them, it is not I who am their accuser.

I.

Far be it from me to wish to attack Piedmontese institutions, or the natural progress of liberty in a nation, or even their ambition for legitimate aggrandizement. No; Piedmont forms a part of that noble Italy whose independence is so dear to us all; and I shall never consider liberty responsible for the crimes of a nefarious policy, or the crying injustice of its usurpations. I am far from pretending that Piedmont had not an important vocation, both before and after the disaster of Novara. By the natural development of liberal institutions and a growing prosperity, by respecting the rights of others, and by concord and union with the only living greatness of Italy, Piedmont might have placed itself at the head of the whole Italian nation, and have brought about, by such a peaceful and noble influence, the true independence and liberty of the whole Peninsula. But she preferred revolutionary methods. It was from the moment when the liberal movement so generously inaugurated by Pius IX. began to propagate itself throughout the states of Italy, that Piedmont declared war against the Church; and far from drawing closer to Pius IX., became the avowed enemy of the Papacy. As if it were necessary to prepare the way for the usurpation of provinces by the oppression and spoliation of the clergy, the establishment of Piedmontese liberty was the commencement and the signal for the bondage and the persecution of religion in Piedmont.

When Charles Albert granted his constitution, the Episcopate of the Sardinian kingdom, as was admitted by one of M. Cavour's admirers, M. Chiala, received with approbation the reforms and the *constitutional statute*. Mazzini himself applauded, on this point, the Piedmontese and Italian clergy. In 1848 he wrote:—" The clergy is by no means hostile to liberal institutions. . . . . Do not attack the clergy; promise them liberty, and they will side with you." Ricotti and others have said, " *Il clero si mostrava, e forse era piutosto propenso alla monarchia costituzionale.*"

How were these sympathies of the clergy for the constitutional monarchy requited? No Piedmontese is ignorant of the laws made by his country against the liberty of Catholics, the liberty of the bishops, against the most unquestionable rights of episcopal authority and teaching, and the most sacred commands of the Church; against the treaties and concordats solemnly concluded with her; against bishops, priests, and religious; even against poor women, the servants of the sick, of children, and of the poor.

Thus, it was at the moment when the liberty of the press was proclaimed in Piedmont (Oct., 1847) that all acts published by the bishops were rendered subject to the *Censure*. A year later (Oct., 1848) lay boards are appointed to superintend the schools and the education of youth in general, their powers extending to religious instruction, catechisms, and the choice of spiritual directors; and it was in virtue of this law that, on the 23rd of October, the minister of public instruction, M. Buoncompagni, since governor of Central Italy, appointed spiritual directors, without consulting the bishops, and replied to the prelates who remonstrated, that if the Episcopate were against him, he had the support of others. In December, 1848, it is decided that the theses for the public examinations in the University of Turin shall no longer be submitted to the bishops for their approbation.

Continuing to carry out their ideas, the Government attempt, in May 1851, to found a state theology; they propose to subject the diocesan schools of theology to the inspection of government delegates, and to oblige the professors of theology in the ecclesiastical seminaries to follow the programmes of the University of Turin. Now, in this University of Turin, whose teaching is attempted to be imposed upon the bishops, after all checks upon it have been taken out of their hands, a professor of canon law then maintained, among other errors, the following theses: The omnipotence of the state over the Church; the impossibility of proving marriage to be a sacrament; that the Church has no right to pronounce upon the impediments to marriage. The same professor accused the Catholic Church, and particularly the Holy See, of having caused the schism of the East; and, as if to open the question of the spoliation of the Papal sovereignty, he disserted upon the incompatibility of the Pope's temporal power with his spiritual. The Holy See, the guardian of faith, and of the rights of the Church, condemned this professor by a decree of the 22nd August, 1851. The Papal condemnation, and the complaints of the bishops, had no other effect, as to the culprit, than to move him, in the same university, from the chair of canon law to that of Roman law.

The doctrine proscribed by the Holy See continuing to be taught in the university, the bishops, as was their duty, warned their clergy of it. How did the ministry treat this salutary warning of the bishops? By a circular (Oct., 1851), in which they signified to all clerks that they could not be appointed to benefices without having frequented these universities.

But all this, and much more, was but the prelude to new and graver changes, and still more audacious measures. I shall only mention the principal: the law which abolished all ecclesiastical immunities, and reduced the number of feasts recognised by law (9th April, 1850); the bill relating to civil marriage (12th June, 1852) ; the law suppressing the religious orders, and confiscating their property (22nd May, 1855); and the violation of all the concordats.

What was the intention of the Sardinian Government in all these measures? What ultimate end was such policy aiming at? What latent designs animated it, whose promotion, it would seem, required to deaden in advance all religious sentiment, and all influence of Catholicism among the people? We shall see in the sequel. In the mean time, I will merely state the facts, remarking, with a French magistrate, M. Foisset, that they wantonly committed at Turin the grievous mistake of the Constituent Assembly in France, namely, the simultaneous establishment of the parliamentary system and of schism; and that in the face of the sympathy which the clergy had expressed for liberal institutions. In a word, they sowed the wind, because they wanted the whirlwind.

II.

But one is not so much struck by what is fatal, irreligious, and schismatical in these measures, as what is almost more painful to observe, the profound duplicity with which the Government acted towards the Holy See. To enter on such a course without even pretending to negotiate with the Holy See, to declare open war against religion, to break publicly and fully with Rome, would have revealed their purposes too clearly; and this did not suit them. They negotiated, therefore; but during the negotiations, continued to act as if they were a mockery; not troubling themselves about the word or the honour of their plenipotentiaries which had been pledged, they settled all pending questions in their own way; they proceeded from encroachment to encroachment, ever gaining ground, never yielding but in appearance, violating past, and rendering future concordats impossible.[1] Thus negotiations were proposed by Piedmont to the Holy Father in an official note, dated the 6th of June, 1848; and before even resuming the conferences which had been interrupted by the dispersion of the sacred college, and the afflictions and exile of the Pope, they voted the law of the 4th of October.

Thus, too, after the law of the 25th of August, 1849, which was the first step towards the expulsion of the religious, and the sequestration of their property; before the Papal protest on the matter, expressed by the Cardinal Secretary of State, in an official note dated the 22nd of September, had even been answered; while, in consequence of the law of the 25th of April, 1848, relating to the royal *exequatur*—another formal violation of concordats—the envoys of Piedmont were officially addressing insulting notes to the Holy See; while other bills, new violations of the rights of the Church, were being presented to the Chamber of Deputies;—it was then (October,

---

[1] The history of these negotiations has been put forth by the Holy See in an authentic statement, published after the Pontifical allocution of January 22, 1855, which places in its true light this diplomacy, with which the Sardinian Government thought to amuse Rome and the Catholics, without wishing or caring to come to any conclusion, and not meaning the concordats it was negotiating. Is it that peace with Rome would have been a hindrance to too many of their schemes? perhaps the annexionist policy felt it necessary first to declare war against the spiritual power before laying its hand upon the temporal.

1849) that Count Siccardi was sent as a special envoy to the Holy Father, to Portici, to inform him that they were ready to resume the negotiations relating to the Concordat, but requiring that, previously, the bishops of Turin and of Asti, guilty of having protested against the encroachments of the civil power, should be directed to give up their sees.[1] Canonical reasons rendering it impossible for the Pope to satisfy the court of Turin upon this head, Count Siccardi left Portici in November, without having said anything more about the Concordat. The Holy Father then deputed, himself, to Turin, Mgr. Charvaz, Archbishop of Sebasta, now Archbishop of Genoa, to explain to the king the grounds of his refusal. The king, in his answer to His Holiness (25th of January, 1850), promised him his protection for the two prelates, and stated that, on a more favourable occasion, the negotiations touching the Concordat should be resumed. One month later (25th of February), how was the king's word kept? By bringing forward the famous *Siccardi* bill, relating to ecclesiastical immunities and legal holidays, the reason alleged being, that Rome, *having obstinately refused a concordat*, the Government were forced to take their measures in consequence![2]

Assuredly, such conduct was monstrous; and I can understand the Holy Father when he says, as he did a few days ago, "If I had, like St. Peter, the power of striking down men of the character of Ananias and Sapphira, and were I to use it, the Vatican would serve as a tomb for all the diplomatists, who have always come to deceive me."

And it should be remembered that all this was done against a Pope who was not only weak and unarmed, but in exile and affliction! So the bishops of Savoy and all those of Piedmont observed in their address to the king:—

---

[1] Exposé des relations diplomatiques.
[2] Exposé des négociations suivies entre le Saint-Siège et le Gouvernement Sarde.

"To break the concordats made with the Holy See, to take no account of the most solemn treaties signed with it by the august predecessors of His Majesty, and particularly by his most pious father of glorious memory in 1841, (Art. 8 of the Concordat of March 27), to unsettle consciences, to hurt and grieve all those who desire to live and die in obedience to the Catholic Church. . . . . And what moment is chosen for all these violations, this formal contempt of the Church, this open rupture with the Holy See, this commencement of schism? A moment when the Father of Christendom, Pope Pius IX., is exiled from Rome, and is drinking the chalice of sorrow in a foreign land!" "Perhaps," boldly added the bishops of Savoy, "if treaties with a great European power were in question, more caution would have been employed; those powers have effectual means of making themselves respected; but Pius IX. has no army, Pius IX. is in exile."

The Holy Father, however, raised his voice, and by his order the Cardinal Secretary of State, in a protest dated Portici, March 9th, 1850, after calling attention to the readiness the Sovereign Pontiff had shown to open negotiations, asked under what pretence important questions had been summarily decided, in a sense directly opposed to concordats; and a law passed, "the general tendency of which was to deprive the Church of the right of acquiring property, which even the constitution of the state secured to her."[1] They could say, no doubt, that some articles had been communicated to the Holy See; but that the Holy See might see that this communication was a mere mockery, they took care to inform it at the same time that the decision of the Government was irrevocable. It is true, too, that the Holy See was invited to resume the negotiations relative to the Concordat, but at Turin only, in order, it would seem, that a pontifical representa-

---

[1] Exposé des négociations suivies entre le Saint-Siège et le Gouvernement Sarde.

tive might sanction, by his presence, the *irrevocable* decisions and laws against the Church.[1]

The law was passed. In vain it had been proposed to suspend its execution until the negotiations with the Holy See had been concluded; the amendment was rejected. Anything that tended to pave the way to an accommodation with the Holy See would have been too much opposed to the policy of Piedmont. The joy of the populace and the revolutionary papers was extreme: there were cries in the streets of "The law of Siccardi for ever!" "Down with the priests!"

Soon after this (12th of June, 1852) came the civil marriage bill, introduced by M. Buoncompagni. On the 5th of July, this bill was passed by the Chamber of Deputies. The bishops remonstrated, in an address to the Senate, asking if it was just "completely to alter and to cancel, by the sole action of the civil power, rules which had been laid down and mutually agreed to by the two powers, and especially the conventions passed between King Charles Albert and the Holy See in 1836." Poor bishops! they were still appealing to justice and the laws of nations!

The Pope, too, in a letter to the king (19th of September), complained that such a bill should have been introduced, "while the negotiations were pending, which had been opened in order to satisfy the violated rights of the Church." The bill having met a sharp resistance in the Senate, was withdrawn, to be renewed at a more convenient time.

III.

I pass rapidly over this and many other deplorable transactions; but the violence offered to the bishops cannot be overlooked. The Archbishop of Turin is seized and dragged before the courts: why? For having ad-

---

[1] Exposé des négociations suivies entre le Saint-Siège et le Gouvernement Sarde.

dressed to his clergy (18th of April, 1850) a circular, in which he traced for them, according to the laws of the Church, the line of conduct they should pursue. A tribunal of three councillors was to decide if there were grounds for a trial. One of them, M. Giriodi, refuses to sit; three other councillors are named.[1] The trial takes place, and Mgr. Fransoni is condemned to be imprisoned for a month, and to be fined 500 francs! Upon this, a captain and brigadier of carabineers present themselves at the archbishop's palace, and order the prelate to follow them to the citadel of Turin. The archbishop, with his breviary under his arm, is led away prisoner by the officers of justice. The Government would have been better pleased if the prelate had voluntarily quitted the city, and he was formally requested by letter to do so.[2] But St. Paul had given him the example of leaving to the authorities the full responsibility of carrying out their own decrees; and Mgr. Fransoni imitated St. Paul. The bishops of Savoy wrote to the archbishop in his prison: "The principles which you have professed, Monseigneur, are those of the whole episcopate; they are those of the Catholic Church. Together with all our priests, we applaud your firmness." (24th of May, 1850). Nothing was attempted against the bishops of Savoy.

M. Siccardi having declared in the Senate, on the 16th, that the great majority of the national clergy regarded the law of the 9th of April as a benefit, the archbishop, from his prison, in a letter dated the 19th, contradicted the offensive assertion: "I cannot imagine," said the prelate, "that any one can hazard such a statement within walls which still echo to the solemn protest of the whole episcopal body of the kingdom!" A few days afterwards, all the bishops of the two ecclesiastical pro-

---

[1] Ami de la Religion, tom. cxlviii. p. 39.
[2] See in the Ami de la Religion, tom. cxlviii. p. 76, the minister's letter and the noble answer of the archbishop. See also the admirable letter of the clergy of Geneva to Mgr. Fransoni.

vinces of Turin and Genoa protested in their turn. "Knowing," say they, "that the immense majority of the ecclesiastics of our respective dioceses are, through the mercy of God, closely united in opinions and sentiments with their bishops, as well as with the Roman Pontiff, the supreme head of the whole hierarchical order, we consider ourselves bound in conscience to declare that we fully adhere to the protest of the Archbishop of Turin, dated the 19th of May, and published in the journals." The signatures follow of the seventeen bishops of the two provinces, and that of the vicar capitular of Genoa, the see being vacant. The bishops of Savoy did the same.

Before long, Monseigneur Varesini, archbishop of Sassari, guilty of the same offence as the archbishop of Turin, suffers the same treatment. "He, too, was accused of having traced out to his clergy the conduct they should follow, for the security of consciences, relatively to the anti-canonical laws, and was judicially summoned before the court of justice of Sassari. Afterwards, a warrant was issued for his arrest, which was to be put in execution by armed force." (Note of Cardinal Antonelli to the Charge d'Affairs of his Sardinian Majesty. The Vatican, 26th June, 1850.) The bishops of Saluzzi and Cuneo having written to the same effect as Monseigneur Fransoni, the Piedmontese Government intimated to them that they must retract; if not, the courts were ordered to seize the property of their sees. (*Gazetta del Popolo*, cited by the Ami de la Religion, t. cxlix., p. 247.)

On the 7th of August, 1850, the archbishop of Turin is again seized by carabineers, and thrown into the prison of Fenestrelles, where the memory still lived of Cardinal Pacca and other confessors of the faith, the glory of the Church. There Mgr. Fransoni is kept in close confinement, his vicar-general is forbidden to write to him, and he is only allowed to speak to his secretary and his servant in the presence of a carabineer. Very shortly, one outrage preparing the way for another, prayers and lamentations even are regarded as crimes; as Tacitus says, *Liber gemitus non fuit:* a chaplain of the prisons had recommended to pray for the archbishop; he is dismissed without a moment's warning. Finally, the 25th of September, 1850, Mgr. Fransoni is condemned to banishment, the revenues of the archbishopric of Turin are sequestrated, and the Catholics are not even allowed to send to the illustrious exile a testimonial of their sympathy and their grief. On the 18th April, 1851, the police of Genoa make a search on board the steamer *Castor*, and seize upon a chalice and a mitre which some Catholics were sending to the proscribed archbishop.

Nor is he the only one who has to suffer imprisonment and exile for the holy cause of the Church: in the same year, 1851, Mgr. Marongini, archbishop of Cagliari, is in his turn arrested, despoiled of his property, and condemned to exile. The exile of these two archbishops has now lasted ten years, as all Europe knows, and all Catholics deplore; and there are at the present moment fifteen sees vacant in the Sardinian states, either by the death or exile of their prelates:—by death, and that for a long time, the sees of Alexandria, Alba, Fossano, Sarzana, and more lately Aosta, Annecy, Vigevano, on the continent—and Nuovo, Ogliastro, Ampusia, and Tempio, Bosa, Bisarcio, in Sardinia; and by exile, those of Turin and of Cagliari for ten years, and the see of Asti for one year. Fifteen bishoprics vacant out of forty-one—that is, over a third; and without the Holy See having once refused canonical institution!

However, the attacks of the revolutionists against the clergy are redoubled. The chamber of deputies rings with accusations against the bishops.[1] Government circulars threaten the priests, and place them all under the *surveillance* of the police; the most odious measures are directed against them; the clergy are even accused as accomplices in the riots caused by the scarcity of corn;

---

[1] Particularly in the meetings of June 10, 1848, August 22, 1849, February 15, 1850, January 10, 1853, and many others.

they are pointed out as objects for the indignation of the populace!

A confidential circular of the intendant of Aosta (3rd division, most confidential circular No. 3) is posted up, in an excess of zeal, by a syndic, an ardent democrat:—
"I have to direct you to observe carefully whether any *pastorals*, or any notices of the kind, should be published or distributed, either publicly or clandestinely; and if any body, without distinction of persons, should let fall observations savouring of insubordination from the pulpit. In any such case, you will inform me of it without delay; you will likewise inform the magistrate of the place, and order the immediate arrest of the author of such discourse."[1] Disturbances had taken place in different towns; a popular demonstration had been made against Count Cavour, at Turin, on the 18th October, 1853, and the elections were coming on. Count Cavour publishes, on the 21st of October, a circular calling for a statistical return of all convents; threatening that if any foreign religious was not given accurately in the list, to have him instantly arrested and conducted to the frontier. And, in another circular (27th Oct.), the clergy were accused, not confidentially, but publicly, of having taken part in the riots relative to the scarcity of corn, and were held up to the vigilance of the police. "The syndics are aware that certain extreme parties are seeking to foment disorders, under pretext of the rise in the price of corn. In some cases the pastors of souls, instead of confining themselves to *their ministry of peace and charity*, have been carried away by party passions. . . . . The syndics should act, in this respect, with due vigilance and zeal. The priests must be carefully watched. . . . . . Words should be taken down, facts recorded, and the law officers should indict. In the more serious cases, the ministers of religion should be immediately arrested."

In this way the popular irritation was to be diverted

---

[1] Ami de la Religion, tom. cxlviii. p. 90.

from Count Cavour. The police act according to these instructions; priests are arrested on all sides, though often released after a precautionary imprisonment, the charges against them being declared void. Thus the Abbé Gagliardi, Lent preacher at Mondovi, was imprisoned for two months, and afterwards declared innocent, on the 17th of March, 1850; thus the preacher, Louis Piola, was arrested on the 13th of September, and set free after forty-five days of unjust confinement; thus the priest who administered the parish of Malanghero was imprisoned from May till September, and then declared innocent; and fifteen priests of the valley of Aosta were accused of having fomented riots, while it was proved on the trial that, on the contrary, they had only interfered in order to pacify the people. The *Armonia*, of 20th December, 1859, contains the long list of the ecclesiastics who had been falsely accused and unjustly imprisoned.

And while bishops are being exiled and priests imprisoned, while the acts of the bishops are stigmatized in parliament, and the whole clergy placed under the *surveillance* of the police, the impious and revolutionary press is allowed to propagate insults of unparalleled effrontery against the clergy, the Pope, and religion in general. That religion which the constitutional *statute* declared to be the religion of the state is continually outraged, shamelessly and with impunity: at Turin, sermons are interrupted by hisses; parodies of the *Via Crucis*, of the *Stabat Mater*, turn our most august mysteries into derision; the complete works of the most scandalous writers are published, with obscene engravings; a "Letter of St. Peter," "Spiritual Exercises for the Clergy," "Pius IX. before God," "Dom Pirlone," &c., are published. . . . The Pope is represented at the theatre and at balls, in the company of abandoned women! An ass's head is drawn, crowned with the tiara; the Pope is represented wrestling, nearly naked; with a thousand other insults. And while the revolutionary papers were thus attacking religion in the most abominable language, and the most obscene caricatures, and were not even interfered with, as the *Bianchi Giovini*—or were acquitted, as had been the *Strega* and the *Lanterna del Diavolo*, a Catholic paper, the *Campana*, was condemned; and the *Armonia*, the *Courrier des Alpes*, the *Cattolico* of Genoa, &c., were suspended. Assuredly, M. Sawzet, in his celebrated publication upon marriage, in 1853, had grounds for addressing this severe language to Piedmont:—" Some fatal influence seems to have blighted Piedmont; the art of engraving seems to vie there with that of printing in corrupting the people by their abominations."

In vain did the Holy Father, in a letter to the King of Piedmont (19th Sept., 1852), remonstrate with Victor Emmanuel on these scandalous excesses. The ministry continued its course, taking good care not to give the Pope any satisfaction; a war against religion, and hostility to Rome, answered too well the purposes of their ambitious policy. As if the insults of the theatres and of the streets were not enough, M. Brofferio—whom the Government afterwards supported as their candidate, in opposition to the excellent M. Revel—applauds the demonstration of the mob of Nice against the bishop; and exclaims, in the chamber of deputies, "Let us show these haughty prelates that the people, too, have their thunders and anathemas."

Of course, in such relations with Rome, the offering of a gold chalice and paten, which the princes of Savoy had always presented to the Holy See for the feast of St. Peter and St. Paul, was suppressed. Ancient courtesies were now out of the question; a very different line of conduct was now imposed, by a minister who was himself grand-nephew of St. Francis of Sales, upon the son of the pious and chivalrous Charles Albert, the royal heir of the illustrious house of Savoy.

Very different ideas prevailed now: a policy was being carried out which called for great resources, and would call for still greater. The treasures and the reserve of Charles Albert were exhausted. The Government was short of money. The Sardinian clergy was not, indeed, rich; they had already contributed to the expenses of several revolutions; still, however, they had something, and could not be allowed to retain it; for the great financial resource of the revolutionary principle is always the same—spoliation. On the 29th of November, the *Courrier des Alpes* contained a letter to the following effect:—" It is alarming to see the forty millions voted last session already gone, before the end of the year, and a fresh loan spoken of. The want of money is hurrying the operations of the commissioners for regulating ecclesiastical property; it is stated that the final and complete expulsion of the Oblates of the *Consolata* is but the prelude to similar proceedings against all convents and churches which possess riches."

I will not speak of the financial measures, which were only the prelude to this plan of spoliation; of the tax, equivalent to a tenth of their net revenue, put (31st March, 1851) upon all houses and buildings of the clergy and religious, except rural buildings and those intended for worship; nor of the tax of half per cent. imposed (23rd May) upon charitable and benevolent institutions, and of four per cent. upon all other religious establishments; nor of the special tax, called mortmain, which the same law charged all the possessions of the Church. Nor shall I dwell upon the secularization of the royal economate, arbitrarily effected, in contempt of two concordats (13th August, 1853); nor upon the circumstance that the municipal council of Chambéry were obliged (March 2nd, 1852) to vote unanimously the suppression, in the municipal accounts, of the part of the salary of the clergy due by the government; finding that it violated, besides treaties, the engagements by which, on becoming possessor of the Church property which was not alienated in 1814, it undertook to become responsible for the expenses of Divine worship.

I have still graver facts to record. The 21st of March, 1853, a law takes from the bishops and invests the Crown with the right of regulating the number of young clerks exempted from the conscription. I have been myself witness, in the diocese of Annecy, in Savoy, to the disastrous effects of this measure. Another decree (May 23,

1853) renders the brothers of the Christian Schools liable to military service, thus opposing an almost insurmountable obstacle to the recruitment of these zealous teachers of the children of the people. The exiled archbishop not being on the spot to protect his seminary, the property of the ecclesiastical seminary of Turin is sequestrated (March 10, 1854); the archbishop, in banishment, remonstrates to no purpose. They were judicious in banishing people before seizing their property.

On the 15th of October, 1852, M. Ratazzi applauded the Carthusians of Collegno for having, *with true Christian charity*, temporarily given the spare part of their house to accommodate some insane patients; on the 10th of August, 1854, the minister turns them out of doors. The Carthusian fathers, having been expelled without notice, were received in a private house: thus, but for private charity, they would have been left in the streets. And so were expelled in turn the religious of the Consolata and of St. Dominic, the priests of the mission of St. Vincent of Paul at Casal, the Oblates of Pignerol, the Servite fathers of Alexandria, who had just sent two of their number to Genoa to replace four other fathers who had perished in attending the victims of the cholera. In vain did the Holy See—with which negotiations were still pending—address to the court of Turin an éloquent protest against such persecutions: it was listened to now as little as on former occasions.

Even women were not spared. In the beginning of the year 1853, an edict had abolished an ancient and peaceful benevolent institution, buried in the mountains of Savoy, the Sisters of Charity, known by the name of Ladies of the Compassion, whose occupation was to teach poor children, and to attend the sick. Thus the nuns of the Holy Cross were expelled from their convent by carabineers, at night, on the 18th of August, 1854. "I thank God," wrote the abbess, "that none of my daughters died in the street." Some years before (Augest 25, 1848), the Ladies of the Sacred Heart had been proscribed throughout the Sardinian dominions; all their houses had been dissolved, their pupils dispersed, and their property, whether in land or money, confiscated to the public treasury.

All this having been arbitrarily effected, the religious having previously been plundered and expelled, it was considered well to promulgate a law, to justify, legalize, and consummate all these iniquities. On the meeting of the Chamber of Deputies (November 25, 1854), the ministry introduced a bill for the suppression of religious communities and corporations, and the sequestration of their property. This law, as unconstitutional as it was unjust, put the seal to the long series of violence and spoliation committed by the Piedmontese government. It was a law based on the most false and fatal principles: for it disallowed to the Church the right of property, a right which even pagan governments had not disputed to her; for, as we have already said, whenever paganism allowed to the Church the right of existing, it also allowed to her the right of possessing; so essentially co-related are these two rights.

The debate was a long and stormy one, and will be remembered as one of the most memorable in the parliamentary annals of Sardinia; the success of the bill was long uncertain. It was denounced by the most solemn protests of the bishops and of the Holy See, and combated in parliament by influential members. The bishops offered to make a generous compromise; but it was carried at length by means of a stratagem. Among the speakers who defended the religious orders and the rights of property, M. Revel and M. Solar della Margarita displayed the highest courage and eloquence. M. Revel, formerly minister of Charles Albert, called attention to the fact that, in the 29th article of the *Statute* (the Constitution) which says, "All property, without exception of any kind, is inviolable," the words, *without exception of any kind*, which are found in no other constitution, had been introduced by the king chiefly for the purpose of securing the property of ecclesiastical establishments. And M. Revel added these words, which caused a profound sensation in the Assembly:—" Most certainly, gentlemen, if King Charles Albert, whose portrait is before us (here the speaker raised his voice),—if King Charles Albert had known how men would one day dare to interpret his intentions and his actions, he would have drawn back that hand which he is stretching out there to swear fidelity to the constitution; yes, gentlemen, he would have drawn it back."

In the Senate, the old Marshal de la Tour and the Marquis de Brignole supported the cause of right with all the weight of their high reputation. But all these noble efforts were without effect; the law, modified by a committee of the Senate, was passed by the two chambers, and immediately sanctioned by the king (May, 1855).

Thirty-five religious orders were proscribed; 7,850 religious were deprived of their property. Neither the learned orders, nor the charitable; neither the humblest, nor the most illustrious, were spared. Piedmont possessed a noble institution, the Academy of the *Superga*, the greatest school of ecclesiastical learning in the kingdom, founded by the discerning liberality of her kings; it was suppressed. The religious of Hautecombe had been the guardians of the tombs of the house of Savoy; the post was a sacred one, but it was not respected.

IV.

I should be wanting to the truth and the dignity of history if I did not say that bold voices were raised to protest against such misdeeds; an energetic resistance was made, as we have seen, in the Sardinian parliament; the deputies of Savoy showed an unswerving fidelity to the cause of honour and religion; and I am happy to render this homage, after so many afflicting details, to these generous advocates of the contemned rights of the Church.

On the 6th of May, 1854, Count Solar della Margarita summed up in an eloquent speech all the grievances of the Catholics, and I will quote from it what follows:—

"What is the state of our relations with the Holy See? We must say what we think on this subject, lest our silence be interpreted against us, and lest it be pretended that we do not dare loudly to proclaim the sentiments of the numerous part of the nation who feel grieved by an antagonism between the Church and the State. A real peace with the Holy See, and the recognition of the principle now so audaciously denied, that concordats with Rome have equal force and oblige equally with treaties made with other powers, nothing but this, I say, can quiet the just and deep alarm of those who ask if this Catholic country is rushing into schism. Brave against a sovereign who has neither numerous subjects nor an army, whose sole defence is the justice of his cause, which is our cause too, his enemies multiply their acts of hostility: they continue a war against him, which, by the perturbation it creates, really involves evils not less terrible than do those wars where blood and gold are poured out like water. In such a conflict easy victories are gained: but what are their results? Troubles and discord in all classes, in all ranks, throughout the whole country.

" While the radicals of Switzerland are persecuting the Church, the pretended defenders, the so-called guardians of our liberty, do not hesitate to imitate them, and while parading their toleration for all other sects, they raise against us the standard of religious intolerance. The statute guarantees the liberty of the individual; but the liberty of the individual does not exist for those who belong to the Church. The statute guarantees the rights of property; but this right is ignored for the property of the Church. The statute establishes the equality of all before the law; but, in contempt of this principle so solemnly proclaimed, the archbishops of Turin and Cagliari have been banished, and still are in exile. I have done. I am unwilling to prolong these sad details, and to unroll before you the long history of these evils. I do not wish to renounce all hope; as long as a ray of hope is left, I will hope."

Unfortunately, this last ray of hope was soon quenched; affairs only grew worse, and the long parliamentary debates of 1855 had the sad issue which we have related.

To conclude.

Laws against the Church, concordats violated, sham negotiations; the violent execution of the law pronouncing the suppression of convents and religious congregations; the tyrannical measures against so many religious and ecclesiastics; the neglect of the Government in paying the clergy the pittance necessary to their bare support; the clergy so impoverished that I have seen numbers of priests in Savoy obliged to borrow money to buy bread, some having received nothing for a year, others for eighteen months; and that a Sardinian paper stated, "We know of curates who receive yearly, in compensation for tithes which have been suppressed, but 50 or 60 francs;" the prolonged and multiplied vacancies of episcopal sees; the obstacles offered to the nomination of canons; the deplorable education bill introduced by M. Lanza; the repeated imprisonment of priests; the circulars of M. Ratazzi, particularly that against the letter of the bishop of Ivrea relative to sacrilegious robberies in churches; finally, the odious accusations of M. Cavour in the Chamber of Deputies against the clergy; all these facts, and many others, superabundantly demonstrate the sad and incredible obstinacy of Piedmontese policy in its hostility against the Church.

This avowed and flagrant hostility was a scandal and a profound affliction to the Catholics of that state, the delight of the anarchists, the triumph of the enemies of religion: the *Avenir de Nice* of the 10th February, 1855, contained these fearful words: "Piedmont has quite gained my heart since I see her make war upon the black gowns. The *wretch* has been but very imperfectly *crushed* by Voltaire. The business must be finished. At all events, it is a comfort to us to see crowned heads setting about this difficult task. Piedmont just now is giving an excellent example." It must be said that such language reveals the peril, as well as speaks the shame, of the government which provoked such homage. And the famous pamphlet *Napoléon III. et l'Italie* was right in calling the policy of Piedmont "an encouragement to revolutionary passions, an embarrassment to consciences, a real and grave danger, not only to Piedmont, but to Italy and the whole of Europe."

That Piedmont has not shrunk from evoking these perils; that it has obstinately continued its persecution of the clergy, and its encouragement of revolution; that it has trampled upon all that is sacred in the pursuit of the objects which its ambition coveted,—these are facts but too clearly established, and which history will lay to the charge of those who were guilty of them. But what were the objects and the grounds of such policy? What final results did it aim at? What were its real motives in breaking with Rome, laying hands on the property of the Church, persecuting the priests, expelling the religious, while it made common cause and linked itself more and more closely with the revolution? Was Mazzini right when he wrote, so far back as 1846, " Piedmont will enter on the right path, from the prospect of the crown of Italy"?

CHAPTER XVII.

PIEDMONT.

SECOND PERIOD:—CONGRESS OF 1856; MEMORANDUM OF COUNT CAVOUR, AND ITS CONSEQUENCES.

I.

However it may be as to the anticipations of Mazzini, all that we have seen having been effected, and these antireligious schemes having been carried into execution, the ground appeared sufficiently prepared. Having, then, kept the Holy See and the Papal states in alarm for eight years; having welcomed all the malcontents and refugees of Italy; having fomented agitation and disturbance by irritating language and fatal encouragement of every description; having grieved the Holy Father by so many outrages, and tricked him by so much pretended negotiation,—on the 27th of March, 1856, Count Cavour thought the opportunity favourable, and brought public accusations against the Pope before Europe, in such terms, that the *Times* declared that nothing said at a Puritan meeting in Edinburgh or Belfast could go further than the diplomatic representations now solemnly made by a Catholic and Italian state. And the *Times* was right.

In fact, Count Cavour asserted that the Papal government was radically bad, and incapable of real or genuine reform. He stated "*the difficulty, or, to speak more correctly, the impossibility,* of a complete reform of the Papal government suited to the needs of the times and the reasonable wishes of the people." In order the better to prove his assertion, he, of all people, ventured to accuse the insincerity and duplicity of the Papal government, and to declare that it would seek and *find a way never to effect its promised reforms, and to elude the beneficial effects of any new arrangement which might be come to.* "It is evident," he added, "that the court of Rome will resist to the last, and *by every means in its power.* It may, indeed, accept *in appearance* civil and even political reforms, *reserving to itself to render them illusory in practice.*" He asserted, in short, that the pontifical government was intolerable, "a permanent cause of disorder in Italy, a scandal and a peril to Europe;" and he hoped "that the congress would not separate without taking all this into serious consideration, and devising a remedy for it."

These charges, and the principles of Count Cavour's *memorandum,* evidently aimed at the total extinction of the Papal power, of *the clerical yoke, the clerical domination,* as he called it; for a power which is *a permanent cause of disorder and anarchy* — I quote his own words— a power which places a country in *a deplorable situation, which only grows worse;* which is *for ever repudiated by its own subjects; which is opposed to any improvement;* which *only apparently* favours anything good, and is ready to use any means to *elude and nullify* desirable reforms; a power which, even if it had the will, is radically *incapable of any reform suited to the needs of the times, and the just desires of its people;* a power which is *a source of perturbation to the tranquillity in Europe, a scandal to Europe, a focus of disorder in the centre of Italy*; a power, in fine, whose *chief supports* are such, that if they are left to it, it is in danger of perishing, and that they cannot be removed *without undermining and upsetting it*, is clearly a power which cannot continue to exist, and must disappear. However, Count Cavour, as yet, only proposed the separation of the provinces bounded by the Po, the Adriatic, and the Apennines, under the government of a *pontifical lay vicar*. But he took care to observe that such a solution could be but *temporary*. He could not flatter himself that such an arrangement could last long: it must necessarily one day bring on another, which at that time he did not venture to hint at, but which is now disclosed. In the mean time it will, said he, "*pacify those provinces, give a legitimate satisfaction to the popular demands, and in this way secure the temporal government of the Holy See, and do away with the necessity of a permanent foreign occupation.*"

And that no argument might be withheld from the congress, and that his representations might gain the favour of the revolution, Count Cavour threw out the most odious and calumnious accusation against the Holy See:—

" Never were the galleys and the prisons more crowded with political offenders; never was there a greater number of outlaws; never were more cruel measures carried out, as is *proved superabundantly by what is taking place at Parma*. Such a government must necessarily keep the people in a state of continual irritation and revolutionary fermentation. Such has been the state of Italy for these seven years."

II.

Of course, we are not taking a purely retrospective view of history, without any reference to present affairs, and the late rising in the Legations: we are rather pointing out the true and evident causes of the evils which soon followed. It would surely show but little acquaintance with the history of revolutions, it would be to estimate inadequately the effect of words and actions, not to feel what excitement such language must have created among a people, and what fuel it must have added to the revolutionary passions of Italy. Was this, as M. Walewski said himself — who committed, by the way, the grave error of bringing before the congress, as its president, the affairs of the Pope, who had no one there to represent or to defend him—*was this to dissipate the clouds which still darkened the political horizon?* Or, according to the fears expressed by the representative of Prussia, who maintained an impartial attitude on this question, was it not rather "*to provoke in the country a spirit of opposition and revolutionary agitation, instead of seconding the good ideas and intentions which had been attempted to be realized?*" Mr. Gladstone declared, too, in the British Parliament, that the policy contained in the protocol tended, not to clear up the political horizon, but, on the contrary, to accumulate fresh storms. Count Buol also replies later to Count Cavour, in a sharp note (18th May, 1856) :—" The enemies of society will not cease their warfare against the legitimate governments of Italy, so long as they find powers which back and protect them, and statesmen who appeal to those passions and those efforts which aim at the overthrow of all authority."

M. Massimo d'Azeglio himself, afterwards military governor of the Romagna, was far from fully approving, in the Piedmontese senate, of the *memorandum* of the 27th of March :—" I must confess that I have some doubts as to the advantages expected from the proposed arrangement of separating the Legations from the Papal states. What is to be done with the remainder of those states? Must the other provinces renounce all hope of reforms? You are proposing, on the one hand, to establish order and concord, and on the other, are sowing the seeds of rivalry and dissension. In my opinion, these things should be left to the action of time; allow this action to operate freely in politics, as the gradual action of the sun produces its effects upon the fruits of the earth."—(Sitting in May 10, 1856.)

As regards international relations, the *memorandum* of Count Cavour was not more to be regretted than the favour which it found with the congress, though it was not accepted unconditionally. The congress in this contradicted itself, and laid down a most serious precedent in European politics. "By a series of inconsistencies as striking as unlooked for," remarked M. de Montalembert, "the rights of nations, which had been so nobly vindicated in the East, were slighted in the West. Powers equally independent and sovereign with the deliberating powers, but who were unrepresented, and had not even received notice of the character in which they were to be made to appear, were placed on their trial before them. It is proclaimed, in the most solemn manner, on the 18th of March, that none of the contracting powers has a right to meddle, individually or collectively, in the relations of any sovereign with his subjects, nor in the internal administration of his states; and the next day the congress constitutes itself the judge of the conduct of these absent potentates, and gives a most improper and wide-spread publicity to its criticisms on their authority, and its censures of their conduct. It begins by asserting the principle of the essential independence and autonomy of sovereigns; to the advantage of whom?—of Turkey, which till then had never been recognized as one of the European family of nations. Then, with the same pen which had just signed this singular innovation, whose propriety was unquestionable, and which had been sealed with the blood of thousands of Christians, the congress records in its acts a violation of the universal, fundamental, and sacred principle; and to the detriment of whom?—of the most ancient and legitimate sovereignty in the Christian world, whose very weakness should secure for it the most scrupulous deference and the most delicate reserve.

The protocol of the 8th of April created a sensation in all the parliaments and journals of Europe.

Count Cavour cannot have been serious in complaining, in his note of the 16th of April, of the little attention which the congress had paid to the Roman question; in deploring "that the assembly, towards which the eyes of Europe were directed, had separated, not only without having in the least relieved the distresses of Italy, but without having held out beyond the Alps a single ray of hope calculated to tranquillize people's minds, and to encourage them to suffer with resignation." The encouragement which he received from the British and Piedmontese parliaments, and the applause of the anarchical journals, proved clearly enough the fatal success of the *memorandum*, how well its import had been understood, and what hopes it had elicited beyond the Alps, and among the revolutionists of Europe. It is known what acclamations welcomed it in England, and what anti-Catholic virulence was displayed on the occasion in her press and parliament; nor have the odious words of Lord Palmerston been forgotten, in which he commends the Mazzinian government of the Roman republic in 1848 as superior to that of Pius IX., declaring that the holy city had never been better governed than during the absence of the Pope. History cannot forget such language, and posterity will unite with the present generation in reprobating it.

In Piedmont, Count Cavour gives an exulting account of his conduct to the Chamber of Deputies on the 7th of May, and to the Senate on the 10th. The Senate pronounces the following resolution:—" The Senate, convinced of the happy results which must follow the treaty of Paris, both as to civilization in general, and the establishment of order and tranquillity in the Peninsula, and fully sensible of how far the policy of the king's government, and the conduct of the plenipotentiaries at the Congress of Paris, have contributed to bring about such desirable results, votes its entire satisfaction."

But to catch the real import and bearing of Count Cavour's proceedings at the congress, one should consult the contemporary numbers of the democratic journals of Piedmont, and see what was their triumph and exultation. " The protocol of the 8th of April is the first spark of an irresistible conflagration," said the *Risorgimento*, Count Cavour's own paper. The avowal was a frank one at least. " For the first time," said the *Opinione*, " a diplomatic congress has admitted the wrongs of governments, and justified the indignation of the people." "We are again espousing the cause of the revolution!" exclaimed approvingly *Il Cittadino d'Asti*, a ministerial paper. Another, *Il Tempo di Casale*, added: "Italy should rise, without waiting any longer for succour from European governments." "If the Italians think they can reconcile themselves to their present condition, well; if not, let them revolt!" exclaimed *Il Diritto di Torino*. "Let them rise, and take care to accept no compromise with the power they revolt against, whatever its nature may be," repeated the *Italia e Popolo* of Genoa, in its 113th number.

As to Count Cavour, he stated that he was ready to give any explanation which might be desired, hinting, however, that he would have to pass over in silence *certain things*, whether from the delicate nature of the questions, or to avoid compromising, by imprudent disclosures, *certain negotiations*, which had not been yet concluded. He named the 6th of May for any questions which deputies might wish to put to him. On that day, the minister, according to the expression of an Italian paper, sowed the dragon's teeth, and delineated the programme, whose realization we have now witnessed. He said that he had presented a note upon the situation of the Pope's states, which had been cordially received by England, and accepted by France. "But," he added, "France is obliged to proceed with caution, for the Pope is not only the temporal sovereign of a state of three millions of people, but also the spiritual sovereign of thirty-three millions of French subjects." The deputy Lorenzo Valèrio, speaking of the language used by Count Cavour in this sitting of May 6th, exclaimed, "Our words, and words *of a far higher importance—those of the President of the Council*—will certainly be heard out of this assembly, and even on the other side of the Ticino. Neither frontiers, nor the bayonets of the police agents which hem in the other provinces of Italy, can arrest their progress."

Count Cavour made a similar speech in the Senate, on

the 10th of May: it was such, that M. Massimo d'Azeglio thought it necessary to recommend the Italians not to revolt yet. "Our debates," said he, "our journals, and all that we say here, pass the frontiers, frustrate the vigilance of the police, and are read elsewhere with perhaps more avidity than at home." It is notorious that M. de Cavour and the Piedmontese agitators had thousands of copies of the speeches then uttered in the Senate and the Chamber of Deputies immediately struck off, and disseminated throughout all the provinces of Italy, along with other revolutionary tracts,—such as the "Piccolo Corriere;" they were sent under cover, as letters; also a protest printed with the title of "Last Protest of the Italians." The Romagna was inundated with them.

III.

The leaders of the revolution, feeling that their time was drawing near, and that M. de Cavour had prepared the way, began to trace out their plan. A sketch of it was found in the papers of Manin ("Manin et l'Italie," Pagnerre, 1859).

In case of a war, of France and Piedmont against Austria, "nothing must be done to displease Piedmont or France, *whatever its government may be*. For instance, as long as the Pope is maintained at Rome by the French arms, we can attempt no insurrection there, as this would oblige us to combat our ally; but if France should decide on overthrowing the Pope, we will second her with all our heart." "The arms of the insurrection should be *joined*, *but not confounded*, with the French and Sardinian arms." Daniel Manin also wrote from Paris to the *Diritto*— "Agitate! agitate!"

To feed and maintain the agitation, addresses and presents to Count Cavour were thought of: the revolutionists of Tuscany presented him with a bust, and saluted him as the avowed champion of Italy; those of the Papal States, Farini and Mamiani at their head, presented a gold medal to the count, accompanied by an animated address.

And the count received all these demonstrations with thanks and encouragement.

From Paris Manin continued his correspondence with Turin; and it is instructive to peruse his letters. The programme which he then sketched, on the banks of the Seine, was—*The Unification of Italy : Victor Emmanuel II. king of Italy!* Manin was disposed to spare the Piedmontese monarchy, for a time, " because it has resisted the eternal enemies of Italy, the Pope and Austria."—(Letter of May 11th, 1856.) And he continued : " Agitate! agitate! Agitation is not exactly insurrection, but it precedes and paves the way for it. . . . . Harass the enemy with a thousand pricks of needles, while waiting for the moment when you can stab him to the heart with the sword."—(Letter of May 23rd.) Again, on the 28th of May, he wrote: " The revolution is practicable in Italy, and perhaps very near!" But he cautions the Romans : " While there is a French garrison at Rome, Rome should attempt nothing."

On the 8th of July, it was proposed to the parliament to fortify Alexandria—" An eloquent evidence of the new and patriotic tendencies of Piedmont," said the *People's Gazette* (11th of July, 1856). The measure was introduced by M. Norberto Rosa, and approved and seconded by Count Cavour, as also the subscription for a hundred cannon for Alexandria, a subscription in which all Italy was to take part. " The Memorandum of M. de Cavour," said *Il Cittadino d'Asti*, " has given a vigorous impulse to agitation, and now we have only to take care that it does not flag, and to keep it up till the decisive day arrives." When, on the night of the 25th of July, 1856, a band of insurgents left Sarzana to provoke a rising in the duchy of Modena, the *Maga di Genova* of the 29th of July defended the attempt, on the authority of Count Cavour: " Did not M. de Cavour state in parliament, in his Memorandum and in his verbal notes, that if things continued as they are much longer, *the Sardinian government would consider itself bound to join with the revolution to rescue Italy ?*" The *Italia e Popolo* of July 30th, 1856, in its defence of the conspirators of Sarzana, writes: "It will be remembered that after the memorable parliamentary discussion, the Sardinian government, in order to rekindle the fire which slumbered in the other provinces of Italy, had the speeches of Cavour and Buffa printed and *disseminated in thousands throughout the duchies, the Romagna, Lombardy, Naples, and Sicily*. Nay, *it excited by its emissaries the inhabitants of these states;* and the words, 'Long live Victor Emmanuel!' were written on the walls and doors of houses at Carrara by Piedmontese agents. Still more flattering and more explicit assurances were given to the partisans of Piedmontese rule who came to Turin."

On the same occasion, *Il Risorgimento*, a paper founded by Count Cavour, writes: "The revolution will never take place in Italy, unless the people are assured of the assistance of Piedmont. It is, therefore, important to keep up among them a firm confidence *that behind the people in revolt will be found the Piedmontese army*." The same journal continues: "The moment the revolution breaks out in any part of Italy will be the signal for a universal conflagration. Austria will interpose, and Piedmont then will have a right to interfere, in order to counterbalance the preponderance of Austria, and it will not interfere alone. Such is, in our opinion, the only possible solution of the Italian question."

Such was the way in which Count Cavour, on his return from the Peace Congress, calmed people's minds, pacified the populations, *ameliorated the anomalous condition of the Papal States, secured the temporal power of the Holy See*, rendering it *independent of foreign support*, and remedied the *disorder and anarchy* of which he accused the Pope's power as the *permanent cause!* Such were the methods he adopted to insure the security and tranquillity necessary to a government from which he called for reforms!

I know nothing of politics, or the artifices or secrets of politicians; but if politics are not altogether foreign to all justice, all truth, all honesty, and all honour, I would demand what name is to be given to the conduct which we have been depicting. You accuse the Holy See; you accuse it in its absence, before all Europe; you dwell upon what you call its *anomalous position*. But, I ask, was, and is, not Europe bound in justice to examine what are the real causes of this anomalous position, who are its promoters, and who are really guilty? I ask, if it is not just to inquire whence the revolutions spring which menance the Pontifical power, and if you are not yourselves, as Lord Normanby expresses it, guilty of high treason against the Holy See, against the rights of Catholics, and the laws of European justice? And to enter into the details of your accusation, you speak of *secularization and the Code Napoléon*, and you pretend thus to explain to Europe the revolutionary perils which threaten the Holy See; but was not the government which fell in France, in 1848, a secularized government, such as you demand at Rome, and which enjoyed the blessings of a Code Napoléon? and did this prevent its fall? Is it not clear to the most humble capacity, that it is your own revolutionary manœuvres for the last ten years, and not the want of a Code Napoléon at Rome, that have caused the dangers which prompt your lamentations before Europe?

Is not Europe still bound, in strict justice, to consider whether, instead of encouraging the agitation of populations, of denouncing governments, and of provoking insurrection everywhere, contrary to the commonest political prudence and honesty, it would not be better to maintain treaties and the faith of Europe which has been solemnly pledged; and to fortify, once for all, by a collective, effectual, and solid protection, the Papal power, precisely because it is weak, menaced, and necessary?

Ah, no! that was not what you wanted at the congress. You were not particularly anxious to see the reforms you called upon the Pope for: they would have been in your way; and accordingly you *declared*, and rendered them at the same time *impossible*. Why, reforms fully adapted to the reasonable wishes of a people, reforms perhaps too extended and too liberal for a people to whom they were strange, had been conceded before the French occupation. Who rejected these reforms, and rendered the occupation necessary? The revolution; the most unjust, base, and ungrateful of revolutions. What has fettered, for ten years, the good-will and generous intentions of the Holy Father? The revolution, encouraged and fomented by you,—a revolution which your support has raised into a standing institution. And what renders necessary, at the present moment, the French occupation, which the Pope himself had asked France to withdraw a year ago? The revolution which publicly burst forth, on the same day as the war, under your auspices.

In fact, while M. Cavour was keeping up an agitation in the Papal provinces, by the occult and incessant operations of his agents, while he was thus directly contributing to the perpetuation of a state of things which he had himself so harshly and bitterly denounced as *anomalous*, another result of his diplomatic aggressions was to embitter the relations of Piedmont and Austria; and to bring about a war, in which his alliance with France and his engagements with the revolutionists justified him in hoping for success.

IV.

Undoubtedly, as I have before remarked, Piedmont might have played a happier part, and taken on her a nobler office. As Cæsar Balbo said, — " As an honest family earns for itself a good reception and rights of citizenship in a town, so Piedmont should moderate her ambition, and content herself with being received as a respectable member of the great European republic. Nowhere, I am convinced, was it easier to establish a free monarchy. For Piedmont is a Catholic and monarchical land; anarchy has there no roots, nor any real power."

To this upright course, M. Cavour preferred violence and anarchy. Immediately after the Congress of Paris, the first words of Count Cavour in the Sardinian Chambers, as we have seen, intimated clearly enough that, the

Eastern question having been hushed, if not settled, the Italian question was soon to take its place, and to convulse and appal the world still more. In his note of April 16, he said, almost in a tone of menace,—" Convinced that they have nothing more to expect from diplomacy, or the efforts of the Powers who affect to take an interest in their fate, the Italians will incorporate themselves, with their southern ardour, in the ranks of the revolutionary and subversive party; and Italy will become anew a focus of conspiracies and strife." We shall see, by-and-by, when treating of the plot of Genoa, in what sense Mazzini understood these words.

Whatever their true sense, however, it is certain that from that time men, whose names notoriously belonged to the revolution, began to flock into Piedmont, where they met with the most gracious reception from M. Cavour. Mazzini had an organ there, *l'Italia e Popolo*. It would appear that he resided himself in Piedmont, where he made, at times, terrible denunciations; he revealed, for instance, that a certain Italian refugee, naturalized in Sardinia, member of parliament, knight of the order of St. Maurice and St. Lazarus, was a regicide, who had attempted to assassinate Charles Albert, in 1833. The man who had recommended this refugee to Mazzini had formerly been president of young Italy, and now lived at Turin, where he was a ministerial deputy, had received decorations, and held a professorship in the university. Farini, the author of the revolutionary proclamations at Rimini, in 1844, was also at Turin, and enjoyed the intimacy and favours of the government, which named him dictator after the insurrection of Parma; his later distinctions are notorious enough. Terenzio Mamiani, the suit instituted against whom at Naples, in 1849, proves him to have been one of the chiefs of the revolution in Italy, was likewise a ministerial deputy, and now is minister of public instruction at Turin. I have been told myself, by French officers, that about half the officers in the Piedmontese army were refugees. I will not do more than mention Garibaldi.

And it was the minister who welcomed and promoted such men that accused the Pontifical government before Europe as a *permanent cause of disorder and anarchy*. And the representative of England seconded such accusations! And Lord Palmerston repeated them in the British parliament, in language yet more odious! Naturally enough, the revolution, finding itself so powerfully supported, began to hatch new plots at London and Genoa. An Englishwoman, an enthusiastic admirer of Mazzini, organized at Genoa the unhappy revolt of June 29, 1857; the shock of which was felt at Leghorn, and which the conspirators of the *Cagliari* attempted to propagate at Naples.

The Piedmontese government prosecuted the conspirators, but Mazzini raised his voice in their defence; the *Italia e Popolo* published a letter from the chief of the revolution to the judges of the Court of Appeal at Genoa, a letter most galling to the ministry, who brought it before the courts; but in vain, a verdict of acquittal was given. Mazzini, in this letter—which was implicitly sanctioned by the judgment of the court—accused the Piedmontese ministers of pursuing *a tortuous and Machiavelian policy*; and designated them, with impunity, as *conspirators, and the abettors of conspiracies*. His words are:—

" I have already exposed the tortuous and Machiavelian policy of the government. It is my duty to insist further upon this point. The government has played the part of an instigating agent. The Sardinian government is at times the enemy, at others the manipulator, of the revolutionary element—conspirator and persecutor by turns.

" Conspirator, as often as it fears to see the Italian party slip completely from its grasp, as often as it sees any likelihood of a disturbance in some other part of Italy, as often as the republican element seems to gain ground. Conspirator, as far as suits its purposes, on the one hand to excite people's minds by some visionary project, or to appear to favour what is threatening to become a reality; on the other, in order to be able to say, in case such a hope is realized, I was with you! and to become master of the movement. Persecutor, on the contrary, as often as a failure affords it an opportunity of weakening more and more that fraction of the party which will not be governed by it; and thus to put in a claim to the favour of absolute governments, which but yesterday it affected to threaten."

But the Genoese agitator did not content himself with accusing the ministry, he brought forward proofs and facts; and the jury considered the testimony of Joseph Mazzini as of great weight in a question of conspirators and conspiracies. He continues:—

"This monarchico-Piedmontese conspiracy lives, or rather agitates in Italy, with no other object but that already pointed out, to thwart every attempt at insurrection, or to appropriate to itself any which may succeed; yet still it continues its intrigues, through its travellers and agents, with obstinacy and duplicity; it carries on intrigues, after a diplomatic fashion, with centres of propagandism and agitation, which I could indicate, with the names and details. Monarchico-Piedmontese committees exist at Rome, Bologna, Florence, and several cities of the Lombardo-Venetian kingdom; and there are secondary centres in several other towns. I could name to you the persons, several of them deputies, who are the agents between the poor dupes and the personages of the government. These intrigues scatter in profusion—as before 1848—encouragements to trust in the house of Savoy, advice to moderate and delay all popular movements, sometimes throw out hints of the deep designs of the Sardinian government, and always hold forth hopes. At times, when the impatience of the dupes, at nothing being done, threatens to break out, they distribute little medals and organize subscriptions. The conspiracy fraternizes with foreign pretenders, and I could mention the names of some who are going to Savoy, with a recommendation, to offer their homage to Murat. But it is not only to him, who is Italian at the bottom of his heart, and in whom one feels confidence at first sight," &c.

Of course, we leave the responsibility of these allegations and facts to Joseph Mazzini, who published them, and to the Genoese jurors, who have, in some sort, confirmed them, by declaring not guilty the letter in the *Italia e Popolo;* but can such revelations be read without sad and absorbing interest, and even without awe? It is difficult not to admit the conclusiveness of Mazzini's argument in what follows:—

"The agitation created by the men of the government is to us nothing but a snare; but it debars them, and you too, gentlemen, if you are honest, from the right of accusing or of punishing.

"Suppose that one of the individuals against whom the public accuser is calling for the severest penalties were to rise and say,—Gentlemen, for what do you propose to punish me? I have but reduced to practice the reiterated suggestions of your government. I have but attempted to procure for it the opportunity which it has sought, to give effect to the longings it has been uttering for ten years, through its agents and its semi-official organs. Was it not the minister who pronounced these solemn words:— *Great solutions are not effected with the pen?* Diplomacy is powerless to change the condition of a people, *it can but sanction accomplished facts?* Did not his journals impress upon us that the *Memorandum* was intended to insinuate a deeper meaning than it expressed? You tell me that all this was mere words; that he who uttered them did not intend that they should be embodied in facts; in short, that the minister was deceiving both Italy and diplomacy. Well, what is that to me? Am I guilty, because, touched by the sufferings of my brethren, and called upon by the friends of humanity, I thought it my duty to prepare to put in practice the creed inculcated on me by the minister, and which was ratified by the voice of my own heart? Which, do you imagine, has acted most uprightly? The minister who, beginning by rousing and stimulating our feelings, draws back, and soon after confirms, in other words, the treaties of 1815; or I, who, embracing his first declarations, was preparing to seal them with my blood, and was marching to join the first champions of the war of emancipation? Judges, what could you answer to such an appeal?"

The conspirators of the 29th of June were condemned nevertheless: but the jurors did not find the words of Joseph Mazzini guilty. As for us, while we respect the first sentence, we may, for the same reason, accept the second.

Some months after the insurrection at Genoa, on January 14, 1858, we had another terrible revelation,—the bombs of Orsini, manufactured in England, burst at the emperor's feet in Paris, and elicited long and deep sentiments of horror. The English people were irritated by what they thought the dictatorial tone of the French government; but they also showed, only too clearly, by their determination to maintain a law which guaranteed the impunity of assassins, by the scandalous acquittal of Simon Bernard, the accomplice of Orsini, and the expressions of popular approbation which were showered on him, the sympathy which is felt, across the Channel, for those whose object is to set the continent in a flame. The letter and the will of Orsini were published, and disclosed strange revelations.[1]

Piedmont, however, persisted in its warlike attitude; a mysterious journey of Count Cavour to Plombières, and his interview with the Emperor Napoleon, were the subject of much curiosity. Certain words, also said to have

---

[1] The *Siècle* of February 28, 1858, published a letter written by Orsini from his prison to the emperor. The conspirator says:— "I conjure your majesty to restore to Italy the independence which her children lost in 1849, by the fault of the French. May your majesty remember that the Italians, and my father among the rest, shed their blood joyfully for Napoleon the Great, wherever he chose to lead them; that they were faithful to him up to his fall; that so long as Italy shall not be independent, the tranquillity of Europe and that of your majesty will be but a chimera." Orsini did not even ask for an armed intervention:—" Do I ask that, to deliver my country, the blood of the French should flow for the Italians? No, I do not go so far. Italy asks that France do not interfere against her; she asks that France do not allow Germany to support Austria in the conflict which will probably soon commence."

been pronounced by King Victor Emmanuel, at a review, assisted in exciting apprehensions.

Still, notwithstanding the mysterious secrecy of the Plombières interview, the evident helplessness of Piedmont, by itself, seemed calculated to allay misgivings; and calm, if not security, had revived in Europe, when, all at once, at the official reception at the Tuileries on the 1st of January, 1859, some words addressed by the emperor to the Austrian ambassador informed Europe that the relations of France with that power had altered.

These words echoed like a clap of thunder in a calm sky; the Bourse took the alarm; public opinion declared against war with extraordinary energy and unanimity. People would not believe it, because they thought it impossible; they foresaw the most alarming contingencies, before which, as they recollected, even the republic of 1848 had recoiled.

In England, the ministry and the opposition agreed in deprecating the intervention of our arms in Italy, and in appealing to treaties; and Lord Derby, on the 3rd of February, in the House of Lords, sharply animadverted on the policy of Piedmont; and declared that her simple and natural course was to attend entirely to her internal improvement; and instead of maintaining an army quite out of proportion with her territory, to trust for her defence to the sympathies of Europe, and to the treaties in virtue of which she held her states, as Austria did hers.

The Catholics were not blind for an instant to the consequences of the Italian war, namely, an explosion of revolution in Italy, and peril to the Papal power: "They who would urge France upon such a course," wrote M. de Falloux (February 25, 1859), "are neither friends to the Imperial government, nor to Italy. They are the friends and accomplices of European demagogy. . . . . Can we forget that those who now advocate so warmly French interposition beyond the Alps, are the very men who opposed it ten years ago by every means in their power, because it would have then favoured the Pope's authority? No; it is not the counterpart of the expedition of 1849 that they demand from the Imperial government; they want their revenge upon the president and the votes of a free assembly." We know now whether the forebodings of M. de Falloux have been justified by events.

Amidst such general alarm, and so general a manifestation of opinion, the French government assumed a prudent and reserved attitude, endeavouring to calm men's minds and restore confidence.

On the 7th January, a note appeared in the *Moniteur*, tending to quiet the emotion created by the emperor's words to the Austrian ambassador: "For some days public opinion has been troubled by alarming rumours, to which the government feels itself bound to put an end, by declaring that there is nothing in our diplomatic relations to justify the fears which such rumours tend to excite." And the emperor, in his address at the opening of the legislative session (7th February, 1859), pronounced himself these words: "The excitement which has been displayed, without any appearance of imminent danger, justly surprises, for it bespeaks an excess, both of distrust and dismay. Far from us be false alarms. Peace, I hope, will not be disturbed."

But the king of Sardinia, on the contrary, had inaugurated the opening of his parliament by warlike language: "Strong in the experience of the past, *let us resolutely meet the contingencies of the future.* . . . . Our position is not devoid of danger, since, while we respect treaties, we cannot be insensible to the cry of grief which rises upon our ears from every part of Italy."

A Milanese refugee, M. Correnti, who had been chief secretary to the government of Milan in 1848, was commissioned to reply to the royal speech, in the name of the Chamber of Deputies:—" Sire," said they, "the elective chamber, encouraged by your approbation and your advice, wishes to offer the only thanks which are worthy of you, namely, to second with promptitude and unanimity the noble resolutions which have been matured in your mind, as they have been in the desires of the nation.

The whole nation will rally round you, and show that it has learnt the antique secret of reconciling the obedience of the soldier with the liberty of the citizen."

Some days later, the Sardinian chambers voted a new loan of fifty millions of francs, proposed by Count Cavour, in anticipation of the war. Refugees flocked into Piedmont from Lombardy, and every point of Italy. The declaration of M. Cavour at the congress was being accomplished: "The Italians will incorporate themselves, with their southern ardour, in the ranks of the revolutionary and subversive party." Piedmont organized them as volunteers; all Austrian deserters were welcomed and enrolled, and Garibaldi (March 20) swore allegiance, as general, to Victor Emmanuel.

Austria replied to these preparations for war by concentrating troops in Lombardy; and Europe continued to negotiate to the clash of arms. While Piedmont and Austria, in the diplomatic notes of Count Cavour and Count Buol, mutually reproached each other with provocations and aggression; while England was attempting to interpose; and Russia was proposing a congress; while the various cabinets were discussing the programme and the conditions of the future congress; while public opinion, in alarm and agitation, was floating, according to the varying phases of diplomacy, from peace to war, and from war to peace, the war at length suddenly broke out, and at the same instant the revolutionary movements, all arranged beforehand, exploded in the states of Central Italy.

This, too, was but the realization of the prophecies and lamentations of M. Cavour at the Paris congress. *It is certain that the irritation, though lulled for a time, will break out again with more violence than ever.* The world saw at length kindle into flame those *sparks of conspiracy and disorder,* so long kept in, and so skilfully fanned, *which the least European commotion would swell into a devouring conflagration.*

CHAPTER XVIII.

PIEDMONT.

THIRD PERIOD—REVOLUTIONARY VIOLENCE.

A MOST serious question here presents itself: one which France is bound in equity, and Europe in prudence, to consider.

It is a question which has already received a sufficient answer in the last two chapters; but it is one of such a character, and relates to so flagrant a violation of the rights of peoples, as well as of those of sovereigns, that we think it necessary to propound it again, in order again to answer it, more thoroughly and decisively.

What was the real cause of the revolutionary explosions which simultaneously took place in Italy? Was it the war? Or was the war simply the unhappy occasion, and Count Cavour their principal and culpable author?

Ought we to view in them a spontaneous expression of the people's wishes? Or had all that we have seen been organized long beforehand, by underhand intrigues and darkly-laid plots? And, at the time, were they not, under the auspices of our victories, and, as it were, under the protection of our flag, violently provoked by foreign agency, and carried into effect by emissaries of Piedmont?

Whether should we consider them, in fairness, as a genuine popular and Italian movement, or as the violent triumph of a faction, and the tyrannical domination of a Piedmontese dictatorship?

When the populations were called upon to pronounce, were they permitted to do so freely? Or did not the dictatorship which had been imposed on them, and the pressure of the revolutionary party, anticipate and stifle any expression of different sentiments? In a word, first in the insurrections, and afterwards in the ostentatious exhibitions of popular suffrage, was not justice glaringly violated, and the people made a tool of? Whether was it the voice of the nation or that of the agitators that was heard? Will there not rest for ever a twofold stigma upon all these transactions—the foreign provocation, and the revolutionary oppression?

The official despatches of the French ambassador at Rome, in 1849, stated that *the great majority of the population were opposed to the movement* which we were combating; *and that the Romans were influenced by the immediate terrorism of bands of foreigners.* In this respect, was it not in 1859 as in 1849?

Well, I affirm, and mean to prove, that the Pope, in his consistorial allocutions and his last Encyclical, had good grounds for calling attention to and condemning the odious plots of *native and foreign agitators*, and pointing out *by means of what men, what money, and what support, the late revolts had been effected, while far the greater part of the population remained as if thunderstruck.* Nor was it groundlessly that a note of the Holy See asserted again (12th July, 1859), " Facts take place daily, before the eyes of the Holy Father and his government, which argue a behaviour more and more outrageous on the part of the Sardinian cabinet towards the Holy See; and evidently reveal an intention to deprive it of an integral part of its temporal dominions. Piedmontese officers are introducing thousands of muskets and cannon, to arm the rebels and volunteers, to augment the disturbance of the revolted provinces, and the audacity of the enemies of order."

No; Piedmont, which now claims the benefit of these insurrections and the annexation of the provinces, could not, as the Emperor Napoleon has done in the case of Savoy, declare to the great Powers that it has arrived at such an aggrandisement neither *by military occupation, nor by encouragements offered to revolt, nor by underhand intrigues.*—(Speech at the opening of the Chambers, March 1, 1860.)

Piedmont has done quite the contrary. Its hand has been in all these revolutions. It has organized, provoked, and hurried them on; and that contrary to the declared wishes of France, which it has disregarded; in opposition to so many declarations of the emperor, which have not even stayed its hand an instant; and in the face of our flag and our victories.

Such is the grave question which here forces itself upon France and upon Europe, and to which palpable facts furnish a most convincing answer. But in order fully to see this, we must enter into details; exhibit carefully the French policy, as it is given in official documents; as well as the conduct of Piedmont, represented by its notorious and public actions.

Undoubtedly, it will one day be a matter of astonishment for historians how an all-powerful ally can have had so little influence over a power which owed it everything, and would have been powerless without it. For my part, without attempting to solve this problem, I shall confine myself to the collection and arrangement of the facts.

I.

We have just heard the revelations of Mazzini touching that monarchico-Piedmontese conspiracy, which had its centres of action at Bologna, Florence, Parma, and all over Central Italy; but perhaps Mazzini, and the jurors who would not condemn him, may not be considered trustworthy.

Well, we will produce something that may: the diplomatic notes of Count Cavour, and his speeches in the Sardinian parliament. We have seen how these notes and speeches were distributed throughout the duchies and the Romagna, in order to keep up the agitation and disturbance which are the forerunners of revolution. We have seen the attitude adopted by the Piedmontese government and its journals, pointing to the sword of Piedmont glittering behind the popular movements. Still, up to this, nothing overt or tangible had been done.

Now, however, we shall see the campaign opened, disguise thrown aside, pre-arranged schemes boldly carried into practice; and all this in a manner as notorious as it was opposed to all international law and justice.

Instructions are sent (March 1, 1859) to the heads of a society in the different states of Italy, which, as is well known, covered all Italy before the war, the *National Italian Society* ;[1] their import was as follows:—1. Before hostilities have commenced between Piedmont and Austria, you are to rise to the cry of " Italy for ever! Victor Emmanuel for ever!" 2. Wherever the insurrection triumphs, he among you who enjoys most public esteem and confidence is to take the military and civil command, with the title of provisional commissioner, acting for King Victor Emmanuel, which he is to retain till the arrival of a commissioner sent by the Sardinian government. Who signed these instructions, or rather this programme, which, as we shall see, was so literally carried out in Italy during the war? A Piedmontese general, Garibaldi; also La Farina, another revolutionist, who had been covered with honours by the Piedmontese government.

At Florence, in what locality was the plot, or rather the unparalleled treason, matured, which issued in the corruption of the grand-duke's troops and his abdication? In the very house of the Sardinian ambassador, M. Buoncompagni, who since has governed in the name of Piedmont, Florence and the states of Central Italy. Here, then, was an ambassador, accredited at a sovereign's court, conspiring against him, and turning his embassy into the head-quarters of the conspiracy! By what name would such conduct be called in any civilized nation? Well, it was publicly, in the British parliament, that Lord Normanby, ambassador at Florence, called attention to this odious fact:—

" Immediately after the expressions used by the emperor of the French to the Austrian ambassador, meetings of the party called 'Constitutionalists,' or 'Piedmontese,' began to be held at the house of the Sardinian minister in

---

[1] *M. de Riancey*, Madame la Duchesse de Parme et les derniers événements.

Tuscany, and a set of pamphlets were circulated among the subjects of the grand-duke by the persons attending these meetings; besides, the most numerous and active attempts were made to seduce the allegiance of the Tuscan troops.[1]

" There have been various accounts of the disposition of the Tuscan troops in favour of Piedmont;[2] but, in fact, it was so unfavourable, that, since the withdrawal of the grand-duke, the Piedmontese government had threatened them with decimation, to prevent them from returning to the allegiance of the prince regnant."[3]

To the evidence of Lord Normanby we may add that of Mr. Scarlett, the representative of Great Britain in Tuscany and at Parma, who forwards the following details to his government, on the 29th April, 1859, that is to say, two days after the revolution at Florence:—

" The Piedmontese minister, Signor Buoncompagni, seems to have been the first leader and director of the late revolt. He was constantly, I am informed, going to, and receiving instructions from, the Secret Committee; and must have been perfectly aware that, by the influence of that committee, the troops had been bribed and tampered with, until their allegiance to the grand-duke was utterly destroyed. His mission to Florence may be the

---

[1] After the grand-duke's departure, the crowd assembled under the windows of M. Buoncompagni, the Sardinian ambassador, who in an harangue, given in the Tuscan *Moniteur, expressed his admiration for the conduct of Tuscany*. Such are the terms in which a minister accredited to the grand-duke speaks of the treason of his army and his subjects. And he added,—" King Victor Emmanuel is deeply interested in the fate of Tuscany; he will take care of public tranquillity, and meet the contingencies of war." Could an ambassador violate more overtly the law of nations?

[2] Twenty-five francs a-head had been distributed to the troops by the ringleaders the day before the revolution.—La Paix de Villafranca et les Conférences de Zurich, par le *Chevalier L. Debrauz.*

[3] Speech of Lord Normanby, formerly ambassador at Florence, on the events of the Romagna, in the House of Peers, June, 1859. —See *l'Ami de la Religion*, of 14th June, 1859.

cause of Italian independence; but as an accredited minister to the grand-duke of Tuscany, his career will not appear very favourably.

"It is my belief that the insurrection which occurred at Parma was only part and parcel of an elaborate Piedmontese conspiracy, aided by the republican party, and having its ramifications throughout every town in Italy" (this is precisely what Mazzini said); "although the success of this movement is now confined to Tuscany, Massa, and Carrara. It will be seen, by the circular I enclose—attributed to Garibaldi, and stated to have been sent to all the committees and sub-committees in the Italian towns, and since published in the *Journal des Débats*—that as soon as ever war became certain, an insurrection was to take place wherever it was possible, and a government immediately proclaimed in the name of King Victor Emmanuel, under a Piedmontese commissioner. It is clear, then, that the plan which had long been prepared, and took effect here, is the link in the chain of a wide-spread conspiracy throughout the peninsula, a work ably promoted by the activity of Piedmontese emissaries."[1]

Thus, then, a vast conspiracy had been organized long in advance by Piedmont, embracing the whole of Central Italy; Piedmontese emissaries are busy everywhere; the day for the outbreaks is named beforehand; they wait but for the declaration of war. Immediately after that signal, Massa and Carrara, Modena, Florence, and Parma, successively revolt. A rising is evidently imminent in the Romagna; after the victory of Magenta, it takes place. Facts everywhere speak a clearer language than any testimony.

---

[1] Further correspondence respecting the affairs of Italy presented to both Houses of Parliament by command of her Majesty, 1859.

In his despatch of February 29, the Cardinal Secretary of State has openly made these charges against the late Piedmontese ambassador at Florence. I am aware that M. Buoncompagni has protested, but he has not even attempted to answer the positive testimony we have just cited.

As to Parma, Mr. Scarlett, again writes to London, to the Foreign Secretary, that the conspirators are kept in check there solely by the popularity of the Princess Regent. In fact, the spontaneous recall of the duchess by her subjects, and her triumphal return, was an unmistakable proof that the revolution which had expelled her was not the work of the country, but that of a minority, who were intriguing with the Piedmontese party. However, M. Cavour did not despair; emissaries from Turin continued to manœuvre in the duchy, and the regent was obliged a second time to withdraw. The conduct of M. Cavour, in other respects, towards the Duchess Regent of Parma, at the beginning of the Italian war, was most odious. In flagrant violation of the neutrality which had been proclaimed, he invades her territory, and occupies Pontremoli with Sardinian troops; on what pretext? He gives himself the singular reason, in a note, in which he accuses the regent, before Europe, of having herself violated the neutrality, by not having prevented, with her 5,000 soldiers, the Austrians from occupying Placenza as a base of operations.

Let us see how the British cabinet viewed this conduct, in their reply to the note. The Earl of Malmesbury, Secretary of State for Foreign Affairs, writes, in a despatch dated June 7th, 1859, to the English minister at Turin, and which was communicated to Count Cavour,—

" The Duchess of Parma has not in any way departed from the strict line of neutrality which she has announced her intention to pursue, and Austria has not set the example of disregarding that neutrality. Notwithstanding these circumstances, the Sardinian government has not scrupled to endeavour to supplant the lawful authority of the duchess, and to occupy Pontremoli by Sardinian troops. But such proceeding, on the part of Sardinia, having no foundation, either on alleged sympathy for a people suffering from misgovernment and tyranny, or on strategetical considerations, can only be looked upon *as a cruel and unwarrantable exercise of force against a small and weak state*, administered by a female sovereign, unprovided with sufficient resources to maintain her independence against an invading army; though anxious to avoid taking any part in the devastating warfare on the borders of her dominions, and striving to the best of her ability to govern her people with humanity and justice."

But, indeed, the similarity of the facts which everywhere took place indicated an identity in the means employed. Was it not everywhere the same programme, arranged beforehand—the programme of M. Cavour and Garibaldi—which was being carried out? Was not the presence and the alliance of the Piedmontese and revolutionary element everywhere visible? And when the protests of the Holy See called the attention of Europe to the intermeddling and intrigues of Piedmont in the provinces which had revolted, did they encounter a single contradiction? No; M. Cavour did not even take the trouble to answer the complaints of the Pope.—(Note of Cardinal Antonelli, May 19. Consistorial Allocution of June 8.)

Indeed, it was no longer mere intrigues and underhand influence that were brought to bear, but something very different. Our victories had emboldened the Sardinian minister; and he carried out his policy with such spirit, that the Pope soon had again to appeal to Europe, as follows:—

" Things have come to such a pass, that Piedmontese troops have already entered the Pontifical territory, and have occupied Sorte, Urbano, and Castelfrano; the Besaglieri and a part of the brigade of Real Navi are there now: their object is to join the rebels in opposing an energetic resistance to the Pontifical troops, sent to maintain our authority, which has been violated in the revolted provinces, and to raise new obstacles to the execution of this just design. Finally, to complete the usurpation of the legitimate sovereignty, two engineer officers, one of whom is a Piedmontese, have been sent to Ferrara to mine and destroy that fortress."

But why be surprised? Were not all these monarchico-revolutionary agitations, these intrigues and this violence, the necessary consequences of the famous notes presented by M. Cavour to the Paris congress, and the execution of his plan for the dismemberment of the Papal states? Does not his haste, in turning to his own account the triumphs of our soldiers, suffice to betray and unveil his policy of plunder? Thus, a revolution corresponds to each of our victories; and no sooner has it broken out, than a Piedmontese commissioner immediately takes the government of the country into his hands, in the name of King Victor Emmanuel; Sardinian troops, in contempt of the rights of neutrals, as well as of all other rights, and despite the protests of the dispossessed sovereigns, invade it; decrees are issued in the name of King Victor Emmanuel; M. Cavour despatches circulars to all the Piedmontese commissioners, declaring that the countries in revolt are, some simply under the protection of Piedmont, others *de facto* annexed, but all henceforth to be governed by it.

It must be confessed that it was something extraordinary to see this minister, while our brave troops were shedding their blood upon the fields of battle, despatching from his cabinet, at Novara or Turin, his commissioners and dictators to all the countries conquered, and even to those destined to remain unconquered.

However, all of a sudden an unexpected event momentarily deranges this current of invasion, and forces M. Cavour to adjourn his plans, at least for a time. The emperor, victorious at Solferino, suddenly halts, and makes peace at Villafranca. Among the grave reasons which brought about this unhoped-for peace, the emperor has himself enumerated the necessity in which he would have been placed "*of openly accepting the assistance of the revolution.*" M. Cavour judges that there is no place for him, now that the march of the revolution is suspended. He retires from the scene.

II.

There is one feature in the occurrences we have been reviewing, as well as in those which remain to be considered, which strikes us as most inexplicable. The official declarations of France strangely contrast with the overt acts of Piedmont: it is difficult to view the latter otherwise than as a continual contradiction of the conservative policy professed by France. It seems, indeed, hard to explain how Piedmont, that ally to whom victory would have been hopeless without us — as was evident from Novara and Solferino,—has been able to carry out a policy so opposed to ours, and to act continually before our eyes, and in the presence of our army, in a manner so contrary to our intentions: it is hard to conceive that a word from France, if firm and distinct, would have had no effect on a Sardinian minister. There is surely some mystery here, which history will perhaps one day clear up. In the mean time, I shall simply relate what occurred. Far from aggravating anything, I shall endeavour to present as doubtful whatever is not absolutely certain; I shall suppress with pleasure, and endeavour to conceal, even from myself, all that conjecture, a too rigorous induction, or an unhappy readiness to censure, might discover; I shall still more jealously avoid whatever may tend to render separations more lasting, divisions bitterer, or reconciliations more difficult. God is my witness, that if it depended upon a word of mine to change the dispositions of those who influence the course of events, and to cause Christian hope to succeed to the evils of revolution,—God is my witness that I would utter it with joy and gratitude. But, as I am here to be an historian only, I shall endeavour to discharge my more modest part with fairness and sincerity.

The declarations, then, of the French government, after the peace as before the war, were explicit: Piedmont could not mistake them; nor could it have more completely disregarded or more openly trifled with them than it has done.

What were these declarations?

The war had broken out; our regiments had already passed the frontier; the honour of our flag was engaged. It was in such critical circumstances that the legislative body opened its session of 1859, and that the government had to expose its policy before the deputies of France. Strong apprehensions as to the possible consequences of the war were expressed, and explanations called for by several deputies, and in particular by Viscount

Lemercier, at the memorable sitting of April 30th. He stated that " he was convinced that the government would not hesitate to satisfy the Catholics of the world as to the emperor's determination, whatever might happen, to see that the independence and the states of the Holy See were respected."

The distinct and categorical answer of M. Baroche, the president of the *Conseil d'Etat*, was as follows :—

" The last speaker has given the answer to his own question, by referring to recollections which the government of the emperor can never forget .... *Any doubt on this head is inadmissible.* The government will adopt all the measures necessary to secure the independence of the Holy Father during any agitations which may break out in Italy."[1]

On the 3rd of May, the emperor spoke himself: a proclamation to the French people announced the war. In this proclamation the emperor gave two solemn pledges; he affirmed that *we were not going to Italy to foment disorders;* and he promised that *the war should not shake the throne of the Holy Father.*

Such were the emperor's words, and such the official policy of France from the commencement. Piedmont could not pretend to mistake it: and, moreover, though insurrections had been projected and organized in advance, still nothing had been done; the difficulty of arresting an impetus once given could not be pleaded. Well, did the declarations of France prevent even one of the revolutions which Piedmont had prepared? No. Has not the word of France been wholly null and void? Yes. Piedmont, by its intrigues and its revolutionary instigations, has been the main agent in overthrowing the esta-

---

[1] M. Baroche added, that "had M. Lemercier not refuted himself, as he had done, the president of the *Conseil d'Etat* would have felt himself bound to express before the chamber his astonishment that such a doubt could have been entertained for a moment as to the conduct of the government."

blished governments in four states, and in depriving the Holy Father of four provinces.

The day after the imperial proclamation, as if to give a still more direct assurance to the Catholics, and to "satisfy the clergy as to the consequences of a conflict which had become unavoidable," his excellency the minister of public worship addressed a circular to all the bishops of France. It ran to this effect :—

"*The emperor has considered the matter before God*, and his well-known prudence, energy, and sincerity, will not be found wanting either to religion or the country. The prince who has given so many proofs of his reverence and attachment for religion, who has restored the Holy Father to the Vatican, *means that the supreme head of the Church shall be respected in all his rights as a temporal sovereign*. The prince who has saved France from the schemes of demagogues cannot become a partisan of their doctrines or their domination in Italy."[1]

Well, what consideration has Piedmont shown for these intentions of the emperor? Has it *respected the supreme head of the Church in all his rights as a temporal sovereign?* Has it kept aloof from the doctrines of demagogy in Italy? To say so would be simply ridiculous. No, Piedmont has taken its stand upon the revolution: it has scouted and usurped the rights of the Holy See; it has commenced, obstinately pursued, and finally consummated the annexation of four of its provinces.

However, while Piedmont and the revolution are about their work, while insurrections are succeeding one another, and Italian sovereigns being dispossessed, the imperial

---

[1] The minister added :—" These practical, generous, and Christian ideas will tend to establish on solid foundations the public order of the Italian states, and to promote a due respect for sovereign power. Such are the sentiments of his majesty ; for which his actions have so often vouched, and which he has again confirmed by the noble manifesto he has addressed to the nation. *They should allay the anxieties as well as prompt the gratitude of the French clergy.*"

government repeats its professions. It repeats them to Italy: in France it repeats them to the religious and other journals; it reiterates them to the nation; it solemnly renews them to the Holy Father himself.

Thus, in his proclamation dated from Milan, June 8, before the revolt in the Romagna had broken out, the emperor said to the Italians: "*I do not come here with a preconceived system to dispossess sovereigns.*"[1] Shortly after, the Pontifical government was overthrown in the Romagna, and Piedmont sent there a military governor.

In France, too, the language of the government continued to contrast with the doings of Piedmont before our eyes in Italy. On the 18th of June, an official *communiqué* to the *Ami de la Religion*, again affirmed, in accordance with all preceding declarations, that "the emperor's proclamation to the French people, as well as the Milan proclamation, had repudiated any *preconceived system of dispossessing sovereigns;* that the emperor had besides formally recognized the neutrality of the Holy Father; that to refer to this declaration was sufficient to enable public opinion to judge *how reprehensible it was to insinuate that France was seeking to disturb the political authority of the Holy Father, which she had upheld ten years before, and which was still under the respectful protection of her arms.*"

At the same time, the *Siècle*, which, on the retaking of Perugia, had insulted the Holy Father and the Church, received, on the 2nd of July, the following *communiqué:* "The *Siècle* newspaper, in its attacks to-day upon the *political power* of the Papacy, and upon the doctrines of which it is the august personification, confounds the noble cause of Italian independence with that of the revolution.

---

[1] It is true that the proclamation also contained the words—"Be soldiers to-day; to-morrow you will be the free citizens of a great country." It is also true that Tuscany was occupied by the 5th *corps d'armée;* and the last manifesto of the Holy See has shown, by the very words of the prince who commanded that corps, the effects of that occupation upon the affairs of the Romagna.

The government of the emperor considers it necessary to protest against such misconceptions, which tend to excite the worst passions, to disturb consciences, and to deceive public opinion as to the principles of the French policy. To respect and to protect the Papacy is part of the programme which the emperor trusts to see realized in Italy, where he hopes to establish order by respecting all legitimate interests. Those journals which represent the import of the glorious war on which we have entered, are abusing their influence to mislead the sentiments of the nation."[1]

Finally, the emperor himself conveyed to His Holiness the most positive assurances that he would protect and uphold, as he had always promised, the temporal power of the Holy See. "Our beloved son in Jesus Christ, the Emperor of the French, has declared to us that the French armies which are in Italy not only will do nothing against our temporal power, but, on the contrary, will protect and preserve it in the Romagna—*tuebuntur atque servabunt.*"[2]

Nothing can equal the distinctness of these declarations, except the persistence and the coolness with which Piedmont has falsified and mocked them. Has it not kept up, carried on, and realized, before our eyes, and contrary to our most express intentions, "a preconceived system of dispossessing sovereigns," including the Holy Father? Has Piedmont, has M. Cavour, respected the neutrality of the Holy Father, according to the formal promises of the emperor? Has he not perseveringly and flagrantly violated, now with subtlety, now with audacity, that sacred neu-

---

[1] The *communiqué* added: "If a sad conflict has taken place at Perugia, the responsibility lies with those who have forced the Papal government to have recourse to force in its just defence. The political independence and spiritual sovereignty which are united in the Papacy render it doubly respectable, and morally condemn such attacks; the government might, if so disposed, have used its legal powers in repressing them; but it prefers to invoke against them the justice of public opinion."

[2] Consistorial allocution of June 20, 1859.

trality which the emperor so loudly proclaimed, and those sovereign rights which he declared were under his protection? Has he paid a moment's attention to that *respectful protection of our arms*, to which the French government alludes?

While Count Cavour is eagerly accepting the dictatorship in the duchies and the Romagna, and exercising it through his commissioners; and while he is encouraging, in guarded language, the proposals of annexation, a note in the *Moniteur* of the 24th of June contains the following declaration:—" The public seems not exactly to comprehend the nature of the dictatorship which has been offered to the king of Sardinia from various quarters in Italy; some have inferred that Piedmont intends, *through the support of the French arms*, and without consulting either the voices of the people or the great powers, to unite all Italy into a single state. *Such conjectures are quite groundless*. The dictatorship is a merely temporary authority, which, while concentrating all powers in the hands of an individual, has this advantage, that *it in no way predetermines the ultimate combinations* which may arise."

It is certainly not easy to imagine, after all the official documents we have cited, how a journal could say, "We defy all those who speak of a guarantee given to the Holy See, to produce a single document, sentence, or word in which such a guarantee has been published."—(*The Siècle.*) We might rather ask if any one can produce a single official document in which this guarantee is not proclaimed.

In short, Piedmont, far from conforming, as might have been expected from an honourable and grateful ally, to such distinct statements of our wishes, has all along contradicted and nullified them. *Let me act, and I will let you speak*, would appear to have been its insulting motto. In fact, who will venture to assert that Piedmont has not, notwithstanding our declarations, sought to *predetermine the combinations* of the future: that it has not attempted to bias, by the united weight of its clubs, its agents, and its armed presence, the resolutions of the revolutionary governments in the duchies and the Romagna? It is quite clear that Piedmont had but one end in view, which it pursued by every means at its disposal; namely, to render definitive and permanent its provisional dictatorship, and to expedite and hurry forward the final annexation, under one pretext or another. The populations, as we shall see, were not fairly consulted, and did not speak freely; the answers of the Sardinian cabinet to the ambassadors of the countries administered by the Sardinian commissioners were neither clear nor frank, and but thinly disguised its ambition; a semblance of popular suffrage theatrically got up before the eyes of Europe, in order to colour and to legalize a revolutionary spoliation: in fine, events were everywhere pressed forward with ominous precipitation, in order to be able to appeal to the grand plea of accomplished facts. It must be added, that France and Europe looked on far too unconcernedly.

III.

A flagrant contradiction, then, was given to the emperor's declarations before the peace of Villafranca. Let us now see how they were respected after that peace.

True, that unlooked-for, but wise and necessary peace, left unaccomplished a part of the emperor's programme; Italy was to have been free,—that is, free from the Austrian yoke, —*from the Alps to the Adriatic.* It seemed a formal disavowal of the aggressive policy of Piedmont, a skilful retreat before the fury of revolution and a threatened coalition, a happy return to the policy followed before the war. M. Cavour was so sensible of this, that he felt his resignation indispensable.

How was this peace, by which the emperor of the French cedes to the king of Piedmont a province equal to his kingdom, yet which is so distasteful to M. Cavour, that he resigns, received by the Piedmontese commissioners in the provinces which revolted? "Tuscans!" says a proclamation on the 13th August, issued by M. Buoncompagni, extraordinary commissioner of the king of

Sardinia, and by the members ef the provisional government,—" Tuscans; the news of events which mar our fondest hopes has filled our souls with sadness! . . . . The *Consulta* will meet to-morrow; the voice of Tuscany will be raised; its appeal will be heard by Victor Emmanuel, in whom our confidence is placed." Such was the gratitude of the Sardinian commissioners towards the emperor and France, which had just sacrificed for Italy the lives of fifty thousand of her sons! Such is the deference shown to our policy! [1]

In fact, where are now the articles of Villafranca and of Zurich? Four points have been stipulated at Villafranca: Lombardy was ceded to Piedmont; Venetia was to form part of an Italian confederation; the rights of the archdukes to the duchies were recognized; and a complete amnesty was granted. Furthermore, the two emperors agreed to employ their influence at Rome, in order to obtain reforms from the Pope, which indeed he was quite willing to accord.

It is clear that the two emperors, by undertaking, in favour of a general pacification, to act as friendly advisers to the Pope, tacitly engaged to fulfil the obligations towards him, which had been publicly contracted before Europe, when, before the opening of hostilities, the neutrality, the independence, and the integrity of his states were so solemnly guaranteed. With what face could reforms have been demanded from the Pope, if it were intended to strip him of his possessions? Besides, in placing the Italian confederation under his presidency, it could not have been intended to offer him a derisive homage, to be followed by spoliation. Common sense and common honesty forbid the supposition.

---

[1] It must be allowed, however, that some of the Turin papers, in particular the *Independente*, took a different view of the consequences of the peace, and that they thanked the emperor of the French, not only for what he had done in Italy, but for what he would allow to be done.

The article relating to the restoration of the sovereign houses indicated still more clearly, if possible, the policy adopted by the two august negotiators. What Piedmont wanted was the monarchical unity of Italy under its own sceptre; what the revolution wanted was a republican unity; what the two emperors stipulated was a federative unity. To this end, it was clearly necessary to repudiate the dangerous support of the revolution. It was necessary to reconstitute power upon solid bases, which might satisfy the legitimate desires of the people, but also preclude those perpetual changes and disorders which always end, with nations recently emancipated, in despotism or in anarchy.

The note in the *Moniteur* of September 9th informed Europe of the condition insisted on as a *sine quâ non* by the Emperor Francis Joseph at the peace of Villafranca, and accepted by the Emperor Napoleon. What had happened in the mean time? No sooner had the telegraph acquainted M. Cavour with the news of the armistice of the 8th July, than, anticipating the intentions of the Emperor Napoleon, he hurried to his head-quarters, to endeavour, if possible, to thwart the negotiations. On the conclusion of peace, he instantly gave notice to the Piedmontese commissioners and the revolutionary government, who hastened to organize (we shall shortly examine in what way) a vote of the deposal of the sovereign and the annexation of the country to Piedmont; the votes took place at Florence on the 16th August, at Parma on the 22nd August, and at Bologna on the 6th of September.

In the note of September 9th, published not before, but after these votes of annexation, the Emperor Napoleon was then justified in complaining that " the destinies of Italy had been confided to men intent rather on petty, partial successes, than the good of the common country, and whose efforts tended not to develop, but to impede the good effects of the treaty of Villafranca." He justly regretted that he had reckoned in vain " upon the good sense and patriotism of Italy," and " appealed to the sound part of the nation." It was with reason that he pointed out to the Italians how they were endangering the peace of Europe by running counter to his policy. In fact, if the archdukes were not to receive back their dominions, "a part of the Villafranca treaty being unexecuted, the emperor of Austria will be released from his obligations with regard to Venetia. If disturbed by hostile demonstrations upon the right bank of the Po, he will maintain himself on a war footing on the left; and instead of a policy of peace and civilization, a state of mutual distrust and rancour will be renewed, which must end in fresh troubles and fresh disasters."

Such language, as might have been anticipated, did not check the Piedmontese policy, which never ceased to aim at the expulsion of Austria from Venice.

But how could the Romagnol deputation which was received by the Emperor Napoleon, as well as the government council, MM. Pepoli, Montanari, Gamba, Albiani, and Pinelli, in their proclamation of August 2nd, give a colour favourable to their designs to the sympathetic words of the French sovereign? What is to be thought of the following extract from a proclamation of Cipriani, the governor of the Romagna? "Let us rather die than yield! Europe looks on us with admiration; the magnanimous Emperor Napoleon is on our side; Victor Emmanuel is the protector of Italian liberty!"[1] What! can those who have falsified all its promises and declarations identify the imperial policy with their own and that of Piedmont?

No; we cannot admit that the imperial policy is to be deduced from the stories of Italian deputations which have been received at the Tuileries, or from the proclamations of insurrectionary governments: were it so, we must necessarily conclude that there are two policies,—one secret and one official. This I, for my part, decline to admit: I mean to go by solemn, authentic documents; and I find

---

[1] Histoire des Etats de l'Eglise depuis la première Révolution, p. 275.

one more, which seems a last effort to stay the policy of Piedmont, which, however, treats it as lightly as the others, continuing to trifle, as unaccountably as before, with its potent ally, and with treaties. The Emperor Napoleon himself writes (20th October, 1849) the following letter to King Victor Emmanuel:—

"MONSIEUR MON FRÈRE,

"I write to your majesty to lay before you the state of affairs, to remind you of the past, and to advise with you as to the best course to adopt as regards the future. The emergency is a serious one; illusions and idle regrets must be laid aside, and the actual state of things carefully examined. Thus, it is now beside the question to inquire whether I have acted well or ill in making peace at Villafranca; but it is essential to turn the treaty to the best account in promoting the pacification of Italy and the tranquillity of Europe. . . .

"A treaty had to be made, as favourable as possible to the independence of Italy, satisfactory to Piedmont and to the aspirations of the Italian people, yet which should not hurt the feelings of Catholics, nor prejudice the rights of sovereigns who had the sympathies of a great part of Europe. It occurred to me that if the emperor of Austria would frankly enter into my views and second me in bringing about so important a result, the causes of dissension which have divided these two empires for two hundred years would disappear, and the regeneration of Italy would follow by common accord, without any fresh effusion of blood."

Then, entering into details, the emperor went over the different clauses of the treaty of Villafranca, particularly insisting upon the honorary presidency of the Italian confederation with which the Pope was to be invested, in order to *satisfy the religious feelings of Catholic Europe,* which had been deeply wounded by the Piedmontese policy, and *to increase the moral influence of the Pope.* The emperor then added:—

"This plan, which I had formed at the conclusion of peace, may yet be realized if your majesty will use your influence in carrying it out. The real interest of your majesty and of the Peninsula is to second me in developing this plan and turning it to the best account; for you must not forget that *I am bound by the treaty.*"

What we have since seen renders it superfluous to add,

that this language of the emperor was, as usual, unheeded; and that Piedmontese policy continued its course. By it the treaties, which bound the victorious ruler of thirty-five millions of subjects, were treated as a laughing-stock.

IV.

The emperor had particularly promised two things with regard to the Papal government: 1. That the neutrality of the Holy Father should be respected. 2. That the dictatorship of Victor Emmanuel should only be provisional.

It was in this sense that even the journals which now advocate the dismemberment of the Papal States, then understood the emperor's purpose, when they were endeavouring to soothe the anxiety of the Catholics, after the revolt in the Romagna. Thus the *Patrie*, now so opposed to the sentiments it then expressed, replied to the *Univers* and the *Ami de la Religion*, as follows: " They forget (these papers) that the French government has expressly declared *that the dictatorship of Victor Emmanuel was merely provisional*, and that the rights of the Holy See had nothing to fear for the future . . . . The provisional dictatorship of Victor Emmanuel is no more a disavowal of the Pope's temporal sovereignty than is the presence of our soldiers at Rome" (June 30th, 1859).

It was M. Massimo d'Azeglio that M. Cavour chose, and despatched to Bologna as Piedmontese commissioner and *military commander*, to exercise there the provisional dictatorship. It must be said that, as military commander, the choice was a singular one. The Sardinian troops arrived at Bologna before M. d'Azeglio, and the revolutionary authorities gave him a most brilliant reception. We find in the " Histoire des Etats de l'Eglise depuis la première Révolution Française jusqu'à nos jours" (a translation from the German, p. 172), that his entry cost large sums of money, and a gratuitous distribution of wine, to excite the enthusiasm of the indifferent and apathetic populace. Before three days had elapsed,

M. d'Azeglio had intermeddled in all sorts of affairs, financial and adminstrative as well as military, and not excepting ecclesiastical. The following is the note which the Pontifical government addressed, on the 12th of July, 1859, to the representatives of foreign powers:—

" *Palace of the Vatican, July* 12, 1859.

"It had seemed to the Holy See that it might remain tranquil amidst the alarms and anxieties occasioned by the present deplorable war, after the repeated assurances it had received: assurances confirmed by the declaration that the king of Piedmont, by the advice of his ally, the emperor of the French, had refused the dictatorship offered him in the provinces of the Pontifical States, which have revolted. But it is painful to find that things are turning out quite differently, and that facts are occurring before the eyes of the Holy Father and his government, which indicate a line of conduct on the part of the Sardinian cabinet altogether unprecedented, clearly showing that it is meant to deprive the Holy See of an integral part of its temporal dominions.

"Since the revolt of Bologna, which His Holiness has already had occasion to deplore in his allocution of the 20th of June, that city has become the rendezvous of a crowd of Piedmontese officers from Tuscany or Modena, who are preparing accommodation for Piedmontese troops. From these foreign states they are introducing thousands of muskets to arm the rebels and volunteers, and cannon, in order to increase the disorder of those unhappy provinces, and the audacity of the enemies of authority. Another fact, which renders the refusal of the dictatorship altogether illusory, has crowned this flagrant violation of neutrality, and this active cooperation in perpetuating the insurrection in the States of the Church. The appointment of the Marquis d'Azeglio as commissioner extraordinary in the Romagna (as appears from the decree of H.R.H. Prince Eugene of Savoy, of June 23, and from the letter of Count Cavour of the same date) is a formal violation of the rights of the territorial sovereign."

And, I would ask, when M. d'Azeglio laid down, in his proclamations to the Romagnols, the strange principles as to the right of insurrection, which the Pope denounced and formally condemned in his letter to Cardinal Patrizi; when, ignoring all acquired rights, and applying to an established society with a legitimate government, reasoning suited only to the case of a new people emerging from a state of nature, he proclaimed the absolute liberty of a people in a political and even a religious point of view;—whether was the representative of Victor Emmanuel, seeking to maintain the provisional character of his dictatorship, alluded to by the Emperor Napoleon, or to detach from the Holy Father even those populations who had remained faithful to him?

Again, was the intention of the league concluded between the revolutionists of Bologna, Florence, and Parma, to uphold the rights of the Holy Father? Who now commands the troops of that league?—General Fanti, at the same time Sardinian minister of war.

V.

But it is in the arrangements made for the elections to the Romagnol Assembly that the sincerity of Count Cavour's declarations as to the provisional character of the Piedmontese dictatorship appears in its true colours, as also the liberty of those popular votes of which we have heard so much. It is true that, having accomplished his task, and, on a hint from head-quarters, M. Massimo d'Azeglio withdrew from the scene, in order to give, as he said, to the inhabitants a full and unrestricted liberty in expressing their wishes; but he took care to leave behind him a successor, Colonel Renaud de Falicon, of Nice, war minister. At Modena, M. Farini did still better; when his office of Sardinian commissioner expired, he succeeded himself as dictator.

I would ask those who view these votes of annexation as the spontaneous and unanimous impulse of the people, if the press was free, and if every one could fearlessly express his opinion? Were the assemblies who pronounced these votes elected by the majority of the population? or was their election the exclusive fruit of the violence of a minority which had seized upon the power? Did not the voting take place under the *protection* of foreign bayonets, in the armed presence of Piedmont? If I open the instructions addressed by Garibaldi and La Farina to the chiefs of the Italian National Society, I find in the 10th article,—" The foundation of clubs and political journals is not to be permitted ; an official bulletin only is to be published." Is not this exactly what was done, especially at Bologna, after the insurrection ? The first step was to suppress all the journals, except the official one.[1]

"The press is shackled and the post-office rifled," Lord Normanby says expressly ;[2] and he proves it by facts. I let him speak for himself:—

" One of the first persons in Tuscany was, even before the elections, sent for by the *préfet*, and asked if it was true he was advocating the return of the archduke; he replied boldly that it was so, for he thought it best for his country. The *préfet* told him that if he did not change his tone in a few days he would send him to prison!

"The Avocato Andriozzi," continues Lord Normanby, " was arrested, with many others, on a charge of conspiring against the existing government. No evidence whatever was produced against him ; but he has since been tried in his dungeon by the *préfet*, on what is called ' *Via economica*,' which means by a secret tribunal, without witnesses or power of defence, and has been condemned to two years' imprisonment in a fortress ! "

The *Times* itself admits this tyrannical pressure :—" This government," it says, " is always ready to pounce upon any paper, pamphlet, squib, or caricature which is distasteful to it."—" Such," adds Lord Normanby, " is positive, and emanates from an authority not to be suspected favourable to the cause. As to the post-office," he continues, " I myself received a letter the other day, sent by a private hand, announcing the appointment of two new officers, called ' *Verificatori*,' whose duty is to open and suppress, at their pleasure, all letters containing anything the government would dislike."

This, truly, is what styles itself a liberal government,

---

[1] Histoire des Etats de l'Eglise depuis la Première Révolution Française, p. 261.
[2] The Congress and the Cabinet, p. 35.

and one favourable to the free and spontaneous wishes of the people!

"Such," the noble lord proceeds to say, "is the intimidation by which the so-called *popular vote* of annexation was obtained! The amount of the population which alone took part in it has been admitted by those who fixed the constituency to have been intended to comprise only one twenty-fifth of the population; and as one-half of those intended to poll refused to take any part, the extinction of the country, the absorption of all its Athenian glories in brave but Bœotian Piedmont, was only voted by one in fifty of the population."

Here Lord Normanby is rigidly accurate, and official figures confirm his testimony. The secretary of the Constituent Assembly in Tuscany, M. Galeotti, has himself positively admitted, in his report, that out of a population of 1,806,740 souls only 35,210 electors took part in the vote of forfeiture.[1]

Well might the noble lord say,—

"The vote was obtained by every variety of intimidation and wholesale corruption, under the protection of the Sardinian flag. The constituency was arbitrarily limited; not more than half of those selected of the classes favourable to the change actually voted. But more; *these electors were never told and did not know for what their deputies were summoned*: and those deputies, on that deliberation or explanation, in a silent sitting of a few minutes, voted the extinction of their country, which during the last five hundred years has boasted citizens proud of that country and worthy of it, somewhat superior to the Piedmontese tools which now fill the benches of the Palazzo Vecchio."

Lord Normanby adds, with the sound sense of honesty and justice, as an excuse for the Tuscans taking no part in the elections:—"It would be hard to expect a people who have never known what political existence meant to

---

[1] La Paix de Villafranca et les Conférences de Zurich, par le *Chevalier Louis Debrauz*, p. 44.

be ready to risk ruin, to say nothing of the dungeon or the dagger."

The atrocities committed at Parma before the eyes of the Sardinian authorities, and which are still unpunished, show what the infuriated passions of a populace are capable of, and confirm Lord Normanby's assertions, where he speaks of ruin, prisons, and daggers. The rigorous intimidation enforced in the Romagna against what were called manipulations in favour of the Pope, and the execrable scenes at Verachio, show too clearly whether opinions contrary to those of the revolution could be expressed with safety. The thousand manœuvres employed to agitate the inhabitants of the Romagna are notorious; and, in particular, the pressure of itinerant agents, who wrote upon the doors of houses, "We are for King Victor Emmanuel," and went about into *cafés* to collect names and signatures, even taking those of schoolboys;[1] while the slightest manifestation in favour of restoring the Pope's authority was rigorously put down.[2]

Things, then, passed in the Romagna precisely as they did in Tuscany; and on this point we have the formal testimony of an English gentleman, Mr. Bowyer, who states, in a letter to the *Times*, that the pretended government of the Romagna exists, in spite of the formal wishes of the inhabitants; that no one is allowed to read, to write, or to utter a word against the reigning faction and the secret societies; that the so-called parliament of the Romagna does not represent a sixtieth of the population; and that the total number of electors allowed is only 18,000, while of this number not a third could be prevailed on to vote by force, intimidation, or bribery.

We could cite many other authorities as to the voting in the Romagna and the duchies; and none of the revo-

---

[1] Histoire des Etats de l'Eglise depuis la Première Révolution Française, p. 274.
[2] Order of the day of General Mezzacapo, dated Forli, August 2.

lutionary journals, whether official or not, have ventured to contradict these assertions.

We learn from the *Journal of Rome* (10th September), that in the Romagna but a tenth of the population was inscribed on the list of electors; that two-thirds of this tenth refused to take part in a vote which must offend the Holy Father; and that, of the third which did vote, several voted for the Papal government.

It is clear that the elections which were paraded as the unanimous work of the population were, on the contrary, the doing of an utterly insignificant fraction.

In the case of Modena, the *Vienna Gazette* has charged M. Farini with having knowingly and intentionally excluded the country population: and he has not denied the charge. But, allowing for such exclusion, it has been proved that there still remained 72,000 electors in the duchy of Modena. Out of this number, how many voted? —scarcely 4,000. Yet what right had these four thousand to force the choice of all the inhabitants of the duchy?

The duchy of Modena had already, in 1848, been called upon to vote its annexation to Piedmont. A spirited Modenese had then the courage to expose, before the Chamber of Deputies at Turin, the way in which the voting was carried on. His petition, presented to the chamber on the 13th November, 1848, speaks in these terms:— "If, gentlemen, you will take the trouble to examine the grounds upon which the annexation of Modena to your kingdom rests, you cannot avoid concluding that act to be illegal; liberty was wanting, the voting was vicious, and there was not a majority: the right of voting was granted to minors, to criminals, to persons degraded and disqualified from all political rights: double votes were received, and innumerable intrigues carried on by those whose office it was to watch over the legality of the voting."

But the Dictator Farini himself has enabled us, in his history of the Roman state, to appreciate the worth of these Italian elections. He himself has informed us of the methods pursued in the elections at Rome to the Constituent Assembly:—"All power was in the hands of the clubs; they alone turned the elections as they pleased; and they neglected no measure to insure the success of their candidates. They used as tools a number of young men blinded by their enthusiasm, and fanatics of the lowest class, whose ignorance supplied the place of courage. They gave out that should the results of the elections be hostile to them, they did not care, and would find means in any case of arriving at their ends." — (The Roman State, by *Louis Farini*. Florence, 1851.) M. Farini adds, that at the elections of the Capitol the agitators were feed from the public treasury, that the numbers were altered, and that in these ways the clubs triumphed. When a man of spirit dared to vote according to his conscience, he was publicly denounced.

So that, according to the Dictator Farini, three principal measures were adopted in order to secure the success of the elections: votes were bought with the public money; the numbers were tampered with; and they who would not vote with the revolution were menaced. It is well known that at the elections to the constituent assembly at Rome a considerable number of voters, instead of putting one ticket into the urn, threw in several, some as many as thirty, filled up with names of all kinds, including those of abandoned women; they merely substituted a masculine termination for the feminine one: and this completed the number of votes required to render the elections valid.[1]

---

[1] At first the bulletins were read out publicly, one by one, after the balloting. But the populace, whose taste for fun and laughter had survived the sad events of those days, had taken care that every now and then the readers should come to some piece of coarse pleasantry, which caused the spectators to forget the gravity which becomes a people who are presiding over their own future destinies. For instance:—"*I vote for Pope Sixtus V., that he may hang you.*" Another: "*For the devil, that he may roast you.*" A third: "*I vote for Master Litta*" (this meant the hangman). A fourth: "*I choose the rope that is to hang you,*" with others of similar taste. These bulletins when read out caused such bursts of laughter, that the criers, pretending that some bulletins were so badly written that

Such is the truth about these aspirations of the Italians, these popular suffrages, which are held up to us as an argument fatal to the rights of the former sovereigns, and as a paramount and unanswerable reason for the annexation to Piedmont.

And now we would ask, Is it not easy to discern for what end Piedmont has been working for the last ten years? Is not the march of her policy now clear? Without her alliance with the revolution, she could not have used it to overthrow the governments which were in her way; without previously oppressing and persecuting the Church and the Holy See, she could not well have plundered them. The Sardinian cabinet has made a profitable speculation of the noble idea of Italian independence and nationality; to them it meant the absorption of all the states and governments of the Peninsula into the Piedmontese monarchy; the declarations of the emperor, instead of meeting with respect, having been obstinately ignored by their insatiable ambition; ignored during the war, and ignored after the peace. And, at the present moment, the chances seem to be in favour of the emperor's reiterated assurances, which the Pope and the bishops received with so much confidence, remaining a dead letter; and that after we have gained six victories, and sacrificed 50,000 of our soldiers! What have we gained in return? We have seen the principles of revolution triumph, monarchies overturned, the Papacy humbled, two hundred millions of Catholics wounded to the quick, long troubles excited in the Church and in the world, and the menace of a new war—as the imperial note of the 9th September states—and of new commotions left suspended over Europe! For it is obvious that, as long as Austria is encamped in her quadrilateral, and

---

it was too difficult to read them publicly, decided that for the future the urns should be opened privately, and the result afterwards published. It was then, probably, that the tampering with the results of the balloting, alluded to by Dictator Farini, commenced.

remains mistress of Venice, Piedmont will pursue her old policy, and Austria will one day try a second time the fate of battles, perhaps not without allies.

But does Piedmont think to chain France for ever to her destinies, and to fall back upon us in all the emergencies which her grasping ambition may create? Impossible: for the emperor, in the same note of the 9th of September, addressed a solemn declaration to Piedmont and Italy: " Let Italy not deceive herself: there is but one power in Europe which will go to war *for an idea;* that is France, and France has accomplished her task."

Such, then, was the deeply-laid and far-reaching scheme of Piedmontese policy: appearing first in a systematic hostility to the Church, and partially enunciated in a European congress; understood from the beginning and welcomed with enthusiasm by the whole revolutionary party in Italy; and finally carried into execution, contrary to our declarations, but by means of our victories. Such was, too, amid the agitations of war, and under the pressure of Piedmontese dictators, the deceit and the precipitation which characterized the first votes of annexation. After a long tenure of the governments, and after new diplomatic phases which we shall soon describe, the annexation has been again, I will not say submitted to, but imposed upon, popular suffrage by Piedmont. We shall see if this second vote was more genuine than the former; we shall give the necessary details as to the manner in which it was organized and taken. But before arriving, I do not say at the final catastrophe of the Italian revolution—for, unless something unforeseen arrests its march, we have not yet seen the end—but at what we may call the close of the first act, let us leave Piedmont for a time, and speak of another intervention, another interference, which has also exerted a fatal influence upon the affairs of Italy. It is time now to speak of England, and the part she has played in this important question.

CHAPTER XIX.

ENGLAND.

I CANNOT avoid speaking here of England; the part she plays in the Roman question is too important to be passed by in silence. But, since I have before me that great and illustrious nation, I shall speak my whole mind about her, openly but not bitterly—not to excite passions, but, on the contrary, to extinguish, if possible, the hatred which has been too long fostered in her bosom, and thus to prepare from afar the reconciliation and pacification of the future.

No! I do not write these pages *to make a blind attack on the inhabitants of the most celebrated island in the world*, to use the expression of Bossuet; and I cannot but join with that great bishop in hoping for better days for England and the Church, and for a reconciliation of which the destinies of the English people and the future of Christian civilization throughout the world have equal need.

"Alas!" said M. de Montalembert, with sound sense and in accents of the most just and lively regret, "the Church is wanting to England, and England is wanting to the Church. With their indefatigable activity and indomitable energy, what would not the English people have done for the faith, had they remained faithful to their religion! What strength, what support, what an abundant harvest would not the Roman Church have found in that race which gave to her in former times St. Anselm, St. Thomas, St. Edmund, the bravest champions of her liberty, and which now devotes to the propagation of a false and powerless Christianity so much wealth and so much perseverence! And in return, what a salutary and blessed influence would not Catholicism have exercised on the heart of the English people, in bending its obstinacy, softening its acrimony, and, above all, diminishing its unyielding selfishness!"

It is under the inspiration of those noble and religious feelings, and with the most sincere and ardent wish for peace and reconciliation, that I take up this delicate and important subject. It is true I shall point out the evident influence on the policy of England of her anti-Catholic rancour, and her manifest injustice and ingratitude towards the Church from whom she received the faith; but, on the other hand, despite present persecution and so much deep-rooted prejudice, I shall express the hopes that it is permitted to found upon the claims of justice, and upon the power of honour over a nation formerly so fruitful in great saints, and always so fruitful in great men; from such a nation we may always hope for a better policy, and a return to truth and justice in a happier future.

The English nation are, assuredly, great in many respects; they possess eminent qualities of mind and character; but it is on account of that very greatness that I am struck with the more wonder and sadness, when I behold the persistency of obsolete rancours and the passions of another age. It is manifest that with some men, at least, in England, the hatred of popery does not grow old; time seems only to add new vigour to it in the hearts of several.

But, may I ask, What is there in the Catholic Papacy that can be to England an eternal reproach or a perpetual danger? The political passions which were formerly mixed up with religious struggles have long since disappeared. The reigning dynasty has nothing to fear from the Catholics: it reckons amongst them its most loyal subjects—I might say its most intrepid soldiers. No pretender to the crown could now shelter ambitious designs under the flag of religion. Three centuries have passed over the usurpation of the Church property, and no one dreams of disturbing its present owners. Why, then, are some Englishmen obstinately bent on stirring up in the nineteenth century all the anti-Catholic passions of the worst days of Henry VIII. and Elizabeth? Why do we see with them this implacable and undying hatred which has no longer any reason for its existence, and which neither religious dogmatism nor political passions can sufficiently explain? Have not Pitt, Canning, Sir Robert Peel, the Duke of Wellington, Lord Macaulay, Lord Lansdowne, proved clearly enough that the duty of true statesmen is not to revive and to perpetuate hatred in the hearts of nations, but to bring back those who are worthy to the ever-glorious and ever-open paths of truth and justice.

There is something truly monstrous in this hatred of Anglicanism. England, unfortunately, is not the only country in Europe spiritually separated from the Holy See; but neither in Prussia, nor in Protestant Germany, nor in Russia, do we see this persevering hatred of which I speak.

For my part, I cannot believe that this hatred has its root in the very heart of the English nation, nor that it is an inspiration of its genius, a consequence of its laws and habits, nor that it can be looked upon as necessary when it is not even profitable to it.

No! such sentiments do not become such a people: they would bind them down to an unjust and inglorious policy, which, I may be allowed to ask them, if it is not time to abandon; and, in doing so, I do not mean to offend Englishmen; I appeal to themselves alone. It is no offence to say to a people: Listen to justice rather than your passions; be guided by your noble instincts, and by your real and great interests: you go astray when you pursue a course unworthy of you, because it is devoid of justice and of greatness. Be what you can be—a just and generous people.

I hope that the noble good sense of the English people will at length understand these things, and will shake off the yoke of ancient prejudices. This enmity will not last for ever; I love to repeat the words of Bossuet: " I cannot believe that this learned and illustrious nation will persist in the hatred she has conceived for the chair of Saint Peter, whence she received Christianity. No doubt God has allowed her to commit such geat excesses only that she may more easily discover her error. Her days of blindness will at length go by, and God will hear the prayers and the groans of His saints."

It is with this wish and in this hope that I begin. I have but one object in view,—it is to place the English face to face with themselves; to ask of them to judge themselves in their consciences, calmly and honestly, and to recognize in what they are doing against Rome old prejudices which ought at length to cease, and an injustice which it would be worthy of them to redeem by a generous reparation.

I.

MALEVOLENT PREJUDICES.

"One must have courage to do justice to England at the present time, and to remain faithful to the admiration with which she has inspired of old the lovers of liberty. In all her relations with foreign nations, her fickleness, her ingratitude, her strange partialities, her revolting selfishness, the abuse of her own strength, her contempt for the weakness of others, her utter indifference to justice whenever there was no interest to be forwarded and no power to be respected,—all these are more than enough to rouse against her the indignation of honest minds."[1]

---

[1] *M. de Montalembert*, on the Political future of England.—M. de Montalembert repeated in this book what he had said eight years before, on the contrast between the foreign policy of England and that of France :—"We, too, have sad pages in our history, but I know of nothing that can be compared with this odious policy. We have, indeed, made foreign nations bear the yoke of despotism, but we had begun by loving it, and taking it upon ourselves. We have even carried, with our bayonets, anarchy and devastation into many countries of Europe, but we had first been intoxicated ourselves with that frenzy we were propagating abroad. But what we have never done, is to keep for ourselves the blessings of order, justice, liberty of the social hierarchy, and to foment and abet

It is an undoubted friend of England that has written those lines. Well, cannot England at length see that the hostile policy she has been made to pursue against the Pope but too well justifies all those reproaches.

It is especially Lord Palmerston that I accuse here. I must say it is in him that the animosity I deplore seems personified. I am told that Lord Palmerston, in religious matters, is more noted for indifference than fanaticism. If so, he is the more culpable in my eyes; for I know of nothing more criminal and more odious, than to affect through policy and personify in oneself passions one does not feel. At all events, it is Lord Palmerston, his baleful influence, his evil genius, his detestable policy, that the Holy See has long had to contend with. Before 1848; during the Congress of Paris; before and after the last war; at all times, and in all places, has Lord Palmerston accused, traduced, and slandered the Holy See.

Before the catastrophe of 1848, I shall only mention the mission given to Lord Minto, "that incendiary excursion," as M. de Montalembert says, "of a semi-official plenipotentiary, everywhere assuming the right to censure publicly the sovereigns, and to inflame populations already so excitable."[1] But during the congress of Paris, what course did Lord Palmerston pursue? And in Parliament, in the speeches he made after the congress, what was his language? I do not hesitate to say, that never in the conduct nor in the language of M. de Cavour himself was there shown more passion or more injustice. For instance, how could the plenipotentiary sent by Lord Palmerston to

---

disorder or tyranny in other countries. No, thank God! France has not to reproach herself with such selfishness or such blindness. I am happy to pay her this homage, not in a mean and narrow spirit of exclusive patriotism, which I have ever condemned, but in obedience to the dictater of my conscience, and to vindicate the outraged majesty of justice, which forces from me a cry of indignation that I had long repressed."—Speech of the 14th of January, 1848, in the Chamber of Peers, on the affairs of Switzerland.

[1] *M. de Montalembert*, Pius IX. and Lord Palmerston.

the congress write these words, as insulting to France as they are void of truth and justice: " The occupation of the Papal dominions *sanctions a bad government.*" And how was it that he was not afraid " of *exciting discontent amongst the people, and a disposition to rebel,*" when he himself urged them on? Was it possible to denounce more openly a sovereign to his people, or to encourage rebellion more expressly?

The official speeches of Lord Palmerston's colleagues were in keeping with the diplomatic notes. We know in what way Lord John Russell commented, in the House of Commons, on the Memorandum of M. de Cavour, and spoke " of the intolerable tyranny of the Roman Government."

If it ill becomes a statesman, speaking in the British Parliament, thus to forget the rights of justice and the respect due to the weak, how are we to explain, except by sentiments too unworthy to be avowed, those persevering attacks on the Pope, and that complete silence about the Government of Austria, whose tyranny M. de Cavour had also denounced in his Memorandum of the 25th of March? What! English ministers had not one word to say against the military dictatorship which weighed upon Lombardy, and they could stoop to the lowest invectives to crush an absent and unarmed Pope?

Lord Palmerston went farther still, and, indeed, passed all limits: he forgot all truths, I might say all decency, when, in the House of Parliament, he—a minister of the crown, and invested with the highest authority a subject can possess in the world—dared to pronounce these words in honour of the revolutionary Government of Rome: " The Holy City was never better governed than in the absence of the Pope."

I may well say, with M. de Montalembert: " The bitterest enemies of England could not wish her a more cruel insult than to see her prime minister thus making himself the posthumous apologist of a government which sprang from and ended in murder."

To what iniquitous comparisons has not Lord Palmerston

been carried away by his blind animosity! Is there in England a man of honour that does not blush when he sets those words side by side with the facts known to the world?

"Before, during, and after the siege of Rome, the dagger was the arm and the symbol of the so-called liberty, and the so-called Roman nationality. The stab that killed Rossi gave birth to the Roman republic, and that *democratic* and *blessed* dagger, as they called it, was carried in triumph and with singing through the streets of dishonoured Rome. And while that new republic lasted, assassination was the usual expedient of the secret societies to keep down the people by terrorism; and priests, officers, and citizens of all classes, were their victims. Nor was one of those assassins arrested or punished under the republic, not even that wretch Zambianchi, the colonel of the *finanzieri*, who had so many unoffending persons murdered at his barracks of San Calisto, and who, the worthy rival of Carrier, caused the venerable priest of the Minerva to be shot in his presence, at the end of a supper at which he had forced that venerable ecclesiastic to be present.—(Vide *Constitutionnel*, Sept. 23, 1849.) After the taking of Rome, they swore, and strictly kept their oath, to assassinate all who showed their joy, or favoured the French army. It is not likely that Lord Palmerston would dare to call into question the honesty of the French commanders. The orders of the day of General Rostolan and General Baraguey d'Hilliers, and many other documents besides, are there to show all the care and energy that were required to prevent the French soldiers themselves from falling under the steel of the assassins."[1]

Such was the government which the prime minister of England dared in the British Parliament to prefer to that of the Pope.

But enough of the past: let us see if what is said and done at the present time in England under the baleful

---

[1] *M. de Montalembert*, Pius IX. and Lord Palmerston.

influence of Lord Palmerston is less iniquitous or less revolting.

Would the English press make use towards the deadliest foe of England, or the worst government on earth, of the insults and calumnies it heaps day after day on the Pope? "Englishmen," says M. de Montalembert, "what would you say if the highest authorities and the most influential men in France were constantly to insult and decry the Anglican Church and its head?"[1] But that is not all: the hand of England, as well as of Piedmont, is but too plainly visible in all that is going on in Italy. Anglicanism, installed at Turin by M. de Cavour, seeks to spread itself over the whole country by the most active propagandism. To what lengths have they not gone? And what do not disclose to us these words of Lord Ellenborough, in his letter to Lord Brougham:—"I am ready, as a peer of England, to send arms to Garibaldi?"

Yes, it must be said, a hatred to the Pope, implacable because he is the Pope, and arrogant because he is weak, is all I can discover in that unbounded animosity, and in that pernicious policy, to which Lord Palmerston seems anxious to give up England, contrary to her true dignity, and consequently to her highest interests. For who does not see that this policy will be without glory and without profit, because it is without danger and without courage? For my part, when I contrast the greatness and power of England with the weakness of the peaceful sovereign of Rome; I shall even say, when I compare the conduct of Lord Palmerston towards the pontifical government with his policy towards other governments, I cannot help wondering how the noble English people have not yet understood that they have been too long made to play a part which degrades them.

"Treat the Pope as if he had two hundred thousand soldiers," said the First Consul to his ambassador at Rome. If the Pope had them, Lord Palmerston would not have

---

[1] *M. de Montalembert*, Pius IX. and Lord Palmerston.

used the revolting language I have mentioned : he took good care not to use it towards Austria, at least before her defeat. He would not have summoned to his bar, contrary to all justice and to all honour, a sovereign from whom he has received no offence, and from whom he has nothing to fear, absolutely nothing : neither military force, for he is without an army; nor even diplomatic notes, for the Pope has no accredited agent at the court of England. You may say what you please against him in your parliament, he is not there to defend himself; and you may say everything with impunity, for he has not, like the United States, fleets to send against yours. You may, you and your press, forgetful in his case alone of the safeguards with which you ever surround the accused in England, put him on his trial without examining his cause, condemn him without giving him a hearing, and dishonour him before all Europe without his having an opportunity to contradict you: you may at your ease insult, denounce, and threaten him with lofty arrogance; but you know how to bend your proud head, alter your tone, and lower your voice, when you are in presence of a power that can look you in the face. But history will one day say whether such conduct towards the weak was glorious, whether such animosity was in any way reconcilable with justice ; and, in fine, whether such a policy was worthy of so great a nation.

You put forward the independence of Italy ; when, may I ask, have you shown real anxiety about it ? Was it in 1848, when Charles-Albert, left to himself, could only say, in the delusion of his blind heroism : *L'Italia farà da se !* —when Venice, in distress, held out to you her hand, from which you turned away, was your flag then seen in the Peninsula, or on the Adriatic ? Was it in 1859, in the last war, when every one of you, statesmen of England, joined unanimously to avert the coming conflagration, and when you, Lord Palmerston, were seen to unite, in order to prevent the war, with the leader of your rivals, Lord Derby, who then inflicted on the policy of Piedmont a sharp censure which you did not hesitate to approve :

"We have intimated to Sardinia," said Lord Derby, "the regret she has caused us, by a course calculated to destroy the sympathies she had won by her late conduct."— (Speech in the House of Lords, 3rd of February, 1859.)

The orator who pronounced those words took pleasure in referring, at the conclusion of his speech, to the unanimity of opinion in the House; and your own language "was neither less precise nor less pacific." You reminded the House that "Austria held Lombardy by virtue of treaties," and you added, that "rights consecrated by treaties ought to be respected." If, then, it had depended on you, Austria would still be at Milan.

But if it is for the political regeneration of Italy that you are concerned, if you are not the enemies of the Pope still more than the friends of Italy, is it not strange that a small state of Italy, that has been governed for the last thousand years by an Italian sovereign, should, with the kingdom of Naples, which you can also attack with impunity, have wholly taken up your attention, whilst you looked on with indifference at the sufferings of Lombardy and Venetia, that were ruled by a sway very different from the mild and paternal government of the Holy Father? It is with that indifference that M. de Cavour bitterly reproached you on the 9th of February, 1859: "The Austrian Alps," said he, "do not allow the groans of Venice and of Milan to reach the heart of England!"

The fact is, you have done but one thing for Italy, and that was, not to draw your sword and shed your blood, but to attack, to insult, to calumniate, without danger and without a possibility of retaliation, the unoffending sovereign of the Roman States, the head of the Catholic Church. And now, when France alone has aided the Italians, and driven back Austria; when she has gained for them six victories, and shed the blood of 50,000 of her soldiers; when she has an undoubted right to say on what conditions she laboured to free Italy: when France has done all this—France, the eldest daughter of the Church; France, who has a traditional policy to support in Italy; who restored the throne of the Holy Father, and by those very treaties which you appealed to in favour of Austria, but which you willingly ignore when the interests of the Pope are at stake. Where can we discover, in all this policy, a semblance of courage, or of the commonest good faith?

CHAPTER XX.

ENGLAND.

HER BLINDNESS AND INJUSTICE.

I.

I SHALL even add: What can England gain by all this? What high interest has she that impels her to wage war to the death on the head of the Catholic Church? For my part, I can perceive none, unless, as the accusation has often been made against her, her selfishness finds its profit in continental disturbances. But if Lord Palmerston made such a calculation, it was no less revolting than fatal; and sooner or later the noble lord would thereby bring down upon his country not only disgrace, but disaster and ruin. Yes, if he had speculated on the peril of European order; if he had undertaken the task of adding fuel on the continent to the still smouldering fire of revolution; if, indeed, we must look upon him as the abettor of subversive principles and of anarchy, his guilty imprudence may cost his country dear. England, in her turn, might learn too soon that tempests cannot be let loose with impunity, and that the revolutionary blasts might one day blow back upon her island the storms she had gathered on the continent.

Can Lord Palmerston declare, before God and before men, that for the last ten years he has given no support to the spirit of disorder, that he has favoured no attempt at rebellion, and, in a word, that he is quite guiltless of all that revolution has done in Italy since 1850? I do not go farther back. Can he, the apologist of that Roman republic to which the dagger that killed M. Rossi gave birth, and the universal aggressor, not of strong governments, but of weak and threatened states—can he, I say, pretend that he has had no influence on the hopes of Garibaldi and Mazzini? Or can he dare to say that England has anything to gain by the success of their sanguinary designs?

But if you are not, as they say you are, the secret abettor of the revolutionists; if you do not trifle, in your selfishness, with the very principles of public order and of European peace; if social authority seems to you worthy of respect, why is it that you delight, not in upholding, but in lowering it, in the person of him who represents the highest moral power in Europe? It is true, indeed, that you do not believe in this moral power of the Papacy; but there are two hundred millions of men in the world who do, and that fact you do not deny. How is it possible that such a fact does not inspire you with some respect for the Pontiff whom those two hundred millions of men revere as the guide of their souls, and the teacher of their faith? Compare your language with that of one of your most illustrious contemporaries, who is a statesman and a Liberal as well as you,—who, like you, has not the happiness of being a son of the Catholic Church, to the greatness of which he has borne witness in the sincerity of his noble heart: M. Guizot loved liberty without ever conspiring with demagogy, and always understood the essential condition of social order—respect: "Catholicism," said he, one day, in one of the highest efforts of his eloquence, "is the greatest, the holiest school of respect the world has ever seen." Such is the sacred power you take pleasure every day in scoffing at, bitterly and unsparingly. Let honest men in England compare dispassionately the noble language I have just quoted with the tone of your habitual attacks, and the unbecoming articles of your papers, and I have confidence enough in their generosity and good faith to believe that they will blush for you and for their nation, whose prime minister you are.

If, leaving aside the interests of Europe, I were to speak to you on behalf of the interests of England, I should ask you whether it is a wise policy wantonly to wound the deepest, most tender, and sacred affections of two hundred millions of men, and of a considerable number of British subjects?

One day in 1848, at the French Tribune, in a memorable debate on the Roman expedition, an orator thus nobly expressed himself, amidst the cheers of the Assembly: "It is a great honour and a great happiness for the French republic to have inaugurated, if I may say so, its action upon the political world and foreign affairs, by preserving the independence of the Head of the Catholic Church; for my part, I congratulate my country with all my heart for having, by doing so, been able to impose a debt of admiration and gratitude on the hearts and consciences of so many millions of men scattered over the world."—(Speech of M. de Montalembert, November 30, 1848.)

Well, the words we have been accustomed to hear from the lips of Lord Palmerston, all that reaches us every day from England on the Italian question, this supercilious language, these wanton insults, these revolting calumnies, wound our hearts and rouse our indignation. Is it no injury, I would say in my turn, to the prospects of a people, to have imposed a debt of ingratitude and injustice upon the justly irritated consciences of all the Catholics upon earth?

Not to speak of other continental nations, are not the vast majority of Frenchmen Catholics? "You boast of your firm alliance with France, and you are right. But do you not fear that your perpetual invectives against the religion she professes will finally weaken this alliance?"

Such were the words M. de Montalembert addressed to you with the soundest good sense, and he added, "Some time ago, during the twenty years that the desperate war lasted which you waged against revolutionary France, you offered a generous hospitality (which nothing ought ever to make us forget) to the French priests and bishops exiled or their faith.

"And now, by a sad contrast, when the highest interests and main strength of your policy lie in your alliance with France, which has now become perhaps more Catholic than she was in the days of Louis XIV., you are not afraid to display on all occasions your deep animosity towards the head and living symbol of the religion she professes.

"And what is true of France is no less so of all the other Catholic nations with whom you have relations to keep up."

Such also were the reflections which the most venerable leader of the Whigs wished to impress on you: "Every country," said Lord Lansdowne, "with Roman Catholic subjects has an interest in the condition of the Roman States, and must take care that the Pope may exercise his authority without being impeded by any temporal influence of a nature to affect his spiritual authority."

"There," added M. de Montalembert,—"there is the truth told you by one whom you cannot suspect, by an Englishman and an Anglican, a politician and not a churchman, a lover of liberty and not of despotism."

It is true, indeed, that the Catholics are a minority in England; but ought not that very fact to be a motive for treating them with regard? However, leaving aside that motive suggested by honour alone, is not the number of British subjects whom Lord Palmerston's conduct towards the Pope grieves and revolts large enough to make it most unwise not to take them into consideration? Who does not know that Catholicism is steadily progressing throughout the British empire? Since Catholic emancipation was won by O'Connell, it is not only in Ireland, but in England, and even in Scotland, and especially throughout the vast English colonies, that the number of dioceses, parishes, churches, monasteries, and Catholic congregations is ever on the increase. What good can come from wounding all those consciences, and irritating all these souls? What are the English Catholics to think of the strange animosity of their Government towards the Pontiff whom they love and revere? What becomes of their freedom of conscience, if the religion which they have a right to profess, is unceasingly insulted and calumniated in its Head by the prime minister of their country?

Moreover, how deep is the wound inflicted by your policy on Catholic hearts, you may see yourselves, by the great public manifestations that have lately taken place in Ireland and elsewhere.

Ireland.—Ah! you have heaped on her oppression and disaster, and there is no people in the world, not even the helots of Sparta, who have been treated by their conquerors with more pitiless barbarity. But I do not intend to go over all the wrongs and misfortunes of that unhappy country, nor to call up in judgment against you the blood you have shed, and the tears you have caused to flow. Ireland has suffered all, and, thanks to God, the dawn of her deliverance has come, at least I hope so: the liberty she has won, stronger than your hatred, will do the rest, with time: Ireland has suffered all with heroic patience, and your horrible tyranny has not disheartened her fidelity.

Well! do you know what is harder for Ireland to bear than proscription and spoliation, than famine and death, than the dreadful emigration which is still her sad lot every day? It is the outrages you offer to the chair of Peter, the wanton insults and base calumnies you shower down on Pius IX. What wounds her to her inmost soul, and makes her feel most keenly all your contempt for her, is your conduct towards the Pontiff, whom she holds in veneration, and who came to her assistance in the days of her most cruel sufferings; she has not forgotten that Pius IX. raised his voice to implore in her behalf the compassion of the Catholic world, when she was starving beside your opulence and disdain. How is it possible that you do not see the deep wound you inflict on the Irish heart by insulting what it loves, and traducing what it reveres? All Ireland was moved when she saw the danger that threatened Pius IX., and by the mighty voice of her meetings she protested against your conduct. At the great meeting of Dublin, so numerous and so enthusiastic, we felt that it was the heart of Ireland that beat in unison with all Catholic hearts in the world;[1] and the loud cheers which generous and faithful Ireland then gave, which were re-echoed by her mountains, and came even to our ears in distant lands, drowned for a while the noise of your fierce and bitter outrages.

The congress was about to meet; the line of conduct you intend to pursue was no secret; and Ireland protested in the way I shall relate. It was a grand and noble spectacle, well worthy to be contemplated, and I wish to give a moment's rest to my soul by dwelling on it.

A young member of the British Parliament presided over the great meeting, and was the first to speak:[2]—

"The moment is come," said he, "to prove that Ireland still retains her ancient faith. (Prolonged cheers.) No true Catholic can hesitate as to the course which it is his duty to take in this crisis in the affairs of the world. All Catholics are agreed in thinking that the preservation of the temporal power of the Pope is essential to the interests of religion. (Cheers.)

"It becomes the duty—the solemn duty—of every Catholic community to raise the voice of indignation, and, if necessary, of condemnation. (Loud cheers.)

"If, then, countrymen, it is the duty of Catholic nations generally to avow their determination to maintain the territorial independence of His Holiness, how much more is it the duty of Irishmen, from the peculiar nature of their position, to be explicit on this point. (Hear, hear.) We are associated with Protestant England—we are said by English statesmen and English writers to form part of a united kingdom, and in the attempt made to overshadow the distinct nationality with which Ireland has undoubtedly been stamped by the hand of God, we are alternately governed by contending factions of oligarchy, that cannot sympathize with us as a people, and that are hostile to us on account of our religion. Hence it is

---

[1] The Right Rev. Dr. Moriarty, Bishop of Kerry, speaking of the emotion of the Irish Catholics and of all Catholics throughout the world, the moment they heard of the threatened attack on the Holy Father, made use of this beautiful expression: "They had risen, as the arm rises instinctively to protect the head when it is in danger."

[2] Vide *Weekly Freeman's Journal*, November 19, 1859.

that at this critical juncture it is imperative upon Ireland to raise her voice, in order that she may preserve her identity among the nations. She must raise her voice loud enough to be heard at the remote ends of the earth, in order that it may be proclaimed that there are even yet five millions of Irishmen faithful, as were their fathers of old, in their allegiance to the chair of Peter. Five millions of Irishmen—" (*A voice:* "Six millions.") "Six millions, if you like—(cheers)—six millions of Irishmen, who disavow all connection with the traducers of the Holy Father, in order that it may be known that the government that would despoil him of his immemorial patrimony, although it may be strong enough to hold Ireland down, is most certainly not the government of her selection. (Cheers.)

"We shall call on Europe to witness that the policy of those men is not our policy; we shall protest, by the memory of those who are gone and who carried the banner of Catholicity in triumph through storms and persecutions, that Catholic Ireland has neither hand, act, or part in the policy that would deprive the Holy Father of any portion of his dominions." (Tremendous cheering.)

Thus spoke The O'Donoghue at the great meeting of the Catholic Young Men's Society in Dublin on the 16th of November, 1859. Later in the evening Mr. Sullivan spoke, and ended a noble speech by these words, which were received with most enthusiastic cheering:—

"Standing here to-night in the capital of this old Catholic land; standing here in the presence of its faithful sons—in presence too of one who well and nobly represents the ancient chieftains of our country—(cheering for The O'Donoghue of the Glens)—standing here, I say, as an Irishman and a Catholic, I lift up my hands and protest against, impeach, and denounce the wrong and outrage offered to the just and rightful, mild and liberty-loving sovereign, Pio Nono. I protest against and impeach it in the name of common humanity, in the name of progress, civilization, social order, and true liberty. I impeach it before heaven, before earth, before God, before man. I am here to say that come what may to that Pontiff, so dear to our hearts, Ireland will ever be found faithful to the Holy See!"

"Here," says the paper from which we extract the account of this meeting, "as Mr. Sullivan retired, the entire meeting rose to their feet, with a deafening burst of cheering, and a scene of indescribable enthusiasm followed; cheering, waving of hats, scarfs, and handkerchiefs, prolonged with apparently inexhaustible fervour, and it was only after a long interval that even partial silence was restored."

Another member of Parliament, Mr. John Pope Hennessy, came forward in his turn :—

"I have come," said he, "three hundred miles to meet you, and willingly, indeed, would I travel from one end of Europe to the other to assist at deliberations such as yours : for what is it we are met here to-night to do? We are met to discharge the greatest task that Irishmen have undertaken since the days of O'Connell; and when I mention his name, and think of the objects of this meeting, I do feel most keenly that Ireland sustained by his death a loss that centuries may not supply. Beneath the dome of St. Peter's his heart is enshrined, and in the sacred cause you are here to defend, that heart, in his lifetime, ever beat with the most filial devotion. (Cheers.) You are, I am happy to say, like your chairman and myself, young men. It is young men we want now (cheers); for when young men sympathize, let us not forget that youthful sympathy is but the prelude to action.

"We have lately seen the anti-papal ranks recruited by one who was a cabinet minister of the late government, Lord Ellenborough. Lord Ellenborough has done us, I think, a good service. In writing to Lord Brougham he said :—'I am prepared, as an English peer of the realm, to send arms from England to Garibaldi.' (Groans.) Now, I want you, as young men, to give to that the proper answer. I know only one answer, and it is this—that not only will you send arms, but that you will send men also. (Enthusiastic and prolonged cheering.) My reply to Lord Ellenborough is a very short and simple piece of advice to you—arm (cheers), arm in defence of the Sovereign Pontiff, the mildest of rulers, one who has for you the deepest sympathy, and who has been so grossly insulted by English statesmen in the face of Europe. Let me tell you, too, that on the day after the publication of Lord Ellenborough's letter I was writing to Lord Brougham about some private affairs, and I took occasion to refer to that letter. I told him, relying on what I know of the Irish people, that if Lord Ellenborough and the other friends of liberalism sent arms to the insurgents in Italy, that the people of Ireland would do what I have now asked you to do. (Hear, hear, and cheers.) I also told Lord Brougham what most of you, perhaps, are not aware of, that Garibaldi, to whom Lord Ellenborough proposes to send arms, was a member of a secret society in Italy, the 33rd rule of which is as follows :—"If the victim whom we as secret judges condemn, escape, he shall be incessantly pursued, and shall be struck, were he to shelter on the bosom of his mother, or on the tabernacle of Christ.' (Sensation, and cries of 'oh! oh!') Now, that is the style of politicians with whom English statesmen sympathize. . . ."

The speaker ended by calling upon Ireland to proclaim aloud her calm but settled determination to defend the Holy See.

It is indeed with admiration that we relate such scenes: our heart is moved by them, and our love for the noble and unhappy country which gave birth to such generous and faithful men would be increased if possible.

II.

Bossuet says somewhere that "when people do not place justice on their side, they always remain weak on that point." Let England forgive me for telling her this is her weakness. Thanks be to God, violated right and outraged justice rise up against iniquity with overwhelming and imperishable force. At the very moment of its ephemeral triumph injustice receives a fatal wound, which sooner or later must unnerve and lay low the conqueror.

And this should console us when we meditate with unavailing sadness on the wrongs which so often triumph here below. Who has not at times been tempted to fear, at the sight of what takes place upon the earth, that this world has been hopelessly given over to the empire of force? But no! justice is not exiled from it for ever. Banished as it often is from public affairs, it takes refuge in the consciences of men: it finds there a stronghold where it may await the day of reparation, when it will inevitably be reinstated in its rightful empire over souls.

These thoughts naturally occur to my mind when I reflect upon the contrast which the Pope and England at this moment offer to the world; when I behold on one side that weak, inoffensive, and unarmed sovereignty, which neither threatens nor oppresses, the only power on earth that blesses; and on the other, that haughty, supercilious, arrogant policy, which, like the stern hero of Homer, *Jura negat sibi nata;* when I behold that imperious hostility, those leagued animosities, those bitter accusations, those unwearied attacks on the august old man who sits in the Vatican: yes, when I see before me this picture, representing in its saddest colours the vile and odious empire of force, the eternal oppression here below of the weak by the strong, ah! it is then my only consolation to remember the inviolable asylum of the human conscience, the avenging tears of oppressed innocence, and the unforeseen but inevitable victory of justice!

This peaceful sovereign of the States of the Church, the father still more than the king of his people, who has done so much for them, for Italy, and for the peace of Europe, and whose benefits have been all turned against himself, he it is who is accused of disturbing the world, of being the cause of dissensions, *the only obstacle to peace*. Yes, you dared to use these words in your parliament. In vain he answered you, "Peace, peace! but who wishes for it more than I? who has done more to obtain it? who represents it on earth if not I?" And you reply, as the wolf did to the lamb, "I say you are disturbing it; and if it is not you, it is yours."

Do we not find this monstrous injustice in all the speeches and invectives of English statesmen against the Holy Father? From their high position, whence they may accuse and threaten with impunity, they condescend to acknowledge that the Pope is *humane and kind*,—a sort of lamb; but they hasten to add, that *those who govern in the name of His Holiness* are wretches, who create disturbances on all sides *by their tyranical acts*.

"In good truth, my lord," said M. de Montalembert to Lord Palmerston in 1856, "tell us where are those tyrannical acts. When, where, how, and by whom committed! Relate them to us, point out the tyranny, and name the tyrants. We defy you to do so: you cannot. You repeat some idle declamations whined forth in your antechambers by unknown refugees or apostates. You would not suffer in England the presence of an official representative of the power which you do not cease to denounce; you are not supposed officially to be aware of his existence; but you are far from honouring him with your indifference. You are without accredited and official agents in the Roman States to report to you what takes place there: but you have there clandestine and more than suspicious agents.[1] .... Since when do you, English, claim the right of condemning people unheard? In this instance, where the destinies of a people and the honour of a world are at stake, and in presence of that august defendant whom you presume to call to your bar, where are your witnesses? Where are your proofs? Where are your scruples? Where are your precautions? What has become of the traditional integrity of your tribunals? Where is your natural sense of right?"

Assuredly these reproachful questions and these withering sarcasms are not uncalled for. When, in fact, has Lord Palmerston treated the sovereign of the Roman States, I will not say with deference, but with common justice? When did he attempt a straightforward discussion, based not on vague and lying accusations, but on a conscientious and impartial study of the facts? Where can we find in those bitter and violent speeches, repeated after him by the English press, even the semblance of impartiality, or the shadow of the forbearance to which, doubtless, a sovereignty is entitled, which so many ages have venerated, and even the schismatical Emperor of Russia has treated with respect?

They speak of reforms; but, candidly speaking, are reforms what Lord Palmerston desires? Or do those desire them whom he upholds in Italy—the revolutionists or Piedmontese? No; it is easy to see, this is not what they want. Lord Palmerston, as well as the revolutionists, have their minds made up: "Whatever Pius IX. may do,

---

[1] M. de Montalembert mentions here a certain Mr. Freeborn, "accused and convicted of *calumny* against France and the French army, in the famous memorandum of the consuls at Rome, which was got up and signed by himself after the siege, in which, with affected regret, the injuries and dilapidations were represented as effected by our artillery, which had been entirely committed by the besieged themselves, whom he honoured with his sympathy and encouragement."

we will use his concessions only to overturn him," said one of their papers on the very day when he issued his *motu proprio* of reform. They have but too faithfully kept their word.

Moreover, the official documents of English diplomacy have themselves informed us that on the very day after the treaty of Villafranca, Count Walewski stated to Lord Cowley that "the Pope had spontaneously declared his readiness to follow the counsels which France might offer him." And in the month of September, when the Duke de Grammont proposed a plan of reforms to the Pope, he was answered "that His Holiness was quite willing to adopt them, provided the integrity of the States of the Church were guaranteed."[1]

After all, I may be allowed to ask Lord Palmerston, why do you assert this right of interference in the affairs of a foreign government only in the case of the Pope, as if his dominions alone required reforms? But, throughout all Germany, I hear loud demands for a great reform in the conditions of the federal compact: has the Emperor of Austria no need of reform in his states? or has Russia none? And what of many other great nations? How is it that you, who are so inquisitorial, so censorious towards the Pope, have no fault to find with other governments? I repeat, it is that they are strong and that the Pope is weak.

But, is your own legislation perfect, and are your political institutions irreproachable? Some two years ago, an omission, a serious omission, was pointed out in the British legislation, which threatened the security of governments: and this reform was proposed,—Lord Palmerston was prime minister, and brought it forward as necessary to his policy; but the country, considering the tone of the French Government as dictatorial, refused its consent, and the noble lord fell from power. But the Pope, though less strong, has an equal right to deprecate interference, and this right becomes a duty when he resists injustice.

---

[1] Lord Cowley's Despatch to Lord John Russell.

And as to the voice of the people, if it is, indeed, honestly, and without sinister motives, that you appeal to it against the Pope, why do you not listen to it elsewhere?

Look at the Sultan, Turkey,—a government and a country that are a disgrace to Europe: look at the Christians of the East groaning under cruel bondage. Has Lord Palmerston ever said of the Sultan what he has dared to say of the Pope? Has he ever asked for the suppression of the decrepit empire of the Turks, as he now asks for the dispossession of the Pope? Does he concern himself about the wishes of those Christian populations of the East, labouring under ill-treatment and oppression, he who makes such a noise about the suspicious votes of an assembly sprung from insurrection, and about a universal suffrage pronounced under the twofold coercion of Piedmontese arms and of revolutionary violence?

"Remember Poland," I would say with M. de Montalembert, "the greatest and most illustrious of oppressed and suppressed nationalities,—Poland, of old the watchword of the liberals of all shades and of all nations. Has its lot been bettered? has its life begun to bloom again? Has eternal justice, outraged by this murder of a people, been appeased? No! And yet you are all silent."

If Lord Palmerston is animated by a zeal for the wishes of population, and not by his hatred of popery, why did he repress, ten-years ago, with implacable severity, the mere symptoms of a revolt in the Ionian Islands, "where," as M. de Montalembert says, "religion, habits, traditions, interests, language,—everything, in short, is opposed to British rule?"

This enormous inconsistency, this flagrant injustice, has been pointed out even in England.

"Within this very year," writes, with the frankness of conviction, a distinguished member of the House of Lords, Lord Normanby, "another assembly has voted annexation to another state; but this is an act which affects the interests and hurts the *prestige* of England. In vain, then, would it be urged that there a parliament is regularly constituted; that we could not complain of the electoral law, for it had been framed by ourselves; that the question of nationality was much more clear and definite; and that it was not here as in Tuscany, a question of the absorption of the purest Italians by a mixed race, for military purposes, but that the desire of Greeks was for union with the kingdom of Greece, a kingdom created by European arrangement, to which we were parties, subsequent to the time when the Ionian Islands were placed under the protection of England. Have we been flattering ourselves that this is a question of which we shall hear no more?"[1] "And it is you who dare at present, on the opposite shore of the Adriatic, to throw all the weight of your unjust partiality into the balance which is to regulate wrongs a hundredfold less grievous, and aversions a hundredfold less justifiable than those which you have drowned in blood in Corfu."[2]

No; you have evidently two mouths and two measures, as the Scripture says. I seek in vain, I shall not say for a motive, but even for a plausible pretext, for what you are doing against the Pope: I can find nothing but malevolent partiality and crying injustice.

Ah! were you in your turn put upon your trial, with what justice might not the solemn injunction of the Gospel be applied to you: "Cast out first the beam out of thy own eye, and then shalt thou see to cast out the mote out of thy brother's eye."

We constantly hear your papers speaking of the *tyranny of the Pope*, of *clerical despotism*, and the *clerical yoke*. Have you, then, forgotten your own history, the history even of late years? Having done what you have done, how is it possible to speak as you speak?

---

[1] The Congress and the Cabinet, by the Marquis of Normanby, K.G. London: John Murray, Albemarle Street.
[2] Pius IX. and France in 1849 and 1859, by M. de Montalembert.

You have just been reminded of the cruelty with which you crushed the revolt in the Ionian Islands. And India! You, who reproached Pius IX. so bitterly with having retaken a city that had rebelled, how did you act in the late war in India? But let us cast a veil over these horrors, the enormity of which a portion of the English press could not help stigmatizing.

At home, in England, Scotland, and Ireland, what have you done? I do not speak of the middle ages, nor of the stormy days of the civil wars, but "hardly a century ago, in the age of philosophy and enlightenment, did you not crush, with the most pitiless barbarity, the revolt of the last partisans of the Stuarts? Did you not put to death the heads of the noblest houses in Scotland, and others less known, with a cruelty surpassed only by the atrocities of Pombal about the same time? And, sixty years ago, when Ireland, almost worn out with six centuries of oppression and suffering, rose up again in rebellion, and opened her arms to the French revolution, did not your scaffolds, the brutal outrages of an unbridled soldiery, and the cold-hearted cruelty of partial judges, exhaust all the horrors that implacable conquest can inflict upon an alien and vanquished race?"[1]

Ah! when a people has before them Ireland—such a name and such recollections—how is it possible that they do not, for very shame, moderate their language.

I shrink from all I should have to relate, were I to give the history of English misgovernment in Ireland. "The policy of Cromwell," says Lord Macaulay, "was comprised in one word, which, as Lord Clarendon tells us, was often in the mouths of the Englishry of that time. That word was extirpation."[2]

"The statute-book of Ireland was filled with enactments which furnish to the Roman Catholics but too good a

---

[1] Pius IX. and Lord Palmerston.
[2] Speeches of the Right Hon. T. B. Macaulay, M.P., corrected by himself, p. 296. London: Longman & Co. 1854.

ground for recriminating on us when we talk of the barbarities of Bonner and Gardiner; and the harshness of those odious laws was aggravated by a more odious administration. For, bad as the legislators were, the magistrates were still worse."[1]

And, in the opening passage of his celebrated history, the same noble author, referring to the events he is about to record, says: "It will be seen how, in two important dependencies of the crown, wrong was followed by just retribution; ..... how Ireland, cursed by the domination of race over race, and of religion over religion, remained, indeed, a member of the empire, but a withered

---

[1] "So great and so long has been the misgovernment of Ireland," says the Rev. Sydney Smith, in the *Edinburgh Review*, November, 1820, "that we verily believe the empire would be much stronger if everything was open sea between England and the Atlantic, and if *skates and codfish* swam over the fair land of Ulster. Such jobbing, such profligacy—so much direct tyranny and oppression—such an abuse of God's gifts—such a profanation of God's name for the purposes of bigotry and party spirit, cannot be exceeded in the history of civilized Europe, and will long remain a monument of infamy and shame to England. . . . The great misfortune of Ireland is, that the mass of the people have been given up for a century to a handful of Protestants, by whom they have been treated as *helots*, and subjected to every species of persecution and disgrace. The sufferings of the Catholics have been so loudly chanted in the very streets, that it is almost needless to remind our readers, that, during the reigns of George I. and George II., the Irish Roman Catholics were disabled from holding any civil or military office, from voting at elections, from admission into corporations, from practising law or physic. A younger brother, by turning Protestant, might deprive his elder brother of his birthright. . . . A Papist was disabled from purchasing freehold lands, and even from holding long leases; and any person might take his Catholic neighbour's horse by paying five pounds for it. If the child of a Catholic father turned Protestant, he was taken away from his father and put into the hands of a Protestant relation. Persons plundered by privateers during a war with any Popish prince were reimbursed by a levy on the Catholic inhabitants where they lived. . . . The greater part of these incapacities," adds the writer, "are removed: but the grand misfortune is, that the spirit which these oppressive laws engendered remains."

and distorted member, adding no strength to the body politic, and reproachfully pointed at by all who feared or envied the greatness of England." [1]

What unhappy Ireland suffered under such a domination, and under the twofold tyranny of barbarous laws, and a still more barbarous administration, it is easier to fancy than to relate. "No," said to me a few days ago an Irish Catholic, "I do not think that a generous Irishman can write the history of his country without blood and tears on every page." "There never has been a country," exclaimed one day, in the English Parliament, the Duke of Wellington, with the accent of emotion we might expect from his great soul,—"there never has been a country in which poverty and destitution have existed to the degree they exist in Ireland!"

What may give some idea of this wretchedness is, that in 1835, the Poor Law Commissioners stated, in their report, that there were in Ireland two million three hundred and eighty-five thousand persons in danger of starvation.

It must be known that in Ireland, notwithstanding the wonderful fertility of the soil, which might, if properly cultivated, support twenty-five millions of inhabitants, as it has been proved by economists, in consequence of English misrule, famines frequently occur, and last generally from three to four months. At all times, the great mass of the people have no other food than the potatoes called "lumpers," which were used in the last century to fatten pigs. In some districts, the peasants eat, in times of distress, a seed-weed called *doulamaun*. The famine begins towards the end of May, when the stock of potatoes begins to run short, and lasts till the end of August, when the new crop comes in.

Such is the wretched food of the poor Irish. With regard to the other details of life, "there are in Donegal," said a Protestant journal two years ago, "about four

---

[1] History of England from the Accession of James II., by Lord Macaulay, p. 2. London: Longman & Co. 1858.

thousand adults, of both sexes, obliged to go barefooted through the snow: pregnant women and aged persons are in constant danger of dying of cold. . . . . It is seldom that a man has a cotton shirt . . . . two persons use the same clothes; when one goes out the other stays at home . . . . but the destitution of the women is still greater, if possible. There are several hundred families in which two or three grown-up girls have but one gown between them."[1]

But without speaking of past times, is not the unspeakable misery which crushed this unhappy country in 1847 sufficient to raise the most terrible accusation against the tyranny of her oppressors? God alone can know the sufferings of those millions of broken hearts. "A great deal has been written," says Captain Mann, in his "Narrative of the Events of 1847," "and many an account given, of the dreadful sufferings endured by the poor, but the reality, in most cases, far exceeded descrip-

---

[1] In 1835, a celebrated French writer, M. Gustave de Beaumont, travelling through the county Mayo, comes to the parish of Newport-Pratt. "Wishing," says he, "to form an accurate idea of the degree of misery in this parish, I entered a great number of cabins, and here are some of the statistical details I collected whilst visiting them:—Out of the 11,761 inhabitants of this parish, 9,338 have no other bed than straw or grass, and 7,531 lie upon the ground. Out of the 206 inhabitants of Derry-Laken, a small hamlet in the parish, only 39 have a blanket for the night; the others are exposed to die of cold as well as of hunger: and whilst I was going through the parish, I found, in the middle of the day, twelve families who had not yet broken their fast for want of food. As to their houses, picture to yourselves four walls of dried mud, covered in with thatch or sods of grass; no chimney, but a hole in the roof, and in many cases the smoke finds no other issue than the door: in the same room are huddled together father, mother, children, and grandfather; no furniture in this wretched hovel, but one bed, made up generally of straw or grass, and serving for the whole family. You see five or six half-naked children squatting down over the dying embers in the hearth, and in a corner a pig, the only inmate that has nothing to complain of, as he delights in dirt. One is at first inclined to look upon the presence of the pig in a cabin as a sign of poverty; but such is not the case, and the destitution is extreme indeed where he is not seen. Such a dwelling is wretched, and yet it is not that of the pauper, but of the Irish tenant."

tion. Indeed, none can conceive what it was but those who were in it. For my part, I frequently look back on it as a fearful and horrid dream, scarcely knowing how sufficiently to express gratitude to the Almighty for having brought this country through it, even as it has."

In a few years, the eight millions of inhabitants that peopled this land, so celebrated for its fertility, were reduced by famine and emigration to six millions. It was a heart-rending sight for those who travelled through the country to see along the roadside the ruins of the deserted cabins and villages. A little later, and the English papers congratulated themselves on the tranquillity of Ireland. She was quiet, indeed; but it was the quiet of the tomb: two millions of the Irish had disappeared. "*Ubi solitudinem faciunt*," says Tacitus, "*pacem appellant.*"

According to the official statistics, 269,253 cabins were pulled down from 1841 to 1851; and, in the single year 1849, upwards of 50,000 families were evicted from their homes, and the lands they cultivated.

In order thoroughly to understand what this eviction means, we must recollect that, from the days of Elizabeth to those of William III., from 1586 to 1692, ten-elevenths of the soil of Ireland have been violently taken from the Catholics, confiscated, and then given to the Protestants. Hence we behold at present the enormous injustice, that the Protestants, who are barely a sixth of the total population of Ireland, are the owners of seven-eighths of the country, and the mass of the Catholics are at their service, to cultivate the land which once belonged to their fathers.

Moreover, the land is let on such conditions, that the *Times* itself said, in 1857, that in Ireland, property was ruled with savage and tyrannical sway; that the landlords exercise their rights with an iron hand, and deny their duties with a brazen face.[1] And the *Times* added, that old age, infirmity, and sickness are there doomed to death.

---

[1] *Times*, 25th of February, 1857.

In the month of November last, two members of parliament, Mr. Maguire and The O'Donoghue, wrote to Mr. Cardwell, the Chief Secretary for Ireland: "The great mass of the tenants of our country have no legal title whatever to the land they cultivate, and, despite old ties and fond recollections, may be driven from it as easily as the cattle that feed on its surface."

And this is done with the iron hand and brazen face which the *Times* spoke of: the landlords, using their horrible right of *legal eviction*, sweep the poor tenants from their land, and reduce them to the most frightful misery,[1] or compel them to emigrate.

---

[1] The most awful poverty is the lot of these unhappy evicted tenants: of their misery we may form some idea from the following facts.

In the Blue Book for 1837, we find that the annual exportations from Ireland amounted to £20,000,000, and that of that sum £15,000,000 were derived from the exportation of cattle, corn, butter, and eggs, which the poor Irish farmers never taste themselves, but sell to pay their rents: for themselves they have no food but "lumpers."

"Millions of Irishmen," says M. de Beaumont, "eat meat but once a year,—on Christmas day."

"One day," says M. Perrand, in his excellent article in the *Correspondent*, of the 25th of March, 1860, on the Irish Tenant Bill, "a tenant of Lord Leitrim's came to complain to him that his demands reduced him to the lowest distress: 'You might as well,' said he, 'cut off my head once for all, as treat me in this fashion.' 'No,' answered the landlord, 'I won't cut off your head, my boy, but I'll shave you as close as possible.'

"In the month of October last, the Irish journals gave us the sad list of the tenants whom a member of parliament, Mr. John A. Wynne, member for Sligo, had evicted from his property for the crime of electoral independence. (*Connaught Patriot*, 22nd October, 1859, quoting the *Sligo Champion*.)

"One of those evictions was made under such circumstances that we cannot pass it by in silence. A man named Bernard Flynn had thought it his duty to vote for another candidate than Mr. Wynne. A notice of ejectment was served. His wife was then dangerously ill; Flynn thought the situation one of a nature to touch the heart of the landlord and his agents. The doctor gave a written certificate that there would be danger of death if the woman were removed,

But, I may be told, has not Lord Palmerston, of whom you complain so bitterly, endeavoured to remedy the evils you deplore? Was it not he who, on the 4th of April, 1856, laid before the House of Commons a bill to amend this frightful state of things?

All that is true; and on that very day he said that "the members of the House must know that Ireland has for a long series of years been the victim of the misgovernment of this country. And it was because Ireland was the victim of sectarian oppression and class legislation that the government were entitled to ask exceptional legislation of the House."

Such were the words of Lord Palmerston. I might also quote Lord Derby, who said, on the 9th of June, 1845, that the remedy for the evils of Ireland is not emigration, but a legislation which should make it the tenant's interest to spend on the land his capital and his labour. "Up to this day," added the noble lord, "this legislation has not been tried, and we are told it is farther off than ever."

If these noble lords have a right to tell me they have spoken of, and promised to do away with those abominable abuses, I have a right to ask them in my turn, What have you done to keep your word? Hitherto, nothing. But, you will say, for reforms, time is required. Well, perhaps so. Yet, except the Sultan, you do not grant to the princes who wish to reform their states that time you

---

and Flynn hastened to show it to the agent. The only answer he received was, 'We have nothing to say to your wife, it is your house we want.' The unfortunate woman was then removed, and died almost immediately.

"It was also on the property of Mr. Wynne that took place the eviction of a poor man who had only made up his mind, after long hesitation, to vote against his landlord. When the notice of ejectment was served, his wife hurried off to the agent to beg for mercy. 'Forgive us,' said she, 'we will not do it again.' 'Off with you, woman,' answered one of the landlord's drivers, with cruel mockery; 'go to your priests, who say they have power to forgive; we have not.'"

claim for yourselves. But, is it indeed time that you want? The horrible oppression of Ireland has now lasted for centuries: even under the reign of James I., Sir John Davies said that the "Irishman was more miserable than a bond slave, because the bond slave was fed by the lord, but in this case the lord was fed by the bond slave." And, in 1859, Dr. MacHale, archbishop of Tuam, wrote again to Lord Palmerston: "Not only do those evils subsist in all their force, but they are even aggravated. .... The evils accumulated by the oppression of past ages extend their influence over the country as widely as ever."

I know that for the last fifty years, without going farther back, there has hardly been a parliament that was not called upon to remedy those evils, so much did they revolt all good men! But we also know that hitherto nothing, as I said before, absolutely nothing has been done. I shall even add that since the beginning of this century, sixteen laws have been promulgated by the British Parliament to consolidate and extend the tyrannical power of the landlords, so bent does the English government seem on persisting in its detestable policy towards Ireland.[1] And you dare to speak of the wrongs of Italy!

And what am I to say of the coercion bills—a sort of martial law—sometimes proclaimed by the British Parliament, probably to better the condition of the Irish? Since the beginning of this century, there have been no less than thirty-three! Here are some provisions of the bill proposed by the government in 1846, at the commencement of the famine, on the motion of Sir James Graham:—

Art. 15. Whoever shall be found outside his dwelling one hour after sunset may be put into prison, and kept there till his trial.

Art. 16. Whoever shall have been imprisoned for such cause, may

---

[1] Vide Bichino, quoted in the Repeal Prize Essay of Alderman Stanton, 1845, p. 76, and the *Law Magazine*, May, 1841.

be punished with fifteen years' transportation, unless he can prove that he had gone out on business authorized by law.

Art. 18. The police may enter any dwelling from an hour after sunset till the following morning.

It was by such means, and under the awful pressure of a tyranny almost unparalleled in history, that in ten years almost 270,000 cabins of Irish peasants have been levelled with the ground; that in one year more than 50,000 families have been evicted; and, finally, that the total population of Ireland, which was 8,200,000 souls in 1841, was reduced to 6,500,000 in 1851, and does not exceed at present 6,000,000. The remainder died of starvation, or emigrated.

Of that fearful emigration, what am I to say?

A writer in the *Edinburgh Review*[1] says, "The emigration of 1846 from the United Kingdom, which was the largest ever known up to that time, amounted to 129,851 persons; the emigration of the first three quarters of 1847 was 240,461; *and almost the whole of it was from Ireland to Canada and the United States.*

"Even this does not represent the full extent of the outpouring of the population of Ireland which took place in this eventful year. From the 13th January to the 1st November, 278,005 immigrants arrived at Liverpool from Ireland, of whom only 122,981 sailed from that port to foreign countries." And a little farther on,[2] he adds, "that of those who emigrated in 1847 from Ireland to Canada, 9,634 died on the passage, at the Marine Hospital, or while the vessels were detained in quarantine."

These are the horrors which are known to all Europe, and of which she has never said a word up to the present, even when assembled in congress! M. de Cavour and Lord Palmerston had other things to think of in 1856.[3]

---

[1] *Edinburgh Review*, January, 1848, p. 291.

[2] Idem, ibid. p. 294, *note.*

[3] When I think of Ireland, I cannot help remembering those words of the Scriptures (Eccles. xiii.) :—

But what is known only to the witnesses of those sad scenes, is the pangs with which these poor people tear themselves away from their friends and the dear old country, to use their own expressions, which they can never cease to love. Amongst the boxes that contained the wretched clothes that still remained to them, there was often one that held a sod of their native village; they hoped to lay it down one day by their hut—in the forests of Australia, or of the Far West, where they go to die— to have the consolation of seeing themselves, and of showing to their children, a portion of a land so beloved.

For my part, when I transport myself in spirit to Dublin and Cork, and picture to my mind the heartrending scenes which accompany the sailing of the emigrant vessels on which so many thousands of poor people are borne off to distant lands, I cannot help thinking that the quays of Dublin and of Cork are the spots of the earth where most tears have been shed.

How often were fathers and mothers seen parting, with sobs and bitter tears, from children, whom they were never to meet again! Old men, broken down by age and want,

---

"The rich man hath done wrong, and yet he will fume: but the poor is wronged, and must hold his peace.

"If he have need of thee, he will deceive thee, and smiling upon thee, will put thee in hope; he will speak thee fair, and will say: What wantest thou?

"And he will shame thee by his meats, till he have drawn thee dry twice or thrice, and at last he will laugh at thee: and afterward when he seeth thee, he will forsake thee, and shake his head at thee.

"The wild ass is the lion's prey in the desert: so also the poor are devoured by the rich. And as humility is an abomination to the proud, so also the rich man abhorreth the poor.

"The rich man spoke, and all held their peace, and what he said they extol even to the clouds. The poor man spoke, and they say: Who is this? And if he stumble, they will overthrow him."

Such are the powerful and their friends .... To the oppressed, I shall say with the wise man:—

"Humble thyself to God, and wait for his hands."

And—"Riches are good to him that hath no sin in his conscience."

accompanying their sons to the vessel, and returning to die alone in their cabin, because they had not strength nor money enough to emigrate! Young women obliged to go off alone and unprotected, amidst dangers to which, alas! they have often fallen victims.

The English papers said a great deal lately of those Tuscan peasants who went to vote, headed by their priests, and gave up to Piedmont the name and glory of their country; they did not speak so much of those Irish villagers that went off, headed also by their priests, as it happened, more than once—exiles never to return.

Poor, affectionate, self-sacrificing people! After this long night you will have your day, for your faithful heart has preserved its youthful ardour and enthusiasm, and the God whom you ever blessed in your sufferings is with you. He remained three days in his tomb, and then He rose again. Irishmen! your three days have been three centuries, but the third is drawing to a close.

However, let us not dwell on our feelings and our hopes, but come back again to the sad discussion we are engaged in. I have a right to ask the English nation, Have not the Irish deep wounds and dreadful wrongs to complain of? And in what is the lot of the Romagna, for which you made show of so much sympathy at the famous congress of 1856, to be compared with that of poor Ireland?[1] I do not say that the Irish ought to separate from you, but I say that you give them by your principles a strict right, and by your Italian policy a most powerful temptation to do so. Well! you will perhaps answer, But we will crush them once more. It may be; but were I to be crushed with them, I shall not be deterred from saying, those who govern a country as you have governed and still govern Ireland, ought to be prevented by common decency from speaking as you speak. No! so long as you shall

---

[1] The Irish have been compared to slaves and helots: but "it would be a lucky day for them," says Mr. Cochrane, "when they might change their condition for that of the convicts of Siberia."

not have removed that beam from your own eye, your sight will not be clear, and you can have no right whatever to judge of the failings of your neighbour. *Ejice primum trabem de oculo tuo!*

If the unheard-of calamities which sweep off the children of unhappy Ireland[1] by hundreds of thousands were to be witnessed but one day in the States of the Pope, if you could only point out there some of the horrible iniquities which still weigh down that Catholic land subject to your sceptre, what dreadful accusations should we not hear in your Parliament and your papers!

You speak of Roman intolerance. But, at the present day, and notwithstanding the tardy concessions you have made at length, does nothing remain of your old penal laws, I do not say in Ireland only, but even in England and Scotland? Do we not still see acts of intolerance which nothing can justify?

What are we to say of your system of *packing juries,* as it is called, to which you occasionally resort when you are specially anxious to obtain a conviction? Some years ago, what a shameful instance of this abuse do we not find in the famous trial of O'Connell? "Unhappily," said Macaulay, in a well-known speech, "you were too much bent on gaining the victory; and you have gained a victory more disgraceful and disastrous than any defeat. Mr. O'Connell has been convicted; but you cannot deny that he has been wronged..... Yes, you have obtained a verdict of guilty; but you have obtained that verdict from twelve men brought together by illegal means, and selected in such a manner that their decision can inspire no confidence."[2]

I know that verdict was afterwards set aside, and we

---

[1] In those last years, from 1851 to 1857, the number of persons who emigrated from Ireland was 932,861, or 11,673 a month, and 376 a day.

[2] Speeches of the Right Hon. T. B. Macaulay, M.P. London: Longman & Co., 1854, p. 312.

had a too rare instance of impartiality; but had you not recourse to the same disgraceful system in April, 1859, in the case of a crown prosecution in the county of Kerry? Only two Catholics could find a place on the jury; and when the jury disagreed, another jury was impanelled, from which *every Catholic was excluded*. This is the more remarkable and the more revolting, as Kerry is almost a purely Catholic county, and of those qualified to serve on juries, the great majority are Catholics. And if I am told that the English government are not answerable for all that, I shall answer that it was Mr. Whiteside, the Attorney-General for Ireland, who did it.

What I wish to be particularly remarked is, that I am not calling your attention to the intolerance of old times, but to cases of most flagrant injustice which we have still before our eyes.

For instance, the Catholic University of Dublin has been established since 1854: since then, the Catholics have been constantly praying for a charter, that their university may be empowered to confer degrees, and hitherto they have not obtained it. If that university gives learning, why do you not allow it to give degrees?

A Catholic cannot be a fellow either at Oxford or Cambridge, and yet most of their colleges were founded by Catholics, and their officers receive large sums of money left for masses to be celebrated for the souls of the founders.[1]

You who cry out against the masses of the Roman Church, what say you to these, and to the money that pays for them?

You speak of the ignorance of the lower classes in the States of the Church: have you forgotten that a dignitary of the Anglican Church declared, not many months ago, that immense numbers, in many districts of England and Wales, "were steeped in worse than heathen ignorance

---

[1] Edinburgh Review, July, 1852, p. 250.

and superstition"? What are your clergy doing? What is the use of all your rich livings?

You who declaim so eloquently in favour of liberty of conscience, why do you refuse the Catholic children in your hospitals, your prisons, and your houses of correction the full benefit of a religious education? Why was the bishop of Glasgow compelled to write a letter in which we read the following statements:—"Of the ninety-four inmates, natives of Ireland, in the principal male reformatory of Glasgow, eighty are Catholics, and no priest is allowed to enter the building upon any pretext whatever. In the year 1858, a poor lad named Mooney was dying in the institution from the effects of consumption, and he implored an old Catholic pensioner, employed to train the boys, but whose Catholicity was unknown to the authorities, to procure for him the presence of a priest of his own religion. The governor of the reformatory refused to grant the required permission; the board of superintendence also refused, and the Home Secretary was subsequently appealed to, but with similar results. One of this poor boy's companions subsequently declared that he had died screaming for a priest."

This letter of the bishop of Glasgow was read by the Hon. Charles Langdale at a numerous and important meeting of the Catholic clergy and laity, held in London on the 8th of June, 1859. Amongst those present were Lord Stafford, Lord Herries, Lord Edward Howard, M.P., Lord Campden, the Right Hon. W. Monsell, M.P., Count Vaughan, the Right Rev. Dr. Gillis, bishop of Edinburgh, the Very Rev. Dr. Manning, Mr. Wilberforce, brother to the bishop of Oxford, &c.

I have now before me the *Times* of October 26th, 1859, containing a letter from Mr. Langdale, and the answer of the *Times*. Mr. Langdale complains "of the local power which, in England, takes the child from a starving parent and assigns it to the custody of a stranger's hand, there to be educated in a faith contrary to its parents's will, or still more painfully invades the last moments of a widowed mother, with the assurance that the law will assign her orphan to a custody, where again it will be educated in a faith contrary to its dying parent's will." The *Times*, in its answer, after speaking of *ecclesiastical tyranny* in Italy, thinks it only fair that, if a parent is unable to support a child from sickness or poverty, and that the child, is placed in a workhouse, "it should be instructed together with the other children, and learn such religion as is taught there as part of its education."[1]

No! till you have done away with, and made amends for, so many indignities, for so many past and present iniquities, you are not entitled to a hearing in questions of justice and oppression.

"By no artifice of ingenuity," says Lord Macaulay, "can the stigma of persecution, the worst blemish of the English Church, be effaced or patched over."[2]

Not many months ago, one of the bishops of the Established Church, rich holders of the lands of Catholic Ireland, committed, by virtue of the existing legislation, such acts of bigotry that an outcry of indignation would have been raised all over Europe, had the like happened in France or in Italy. I speak of the sixty Catholic families upon whom notices of ejectment were served, and of the Christian Brothers evicted by Lord Plunket from the plot of waste church land on which their school had been erected, at a cost of £800, for the education of the Catholic poor: children, parents, religion, justice, nothing was listened to.[3]

---

[1] It has been proved that the great Foundling Hospital of Dublin gave in this manner, in the space of 134 years, 56,000 children to Protestantism.

[2] *Edinburgh Review*, September, 1828, art. Hallam's Constitutional History.

[3] "As a non-Catholic member of the community," says Mr. William Smith O'Brien, in a letter to the Most Rev. Dr. MacHale, which I read in the *Freeman's Journal*, October 18, 1859, "who feels a deep interest in everything that concerns the welfare of Ireland, I have no hesitation in declaring that I consider the proceedings of the Protestant bishop, in regard to your Catholic schoolhouse, as *an act of simple robbery committed under the name of law*."

I say, with Lord Macaulay, " I am not speaking in anger, nor with any wish to excite anger in others; I am not speaking with rhetorical exaggeration; I am calmly and deliberately expressing, in the only appropriate terms, an opinion which I formed many years ago, which all my observations and reflections have confirmed, and which I am prepared to support by reasons, when I say that *of all the institutions now existing in the civilized world, the Established Church of Ireland seems to me* the most absurd." [1]

" Is there anything else like it?" says the same eloquent speaker a little further on,—" was there ever anything else like it? The world is full of ecclesiastical establishments: but such a portent as this Church of Ireland is nowhere to be found. Look round the continent of Europe. Ecclesiastical establishments, from the White Sea to the Mediterranean; ecclesiastical establishments, from the Volga to the Atlantic; but nowhere the church of a small minority enjoying exclusive establishment . . . . . *In one* country alone is to be seen the spectacle of a community of eight millions of human beings, with a church which is the church of only eight hundred thousand." [2]

Sydney Smith expresses himself on the same subject in terms perhaps still more energetic :—

"This is English legislation for Ireland! There is no abuse like it in all Europe, in all Asia, in all the discovered parts of Africa, and in all we have heard of Timbuctoo! It is an error that requires 20,000 armed men for its protection in time of peace; which costs more than a million a year; and which, in the first French war, in spite of the puffing and panting of fighting steamers, will, and must, break out into desperate rebellion." [3]

---

[1] Speeches of the Right Hon. T. B. Macaulay. London, 1854, p. 380. [2] *Idem, ibid.* p. 382.

[3] The Works of Sydney Smith. London: Longman & Co., 1854, vol. iii. p. 531.

Those are not my words, but the words of your fellow-countrymen and co-religionists: it was Englishmen, and Protestant Englishmen, that published those sentiments to the world! And the reason they do so is, that neither national nor religious prejudices can stifle, in honourable and noble hearts, a cry of indignation at the sight of such enormities.

For my part, I hope most sincerely there will be no revolt in Ireland; but I hope, also, that the honour and good sense of the English people will not permit them to disgrace themselves for ever by such extraordinary injustice! One day there will be peace for all in truth and in justice: God grant the day may soon come! Yes, noble Catholic land, old island of saints, brave and patient Ireland! the world has known thy sorrows, admired thy constancy, applauded thy unshaken fidelity to the religion of thy fathers; and there is not a generous heart upon earth that did not hail with joy the first signs of thy resurrection, and of the new era of liberty inaugurated by thy O'Connell! England has learnt at length to blush for her long iniquity; and if too many remains of ancient intolerance still subsist, the liberties thou hast won must soon make them disappear for ever. No, such abuses cannot endure in this age. The private interests of a rich and powerful clergy cannot screen them much longer from the indignation of good men. And when once this abuse is abolished, England will be the first to congratulate herself, and she will then acknowledge the truth of these words of one of her most celebrated statesmen:—

"I love the Irish nation," said Charles Fox, at the beginning of this century. "I know a good deal of that people. I know much of Ireland from having seen it; I know more from private friendship with individuals. The Irish may have their faults, like others. They may have a quick feeling of injury, and not be very patient under it; but I do affirm that, in all their characteristics, there is not one feature more predominant, in every class of the country, from the highest to the lowest order, than gratitude for benefactions, and sensibility to kindness. Change your system towards that country, and you will find them another sort of men. Let impartiality, justice, and clemency take place of prejudice, oppression, and vengeance, and you will not want the aid of martial law, or the terror of military execution."

CHAPTER XXI.

ENGLAND.

RELIGIOUS PACIFICATION.

There is another reparation which the world expects, another act of justice, which the Church hopes for from the honour of the English people. On the day they shall at length acknowledge that the Catholich Church, from which they are so unhappily separated, does not deserve their hatred nor their disdain, any more than Ireland which they have so cruelly wronged; on the day they shall understand that the august Pontiff, whom two hundred millions of men love and venerate, is worthy of the regard of a great nation, were it only on account of his very weakness; on the day they shall consent to treat him and us with common justice—on that day, prejudice and intolerance will suffer a great defeat, and a great act of reparation will be accomplished upon earth.

And to obtain that result, all we ask of England is, not to forget entirely bygone days, and the most religious and touching passages of her history. Instead of seeking in the contentions of the present day groundless motives for the gratuitous hatred she bears us, had she not better go back to other times, and rise with us into a region calm and serene, where no cloud may overcast our meeting, and our hands join with all the fervour of hope ! Is there amongst men a more revered and beloved memory than that of St. Gregory the Great, to whom England owed the blessing of the faith and the pure light of Christian civilization ? Moved even to tears at the sight of the young Angles, who were sold as slaves in the Roman *Forum*, and who appeared to him beautiful as angels, this great Pope resolved to rescue their country from the chains of barbarians and the darkness of heathenism; and therefore he sent to their land the holy monk Augustine with his missionaries.

The history of the Church contains nothing more beautiful than the landing of Augustine in Kent with his forty companions, who, headed by the cross and the image of the great King our Lord Jesus Christ, offered up vows to heaven for the conversion of England.[1]

Bertha, the daughter of Charibert, king of Paris, brought over King Ethelbert, her husband, to Christianity : our kings protected the new mission; our bishops had also their part in this admirable work, and the archbishop of Arles consecrated St. Augustine. St. Lupus of Troyes, St. Germanus of Auxerre, our most illustrious predecessors, esteemed it ever an honour to visit the Church of England, and to become the friends of its bishops. And it was thus that the English Church was founded and raised up. And it is those remembrances, which we can no more blot out from our hearts than from our histories, that make us still hope for peace and better times: *in spem*—I shall never consent to add, *contra spem*.

In the mean time the new Church, strengthened by the care of Pope Boniface V. and Honorius, was becoming celebrated throughout the world. Miracles and virtues flourished there, says Bossuet, as in the days of the apostles ; nothing was more admirable than the wonders of her conversion; nothing more glorious than the piety of her bishops, her religious, and her kings. Edwin em-

---

[1] *Bossuet*, Universal History.

braced with his whole people the faith that had made him victorious, and he converted his neighbours. Oswald acted as the interpreter of the preachers of the Gospel, and preferred his title of Christian to the glory he had won on the field of battle. The Mercians were converted by the king of Northumberland: their neighbours and successors followed in their steps, and their good works were incalculable.[1] I do not speak of Alfred the Great, St. Edward, and so many others.

The English Church was fruitful at that time, and gave birth to other churches. St. Wilfrid, bishop of York, went to convert Friesland; Winfrid, as a token of all the good he had done, received from Pope Gregory II. the name of Boniface, and became the apostle of Germany. To recall the names of St. Dunstan, St. Edmund, the Venerable Bede, Lanfranc, St. Anselm—the latter two given to England by Italy,—and, in fine, the glorious name of St. Thomas of Canterbury, is it not to celebrate learning and virtue, charity and apostolic courage?

During a thousand years, that is, for a period three times the length of that which has elapsed since she became Protestant, England remained united to her mother, the Roman Church. In that lapse of time, what benefits did she not receive from her! In the middle ages, the preservation and progress of civilization were, in England as everywhere else, the work of the Catholic clergy. And the remains that are still to be seen on all sides throughout the land bear witness to the ancient and glorious empire of Catholicism. If my testimony in this matter were looked upon as suspicious, I might offer to Great Britain that of one of her most illustrious sons, perhaps the ablest English writer of our days, Lord Macaulay, who was three times a member of a Whig administration, twice a cabinet minister, and created a peer of the realm a short time before his lamented death, not only in consideration of his parliamentary services, but of the lustre

---

[1] *Bossuet*, Universal History.

he had shed on English literature. If this great statesman did not come to know the truth of Catholicity, he rose far above the prejudices and the hatred of which I have shown to England the blindness and injustice, and wrote on the Catholic Church pages on which his fellow-countrymen ought to meditate. For instance, he admitted, in the following terms, the beneficial influence of the Church during the ages which preceded the revival of letters:—

"The ascendancy of the sacerdotal order was long the ascendancy which naturally and properly belongs to intellectual superiority. The priests, with all their faults, were by far the wisest portion of society. It was, therefore, on the whole, good that they should be respected and obeyed. The encroachments of the ecclesiastical power on the province of the civil power produced much more happiness than misery, while the ecclesiastical power was in the hands of the only class that had studied history, philosophy, and public law, and while the civil power was in the hands of savage chiefs, who could not read their own grants and edicts."[1]

It was also Lord Macaulay that wrote on the Catholic Church the following eloquent page, which may well inspire all honest minds with admiration and love, or at least with moderation and respect:—

"There is not, and there never was, on this earth a work of human policy so well deserving of examination as the Roman Catholic Church. The history of that Church joins together the two great ages of human civilization. No other institution is left standing which carries the mind back to the times when the smoke of sacrifice rose from the Pantheon, and when leopards and tigers bounded in the Flavian amphitheatre. The proudest royal houses are but of yesterday, when compared with the line of the Supreme Pontiffs. That line we trace back in an unbroken series from the Pope who crowned Napoleon in the nineteenth century, to the Pope who crowned Pepin in the eighth; and far beyond the time of Pepin the august dynasty extends, till it is lost in the twilight of fable. The republic of Venice came next in antiquity. But the republic of Venice was modern, when compared with the Papacy; and the

---

[1] History of England from the Accession of James II. By Lord Macaulay. London: Longman & Co., 1858, p. 48.

republic of Venice is gone, and the Papacy remains. The Papacy remains, not in decay, not a mere antique, but full of life and youthful vigour. The Catholic Church is still sending forth to the furthest ends of the world missionaries as zealous as those who landed in Kent with Augustine, and still confronting hostile kings with the same spirit with which she confronted Attila. The number of her children is greater than in any former age. Her acquisitions in the New World have more than compensated her for what she has lost in the Old. Her spiritual ascendancy extends over the vast countries which lie between the plains of the Missouri and Cape Horn—countries which, a century hence, may not improbably contain a population as large as that which now inhabits Europe. The members of her communion are certainly not fewer than a hundred and fifty millions, and it will be difficult to show that all the other Christian sects united amount to a hundred and twenty millions. Nor do we see any sign which indicates that the term of her long dominion is approaching. She saw the commencement of all the governments, and of all the ecclesiastical establishments, that now exist in the world; and we feel no assurance that she is not destined to see the end of them all."[1]

I take peculiar delight in quoting this great man, whose generous impartiality soared so far above the prejudices of his fellow-countrymen, and the shallow judgments of vulgar writers, and whose example proves, a great deal better than I could or would attempt to do, how much base ingratitude is mixed up with that unaccountable hatred which I now beseech England to abjure. For it was by reasoning on positive facts, and after an enlightened and impartial study of history, and guided by his immense learning, that Lord Macaulay formed his opinion concerning the beneficial influence of Catholicism in his country.

There are, indeed, many other English names that would bear witness to the truth of my statements. Dr. Newman, Dr. Manning, the two Wilberforces, all those noble hearts, who, giving up so generously fortune, honours, their youthful friendships, worldly interests, the most inveterate prejudices, and the dearest affections, devoted themselves to the cause of truth, and rendered to the Catholic Church, in those works where their undisputed learning shines

---

[1] *Edinburgh Review*, October, 1840, p. 227.

forth, a homage of which no one has hitherto called into question the heroic sincerity,—all those great men, I say, thought as did Lord Macaulay; but, more consistent than he, they moved on in the path of light, and their conversion is assuredly the most glorious testimony that can be given in favour of Catholicism. However, error and prejudice would except to their testimony, by reason of its source; and, therefore, I have preferred appealing to Lord Macaulay, who remained a Protestant, notwithstanding all the respect and admiration he professed for the Catholic Church: at any rate, every one must admit that words such as I have just quoted could only have been dictated by the most conscientious conviction.

There are in the works of this illustrious historian many other pages [1] which I recommend to all Englishmen, and to all true lovers of freedom and human dignity.

---

[1] I may be allowed to copy from the beginning of his history the following passage, in which Macaulay shows in Catholicity an influence and operation worthy of something else than insult and disdain:—

"It is remarkable that the two greatest and most salutary social revolutions which have taken place in England, that revolution which, in the thirteenth century, put an end to the tyranny of nation over nation, and that revolution which, a few generations later, put an end to the property of man in man, were silently and imperceptibly effected . . . .

"It would be most unjust not to acknowledge that the chief agent in these two great deliverances was religion; and it may perhaps be doubted whether a purer religion might not have been found a less efficient agent. The benevolent spirit of the Christian morality is undoubtedly adverse to distinctions of caste. But to the Church of Rome such distinctions are peculiarly odious, for they are incompatible with other distinctions which are essential to her system. She ascribes to every priest a mysterious dignity which entitles him to the reverence of every layman, and she does not consider any man as disqualified, by reason of his nation or of his family, for the priesthood. Her doctrines respecting the sacerdotal character, however erroneous they may be, have repeatedly mitigated some of the worst evils which can afflict society. That superstition cannot be regarded as unmixingly noxious which, in regions cursed by the tyranny of race over race, creates an aristocracy altogether independent of race, inverts the relation between the oppressor and the oppressed, and compels the hereditary master to kneel before the

True, indeed, it is not a son of the Catholic Church that speaks in these pages, as many of his sentiments show most clearly, but a man of high intelligence and noble heart, who is not carried away by blind hatred, and has courage to do justice to whom it is due: it is in that spirit, and with those feelings, that I conjure Englishmen to examine and judge us: and in their history, and throughout the land they live in, they will find many other proofs of the benefits conferred on them of yore by Catholicism, which ought to open their eyes, and show them the ingratitude of so unjust and persevering a hatred. "The most venerable institutions of England," it has been said by an illustrious Catholic, whose testimony the English may well receive, for he has done homage to their greatness more than any one else in France,—" her most popular and purest titles of glory, are connected with Catholicism. Trial by jury, parliament, the universities, were established in those days when she was the dutiful daughter of the Holy See. It was Catholic barons that extorted Magna Charta from King John, and Catholic Irishmen that constituted the main strength of the English armies in the Peninsula and the Crimea. Except Queen Elizabeth, the only sovereigns

---

spiritual tribunal of the hereditary bondman. To this day, in some countries where negro slavery exists, Popery appears in advantageous contrast to other forms of Christianity. It is notorious that the antipathy between the European and African races is by no means so strong at Rio Janeiro as at Washington. In our own country this peculiarity of the Roman Catholic system produced, during the middle ages, many excellent effects. It is true that, shortly after the battle of Hastings, Saxon prelates and abbots were violently deposed, and that ecclesiastical adventurers from the continent were intruded by hundreds into lucrative benefices. Yet even then pious divines of Norman blood raised their voices against such a violation of the constitution of the Church, refused to accept mitres from the hands of the conqueror, and charged him, on the peril of his soul, not to forget that the vanquished islanders were his fellow-Christians.

"The first protector whom the English found among the dominant race was Archbishop Anselm. At a time when the English name was a reproach, and when all the civil and military dignitaries

whom the people remember are Catholic kings:—Alfred, Edward the Confessor, Richard the Lion-hearted, Edward III., Henry V. The cathedrals, the churches, the castles, all those ecclesiastical and feudal buildings, which England restores or preserves with such religious care, are exclusively the work of Catholic generations. The fervent piety of the converts to Catholicism finds heaven peopled with English saints, from St. Wilfrid and St. Boniface to St. Thomas of Canterbury." [1]

And when I recall the benefits which Catholicism conferred on England, and which she seems to have forgotten, I wish to say but one thing to the English: You have broken the time-honoured tie which bound you to Rome and to unity; you have insisted upon having, contrary to the order of Christ, your religious independence; you have got it, and what has been the consequence?—you know as well as I. " Religion," says Bossuet, " was with you purely political; you obeyed the wishes of your kings, and your faith was fashioned to their caprices." It was a great misfortune; it was a great misfortune for you and for the Church; it was the most humiliating slavery of souls in the freest country in the world. Well! we still hope, with

---

of the kingdom were supposed to belong exclusively to the countrymen of the conqueror, the despised race learned, with transports of delight, that one of themselves, Nicholas Breakspear, had been elected to the papal throne, and had held out his foot to be kissed by ambassadors sprung from the noblest houses of Normandy. It was a national as well as a religious feeling that drew great multitudes to the shrine of Becket, the first Englishman who, since the conquest, had been terrible to the foreign tyrants.

"A successor of Becket was foremost among those who obtained that charter which secured at once the privileges of the Norman barons and of the Saxon yeomanry.

"How great a part the Catholic ecclesiastics subsequently had in the abolition of villenage we learn from the unexceptionable testimony of Sir Thomas Smith, one of the ablest Protestant counsellors of Elizabeth. When the dying slaveholder asked for the last sacraments, his spiritual attendant regularly adjured him, as he loved his soul, to emancipate his brethren for whom Christ had died."

[1] M. de Montalembert, on the political future of England.

that great bishop, that the days of delusion will pass by, and that *so learned a nation will not always remain blinded by error*. At least, if the dawn of truth is still far off, may that of justice soon come, and *let not England persist in her hatred*. Without speaking of the eminent scholars of her great universities, whom, as Bossuet foretold, "*their respect for the Fathers, and their profound and unwearied study of antiquity, have brought back to the doctrines of the first ages*," how many other distinguished Englishmen, though still attached to the Anglican Church, protest against the persistence and ingratitude of this hatred, and begin to speak of the Roman Church without passion, and even with a grateful heart.

Nor is it even necessary to go back to ancient times to find motives which should induce the English to alter their conduct towards the Papacy, and to lay by their implacable and gratuitous hostility: the recollections of our own times ought to suffice. Since the English, at the beginning of the nineteenth century, contributed, in concert with the other great powers of Europe, to the restoration of the Papacy, what wrong have they had to avenge on the Roman Pontiff? I might even recall his claims to their deference and respect. The noble conduct of Pius VII. towards them would seem to deserve a better requital. When the Emperor Napoleon wanted to draw him into the continental league against England, and to prove to him that this heretical nation, so hostile to the Church, was in no wise entitled to his affection, what did the mild and courageous Pontiff answer? It has surely not been forgotten. A few years before, during the famous discussions which took place in the British Parliament on the emancipation of the Catholics, a member of the House of Lords, imbued with those prejudices which are still so strong in some of the English statesmen of the present day, used the following words:—"I believe, nay more, I am certain, that the Pope is but a wretched puppet in the hands of the usurper of the throne of the Bourbons; that he dare not stir without Napoleon's order, and that if the latter asked of him a bull calling on the Irish priests to rouse their flocks to insurrection against the English government, he would not refuse it to the despot." Now, to use the expressive language of M. de Maistre, "The ink certainly was scarcely dry on the paper that informed us of this strange conviction, when the Pope, summoned with all the authority of menace to favour the designs of Bonaparte against the English, answers that, being the common father of all Christians, he could have no enemies amongst them: and, rather than comply, he lets himself be insulted, driven from his capital, and thrown into prison, and begins that long martyrdom that entitles him to the respect of the entire world." Why must we except England?

What real motive, I ask it again, can they plead for this ill-will, for this inexorable animosity? In what has Rome, directly or indirectly, thwarted the policy, or hurt the interests, of the English people? I am told that the great, the national grievance against the Papacy is the re-establishment, in 1850, of the Catholic hierarchy in England. Well, I ask, What man of sound sense and common honesty ever thought that the Established Church was threatened by this hierarchy? Was it not English pride much more than Protestant faith which broke out with such violence? Interested and clever politicians turned to account those noble instincts of English patriotism which sometimes degenerate into unworthy defects; and Great Britain rose up against what was represented as the usurpation of its land and Church by the Catholic episcopate. But, in reality, what was then done was but a homage paid to the institutions of free England, a mark of confidence in the liberty of English citizens, an act by which the constitution was not threatened, and no one should have been rendered uneasy. How was it possible to misapprehend so simple and inoffensive a use of the first of all liberties?

The English would fall even below Russian intolerance, were they to proscribe the Catholic religion: but this religion cannot exist without the fundamental conditions of its existence, its spiritual hierarchy. The episcopate is essential to it; you must accept it: but is it not better that it should be amongst you in its hierarchical, recognized, and normal form, than in the anomalous one of apostolic-vicariates?

But should you not rather commend the new arrangement proposed by Rome? Although bishops are subordinate to the Pope, as they ought to be, they are, in one sense, less directly dependent on him than vicars-apostolic, who are nothing but his revocable delegates. There was no violation of the English law, no challenge, no threat: and all the lovers of liberty throughout Europe saw, with amazement, the bitter prejudices and the passions of another age which then broke forth in England.[1]

"All that has been said, to frighten Protestant states, of the influence of a foreign power," says M. de Maistre, " is a vain chimera, a bugbear got up in the sixteenth century, and which has no meaning in ours. The age of passions has gone by; we can speak to one another without hatred, and even without anger."

"The English," adds the same writer, "in their prejudices against us, are only mistaken with regard to time: their infatuation is a mere anachronism. They read in some Catholic book that heretical princes are not to be obeyed: immediately they are frightened, and raise the cry of No Popery. All this flame would soon be quenched if they deigned to look at the date of the book, which would be surely found to coincide with the sad epoch of religious wars, and changes in dynasties."

In good truth, is Catholicism opposed to a single one of England's institutions, to her prosperity, to her love of liberty? Read over the pages of Lord Macaulay, which I quoted to you just now. Why should not an English Catholic be as faithful to his country, as true an Englishman as any other? For my part, I cannot discover the

---

[1] The English themselves seem to be aware of their injustice, for the *Ecclesiastical Titles Bill* has been a dead letter since the day it was passed.

shadow of a reason. Assuredly the author of the work, "On the Political Future of England," is one of the most devoted, one of the most dauntless lovers of liberty, and it was he that said to the English :—

"The glory of the Catholic Church, one of the conditions and consequences of her immortality, is to be all to all, to adapt herself to the institutions, the manners, the ideas of all countries and all ages, to whatever is not incompatible with faith and Christian virtue, and to allow all her children to have, as it were, a home, to possess a patrimony of their own within the pale of her matchless unity, which triumphs over, and survives all earthly institutions only by its elasticity and its universality."

I shall therefore say, with confidence, to the English, when they have mastered themselves and their prejudices, Reflect, in the calm of your consciences, how strange were the prejudices which you have hitherto obeyed, and how glorious it would be for you to do justice at last to that church who was your mother in the faith! Three centuries ago you were the first and fiercest enemies of unity! What an honour it would be for you to establish it again in Europe. It would indeed become your greatness to raise up the standard of Christian unity, and to bear it beyond the seas over those lands which are waiting for you, and expect you from afar! It would be a sacred and immortal period in your history, a new era inaugurated by you in the annals of mankind!

Happy they to whom it shall be given to behold those better times which, perhaps, are not far off! Happy they whose lot it shall have been to prepare them, even by their aspirations and their prayers!

This I have attempted to do, feebly indeed, but to the best of my power, and in all the sincerity of my heart. I have not come to sow disunion where such painful antagonism already exists; these pages are only a call to peace in the name of liberty and of justice.

The day will come, I hope,—for truth cannot be obscured for ever; the day will come, and who can prevent it? Is it not an absolute necessity that it should? This enmity between two great powers, that seem made for one another, is too grievous and too bitter not to create a longing for pacification, nor to suggest kindly and honest reflections, conciliatory words, and, finally, to bring about a generous and welcome reparation.

Yes, the hour will come, nay, has come, to understand one another, and to argue no longer with passion and bitterness, but quiet, confidence, and respect.

The reconciliation would be happy in proportion to the sadness of the separation. When two great influences, which had been enemies, cease their strife, they both prosper in peace; they expand freely, each in its vast and noble sphere. The most precious resources, the noblest gifts of humanity, all that is grand and fruitful, then find a wide and glorious space for its development, where progress is arrested by no impediment.

What good accrues to the world from the continuation of conflicts, from the deepening of hatred, from the adjournment of reconciliation? Eternal dissension between the noblest nations, is civil war within the very bosom of humanity! And alas! victories cost as dear to the victors as to the vanquished! and England has made this sad experience perhaps oftener than any other nation. Is it not time that such scenes should end?

Assuredly, when so many new links of connection tend to draw mankind closer together, is it not time to effect a deep and hearty union of minds and hearts? We are making commercial treaties; perhaps we shall soon see treaties of navigation; would it not be better still to ratify a grand and novel treaty of faith and charity, in unity, for the propagation of the Gospel throughout the world?

Yes, I would say to you, my brethren of England, with emotion and with love, if one day your prejudices were to cease, your eyes to open to the light, your hearts to be softened by the sweetness of the Gospel; if you were to be reconciled with the Church, the past would be forgotten, and your glory be unstained; no more accusations of abetting the disorders, the revolutions, and the troubles of so many nations, would be raised against you: those voices would be silenced which for ever question your disinterestedness, and taunt you with selfishness. Ireland would no longer be a thorn in your side; she would no longer be pointed at as your eternal reproach and opprobrium. Your influence in the councils of Europe would then be more respected and powerful. What could you not then do for the peace of the world; and at this moment what could you not do for Italy? What could not France and you effect, if, rendering a tardy justice to the Pontiff, who is in reality the best friend of unhappy Italy, and the most essential to her prosperity and independence, if you were to agree to rescue the Italian cause from the oppression of the nefarious party which is undoing Italy and shaking Europe to its centre?

But, alas! I am allowing myself to be carried away by hopes and longings I too fondly cherish. "A reconciliation has not been yet accomplished. The spirit of evil still triumphs. The bond which had united England to Rome for a thousand years has been violently severed. Rome and England are still at war. Thus two souls made to love one another, but divided by some fatal error, in some unhappy moment, become strangers to one another, and carry on a life-long combat throughout a course where union would have crowned them with prosperity and joy. And yet, a ray of light, an accident, one of those junctures where the mysterious hand of Omnipotence is discerned, would be as powerful for good, as a moment had been for evil: and of all the reconciliations which the world has witnessed, this would be the happiest and most fruitful."[1]

Shall it one day be our lot to see it? For my part, I will hope for it, and, two centuries after Bossuet, it gratifies me to share his generous illusion when he said, "I will hope, as do wiser men, that the days of blindness are drawing to a close, and that it is time for the light to dawn." Indeed, schisms and heresies can never be more

---

[1] On the Political Future of England, by M. de Montalembert.

than transitory scandals; because, being the work of man, they are unsustained by the only force which can conquer time. Twelve centuries have now passed over the last ruins of that powerful Arian heresy, which seemed, at one time, destined to last for ever; and the error which for more than three hundred years disputed with the Catholic Church the empire of the world, exists now only in the annals of the wanderings of the human mind.

If, however, worldly wisdom were here to object that my impatient hopes prescribe too narrow a limit to the action of time, and that the wished-for return of England to Catholic unity is an event not yet mature, then, without giving up those hopes, I would offer these last suggestions to the English nation; I would propose to them this compromise, if I may use the expression, on behalf of the peace which is so dear to our hearts:—

Nothing in the world, I would say, is so strange and repugnant to all Catholic ideas as to see a woman invested with spiritual supremacy; and it inspires us with pity to see your Queen Victoria the legal and unlooked-for heir of the noble title of Defender of the Faith, awarded, perhaps too precipitately, by Pope Leo X. to Henry VIII. Still, together with our Catholic brethren of the three kingdoms, we cannot but personally respect that queen, the worthy object of your affection, and we feel pleasure in rendering homage to her royal qualities, and to the domestic virtues of which she is, on the throne, such a noble model. Well! what we ask from you in return is to respect too the virtues, the august old age, and, as we already said, the weakness of the Pontiff-king, in whom you may not indeed acknowledge the supreme prerogatives of the successor of Peter; but whom the rights of an ancient and venerable sovereignty, the unanimous sentiments of the Catholic world; the prayers and the sorrows of Ireland, the most honoured recollections of your own history, and, I shall add, his very trials, the bitter portion which has befallen him, and the indescribable grace which suffering lends to virtue, recommend to your justice, to your generosity, and to your respect.

At present, I ask for nothing more: charity, patience, prayer, learned and friendly discussion, the preaching of the Gospel, the study of the Fathers, the groans of the saints,—the grace of God will do the remainder for your happiness and the progress of civilization, of which France will be glad to share with you the immortal glory.

Will you refuse a peace, offered on such fair conditions?

CHAPTER XXII.

THE DISMEMBERMENT.

WE are now come to the vital question, and right in front of the revolution. Our work must draw to a close.

In the preceding chapters we have shown the profound reasons which prove the providential legitimacy and the religious necessity of the temporal sovereignty of the popes. We have shown the indisputable right of the Supreme Head of the Church to the possession of the Pontifical States, and the inviolability of those august titles, that have been consecrated, during so many centuries, by the law of Europe and the veneration of the faithful.

We have also related, as history will hereafter, the origin, the causes, and the first attempts of the revolution which, during the last war, broke out of a sudden in the States of the Church. We have seen the part played in those great and sad events, by Piedmont, England, and France.

Doctrine and fundamental principles, history and indelible facts, policy and its different stages—we have endeavoured to leave out nothing in this great and important study.

These pages were printed, and were on the eve of publication, when the recent vote of Central Italy, the acceptance of this vote by Piedmont, and the silence of Europe, have consummated, for awhile at least, the iniquity we should have wished to avert. We have published them, nevertheless, because the principles which have been scandalously sacrificed still subsist, and will rise up again victorious, when their day comes; and also because the true history of this memorable spoliation will always carry with it useful lessons.

No; what is called the Roman question is not settled by the annexation of the Duchies and of four provinces of the Pontifical States to the Piedmontese crown. It is neither settled for the Catholics, who protest with all the energy of their soul, nor for the revolutionists, who wish that more had been done, and done differently, and for the benefit of a power dearer to them than the Piedmontese throne. The formidable question still remains as a cloud overcasting Europe, because violated justice is still justice, and principles, though trodden underfoot, will rise again, sooner or later, at the time appointed by Providence, and also because the passions that are victorious are satiated. Of this they make no secret, and already they cry out loudly for the final solution which policy is putting off for the present—the total suppression of the temporal authority of the Papacy.

Nor does this surprise us: the irresistible logic, the necessary connection of principles and facts do not allow of a moment's doubt to good and enlightened men. To many worthy but unenlightened people, the present partial dismemberment of the States of the Pope is, no doubt, a fact to be regretted, but of slight consequence; but to whoever discerns and understands, it is an immense, decisive, and disastrous fact; it is the whole Roman question. To limit the question to the four separated provinces, is not to see the effects in their causes, nor the consequences in the principles; it is to stop at the surface of words and things. No; the Pope's whole dominions are here at stake; for the principle, in the name of which he is partially despoiled, is the same which calls for his entire dispossession, and the right which the Pope would sacrifice by giving up the separated provinces, would place at the mercy of all the irreligious and anarchical passions the grand principles of European and universal law, without which the Pontifical sovereignty has no longer any foundation in the world, and every throne in Europe would be shaken.

In vain do they urge historical considerations to induce Europe and the Pope to resign themselves to this sacrifice. Never, in the past, was the question put as it is now. Never, in any of the changes which the Pontifical States underwent, in the course of ages, did men invoke the principles which are appealed to now. At present the whole is in question. Whether they will or no, what has been done will lead them on farther—shall I say, than they think, or, than they wish? God alone knows. But what human foresight may assert is, that in this fatal career, it has scarcely ever been possible to stop; it is easy enough to enter on it, but none can say where or how it may end.

This is what the Pope lately stated himself, with all the luminous evidence of good sense and good faith, by answering to the objection taken from the treaty of Tolentino. "The Holy See had then to meet only the violence of a material fact, but at present it has to contend with an odious principle, which is authoritatively urged against it. Now, material force is only a fact. Of its nature, it is limited, and its action is only felt in a narrow sphere, which it cannot exceed; but it is quite different with principles. Of their nature, they are universal, and extend to all things; their fruitfulness cannot be exhausted; they never stop at the point where men wish to limit their action, but they imperatively claim to be applied to everything."

I repeat it: do what they will, they cannot stop. The dismemberment accomplished in this way, calls for other dismemberments. One member is first torn away, and then another, and then all; and then follows death. As

Bossuet says: "Principles cry out, Onward, onward;" the revolutionary menaces forbid to pause, and men hurry on until they meet the precipice, and are hurled into it by the avenging hand of God. Moreover, the future will teach presumptuous men, and sooner perhaps than they imagine, whether the present settlement of the Roman question is final or momentary,—whether it is war or peace, the stability of order, or a long and radical perturbation.

It is, then, not only for the present, but also for the future, for the time when these questions will be raised again, that I wish to set down, not in fugitive pages, but in a book that may remain, the invincible reasons that have made me stand out to the last for the inviolability of the pontifical right, and that dictated to Pope Pius IX. that noble refusal which history will celebrate, and which the Holy Father expressed with no less firmness than mildness in these beautiful words of his Encyclical Letter: "Relying on the aid of Him who said, 'In the world you shall have distress; but have confidence, I have overcome the world;' and again, 'Blessed are they who suffer persecution for justice sake!' We are ready to walk in the glorious steps of our predecessors, and, after their example, to suffer the severest and most bitter trials, and to sacrifice even life itself, rather than ever abandon the cause of God, the Church, and of justice."

Let us then enter upon the subject.

THE THEORY OF SPOLIATION.

The spoliation of the Pope by the dismemberment of his provinces was so evidently a work of intrigue and violence, so tainted in its very source, that men could not but feel the want of colouring and justifying it. They have therefore appealed to principles, and contrived theories; and these theories and principles are precisely those which do not permit to halt in mid career, and call for a total usurpation, as well as for a partial spoliation.

As to the spoliation itself, they long hesitated about the way of accomplishing it, and also about the sanction to be given to it. They first asked for, and then laid aside, a European congress; they tried to bring the Pope to the voluntary surrender of his dominions; they wavered between an unconditional annexation to Piedmont and a sort of lay Piedmontese vicariate. Were they to invade at once the whole Pontifical territory, or only the Legations and the Marches? or were they to leave to the Pope only Rome and the Roman Campagna? They finally committed the decision of these momentous questions to the doubtful votes of a people, tired of anarchy, and that had been ruled for eight months by the revolutionary faction, and the armed promoters of annexation.

The first theory of a dismemberment of the States of the Church was expounded in a celebrated pamphlet, the author of which was unknown, but which created an immense sensation, and wrung from all Catholic hearts throughout the world a loud and unanimous burst of reprobation. At first sight, this pamphlet seemed only to ask for the separation of the provinces that had rebelled; but the principles it laid down went far beyond this conclusion, and undermined the very foundations of the pontifical power. Under the question of the Romagna, it comprised and settled the ultimate question which the revolutionary press boldly stated soon after, and which impending revolutions will soon inevitably propose—the utter ruin of the sovereignty of the Holy See. The truth must be told. The high origin which men affected to assign to this pamphlet, the wide circulation that was provided for it, the mystery of its source, everything, in short, contributed to make it a terrible attack on the very principle of the temporal power of the Pope; and, indeed, it was more dangerous than an open attack, for a momentary triumph of force is not irreparable, but the powers that are brought into discredit and ruined in their principle, are ruined for ever.

It was my duty to oppose, and I opposed with energy and

unsparingly, this perfidious work, on its first appearance. As far as in me lay, I exposed its subterfuges and unmasked its sophisms; and if I cannot help repeating here something of what I then said, it is that I look upon what is going on at present in Italy as the triumph of the pamphlet, and that we are advancing with rapid strides towards the great end it pointed out. As the revolutionary press says, loudly and distinctly, what has been done is but a first step in the way that has been chalked out: Piedmont cannot stop short in so grand a career, said M. Seracco a short time ago, with the unanimous approbation of the Piedmontese Chamber. They will, therefore, soon go to work again; the consequences of the principle that has been laid down will be developed, and the same theories will be invoked to justify new crimes.

At all events, I have done what I could, that, when these theories are again advanced, a refutation may be at hand: the protests of the French bishops and of the whole Catholic episcopate will yet speak; and right, though to-day unheeded, may, to-morrow, be reinstated. No, I shall yet hope that our struggles for truth and justice have not been unavailing.

I said at the time, and I will here repeat, that I rarely met in my life with pages where sophisms, flagrant contradictions, and, if the whole truth must be told, the most palpable absurdities, were solemnly laid down as principles by a publicist, with more self-confidence, and a more perfect conviction of his own powers and of the simplicity of his readers, than in that famous pamphlet.

An enormous and radical contradiction struck one at first sight. The author styled himself a sincere Catholic, spoke only of his respect and love for the Church, and *wrote but to save it*; yet his first panegyrist was the *Times*, and the revolutionary and infidel press of Italy and of France hailed his work with unanimous commendation. I can well understand why it was so: as a *sincere Catholic,* and reasoning in this point of view, he proclaimed the temporal power of the Pope to be indispensable; but, at the same time, he did all in his power to prove that it was impossible. He extolled, even more than we, the divine character of the Pontiff; but it was to use it as an argument against the sovereign. No one could have confessed more explicitly how absolutely necessary this power is for the liberty and honour of the Church; no one could have striven more assiduously in every way, to prove its utter impossibility, not only politically, but even morally and spiritually.

The pamphlet laid down as a principle, "This power can be possible only if it is exempt from the ordinary conditions of power, from all that constitutes its activity, its development, its progress." Exactly what M. de Cavour had said at the congress. But, I may ask, who can live here below, exempt from all the ordinary conditions of existence? What is this *activity, this development, this progress of power*, which you declare to be radically incompatible with the pontifical government? Is it the activity, the development, the progress of good or evil? What do you mean by it?

First of all, " *the pontifical government,*" you say, " *must exist without an army.*" And wherefore? What principle prevents it from having an army, not to attack others, but to defend itself, and protect public order? Why should it be refused the right of legitimate self-defence? I know, indeed, that it existed for many centuries without an army, and that its position was honourable enough in Europe, and in the world; but now things are altered. After the revolutionists have set all Italy on fire, and sixty years of political and social convulsions have perverted all notions of right, and disturbed European order, armies of five hundred thousand men become necessary in time of peace to the most powerful states: at Rome, as everywhere else, "*material force must make up for the insufficiency of moral authority.*" In such times, why should not the pontifical government have a force to protect order and justice in its states? Fénélon and Bossuet wished Christian princes to be the fathers of their subjects. Did they mean thereby to take out of their hands the sword of the law, and to disarm justice?

You ask, How can the man of the Gospel, who forgives, be the man of the law, who punishes? and you remind us that the Church is a mother. But, as the bishop of Perpignan asked you, in his turn, " Are we discussing a question of doctrine, or a question of feelings?" Are you, then, unacquainted with the simple, elementary distinction between charity and justice? The virtues are not sisters at war with one another. Does the Christian magistrate cease to be the disciple of faith and the man of the Gospel, because he is the man of the law, and the defender of society?

Moreover, is there on earth, or in heaven, a power that always forgives? Such power would be imbecility! Saint Louis, who established and administered so firmly justice in the kingdom of France, was, nevertheless, *the good and holy king*. Louis XII., to whom history ascribes the merit of having been a good dispenser of justice, was called, nevertheless, *the father of the people*.

Is it not in behalf of the good, and to defend them against the wicked, that justice should be made to reign? And how does that interfere with the due exercise of the evangelical charity which pardons?

But has paternal and maternal authority, instituted to bless, never any other more painful duty to discharge? Does not maternal love itself, when it has been outraged and overcome, let fall on the guilty a curse, terrible because sanctioned by God? *Maledictio matris eradicat,* says the Scripture: yes, the curse of a mother roots up, and kills. And therefore it has been said to you: " If the tears of the Church move only her dutiful children, and if her thunders appal those only whom they do not threaten, they are, nevertheless, the tears of innocence and the thunderbolts of justice. Neither do the former always remain unfruitful, nor the latter always powerless."[1]

---

[1] M. de Montalembert—Pius IX. and France.

And besides, does not God, the Father of men, sometimes punish and curse ungrateful children? Is not God, who is love,—*Deus charitas est*, justice also, and is he not called the God of judgment?

You would, then, wish to deprive us even of the right of self-defence, because we are Christians!

No, you answer, we do not intend to go so far; but still we maintain that *"the temporal power of the Pope is only possible without activity and progress; it must live without magistrates, — and almost without a code, and without justice."* And why so? "Because *under this government dogmas are laws.*" Assuredly, the answer is a strange one. What! do Catholic dogmas dispense any nation from having laws and a code of justice? Or is it, that good laws and a good administration of justice are incompatible with Catholic dogmas? It would be hard to offend more wantonly common sense.

In spite of everything, added the author, *" its laws will be bound down to the dogmas; its activity paralyzed by its traditions; its patriotism condemned by its faith."* The pamphlet, "Napoleon III. and Italy," had already said: "Canon law is inflexible as the dogma." But, why do you wrong us so outrageously? I asked it at the time, and I ask it again, of this Frenchman, who calls himself a *sincere Catholic:* Since when does faith condemn patriotism? For my part, I undertake to prove that, during ten centuries, there were not in Italy more patriotic Italians than the Popes; and what I say has been proclaimed by Cæsar Balbo, an Italian patriot, worthy of that glorious title: without the popes, Italy would long since have become German.

Indeed, I know not if the author understood his own meaning, when he wrote that, *" under that form of government dogmas are laws."* Of course, dogmas are laws for the understanding; but civil laws have ever been distinct from religious dogmas; and when the writer spoke of the dogmatical inflexibility of canon law, he was completely ignorant of the first elements of the things he treated of, and of the very language he tried to speak.

"*The Pope*," added he, "*must*, on account of those dogmas, *submit to remain always stationary.*" What! you call yourself a Catholic—you do not allow us to doubt it for a moment,—the inflexibility of dogmas is, therefore, in your creed as well as in ours: do you think you are, on that account, comdemned to remain stationary? In your country, does the inflexibility of dogmas impede the progress of all material improvements, of agriculture, of trade, of industry, of electric telegraphs and railways? England had anticipated us in all that. Would she have had a right to say to us: It is the inflexibility of your dogmas that hinders the establishment of telegraphs and railways in your country? Fortunately, other Catholic countries were not behind England in these respects, so that this splendid argument was refuted before it was thought of.[1]

But there are other improvements besides material ones. In what is the inflexibility of dogma prejudicial to art, to science, to literature, to all intellectual and moral progress; and how can you presume to say, "The Pope can never profit by the conquests of science, and the progress of the human mind; his laws are chained down to dogmas?"

It is like a dream to read such things!

It was these dogmas, these popes chained down to

---

[1] What is there in Rome that renders it so utterly incapable of all progress, that it must be destroyed and not reformed? What! is this fatal immobility more fatal than that of the Turks? Here is the phrase used, I shall not say the idea; let whoever can, make out its meaning:—" At Rome, theology chains down progress. The dogmas are laws, and render the laws as unchangeable as they."

Which means, I suppose (for we must be clear and precise), that in Rome, as God is in three persons (a dogma), the mortgage regulations (a law) cannot be altered.

Or, in Rome, as God created heaven and earth (a dogma), the Jacquart-loom (an improvement) cannot be introduced.

Or, again, in Rome, as the Church is one and apostolical, steam-navigation cannot be allowed.

If that is not the meaning, let them mention a single dogma of the Church incompatible with any serious improvement.—*Vide* the excellent article of M. le Comte de Champagny, in the *Ami de la Religion*, from which I have made this extract.

dogmas, that conferred on you, and preserved all those blessings for you, ungrateful Italy, and for you, Europe, forgetful of your most sacred interests!

Such are the absurdities which have been echoed all over the world! Such are the ridiculous calumnies which the French public have been asked to believe!

It is not with the obstinate zeal of a devotee that I say these things: Voltaire and M. Chateaubriand said them before me: "*Europe owes to the Holy See its civilization, a part of its best laws, and almost all its arts and sciences.*" Our adversaries themselves have said the same thing elsewhere; but self-contradiction does not embarrass them much.

Was it the inflexibility of canon law or dogmas that chained down Pius IX., when he gave to the Italian princes the signal of reforms, and to the people of the Roman States those liberties which the revolutionists so soon availed themselves of to upset his throne? As M. Saint-Marc Girardin said so well with Cæsar Balbo: "The great national movement in Italy began with the temporal power of the popes. Did Pius IX., when he strove to place new institutions beside the venerable authority of the Papacy, cease to be a pope? Did he, in any way, derogate from the immutability of Catholic dogmas? Or, was he then no longer a prince? Was he not acting by virtue of his temporal authority? The Popes may be very intelligent and civilized princes without being, on that account, unworthy priests. They may introduce political and administrative reforms without injuring the Catholic faith."

It is idle to talk to us of religious toleration; is there not a state religion maintained in those countries where political liberty and constitutional institutions prevail? Is civil toleration contrary to any dogma of the Gospel? Do not, then, seek to persuade us that there is any radical incompatibility in what is a mere question of prudence and expedience. The Decalogue is inflexible: but is it not so as much for you as for all others? Are there in the Decalogue any laws which you would dare to touch?

And if any of your laws were contrary to that divine code, would they not be *de jure* null and void?

It was said to you with truth; the logical consequence to be drawn from your reasoning is that no one would be fit to reign in the world but desperadoes without law or honour.

No, said the pamphlet; in spite of all that, "*the activity of the Pope will be paralyzed by tradition.*"

But of what tradition did it speak? Which is the Catholic tradition that paralyzes any praiseworthy activity?

It is an old tradition, it is true, in Christianity, that trade and industry must respect the laws of justice, and that writers must respect the laws of truth;—is this paralyzing trade, industry, or intellect?

And what did the writer mean by antitheses such as the following: "The Pontiff is tied down by principles of the divine order which he cannot violate. The prince is bound by exigencies of the social order which he cannot disavow."

But since when are the social and the divine orders at war with one another? What is the social order, and how are we to understand it? Is not human society also of divine right? What is this novel incompatibility which, after eighteen hundred centuries of Christian civilization, you come to proclaim between Christianity and social order?

Do you not see that you are repeating the most odious accusations of ancient paganism? As Tacitus said formerly, you accuse the Church of being the enemy of mankind, *odium generis humani:* but now, it is no longer from Rome, nor from Italy, nor from Europe, but from the whole world, that the Catholics must be expelled!

Whoever you are, Rousseau is your great master in social and religious systems; but Rousseau was more frank than you; he distinctly declared, after having, it is true, declared quite the contrary,—but what matter contradictions in these deplorable times, when all public spirit has sunk so low that hardly do the most absurd contradictions find a contradictor,—Rousseau distinctly declared that a Christian people is incapable of progress, and that, too, on account of its dogmas.

Is that what you meant by opposing the divine to the social order, by proclaiming that dogmas condemn to immobility?

. No, we shall not let ourselves be imposed upon by such absurdities!

There is, as was said at the French tribune, the revolutionary progress of the ball which rolls about in every direction, and never stands still; and there is the immobility of the milestone, which never stirs. We wish neither for one nor for the other.

. But there is also the glorious immobility of the sun, fixed in the centre of the universe, vivifying and illumining all things, around which the earth and the heavenly bodies move in majestic order, and whose light never fails. Such is the image of Catholicism.

These were the strange principles on which the celebrated pamphlet based its system of dismemberment, or rather of utter ruin for the Pontifical sovereignty; the odious preambles of an odious judgment; a sentence of incapacity passed on the Pope; wretched sophisms, by which writers deceive themselves and the public, and lead on governments to perdition.

In reality, it was the abolition of the temporal power of the Holy Father that such principles proclaimed; notwithstanding all the efforts of the pamphlet to cast a veil over it, this odious purpose involuntarily transpired.

In vain did the writer begin by saying, "We wish the congress to admit as an essential principle of European order, *the necessity* of the temporal power of the Pope. *That seems to us the essential point.*"

That *essential point*, that *necessity* so expressly declared, did not prevent the author from maintaining, soon after, that the temporal power of the Pope is neither essential nor necessary to anything whatever; that it is a temporal interest in no way affecting the spiritual, and which religion has no need of.

What matter, as I said before, contradictions? These fine professions of feigned respect did not surprise us; before robbing the Pope, and declaring him incapable of reigning, it behoved at least to do him homage, *to kiss his feet and to tie his hands*, as Voltaire said in the eighteenth century. In the nineteenth, they wish to take off, in mercy, his crown of thorns.

"As to the territorial possessions," they said, "what is of importance is that he should keep the city of Rome. The *remainder* (not only the Romagna, but the *remainder*) is of secondary importance."—"*Only the remainder!* that touch completes the picture," exclaims the bishop of Perpignan.

Well! we have it at last! Rome and the gardens of the Vatican; we were prepared for this; we were aware it had been said.

This is what M. Dupin repeated not long ago in the Senate: "Those provinces," said he, "have never constituted but very imperfectly a real domain for the Church, whose essential seat is Rome and the Campagna."

The temporal sovereignty of the Holy See would thus be soon reduced to the city of Rome and its *suburbium*. Nothing could be better; for, as the author of the pamphlet very wittily added, "*In what can square leagues contribute to the greatness of the Sovereign Pontiff? Does he need extensive territories to be loved and respected? The smaller the territory, the greater will be the sovereign.*"[1]

The Papal dominions being thus curtailed, and the Pope

---

[1] "It is not enough to have taken away one province from him: if he still has two he must be deprived of one: he will be so much the greater. Do not pause; rob him of that last province: must you not always labour for his greatness? He still has Rome, but Rome is too large: when he shall retain but a part of Rome, his spiritual sovereignty will have made new progress. Take from him this part, shut him up in the Vatican: his spiritual power will be as wide as the world. Expel him from the Vatican, cast him into a cell, he will be greater than the world!"—*M. Nettement*, in his eloquent refutation of the pamphlet "The Pope and the Congress."

seated, as the pamphlet says, immovable, *on the holy rock*, he must be watched over and protected. To that end, *there shall be an Italian militia, chosen from the élite of the federal army, and whose mission will be to insure the tranquillity and inviolability of the Holy See.* As he cannot have an army, he must, to be free, have guards.

And that all may be perfect, " *a municipal liberty, as extensive as possible, must free the Pontifical Government from all the details of administration.*"

Thus, the Pope will reign, the Commons will govern. This is the compensation offered to those whom the pamphlet calls *the disinherited of political life* (*les déshérités de la vie politique*).

Finally, and to crown the system, the Papacy shall be pensioned by Europe, as priests are by the State. It will have in this way *a large revenue*.[1] The Pope would thus

---

[1] The wretched sophistry and the contradictions of the pamphlet have been luminously set forth by the bishop of Perpignan in the following page:—" Two opinions are in the field : the one wanting to restore everything to the Pope, the other wanting to take everything away from him. I know the way to arrange all that by a third ingenious theory, which holds a just medium between the other two. Why do the Catholics wish for the maintenance of the temporal sovereignty of the Pope ? Because the political independence of the head of the Church is necessary to the Church. I am quite of their opinion, and am as anxious as they can be for the maintenance of this temporal power : I call God to witness ! Why are *the others* (les autres) anxious for its destruction ? Because they say the political power of the Pope is in itself a bad and dangerous thing. Candidly speaking, I am of their opinion.

" But then, how are we to find a point on which the Catholics will agree with *the others ?* It seems difficult, and yet it is extremely simple. It suffices to reduce the temporal sovereignty of the Pope to *a shadow*, and to obtain from Europe a solemn declaration that *this shadow is inviolable.* That being laid down, it is evident, in the first place, that this sovereignty will not be done away with : for a shadow is something. But this something can make no one uneasy ; for what harm can a shadow do ? Who will fear the power of a shadow ?

" *The others* will then be perfectly tranquillized, whilst the Catholics will be most happy to see the sovereignty of the Pope borne up,

be changed into the first high functionary of public worship in Europe, whose quarterly salary might be stopped when it should please or suit his paymasters.

For my part, I have no hesitation in saying, I prefer black bread and the catacombs. We will not give them to you, I have been answered; you get on too well with them. In that case we shall take them.

But I must leave aside my feelings and my thoughts.

We now see to what would be reduced, in the end, that sovereignty of which the author of the pamphlet said so pompously in the earlier pages:—" In a religious point of view, it is essential that the Pope should be a sovereign; in a political point of view, it is necessary that the head of two hundred millions of Catholics should belong to no one, that he should be subject to no power, and that the august hand which governs those souls should not be tied down, and should be able to rise above all human passions. If the Pope were not an independent sovereign, he would be a Frenchman, an Austrian, a Spaniard, or an Italian, and the title of his nationality would take away from him his character of Universal Pontiff. The Holy See would be no more than the support of a throne at Paris, Vienna, or Madrid . . . . It is of importance for England, for Russia, for Prussia, as well as for France and Austria, that the

---

in its character of shadow, into a superior region, far above the inconveniences of reality. Everything is thus made smooth and easy, all interests are reconciled, and the temporal sovereignty is saved, to the satisfaction of everybody.

" All that is as clear as noon-day: if you do not see it, you are the blind friends of the Papacy; if you will not allow it, you are its open enemies: make your choice."

" Shall we be told now," adds Monseigneur Gerbet, " that we made use of an improper term, when we said it was wanted to reduce to *a shadow* the temporal sovereignty of the Papacy? Is it not evident that the Head of the Universal Church would be lowered to the *legal condition of the Dairi of Japan? Rome would be the Meaco of the Catholic world.* We have not spoken of the millions that are promised to the shadow: we shall therefore add, that our account may be complete, that the author of the pamphlet proposes to make of the Pope *a gilded shadow.*"

august representative of Catholic unity should neither be constrained, nor humbled, nor subordinate."

After those fine propositions, lest he should be *constrained*, a portion of his states was violently taken from him. Lest he should be *humbled*, he was placed in the position of the father of a family, whose children get him declared incapable of managing his affairs, on condition that they shall pay him a yearly allowance, with this difference, however, that there will be no tribunal to oblige them, if one of them refuses to pay his share. Finally, lest he should be *subordinate* or *dependent*, he was condemned to have no means of his own, and to lie at the mercy of everybody—of his Roman subjects, if ever they rebelled; of the Roman municipal council, if the Pope happened to displease them; of the federal army, who, if the Pope was ever forced by his conscience to thwart the wishes of the Federation, might throw him into the castle of St. Angelo on the first signal of their sovereigns: and I shall add, notwithstanding my respect for the great Catholic powers, at the mercy of France, Austria, and Spain; for no one can answer for the impossibility of revolutions, nor for discontent and caprices too easily foreseen.

Humiliation and dependence, debasement and servitude, were, then, what they wanted, " *to secure to the august head of Catholicity his safety and greatness*." And the author was " *pious but independent*," " *a sincere Catholic*"*!*

Moreover, towards the end of his pamphlet, he pointed out, with religious solicitude, their new duties to the few hundred thousand souls whom he still left as subjects to the Pope. After refusing to the power of the Pope all the ordinary conditions of power, he wished, in order to conciliate everything, to refuse the people all the ordinary conditions of a people's existence. He made of Rome a city by itself, a sort of monastery where the Pope was to be shut up, as imbecile kings sometimes were, formerly, in some convent; and of the Roman citizens a monkish people, " a people far removed from all the interests and passions that disturb other peoples, and consecrated exclusively to the glory of God; a people without any other occupation but meditation, the arts, the recollection of a glorious past, and prayer; a people passing a life of quiet and contemplation in a sort of *oasis*, where political passions and interests were not to be allowed to enter, and enjoying the sweet and calm prospects of the spiritual world, each individual of this people having, however, the honour of calling himself a Roman citizen, *civis Romanus.*"

Admirable! What delicate pleasantry! But if, notwithstanding your poetry and your flattering irony, this people understood differently its title of Roman citizen; if they one day had enough of your *oasis* and these *sweet and calm prospects of the spiritual world;* if it did not please them always to live in a monastery; if they grew tired of being, as you say, "for ever disinherited from that noble part of activity which in all countries is the stimulus to patriotism, and opens a field to the highest moral and intellectual faculties of man;" if, in fine, they would no longer submit to the Pope's rule, what would you do? —you would compel them, for here you allow of compulsion. And what will become of the people in this strange and unprecedented existence you have invented for them? .... But what is that to you? you will not live there; but the Pope will, and such a life is very well for him. As the Pope is a father, and the Church a mother, they can live, you say, surrounded by the hatred and insults of their subjects, who will be reduced, by your preposterous and abominable system, to be as Pariahs in the very heart of Italy, and the last of men kept down to a life of meditation and prayer, which they loathe.[1]

Such is your aim. Why did you not say so from the beginning, and without circumlocution?

Fortunately, this will not come to pass! Such a system

---

[1] It was curious to read the English papers of the time, who persisted, cleverly enough, in looking upon the pamphlet as a manifesto of the French government.

could never triumph in a great council of Europe, especially if it were held in Paris, and if Catholic and victorious France were called to the honour of presiding over it. No, France would not allow it; she would not allow it to be said that it was to obtain such a result "that she had run the risks of a great war, won four victories, lost fifty thousand men, spent three hundred millions of francs, and shaken all Europe."

Enough, your object is exposed. It is worthy of the absurdity of your principles, and the iniquity of your means.

"To treat a power in this way," said the *Presse*, candidly, "is to declare it abolished." But to destroy at one blow the Pontifical power would have been an act of brutal violence, to which the world is not yet accustomed; to carry off the Pope from Rome can scarcely be again attempted; to proclaim his incompetency in his provinces by suppressing his power there, and his competency at Rome while degrading him, was too precious an invention for the discoverer not to share with the world, while he flattered himself that he arrived at his end with little noise, smoothly but infallibly.

It was the same policy as in 1809, with the only difference that in 1809 the Pope was carried off by violence, and that the pamphlet merely proposed to extinguish him in Rome.

Another pamphlet, which has also been famous in its way, *The Roman Question*, arrived at the same conclusions:—

"At the worst," said the pamphlet, "the Pope would still keep the city of Rome, his palaces, his temples, his cardinals, his prelates, his monks, his princes, and his lackeys. Europe would send food to this little isolated colony.

"Rome surrounded by the respect of the universe, as by a wall of China, would be, as it were, a foreign body in the centre of free and living Italy."

Moreover:—

"Princes will study history. They will see that the strong

governments are those who held religion with a firm hand: that the Roman senate did not grant to the Carthaginian priests the privilege of preaching in Italy; that the queen of England and the emperor of Russia are the heads of the Anglican and Russian churches, and that Paris ought logically to be the metropolis of all the churches of France."

One must confess all this would be amusing if it were not frightful, and that we have skilful adversaries. We exert ourselves to prove to them that the Pope must be free, independent, respected, a sovereign: they answer that he must undoubtedly, and that they proclaim it as loudly as we do ourselves: and to that end, what do they do with the Pope? They make of him a sort of deaf and dumb idol, chained down in the middle of ancient Rome, "immovable on his holy rock."

These gentlemen have, I must confess, a strange way of interpreting "*Tu es Petrus, et super hanc petram.*" But let them take care: it is written of that rock that it will crush whomsoever it falls upon. *Super quem ceciderit, conteretur.*

We labour to prove to them that Rome, that Italy, that Europe, cannot do without the Pope, and they answer us: We are entirely of your opinion, and we shall keep so well the Pope at Rome, in the centre of Italy and of Europe, that he cannot escape from us. We shall keep him there in such a close embrace, that no one can question either our love or his power. There is but one difficulty in all this—it is, that the best-contrived schemes do not succeed very well against God. God from the high heavens watches over His Church, and by unforeseen plans, or, if necessary, by His thunders, as Bossuet says, delivers her from the greatest dangers, and baffles earthly skill. He enlightens when He pleases human wisdom, so short-sighted by itself; and, again, when it turns aside from Him, "He gives it up to its ignorance, He blinds it, and dashes it to the earth; it is entangled in its own toils, and ensnared in its own precautions. The days of trial go by, and the Church remains. It has often been seen, and will be seen again."

You think the Pope is vanquished, because within these

last few months his provinces have been made to rebel
against him. Your views are narrow, allow me to say, and
your prophecies show little penetration. We do not yield
so easily. The Popes have gone through other trials, and
still hold out. You think the Pope is ruined, because the
revolutionists, after adding to his expenses, declare his
finances to be in a bad state; and on that account you
offer him a maintenance. Well! it is not from your hands
he will accept it: you would be too haughty benefactors;
one day, perhaps, you might taunt him with your munificence, or make him pay too dear for it.

An alms! Ah, if the Father of the Faithful is to be
brought so low, he will receive it with a better grace from
the hands of the poor than from you. Five hundred bishops
throughout the world, who have raised their voices in his
behalf, would collect, if it were necessary, the old and
venerable tribute of the Peter-pence; and the Catholic
world would give him soldiers, if he wanted them.

Do you think that Christian blood has ceased to flow in
our veins, and our hearts to beat in our breasts? Beware,
you will wound us at last. I do not know if our eyes
required to be opened; but you succeeded admirably in
doing so.

At all events, we hope and we pray, full of bitterness at
the deeds of men, but full of confidence in the succour of
Omnipotence.

CHAPTER XXIII.

THE DISMEMBERMENT.

THE THEORY OF SPOLIATION.—CONTINUATION OF THE SUBJECT.

Such, then, were the sad conclusions which were deduced from odious and fallacious principles, applied to the question of the Romagna, and thus were they paraded on the eve of a congress, which was to give a final and irreversible decision. In examining the practical reasons which were to influence that decision, the author was not more happy than in his statement of theoretical principles. These practical reasons have been so often insisted upon since, that it will be well here to dwell upon them in detail. The author begins by invoking the *authority of the accomplished fact*. Ah! the accomplished fact is now at once the sword and shield, the means and the argument of the revolution. Well, it is therefore doubly necessary to hinder the accomplishment of such facts; and, before the appearance of the pamphlet, I had myself called attention in my "Protest" to the indifference of those who stood and looked on, while others were precipitating events with ardour, in order to be able to appeal to accomplished facts. We know, indeed, the way in which these facts were accomplished; we know what agents and what funds were employed in the Romagna. Lord Normanby, Mr. Scarlett, and others, have told us all. And the writer of the pamphlet knew all this as well as we; only it suited his purpose to ignore it. However, it is important that the world know the truth upon the matter; and we shall continue to proclaim it, as the Holy Father himself has been obliged to do, repeatedly and emphatically.

All that we had asserted has been recently confirmed by the Encyclical of the Holy Father, and again by the reply of the Pontifical government to the circular of M.

Thouvenel of the 8th of February. "It would seem," says the Pontifical despatch, "that the French Minister of Foreign Affairs had not inquired fully enough into the facts, when he stated that, by the mere fact of the Austrians retiring, the inhabitants of the Romagna found themselves independent without any need for foreign support or agitation. The truth is, that no sooner had the garrison withdrawn, than the revolutionary party, which had everything ready, owing to its previous manœuvres, and was emboldened by the proclamation of one of the belligerents, seized upon the power, and imposed its yoke upon the people, who still continue under the same tyranny. Perhaps it is not going too far to say that there is not a capital in Europe where what has happened at Bologna would not occur, if the garrison which protects it were suddenly withdrawn."

But apart from any particular circumstances—such as the Piedmontese intrigues and a revolutionary terrorism—what is the theory of the accomplished fact, as laid down in the pamphlet, but an elevation of injustice into a principle, and a substitution of brute force for right? The writer appeals to an argument as novel as it is replete with danger, when he opposes to the authority of the Pope what he has presumed to call the *authority of the accomplished fact.* "The Romagna," he says, "has been separated for some months, in fact, from the Papal government. Thus this separation has in its favour the *authority of the accomplished fact.*" This fact, then, this disgraceful fact, is now appealed to as an *authority* against a right recognized and proclaimed by France and the rest of Europe. We have long been aware, indeed, of the violence and brutality of accomplished facts; but hitherto we had not heard of their *authority.*

Authority, that grand and sacred idea, founded upon law and right, and which is one with them, how has it been dishonoured! It is now declared to spring from infamy and wrong! Such is the strange source and foundation assigned to it, such the bad company in which we are to seek it. I can understand that, after expressing such a sentiment, the author should not have hesitated to propose to a European congress to sanction such enormities, and to state that its task would be a light one, merely " *to record an accomplished fact.*"

So that, for the future, an insurrection kept on foot for a few months by the hirelings and the revolutionary ambition of a neighbouring state, is to be looked upon by Europe as a glorious *fact,* soon rising into a *right,* which must not be further discussed. To record it is sufficient. Let a revolt only be kept up for six months, and a venerable right, numbering more than a thousand years, founded and sanctioned by all European nations, ceases *ipso facto* to exist!

But passing over the question of right, and the violation of moral and social law, is not history against you here? How many accomplished facts have been reconsidered and differently arranged, at all periods, in Europe. Had not the oppression of Greece been an accomplished fact for centuries when France broke her chains in 1827? Without going further, had not the French republic been an accomplished fact for four years on the 2nd of December, 1852? When we laid siege to Rome, was not the Roman republic an accomplished fact, and a more decisively established one than the present, for the Pope was then at Gaeta, and now he is at Rome; and the Roman republic had constituted and defended itself, while Central Italy was and is still occupied by foreign armies? On the 18th Brumaire, had not General Bonaparte a constituted government and an accomplished fact before him?

Moreover, the fact was so far from being accomplished when the pamphlet appeared, that Piedmont had not yet accepted the annexation which had been voted, and the new state of things was universally regarded as temporary.

It may be said, however, all this is very well upon paper, but in practice one must accept an accomplished fact, when it cannot be annulled; our advice having been spurned, and armed interference being inadmissible,

I will answer, with one of my colleagues, Mgr. de Perpignan: "No, I do not accept this alternative; even supposing that the fact cannot be annulled, I deny that we are forced to accept it. There is evidently another attitude, another course which remains to be taken; to proclaim the right in firm and distinct accents, to refuse to recognize anything which has been done contrary to it, and to maintain such refusal in all its political consequences. The reasoning of our opponent is the sophism of incomplete enumeration, employed to the prejudice of a right which he recognizes himself. The grand mistake of this advocate of organized and armed rebellions is, that he seems to believe too much in the justice of force, and not enough in the force of justice. In the latter, however, we shall persist in believing, till it is proved to us that Europe, in spite of her vaunted progress, has fallen so low, that she must either accept an injustice, or avow her helplessness."

And, what is most inconsistent and iniquitous in all this, the congress was declared, at one and the same time, with regard to the same legitimate sovereignty, helpless to maintain its rights, and omnipotent to overthrow it!

For the omnipotence of the congress was the means proposed, to elevate the accomplished fact into a right: its omnipotence, when opposed to the weakness of the Holy Father!

"*A congress has every power*," it was said; but as it was well answered, has it therefore every right? One may be omnipotent and yet commit injustice.

A congress omnipotent! Thus a congress might at pleasure decree annexations, destroy autonomies, take away provinces, and bestow them upon others; take Ireland from England, Alsace from France, Sicily from Naples, Geneva from Switzerland, &c. And no law or justice is superior to its omnipotence!

You expressly admit that the insurrection in the Romagna is "*a revolt against right.*" The accomplished fact was then unjust: well, if one is weak like the Pope, one may submit to an unjust fact; but when one is omnipotent like the congress, *one cannot record it,*—at least, without dishonour.

The congress would not have dishonoured itself; and, for my part, though the pamphlet sought to hamper it beforehand, and to trace out for it its course, I should still have felt implicit confidence in the great minds, the illustrious diplomatists whom Europe was sending there. The congress, on the eve of its meeting, was dispersed; and I regret it. It would not have accepted the office proposed to it; which was to sanction injustice and rebellion, solemnly to introduce the revolutionary principle into European law, to insult all sovereignties, to consecrate brute force, and basely to abandon weakness. What were the arguments by which, as was supposed, it was to be conducted to such a resolution?

It was said, "*Europe, which sacrificed Italy in* 1815, *has a right to save it in* 1860." Thus to save Italy was to deliver it from the authority of the Pope!

It was added: *Europe, in* 1815, *gave the Pope* the Pontifical States and the Romagna; *in* 1860, *she may come to a different decision.* But can any one name one of the sovereigns who were dispossessed of their states before 1815, who will admit that the Congress of Vienna *gave* him his dominions, and that a future congress may take them away? Does the king of Sardinia, for instance, all whose provinces were then French departments, recognize the right of a congress to restore them to France?

Europe, in 1815, was emerging from a long earthquake—from wars, revolutions, and conquests. She meant to restore the rights which had been violated.

Moreover, what did you mean by pretending, in the name of *European jurisdiction,* to forbid a Catholic power from offering aid to the Pope?

What, then, was it that France did in 1849? Did she not bring back the Pope to Rome? What was then the behaviour of Europe herself? Was she not present with Pius IX. at Gaeta, in her representatives?

Will you inform us why a European, a Catholic power,

should be prohibited from upholding a sovereign whom all Europe recognizes, a sovereign who is the supreme head of the Catholic Church?

Will you inform us on what grounds attacks are to be sanctioned, while defence is to be prohibited?

At what period did civilized Europe decide that the weak have no right to protection or assistance?

It was on this ground, however, that an ancestor of Victor Emmanuel, in 1818, whom revolutionists had dethroned, was restored by the intervention of a great power.

You have informed us that France cannot aid the Pope. " As a Catholic nation, she cannot consent to compromise so seriously the moral power of Catholicism. As a liberal one, she cannot consent to force a people to submit to a government in opposition to their wishes."

Ah! the argument is an old one. In 1848 and 1849 we had men as uneasy as you about the moral power of Catholicism, and who could not bear that France should destroy the Roman republic; thus prejudicing the rights of peoples, and contradicting its own principles. These men spoke of filing an accusation against the President of the republic, and even rose in arms in the streets, to avenge, as they said, the violation of the constitution. Their names were Ledru Rollin, Louis Blanc, Caussidière, Pierre Leroux, Sergeant Rattier, &c. It was they who then pleaded the cause of Mazzini and Garibaldi against us.

Well, the Roman expedition was carried without them, and in spite of them; and M. Dupin has just declared to the senate that the restoration of the Pope by the French armies, in 1849, is one of those speaking facts which can never be effaced from the hearts of Catholics. It is true that this does not prevent M. Dupin from adopting the strange opinion of the pamphlet as to the injury we should do the moral power of Catholicism, if we went to the aid of the Pope.

But it is again objected to us that the Pope has not granted the necessary liberties to his subjects; and that they have, therefore, revolted. To this I have two very plain answers to give.

First, if there are any new liberties, practicable and advisable, to be accorded in the Papal States, such grave questions are not surely to be discussed amidst outrages and revolutions; but, on the contrary, in a spirit of conciliation on both sides, with a friendly understanding between liberty and authority, so difficult to realize in these stormy times. Even in France, have all difficulties of this kind been yet resolved?

Secondly, the Pope is bound, like all temporal princes, and more than they, to study the welfare of his subjects, and to dispense to them, in just measure, the benefits of a wise liberty with those of a regular and paternal administration. Well, Pius IX. has not been wanting to these duties; M. Saint-Marc Girardin lately referred to the noble testimony borne on this head to Pius IX. by Count Cæsar Balbo, in the Sardinian parliament:—" The important act which was the initiative of our restoration, the immortal act of amnesty originated, not from Pius IX. as Pontiff, but from Pius IX. as Prince; the amnesty and the reforms owed their being to the sovereignty of Pius IX.; his sovereignty, his temporal power, was unquestionably the germ of our great national movement. Whatever varying phases that movement may hereafter present, it is certain that its source was the temporal power of the Popes." As I have already said, when Pius IX. left Rome, on the approach of the bands of Garibaldi, he might, on first touching foreign soil, have solemnly called to witness the city which had expelled him, and the whole world with it, that he had done, of his own accord, more for the liberty of his people than any other European sovereign had then done.

But our opponents rejoin, " You are attributing to us intentions which we disclaim; we are seeking to preserve his spiritual authority by abandoning to the flames a part of his temporal power. After all, *the territory of the Church is not indivisible.* No one proposes to deprive the Pope of his temporal dominions; the question is, whether they may not be curtailed."

I will reply with Father Lacordaire, whom you have slanderously represented as an ally of your unhappy cause:—" What would France say if it were proposed to degrade her crown? Territory is divisible, but right is not. Territory is a field which may be parcelled out; but honour is an idea which must either remain intact or perish."

I would add,—Where is the territory which force or a triumphant insurrection cannot divide? Is there a single nationality, sovereignty, or property which is naturally indivisible? The principle you are laying down is a perilous one; take care that it does not turn against yourselves.

Is it not because Poland was not naturally indivisible that it was so miserably parcelled out between Russia, Prussia, and Austria? And France and the rest of Europe stood by, in the enlightened eighteenth century, and congresses have vainly protested or tacitly acquiesced.

The argument, however, has become fashionable; and, the other day, was complacently advanced in the Senate by M. Dupin. And, by the way, what was M. Dupin's object in telling us that these provinces were the latest addition made to the Papal States, first by war, and afterwards by negotiation? First of all, this is a formal contradiction of history. The Legations constituted precisely the ancient Exarchate of Ravenna, which was given to the Holy See by the Frank kings. But, even granting the truth of his statement, what does it prove? What would be said if a member of the English House of Lords were to advocate the separation from France of Alsace or Lorraine, on the ground that they were the last provinces we had acquired? No; it is absurd for M. Dupin to insinuate that for this reason the Pope has not now a full, real, and incontestable right to those provinces. In the words of a celebrated writer:—" The Romagna is a perfectly legitimate possession of the Pontifical government, and belongs to it by a title sanctioned by history and by treaties;" and, as the emperor himself has said in his letter, " The powers of Europe must admit that the rights of the Holy See to the Legations are indisputable." The emperor, as well as the rest of Europe, saw here "*one of those established rights, to which the most profound respect is due.*" [1]

Unhappily, to the grief and scandal of the Church and the friends of order in Europe, such respect has been wanting on the part of a monarchy, which has been hurried by its ambition into a contempt of all rights, a neglect of all its duties, and, I will add, all its true interests.

I fully concur in the following sagacious and profound reflections of the bishop of Perpignan:—" I can understand that a revolutionary dictatorship, which declares war against all monarchies, like the Convention in France, should publicly exult in the overthrow of the legitimate power in the countries which it had excited to revolt; but that a government which calls itself monarchical should solemnly accept, from its throne, in the face of the world, a call to approve and profit by the overthrow of another government, with which it is at peace, and whose independence it had promised to respect; that it should congratulate the perpetrators of the deed, caress, extol, and exhort them to persevere, promising them its support in the counsels of Europe—nothing like this can we recall in the history of civilized nations. If such an enormity pass unpunished, if—what can never be—it receive a general sanction, one would be moved to ask whether all shame, as well as all good faith, had not taken leave of the political world."

---

[1] It is also contrary to history to say, as the dictator of Bologna has done, that "the temporal power of the Popes has undergone in the course of ages various and essential modifications." On the contrary, it has scarcely at all varied, and the Pope is perhaps the only sovereign in Europe who now possesses nearly what he did a thousand years ago.

CHAPTER XXIV.

THE DISMEMBERMENT.

THE RELIGIOUS QUESTION.

I.

THE idea of a European congress was soon abandoned; the prudence of submitting the question of the dispossession of the Pope to the decision of Europe appeared questionable; people were scarcely sanguine enough to hope that such an assembly would take upon it to sanction insurrection, and to lay down a precedent of spoliation. The question then entered a new phase: a voluntary cession was demanded from the Holy Father by the emperor, in his letter of December 31, 1859; inexorable necessity being still the great argument appealed to.

The Holy Father's reply was what might have been expected from that mild but firm Pontiff; and an encyclical immediately informed the world of his refusal, and the motives which had imperatively prompted it. He said:—

"The most noble emperor counsels us voluntarily to forfeit our claim to these provinces, pleading that he can see no other means of remedying the present disorders. We have not delayed to reply to him; and, with the apostolic liberty of our heart, have declared to him that we could in no wise comply with his advice, inasmuch as it presents insurmountable difficulties connected with the rights of the Holy See, which belong, not to the hereditary succession of a royal family, but to all Catholics.

"We have declared that we could not cede what belonged to the Church, not to us; and that to sanction and approve the insurrection in the Emilia would urge on the native and foreign agitators in the other provinces of the Pontifical States to renew the same attempts, encouraged by the success of the former rebellion.

"Finally, we have informed the emperor that we could not abandon those provinces without violating the solemn oaths which bind us, without exciting complaints and risings in our other provinces, without deserting our duties to all the Catholics of the universe, and, moreover, without prejudicing the rights, not only of the Italian princes, who have been unjustly dispossessed, but of all the princes of Christendom, who could not behold with indifference the triumph of most dangerous principles, which we are now asked to consecrate."

One of the most generous champions of the Pontifical independence, M. Augustin Cochin, has well summed up in a few words the unanswerable reasoning of the Pope's reply: "A sacrifice which might lead to poverty, if justifiable, and favourable to the peace of the world, would be an act of virtue," worthy, undoubtedly, of the Vicar of Jesus Christ; "but a sacrifice involving the violation of an oath, the consecration of rebellion, the abandonment of the rights of others, and which must compromise even what is retained, would be an act of weakness," of which the Sovereign Pontiff is incapable.

Another eloquent and fearless defender of the Holy See, Prince Albert de Broglie, has expressed the same ideas, as follows:—

"It is clear, from what has been proposed to the Pope, and what is publicly proclaimed throughout Europe, that what is asked from him is not the mere cession of a province, but an avowal of his own indignity; he is asked to sign the act of his own degradation, an act which will be executed wherever the Papal arms, the tiara, and the keys are still displayed. It is the whole human power of the Papacy; that fabric which has withstood the action of time, which has survived so many usurpations of despotism, and so many popular revolutions, sanctioned by the homage of all the high-minded statesmen of Europe, and under whose shadow so many millions of consciences have reposed in freedom for a thousand years; which is now undermined to the centre, and is tottering to its fall. The point which is now argued is not in what way the head of the Church is to govern, nor who are to be, or not to be, his subjects; but whether he is to descend from the rank of sovereign, and to choose between the lot of a subject and that of an outcast."

However, the encyclical was accused with having introduced considerations foreign to the controversy, with viewing the subject in an exclusive manner, and converting a purely political question into a religious one. The same grounds were alleged for very unwarrantable censures, condemning the zeal and emotion which the Catholics displayed, and the public protests they had made.

To the impossibility proclaimed by the Holy Father were opposed the origin of his oath, a few historical precedents, and certain instances of partial dispossession or voluntary renunciation, but without replying to the fundamental and irrefutable arguments of the encyclical.

But a close examination must convince us that the Holy Father, far from looking at the question from an exclusive point of view, had, on the contrary, most perspicuously distinguished and pointed out its double aspect.

In fact, no one has ever asserted that the terrestrial rule of the Holy See was of a spiritual nature; what is earthly is earthly. It has only been said (and our most avowed antagonists have agreed with us in saying) that the question of the Pope's temporal power concerns religion, and that in this sense it is a religious question. Why? Because that temporal power has a religious use, a religious purpose; it is necessary, not politically, but religiously, because it insures the spiritual independence of the Pope, who, as has been so well remarked, *is a Prince only because he is a Pontiff*. And with the spiritual independence of the Pope, the liberty of the consciences of all Catholics is secured, which must suffer, if their guide were not in the possession, the evident possession, of his liberty; if the supreme doctor of their faith were himself oppressed and dependent.

All this I have superabundantly demonstrated in the

earlier chapters of this volume. I have cited, besides, the most eminent Catholic theologians, Protestants, philosophers, publicists, heterodox sovereigns, and statesmen, all admitting and recognizing, with us, the paramount nature of the religious and spiritual interests involved in the question of the temporal power of the Papacy. And I must confess, for my part, that I cannot understand how any one can now publicly affirm that *it is a merely political question, which in no way concerns religion.*

But our present opponents, who with monstrous inconsistency, for which their motive is but too plain, will not see in the dismemberment of the States of the Church anything but an exclusively political question, have been obliged to make admissions which condemn them. The pamphlet, *Le Pape et le Congrès*, having propounded the question, "Is the temporal power of the Pope *necessary* to the exercise of his spiritual?" answers: "*Catholic doctrine* here agrees with political reasoning in giving an affirmative answer. It is *necessary* that the chief of two hundred millions of Catholics be dependent on none." And the pamphlet, *Napoléon III. et l'Italie*, stated as decisively that "the cause of the Pope involves *the greatest religious interests* of Europe;" and that "the political power of the Papacy is *necessary* to its independence, and on account of the greatness of its spiritual mission."

It must be allowed that it is not difficult to argue with opponents who thus contradict themselves; yet, unhappily, such contradictions create, in practical matters, unexpected and disheartening difficulties.

Every one knows the expressive terms in which the first emperor declared that the Pope's temporal sovereignty was indispensable to the exercise of his spiritual power, adding that it was *the work, the glorious work, of centuries.*

A man must assuredly be in an awkward dilemma, and feel strangely puzzled for arguments, who, in opposition to every authority as well as to common sense, can volunteer the novel assertion, that the question of the Pope's temporal power is an exclusively political one, in no way concerns religious interests, and bears only upon *lay and material affairs*.[1]

The Papal government, in its reply to the French Minister of Foreign Affairs, maintains, with unanswerable logic, the essentially spiritual character of the question:—

"Without referring to the manner in which the Pontifical States were formed, under the influence of religious motives, and for an essentially religious end, the very name of these states, the States of the Church, a name so thoroughly in accordance with their real destination, the securities and the means which they afford the Vicar of Christ for preserving the independence necessary to the exercise of his apostolic ministry, the patrimony which they furnish to the head of the Church, who, unlike other sovereigns, who declare themselves, as princes, the heads of their churches, is a prince only because he is a Pontiff, all these considerations should suffice to demonstrate that the present question is essentially a religious one, and has an intimate connection with the most vital interests of the Catholic Church, and with those of all her members, both in general and in particular."

And such was the sentiment of all Catholics; their souls kindled, and they instinctively assumed an attitude of defence: and those are really to be pitied who, like M. Dupin,

---

[1] One of my colleagues, the bishop of Perpignan, whose moderation has been eulogized by our opponents, and whose talent and firmness I, for my part, also admire, has likewise energetically refuted the preposterous assumption that the question is simply political, and in no way concerns religion. "What! the temporal sovereignty of the Pope, instituted to insure the liberty of his universal mission, is not a religious question! The violation of the faith sworn to him, of the oaths of fidelity made to him, not a religious question! The excommunication pronounced by the last general council, the Council of Trent, against all who violate the ecclesiastical dominions, not a religious question! The demonstrations of impiety stirred up by the chiefs of the spoliating faction wherever their footsteps pass, are not religious questions! In its causes, in its immediate effects, and its future consequences, the present state of affairs vitally involves the very highest interests of religion."

can only see, in such a noble and religious solicitude, the vulgar anxieties of *shareholders in alarm about a common fund*. The Pontifical despatch continues:—

"Now, if the interests of the Catholics are deeply involved in this question, it follows that they have a right, nay, that they are bound, to take a greater part in its discussion than if it were of a purely political nature. Is it not clear, that the fact of the separation of the Romagna, and still more, the evils which must flow from such a wrong and unjust precedent, must prejudice the rights of all Catholics, as far as they have a right, in the present order of things which Providence has established, to see their supreme doctor uncontrolled by any human authority, and fully independent in the exercise of his apostolic ministry? It was but just to warn Catholics of the injury with which they were threatened; and such warning could only be given under a religious point of view, for the right we allude to is based upon religion; its exclusive object being the dignity and independence of Catholic consciences.[1]

"The Holy Father was then bound to declare to the Catholic world the real state of the question; and in his encyclical, the political and the religious questions have not been confounded, but carefully distinguished. The religious question is there treated separately, and at the same time it declares to all, the celestial mission which the Vicar of Jesus Christ has received, of reminding sovereigns and people of the eternal rules of truth and justice. As to the multitude of the faithful, His Holiness has sought from them no other assistance than their prayers."

Who here takes the most narrow and exclusive view, the Pope, or they who persist in asserting, with regard to a controversy which evidently concerns, deeply and vitally, religious interests,—which, indeed, they have admitted as

---

[1] A writer, thoroughly devoted to the government, wrote as follows in a ministerial paper, some time ago:—"Rome is not only the natural capital of Catholicism, but also, in equity and according to good sense, the property of the Catholic world."—*Le Pays*.

distinctly themselves as we, that the question between the Pope and the emperor is an exclusively political one?

In vain has reference been made, in support of this assertion, *to the confusion of the two orders, civil and religious,* caused by *the theocratic tendencies of the early ages of the Church.* History says the contrary. Neither did the Christian emperors, from Constantine, accept such confusion, coming from the popes; nor did the popes accept it, coming from the emperors. In reality, the distinction between the two powers was ever taught and professed by the popes; it is formally laid down by St. Gregory the Great, by Gregory II., by Symmachus, and St. Gelasius. I have before cited the letter of the last-mentioned to the Emperor Anastasius: " This world, august emperor, is principally governed by two powers, that of the pontiffs and that of kings .... The ministers of religion obey your laws in all that regards the temporal order, because you have received your power from above; but in what regards religion, you confess that you have no right to control them by your will, but are bound to hear them."

We find the same doctrine distinctly stated in one of the *Novellæ* of Justinian. They have always been familiar to the Catholic Church, and indeed were introduced into the world by her; for, before the Catholic Church, no spiritual power existed independently of the temporal, which then arrogated all authority to itself.

"The separation of the two powers," says M. Thouvenel, "is an advantage to the world." This, for my part, I do not deny; but it is an advantage contingent upon one condition, which alone can prevent the oppression of men's consciences, by opposing the otherwise inevitable absorption of spiritual power by temporal; and that condition is, the temporal and spiritual independence of the supreme head of the Church.

As M. Odilon-Barrot well remarked in 1849, " *It is in order that the two powers may be separate everywhere else, that it is necessary they should be united at Rome.*" Otherwise, disputes are unavoidable, the spiritual power must be in bondage to, or even altogether absorbed by the temporal, as history has proved, and as is now seen at Constantinople and Moscow.

I say, with M. Barrot, *united*, not confounded; for they remain distinct. But it does not follow that they are altogether foreign to each other, that they have no connection, or that one may be overturned without affecting the essence of the other.[1] Cæsar Balbo had replied in advance to these strange deductions from true premises: "Doubtless the temporal power is not of the essence of the spiritual;" children could tell us that; "but it is indispensable to its exercise," to the necessary liberty and independence of the spiritual power. In a word, as the Pontifical despatch so well expressed it, "The Pope is a prince, because he is a pontiff:" he is a king, because he cannot be a subject, because our souls and bodies would be in subjection with him.[2]

And this you have all confessed and proclaimed your-

---

[1] This reasoning is to be found in the *Memorandums* of Cipriani and Pepoli, in the French diplomatic despatches, and in the speeches made in the Senate. All present the most remarkable analogy on this point.

[2] This is the period to which Prince de Broglie called attention some time ago, in energetic and eloquent language. After giving a description of the imperial system in France, that powerful organization, which has a thousand arms in its ramifications, and a single head in its centralization, whose will is executed with the rapidity of lightning, and which, by a sage combination of old with new legislation, retains in its grasp all the sources of and all the checks on, social activity; the administration of justice, the press, and the financial resources of the country—he adds: "I know of but one equal to this power, which is, however, superior to it as well,—the power of the Catholic Church. I know of but one authority which is not dependent on it; and that is the Church. I know of but one door of which it has not the key; that is the conscience. It is not difficult to conceive that in presence of such a power it must be hazardous to lower, if only by a little, the only head which is on a level with it, and can look it in the face; or to concede to it any fresh advantage over the representative of the only domain upon which it has been, as yet, unable to intrude. And such danger ought to seem more pressing to those who do not believe in the promises made to the Church."

selves; and if you are now recanting, and contradicting yourselves, you are actuated by expediency, not by a love for truth.

At all events, it is clear that nothing but the imperative voice of his conscience could have dictated to so peacefully disposed a Pontiff so formal a refusal, or repressed upon the lips of a sovereign who had been so severely tried, the word, the only word, which instantly—at least so he was told—would have ended the strife, and lulled the storms which threatened him.

Vain were the efforts made to shake the *non possumus* of the Pope, and to invalidate the oath by which he declared his conscience bound. M. Dupin has stated that that oath was never imposed on the popes till 1692, in order to check the abuses of nepotism. But, a hundred years before Innocent XII., Innocent IX., in the bull *Quæ sub hac sancta*, in 1592; before Innocent IX., Sixtus V., in the bull *Quanta apostolicæ*, in 1586; before Sixtus V., Gregory XIII., in the bull *Inter cætera*, in 1572; before Gregory XIII., St. Pius V., in the bull *Admonet*, in 1567; and before St. Pius V., all the popes to whom he refers, had spoken the same language. And, moreover, the repression of a petty and particular abuse is evidently inferior and subordinate to the grand and universal obligation of the popes to preserve intact the states of the Holy See.[1]

Vainly, too, were appeals made to the past, and history ransacked for precedents. Why? For what object?

From the harshness and contumely of Louis XIV. towards Innocent XI.; from the annexation of the country of Avignon to France in the revolution; from the spoliation inflicted by force of arms at Tolentino; from unjust

---

[1] See M. Dupin's speech in the Senate. Having paid a deserved tribute to M. Dupin in this volume, it will be perhaps allowed that I have a right to say here what I think of his late speech. However, I will not do so in this place. A fitting answer to such a speech could not be given in a note.

compensations sought by such or such a power, at such or such a date; what conclusion was it endeavoured to draw? Was it the exclusively temporal character of the present question of dismemberment? But these facts cannot change the nature of things, and all that we have proved as to the great spiritual interests it involves still holds. Was it the legitimacy of the annexation, once it is consummated? But, "accumulate as many unjust facts as you will," replies the Holy See, with unanswerable logic, "you never can extract from them one just fact." Was it the possibility of the abdication demanded? But in that case you should prove that the precedents you cite bear in some way upon the present question. You have not done so, and you could not. In 1797, by the treaty of Tolentino, about which so much is said, the Pope yielded to *a fact*, to war, to superior force; but to-day, by voluntarily giving up his provinces, he would be recognizing *a principle* which tends to destroy his power altogether. "Pius VI.," says the Pontifical despatch, "under circumstances wholly different from the present, had to deal with irresistible violence and overwhelming material force; but were the reigning Sovereign Pontiff *to acquiesce in a pretended principle*, he would thereby virtually abdicate the sovereignty of all his states, and authorize a spoliation opposed to all the rules of justice and reason. The instance adduced by the French Minister of Foreign Affairs conducts them to a conclusion directly opposed to that which he had in view."

I must add, that to revive the recollections of Tolentino, is not to remind the world of a good faith and an uprightness which did us honour. The precedent was the less conclusive, in that Pius VI. was shamefully deceived; by yielding, he hoped to preserve the rest of his states, and two years after he died at Valence, stripped of everything.[1]

---

[1] Pius VI. asked his persecutors, with touching meekness, at least to allow him to die at Rome. "You may die where you are going," answered Haller, the agent of the Directory. Pius VI. died at

General Bonaparte wrote to the Holy Father, on the 1st of Ventôse, year V.: "All Europe knows the pacific intentions and virtues of your Holiness. The French republic will be, I trust, one of the truest friends of Rome." And he wrote, on the same day, to the Directory: "My opinion is that Rome, once deprived of Bologna, Ferrara, the Romagna, and the thirty millions which we are taking from it, can no longer exist; the whole machine will go to pieces of itself."[1] General Bonaparte was at least clear-sighted enough to see the importance of the provinces which were torn from the Holy See.

It is, then, undeniable that the question, in the form under which it has been propounded by events and by the insurgents, is not a simple question of fact, but one of right; that, in the present case, it was not the acceptance of a fact, but the abandonment of a principle, which was demanded from the Pope; of a principle all-important, and which must carry everything with it in its ruin.

Again, when Rome pleaded that "the Pope cannot do what is asked from him, because the reasons for abandoning the Romagna apply equally to the rest of his states: such renunciation would imply the renunciation of the

---

Valence, having pronounced a touching prayer, which was heard both by God and men:—" O Lord Jesus Christ, behold before Thee Thy Vicar, the Pastor of the Catholic flock, a captive and a mourner, joyfully dying for his sheep. From Thee, O tender Father and Master, I beg and ardently implore two last graces: first, that Thou wouldst grant the most ample pardon to all my enemies and persecutors, and to each of them in particular; secondly, that Thou wouldst restore to Rome the chair and throne of St. Peter; to Europe peace, and especially to France, which is dear to me, and which has ever laboured for the good of the Christian Church, Thy holy religion."

[1] It is true that, on its part, the French government sent these instructions to its general:—" You will shake the tiara of the pretended head of the universal Church." And again: " You have two objects to keep in view; to prevent the king of Naples from marching on Rome, and to foster, far from discouraging, the good dispositions of those who may be of opinion that it is high time for the reign of the popes to end."

whole patrimony of the Church;" no reply was given, either in the diplomatic despatches, or in the speeches in the Senate and the *Corps Législatif.* No more were these arguments answered: " The Pope cannot, because, being the common father of all his subjects, and king of his twenty-one provinces, he is bound either to procure for all what is required from him as a benefit for the four provinces of the Romagna, or to ward off from these the evils which he would grieve to see inflicted upon the others; he cannot, finally, because of the scandal which would result, to the prejudice of all Christian princes, and of civilized society in general, if felony were to be crowned by prosperity and approbation."

If there be persons who may smile at these words, for my part, I honour them; and I do not hesitate to say, that, in my opinion—even apart from the great spiritual interests which here take precedence of everything else —so grand a view of political duties, investing them with all the solemnity of the highest questions of morality, elevates them into his jurisdiction, who has received from God the exalted mission of enlightening souls and guiding consciences.

II.

No; the plan of a voluntary renunciation was no solution to the question; it was an expedient, by which nothing could be saved, yet which must compromise the whole. It was wantonly to sacrifice an indisputable right, and a capital principle. It was, under the circumstances which had occurred, morally an abdication, entailing rapid, inevitable, and irretrievable ruin. It was necessarily a pledge, not of order and peace, but of war and confusion. By it a passing difficulty might have been evaded, speedily to reappear under a form more pressing and perplexing than even what we now behold.

In fact, the pretext for a quarrel with the Pope is not the extent of the Pontifical States; it is of a very different nature; by dismembering his states, the grievances, real or imaginary, of his remaining subjects, would not be redressed; but, on the contrary, sanctioned, and thereby aggravated; affairs must continue in the same, or a worse state than before: the Pope, stripped of a province, and the *prestige* of his firmness and moral courage gone, would be simply left surrounded by the same enemies and the same dangers, or probably greater.

It was, therefore, here most essential not to be led away by appearances, or by a semblance of conciliation and generosity: it would have been foolish to mistake, through impatience or faint-heartedness, for a salutary concession, what was simply a bootless and fatal sacrifice of a sacred and indisputable right.

Undoubtedly the states of the Holy See might, like any others, have had different territorial boundaries from what they have; the Romagna might not have belonged to it: but, as it is, it does belong to it; in the name of what principle do you propose to take it away? By taking it away, what dangers do you obviate? What new principle of right are you inaugurating? Such is the real question.

The Pope, it is true, can but feebly defend his rights; yet, when weakness has justice on its side, it is only the more worthy of respect. Now, as a bold and eloquent writer has just inquired, " Is there a sovereignty in Europe which rests on a more ancient basis, or can refer to a more unexceptionable origin than the Papacy? Is there one which has weathered ruder trials, which has been oftener accepted and approved by the voice of its people, or which, finally, has been more solemnly guaranteed by treaties, which it has not violated, and which, even humanly speaking, none have a right to violate to its prejudice?" And, relatively to the very provinces in revolt, I will repeat the emperor's declaration, that "*the European powers must admit that the right of the Holy See to the Legations is indisputable.*" Its possession of them is, therefore, guaranteed by the public law of Europe. Assuredly, no existing sovereignty can refer to more solid and better-established titles, merely in an historical and political point of view, setting aside the religious argument entirely.

But what is there which may invalidate a right of sovereignty? Is it war? But the belligerent powers had solemnly proclaimed the neutrality of the Holy See; the Holy Father has strictly observed that neutrality, and France has declared that she would protect the Holy Father and his neutrality against all attacks. It is a thing never heard of, that a war should entail the spoliation of a power declared neuter by the belligerents, and taken under the special protection of the conqueror. Is it the discontent of the revolted provinces? On this point, I will say freely, not meaning to express a stricture, but merely to state a fact, that if these provinces have passed from a real or factitious discontent, to insurrection, the occasion was our entry into Italy. From the first, the danger was foreseen and distinctly pointed out by the Catholics; and it was in order to avert it, and to warn the revolution that we did not mean to serve its ends, that the French government solemnly declared that it was not our intention, in entering Italy, *to foment disorder or disturb the power of the Holy Father; and that his rights continued guaranteed in all their integrity.* Such was the formal assurance repeated to the faithful by all the bishops of France, with unhesitating confidence.

We have, therefore, imposed on ourselves a responsibility which we cannot shake off; our word has been given,—how can we refuse to keep it? A responsibility once incurred, continues; and has not our promise become futile, if, what was apprehended on the one hand, and disavowed upon the other, is to be carried into effect before our eyes, and in opposition to our demands?

I ask if it is worthy of us to stand by and behold the final dismemberment of a sovereignty which we had taken under our protection, and which had a right to count upon us. This, indeed, is all that the revolution wants. Its journals have told us that it views with gratitude and satisfaction, not only what we have done for Italy, but also what we may allow to be done. It asks us to hold aloof—it asks for nothing more. We had said that *we would not accept its co-operation;* but if now we passively acquiesce, we shall have lent it ours.

No; it was France, the first Catholic nation in the world, which founded the temporal sovereignty of the Pope, and has been its unfailing supporter. Ten years ago she restored it, and for ten years she has upheld it. Before the late war, she gave her guarantee for its integrity. She has never asked the permission of Europe to fulfil her immemorial duty; she might as well have asked for the permission to call herself France.

Public promises, traditional precedents, and services already rendered, oblige the French government to such a line of conduct. It is powerful enough to maintain it before Italy or before a congress. It stands in need of no permission from Europe, and Italy can refuse it nothing. No one has prevented Piedmont from doing as it listed; who shall forbid France from executing her mission?

But to console us for the present dispossession, and to render us easy as to the future, we are promised a guarantee for the remainder of the Papal States. We are told that Europe, in return for this sacrifice to the insurrection, will guarantee to the Holy Father *the peaceful possession of the States of the Church.* What! has he not already this guarantee? At the present moment all the powers of Europe are solemnly bound to maintain the integrity of these states; and the Pope might call upon them to do so, in the name of treaties and of public European law. Yes, if there is still a public law in Europe, the Pope might to-day summon France, England, Russia, Prussia, Spain, Sweden, and Portugal to execute the guarantees to which they have pledged themselves by oath.

Any guarantee which may now be offered him must be given under less solemn circumstances, and would assuredly carry less weight: and if the existing European guarantee is of no avail, what is the new security held out to him, but paper upon paper?

Europe is to guarantee to the Pope the peaceable possession of the remainder of his states; but either Europe has, or has not, the right and the power to secure his states against revolutionary aggression. If Europe has such right and power, why does she not now exercise it? If she has not, how can she exercise it by-and-by? If she has this right as regards the whole, which is undeniable, I cannot see why she has it not, with regard to a part. If, again, Europe has no right to guarantee to the Pope those provinces over which she, nevertheless, *admits that his rights are indisputable,* what right can she have to secure to him the remainder?

These are the conclusions of good faith and common sense: the right is as certain for the whole as the part, for the present as for the future; and as to the means, I have already pointed out that a right, when recognized and proclaimed by the whole of Europe, acquires a force before which all resistance collapses, more readily than we might imagine. In the words of M. Villemain, "The victorious power which has interfered in Italy would not need to employ force against any of the insurgent districts. If it merely refuse to recognize any transfer of power, a state of things must cease to be, which never could have long subsisted, and which is contrary to the interests of France."

But if the revolution is allowed to pursue its course, if it is to remain unchecked, I do not say by force of arms, but by a firm assertion of right, by a distinct refusal to recognize an unjust dispossession, an impolitic and violent dismemberment, how can any effectual guarantee be given as to the future?[1] What! at the very moment when you declare the existing guarantee futile, you promise a new one: what confidence do you imagine it can give us?

Here is already an organ of the English ministry, the

---

[1] M. Cochin, too, ably remarks: "Are we to call for another Roman expedition? Not at all. It is sufficient to ask that the Holy See be treated as Denmark or Portugal would be. No violent measures are requisite. It is not even necessary that a congress should meet to discuss an indisputable right. Let no power recognize the annexation of the Romagna to Piedmont, let France set the example, let Piedmont not usurp what is not hers, and one may foresee that in a few months the dispute between the sovereign and his people will inevitably end in a compromise, which may satisfy all rights and settle the complaints of both parties."

Morning Post, declaring that England *will guarantee nothing*. When citing this expression of Lord Palmerston's paper, I do not mean to say that here are opponents of the Church, whose conduct is guided by the passions of the moment, politicians without principle, without respect for themselves or others, the slaves of circumstance; but I cannot help recollecting that Lord Palmerston, in a despatch to Lord Ponsonby, in September, 1847, stated that the integrity of the Roman States ought to be considered as an element essential to the independence of the peninsula.

However, I do not yet despair of the efficacy of European law, as recognized and proclaimed; provided Europe do not abdicate its rights, by permitting them to be trampled under foot; and provided she refuses to recognize force as the only right.

Moreover, the minister of the Holy See has justly asserted, that if the Sardinians and all foreign anarchists had been removed from the Romagna, the Papal government could have maintained order there, without other resources than it possessed. Indeed, it is self-evident that if Count Pepoli and the other revolutionary Romagnols had thought that the people were with them, they would not have sought so eagerly and obtained from Piedmont troops, commissioners, functionaries of all kinds, police agents, and all the paraphernalia of the Piedmontese dictatorship.

In fact, as one of the most distinguished representatives of France had already shown, "The revolutionists of Italy invariably rely on foreign aid for the accomplishment of their plans. If such support failed them, they would resign themselves to their present situation more readily than might be imagined. The English and Sardinian press should cease to stimulate their passions, and the Catholic powers should give marked proofs of their sympathy with the Holy See. But it would be vain to hope that such virulent enemies of the Holy See should desist from their attacks" while they continue to receive such encouragement.

We see, in these judicious reflections, what might have remedied the evil. But to expect that a sacrifice made to the revolution will restore order and peace to the Pontifical States, would be a sad delusion. The Pope, by yielding up his provinces to the revolution, would sign his abdication, and the irreparable ruin of his sovereignty. To approve and consecrate to-day the revolt in the Romagna, would be to desire the other provinces to revolt to-morrow in their turn. If one province has a right to rebel, why not another?

Not only is the right the same, but the cases are identical. Moreover, the danger would be imminent; the conflagration is too close at hand. To speak plainly, the example would be too good not to follow, and the success too flattering not to dazzle new competitors.

What! do you fancy that the storm would suddenly subside, as if by enchantment, because the Pope had given his fiat to the insurrection, because a triumphant rebellion had received his sanction?

Garibaldi, it is true, is not just now threatening the Papal frontier; he has given in a temporary resignation; but he is still addressing to the revolutionists, not only of the duchies and the Romagna, but of the other Papal States and of Italy in general, proclamations,[1] exhortations, and calls to arms, which we read every day in the

---

[1] All the papers have published, and as far as I am aware, without contradiction, the proclamation of Garibaldi to the students of Pavia; it contains the following exhortations : "Every man upon this earth should snatch the paving-stones from the streets, and avenge upon these miserable hypocrites in black soutanes the woes, the insults, and the sufferings of twenty generations. Yet this cursed race—but a yet more terrible enemy exists, the most formidable of any;—formidable because diffused among the ignorant masses, which it hoodwinks by its lies!—formidable because sacrilegiously wrapt in the cloak of religion!—he smiles upon you with a satanic smile—he is slippery as the serpent when preparing to bite!' And this most formidable enemy, my young friends, is the priest! with scarcely an exception, under whatever form he appears!"

newspapers, and in which he represents the Papacy as *the gangrene of Italy, which must be plucked out at any price,* declaring that no pause should be made till the whole of Italy is in revolt: and for this he asks for a million of muskets from the revolutionists of Europe.

And while these muskets are being got ready and forwarded, the British press is generously insisting that France ought to withdraw her troops from Rome.

It is manifest, then, that the renunciation proposed to the Pope was not a solution; it would have left Europe in amazement, Catholic France in grief, the Italian revolution triumphing in the north and smouldering in the south; and the Pope, pressed and invested by it on all sides, would have remained in more imminent peril and closer to the verge of the precipice than ever. By signing his own degradation, he would merely have given his sanction to insurrection. From that time forward discord and disturbance would have taken a wider range, after right had been sacrificed; whereas at present, owing to the firmness of the Pontiff, right still abides.

I again affirm that, supposing the circumstances just as they are at present, the sacrifice of the Romagna, or any other revolted province of the Papal States, would not merely have been useless, but must logically and fatally have entailed the total ruin of the temporal sovereignty of the Holy See; and its consequences would not have even ceased there. Nor would its operation have been slow; for, in our day, revolutions are not long about their work.

Moreover, the revolutionists were alive to this, and some of the more plain-spoken openly stated their opinion. " This is but the first stage," said the *Siècle;* " the second will bring us something better." " It is but the first step," said another journal, " but it is a great one." Yes, this was just why it was a step that should not have been taken; because it led straight to where men did not intend, and ought not to go.

But, it is again asked, Are we to take no account of the discontent of the Italians? I answer, first, Have they set themselves free? If it is we who have set them free, we have surely a right to specify to them under what understanding and on what conditions we have done so. They cannot insist on our conceding to them, contrary to the ancient faith of France and her most evident interests, a right to degrade and curtail the sovereignty of the common Father of the Faithful, and that we should make ourselves the tools of English Protestantism. The *Times* has stated that it was gratifying *to think that Protestant England should find hearty and effectual support from the emperor of Catholic France.* Yes, such offensive and unwarranted imputations may suit the *Times,* but how painful they are to us.

Let the Italians and their friends—the revolutions which have succeeded, and those which are in preparation—reflect, too, that if, as they imagine, the reign of democracy is at hand, democracy, of all possible social arrangements, stands most in need of Christianity. Its partisans would, then, be sadly imprudent to create a breach between them. They will see into what their democracy will develop, if they bind or repel the hand which bears the Gospel. As for the Church, she fears not such conflicts; she obtains in them an increase of glory; those for whom she mourns are not her defenders, whose ardour and generous devotion are only enhanced by danger, but her assailants, who are estranged from her and lost for ever.

But, as to the discontent of the Italians, I would also ask, what Italians are alluded to? A great noise has been made about the voice of the Italian populations. Assemblies, the offspring of the revolt, have pretended to express in their votes the wishes of the people; and deputations from those assemblies have laid these votes at the feet of a new sovereign. A great deal has to be said about these votes, and we shall by-and-by have to consider them.

At present, however, can what is passing in Italy allow us to doubt for a moment as to the import of the proposed dismemberment? It is too clear that the utter ruin of the Papacy is contemplated. In the intoxication of success, Piedmont no longer conceals her intentions; the time of disguise and mystery has passed away. " May our glorious king accept, may Italy too accept, *the oath* which we take on this grand and solemn day, *not to stop short in so grand a career.*" Such is the language used by the deputies of Turin, when sanctioning by their votes the royal decrees relative to the annexation of Central Italy.

The address to the king is not less significant. Having spoken of the new destinies of Central Italy, and the sufferings and troubles of the rest of the peninsula, which daily become more notorious, it adds—" *The moment has arrived for the whole of Italy to have a common destiny.*" (Sitting of April 14.) So all the states of Italy are to have henceforth a new and common destiny. Those as yet unannexed to the Piedmontese kingdom form, by their *sufferings*, too painful a contrast to the lot of the others; that contrast must be effaced; who can *stop short in so grand a career?* *The moment has arrived* to hurry the whole of Italy, from Turin to Rome and Palermo, into a universal revolution.

If such provocations and such unambiguous signals of revolt issue from the Piedmontese Parliament, why should the revolution use more measured or guarded language? Read the following proclamation, and say if a doubt remains as to the projects of the revolution in Italy. The storm cannot be far distant, when we can already see the first lightnings play on the verge of the horizon :—

NATIONAL ITALIAN SOCIETY.

" *To the soldiers of the Pope and of the Bourbon of Naples.*

"The *Italic* kingdom is now firmly established. The tricolour, that sacred banner, waves glorious from Susa to Rimini, from Sondrio to Cagliari, from Ravenna to Leghorn. The Emilia and Tuscany have chosen to be Italian. The Marches, Umbria, Naples, and Sicily would certainly have followed this example, had not you prevented them. Who is it then that retains the south of Italy in fetters? Who renders that unhappy land the most miserable in Europe, if not you, Italian soldiers of the Bourbon of Naples and the Pope? You alone prevent Italy from rising to the front rank among nations.—ITALY AND VICTOR EMMANUEL! that is our cry.

" *Turin, March 22, 1860.*"

This document bears the signature of La Farina, an especial favourite of Count Cavour.

What room remains for doubt, when the men who publish such proclamations, when the members of the National Italian Society, whose manifesto we have just seen, express in their addresses to the head of the new Italian kingdom their desire for a complete and absolute *unification* of Italy, in spite of all rights, and at the expense of all sovereignties, and when the king's prime minister replies to them as follows :—" The government of the king can but applaud the sentiments you express; he cannot conceal his satisfaction, seeing the Neapolitans and Sicilians determined to unite, in order to carry out the great work commenced by Piedmont, the regeneration of Italy."

Sicily has responded to these revolutionary war-cries from Turin, by taking up arms. And while the conflict was raging, and blood flowing, incendiary proclamations to the following effect were distributed at Naples:—

" NEAPOLITANS,—At the very moment when King Victor Emmanuel was pronouncing in the Sardinian Parliament his solemn declaration as to the present and the future of Italy, our brave brethren of Sicily were shaking off the degrading yoke which has long oppressed and shamed us. The initiative of the movement was bold, the struggle gigantic. The flag of Italy floats over the barricades of the invincible Palermo. Our hour has come. To overturn the government is the grand duty which presses on us at this critical moment."

And, but yesterday, that *flag of Italy*, wrapped in funereal crape, was carried before King Victor Emmanuel, at Florence, by the rufugees of Rome, Venice, and Naples, who came to ask him to fight in their behalf. *The news*, he answered, *are not as favourable as you think:* and, for his part, he would only interpose when called upon by the majority of the populations in insurrection.

Finally, to the mayors of towns, who offer him *their money and their arms* for the regeneration of Italy, he answers *that he accepts them:* and adds, his hand upon his sword, "*In the name of God, we will go through with it!*—Viva Dio! *andremo al fundo!*"

Thus, the tide of revolution is swelling every day. How long will it be before the dykes which keep it in give way? And if it overflows, where will its ravages stop? What the Pope and the Catholics had foreseen is coming to pass; and it at least justifies, for ever, their warnings and their unflinching resistance.

CHAPTER XXV.

THE DISMEMBERMENT.

THE EUROPEAN QUESTION.

HITHERTO we have been viewing the question of the dismemberment solely from a Catholic point of view; but it has another important bearing. Feeble and imperilled as is the power of the Roman Pontiff, it is still of so general an importance, and so interwoven with other most momentous matters, that everything else seems unsettled when it is questioned, everything trembles when it is shaken.

In reality, the grandest principles of public law are here on their trial; and for this reason we have just seen Catholics, Protestants, and philosophers leagued under the same standard, to the amazement of short-sighted journalists and shallow politicians: just as, in 1849, the most distinguished partisans of order, whatever their political watchword, and even their religious creed, united with like cordiality in the defence of the Sovereign Pontiff, so again to-day, notwithstanding a few sad but not unexpected desertions, their accord is equally striking.

But, without dwelling on these cases of interested defection, let us state the question fully.

What really is serious in the present Italian revolutions, is far less the remodellings of territory, the annexations or disannexations which are being effected, than the new-fangled principles of public law which are broached, and inculcated upon listening Europe. It is nothing less than the whole of received European law which is undermined by and totters under these attacks upon Catholicism.

Not only are the ancient limits of all nations menaced; not only is an ominous panic as to the fixity of tenure of territory becoming rife in Europe; the danger is yet deeper and more vital; government itself is now abandoned to the caprices of a popular vote; the very principle of power is aimed at; and, consequently, social peace and European order are radically compromised by the principles now in vogue. This the Holy See has discerned, looking down upon political questions from the commanding ground of eternal moral truth: for this reason, too, it perceived a connection between the *purely political* question of the duchies and the *political and religious* question of the Romagna; and this justifies me in speaking of the simultaneous overthrow of Catholic and European law.

I do not mean, however, and I wish here distinctly to say so, to compare the annexation of Savoy to that of the Romagna. France has not, as stated in the imperial address of March 1, fomented a revolution in the country which is giving itself to us; she has not employed a military occupation, nor provoked an insurrection; she has proceeded to the annexation with the consent of the legitimate sovereign, and after having consulted Europe.

But the annexations, as effected by Piedmont, are the triumph of the revolutionary principle and the inauguration of a new right, as fraught with peril to the people as to sovereigns themselves. It would be a delusion to confine our view to the revolutions which are now in progress; a way is being paved for revolutions more widespread and overwhelming.

For, in fact, two weights, two measures cannot be applied to human affairs. To grant to one people what is refused to another, to proclaim a principle here which we should tremble to apply elsewhere, is a contradiction which political speculators may tolerate and uphold for a time, but which the logic of revolutions, no more than truth and justice, will never admit.

When has Europe laid down, that political dissatisfaction, fomented by the ambitious views of some and the revolutionary visions of others, gives a province a right to insurrection and separation? If so novel a right is to be introduced into the international code of Europe, is it not easy to see whither it must lead? If any are to have such a right, why not all? If, for instance, Prussian Silesia one day should complain, and demand a separation, what would Prussia say? If Franche Comté desired to separate from France and become a Swiss canton, as many proposed in 1830, or if Corsica called for its annexation to Italy, what would France say? If Jersey and Guernsey wished to be annexed to France, what would England say? Again, would Lord Palmerston admit that if war broke out between England and France, for instance, such or such a part of the United Kingdom which could point to grievances of greater or less gravity, thereby acquired a right to revolt and throw off British rule?

Or if, in time of peace, the French were, just as England has done in the case of Italy, to subscribe for a million of muskets for the Irish, would the prime minister of England think it perfectly natural?

No, no; when we lay down a principle, we must not shut our eyes to its consequences. It is because a great principle is invoked to justify the violation of a great right, that the Pope and the Catholics have inflexibly maintained the right and resisted the principle.

I repeat, those who imagine that only a province more or less is affected by this portentous question, deceive themselves. Once more, it is not the fact which is so deplorable, as the principle in the name of which it is accomplished.

Moreover, when a fraction of a people set about detaching themselves from the nation of which they form a part, to incorporate themselves with another state, not only is the right of the sovereign infringed, but the territorial right of the nation violated. Thus, by the annexation of the Romagna to Piedmont, the States of the Church are dismembered, not by the general act of the Roman people, but by that of a province, which has not consulted the state on which it depends. As M. Sauzet observes, this is a singular application of universal suffrage. He asks, "Ought not, before detaching these provinces from the common bond of union, the universal suffrage of the state of which they form an integral part, as established by treaties as well as by immemorial usage, to have been consulted? Henceforth is a simple wish on the part of a province which hankers after separation to suffice to sever bonds formed by mutual engagements and ratified by the operation of time? If so, majorities will be as little obeyed as minorities are protected; traditions, institutions, the respective boundaries of empires, the mutual engagements of kings and peoples, may be annulled by the caprices of a popular deliberation. Republics will be as little protected as monarchies; confederations as military states. Basle may break from Switzerland to offer itself to Germany; New York from the great American union to form an independent republic. The most powerful as well as the humblest societies will find their peace, their resources, and their very existence continually imperilled."

These anomalous annexations, therefore, seriously compromise the equilibrium of Europe. Europe, in fact, forms a society, whose parts hang together, each contributing to sustain the whole. Neither can a province mutilate at pleasure the political corporation to which it belongs, nor a nation disturb the equilibrium of the general society of which it is a member. Thus, in 1830, Belgium was not allowed to amalgamate itself with France. Europe decided to the contrary. It must be admitted that there are principles which overrule private interests, and from which we cannot arbitrarily derogate. Treaties and laws themselves take for granted this mutual dependence among nations. As M. Sauzet correctly observes, " we must choose between the sanctity of engagements and endless disunion and partition."

Some vaguely dwell upon incapacity and reforms, to justify the dispossession of the Pope, and tell us that the revolution in the Romagna is an exceptional and unimportant case, which must be passed over! But if the capacity of every government is to be put on its trial, if reforms are to be an adequate pretext for abolishing a sovereignty, where will such an examination of conscience end, made, too, by the subjects themselves, or by interested neighbours? What a loophole does it not afford to revolutions in every state in Europe![1] As to the Pope, I shall shortly consider the grievances which have been so much harped upon; at present, I shall merely ask, Is there a throne in Europe which has been filled by so many men of genius as his? What is to be thought of the capacity of Leo the Great, Gregory the Great, Gregory VII., Gregory IX., Leo IV., Alexander III., Innocent III.; or, in modern times, of Nicholas V., Paul III., Paul V., Julius II. even, and Sixtus V., among many others?[2]

---

[1] "It is idle to repeat that a sovereign should be sustained by the adhesion of his subjects. The vast suffrage which founded the present power in France does not render the support of an immense army superfluous. If Alsace wished to separate, regiments, not arguments, would be despatched there. Are Ireland, the Rhenish provinces, or Poland, bound to England, Prussia, and Russia by chains of love? Is the parliament of the Ionian Islands less unanimous or less competent than that of Bologna?"—*M. Cochin.*

[2] Are we to consider also as inferior politicians, Cardinal de Richelieu, who humbled the house of Austria; Cardinal de Fleury, who gave us Lorraine, by the peace of Vienna; and Mazarin, who consummated the union of Alsace with France, and also negotiated that of Roussillon and Artois, and fourteen towns in Flanders and Hainault? To go farther back, look at Hincmar of Rheims, Suger, the immortal minister of Louis VI. and Louis VII., called the father of his country; and the Cardinals d'Amboise, de Lorraine, du Per-

Do our opponents believe there is as hopeless a divorce between virtue and genius, as a late pamphlet has ventured to pronounce between Christian faith and civilization?

But enough of this; it is not only the Pontifical administration, or the independence of Italy, which are now in question: European order is menaced, and a traitorous and deadly weapon has been forged for its enemies.

There is ground now for asking if it be patriotism to cut one's country in two, to satisfy a caprice; if it be lawful to revolt and deliver up a province to a neighbouring sovereign; if a conspiracy unblushingly stirred up and sustained by foreigners can truly be called a national movement.

The congress we were looking for has not met; but perhaps one may meet hereafter. Well, whatever the nations which compose it, Russians, Swedes, Prussians, or English, with French, Austrians, and Spaniards, I shall feel the fullest confidence in their decision, provided the plenipotentiaries do not forget the first article of the moral law: Do not to others what you would not wish done to yourselves.

But, after all, the Pope has not granted any reforms! First, this is not true; as I have already proved, and shall soon have occasion to show again; but ought the Pope, as part of these reforms, to cede his provinces, and make of the ancient Romagna a new Piedmontese department? Ah! Piedmont and the writers who are for ever vaguely

---

ron, d'Ossat, and the Chancellor Duprat. Cardinal Ximenes and Alberoni, in Spain; Cardinal de Granvelle, in the Low Countries; Wolsey, in England; Commendon and Possevin, in Germany; in Switzerland, Matthew Schinner, Cardinal of Sion; at Rome, Cardinal Albornos and Consalvi; with many others, assuredly have governed their country, or represented their sovereign abroad, creditably enough.

It may be said the Church produces no Ximenes or Sugers nowadays.—I answer, with an historian: Are the councils of kings encumbered with Sullys, Oxenstierns, Colberts, or Pitts?

declaiming about reforms, would be very sorry to see them realized; they would feel sadly disappointed if every pretext for their attacks were to disappear. Reforms are not what they wanted; their object was a more definite, but less honourable one—to possess themselves of a province.

A German comes to Strasburg and decries the institutions of France; he is perhaps abusing hospitality. Still he is free to do so; his strictures may be bad taste, without being crimes. But if he stirs up the inhabitants or the garrison to expel the prefect, he is a felon. If he comes as the agent of a neighbouring prince to excite a revolt in Alsace, that prince is a usurper. He may declaim about liberty like a knight-errant, but he is respecting justice like a pirate. Everything done under his compulsion is null and void.

These men promise wonders to their dupes; they persuade them that, under a new master, they shall no longer suffer. Those who yield to such enticements will repent it. But even were such expectations well founded, if the change were for the better, the injustice would remain.

It is, we are told, the new right of peoples! Yes, of those of South America. Probably Texas is better pleased to belong to the United States than to Mexico: yet the voice of a great American citizen, Channing, was raised to denounce as a monstrous iniquity the pretended *war of independence*, which transferred Texas to his country. It cannot be said here that it is a bishop defending exploded and mediæval ideas; it is a republican who speaks: "But if every town or every canton may declare itself a sovereign state whenever it suffers a wrong, society will be ever in convulsion, and history will be merely a relation of sanguinary revolutions.... Nothing easier for a people than to draw up a list of grievances; nothing more fatal to them than to revolt whenever a complaint is not attended to."[1]

---

[1] Channing continues :—"In the army of 800 men who gained the victory, broke the Mexican forces, and made their chief a

There are those who have not shrunk from mentioning the Papal government in connection with that of the Grand Turk. Let us admit, for an instant, this unbecoming allusion. Did not England and Piedmont unite with France to prevent the Christian subjects of the Grand Turk from seeking good fortune under the sceptre of the Czar? The Turk was supported, not because he was the Turk, but because he was oppressed. At present England and Piedmont propose to despoil the Pope, although he is oppressed, because he is the Pope.

But our opponents rejoin, We go upon the same principle in upholding the Grand Turk and dispossessing the Pope. By maintaining the integrity of the Ottoman territory, we saved the equilibrium of Europe, and the peace of the world; while the possession of the Romagna by the Pope was an unending source of disorder and perturbation to Europe.

I have shown, at length, that the cause of revolutionary perturbation lies elsewhere; but let it pass. Well, you fancy that all this would have grown calm, as if by magic, because the principle of insurrection had triumphed, because revolt had been transformed into right! No; after having let loose such fiery passions, to flatter oneself that it would be possible to appease the genius of revolution in Italy and Europe by throwing to it, as a prey, a part of the Papal States, would argue but slight knowledge of human nature.

Garibaldi is calling upon the revolutionists of Europe

---

prisoner, there were not found more than 50 Texans who had wrongs to avenge upon a field of battle. In this war, the Texans are a mere name, a pretext, which the adventurers of another country have used to screen themselves while about their work of plunder. There are crimes, whose enormity touches on the sublime: the taking of Texas by our countrymen is entitled to that honour. Modern times afford no instance of pillage committed by individuals on so great a scale. It is nothing less than the ROBBERY OF A STATE. The pirate seizes a ship; our colonists and their associates are not content with less than an empire."—*Letter to Mr. Clay.*

for a *million of muskets*. Well, I would ask, in my turn, What steps is Europe going to take to protect the Roman States and the rest of Italy against this million of muskets? I will even put a more serious question: What steps will Europe take to defend herself against this million of revolutionary muskets, when the hour of the conflagration comes? Garibaldi has resigned his commaud; but he is in the Sardinian parliament; he speaks and protests, and that not alone; we know what he and his call for. The whole of that parliament, indeed, has just declared to the king that they could not stop short in so *grand a career*. Sicily has already risen; an explosion at Naples is not improbable, as the result of the machinations of Piedmont, and of the revolutionary successes in the north.

We are told that we must take account of nationalities: I will answer by borrowing the sentiments of Mr. Gladstone: "I am sensible of the respect due to the idea of nationality, when confined within the limits of what is possible and just. But they who, disregarding times, persons, circumstances, or *consequences*, in a word, profoundly indifferent to all existing facts, think that sentiments of nationality alone are to dispose of the affairs of mankind, are madmen. I will add, that the doctrines of nationality, enunciated in certain terms, become doctrines of disorder and anarchy."

Lord Granville, in the Upper House, used similar language: he stated that the Italians were not agreed among themselves; that some wished for despotism, some for constitutional monarchy, and some for the wildest republics. Also, that the means they employed were as dissimilar as the ends: some were for continual agitation, others for war, and others for assassination in its most odious form. Was this last statement of Lord Granville suggested to his mind by the following expression of a Piedmontese deputy: "Let Europe take warning, and not attempt to break our sword in our hands; for a broken sword becomes a dagger. — UNA SPADA SPEZZATA DIVENTA UN PUGNALE."

It is said that we must sacrifice something to the fire.

I answer, Certainly, if it will extinguish the fire; but such is not the nature of the revolutionary fire.

We in France have learned, by sad experience, that it is not always safe to place arms in the hands of the masses: and so the government judged, when it disarmed part of the people of Paris.

The present revolution is not Romagnol, but European. It is the most malignant form of revolution, that which was crushed by the First Consul. The men who cheer Garibaldi and Mazzini are everywhere; the hands which are waiting for the muskets are everywhere.

I do not intend to exaggerate; I do not mean to say that all the Romagnols are Mazzinians. I know that there are in Italy a number of honest and noble hearts, which justly and sincerely long for the legitimate independence, the glory and prosperity of their country. But we cannot blind ourselves to the advance of demagogy: in Italy, it triumphs; in France, it applauds; in Europe, it hopes. And what encouragement for it if, by the consent of Europe, "an ancient and rightful sovereignty, notoriously weak and inoffensive, confirmed by centuries, and sanctioned by existing treaties, be mutilated and reduced, at pleasure, by disturbances fomented and directed by designing foreigners! Such a simplification of European law is fraught with grave consequences to every established throne. Let all the sovereignties in Europe, all the reigning houses, understand that henceforth there is no real right resulting from the duration, the unbroken descent, or the moderation of their power; that their only true right is their present force, the number of their soldiers; and, in novel or doubtful cases, right is the result of a universal suffrage,"[1] which may, as we have seen in Italy, be a compulsory and erroneous test of the popular will.

Yes; on the day that Europe ratifies the annexation of the Romagna to Piedmont, the most ancient and venerable of sovereigns will have fallen by an iniquitous aggression;

---

[1] *M. Villemain*, l'Europe et la Papauté.

the principle of compulsory abdication will be recorded in the law of nations, and the past and present policy of Europe will be annulled. For what sovereign is here dispossessed? Who is it confessedly intended to reduce shortly to complete abdication? Is he a foreign prince? No, for the sovereign of the Roman State is Italian, thoroughly Italian. If the separated provinces, integral parts of a state restored by France, and recognized by Europe, are allowed to detach themselves from it by violence, and amalgamate themselves with another; if such a right is recognized and sanctioned by sovereigns themselves, we will say that not only the principle of the inviolability of the Pontifical dominions perishes, but the revolution makes its triumphal entry into public European law; the bases of all treaties are shaken; the principle of authority, the safeguard of social order, is overthrown; sovereignty is humiliated, and spoiled by sovereignty; and this in Europe, where the soil, undermined by so many revolutions, still trembles; and anarchical passions, though overawed for a moment, never cease to swell.

Moreover, the most shameful, as well as the most dangerous, feature of this revolutionary triumph, is that the sovereignty which is thus to succumb is not only sacred and venerable in the eyes of Catholics, but is also that which is most deserving of the sympathy of every civilized nation, because of the principle of moral dignity which it represents, and that which is most worthy of assistance and respect, because it is weak, innocent, and oppressed.

In truth, the more I reflect, the less can I understand this new right of sovereigns, which entitles them to reform their neighbours, and if they refuse, to seize upon their states. The influence of free institutions in a country may extend beyond its frontiers; public opinion may applaud and diplomacy second it; all this is but fair: but an occupation by the bayonet, on pretence of governing better, is too like enslaving a free people under pretence of conferring a benefit upon them: and, happily, such a proceeding has not yet found a place in the practice of the law of nations.

However, as, in the depressing times in which we live, so many fluctuations, in opinions as well as facts, occur; as reason and the moral sense appear so easily warped and altered; as the most commonplace truths fade so rapidly from the conscience, it is well to hear, on these grand principles of public law, men whose opinions are, from one reason or another, entitled to some degree of respect. The following are the sentiments expressed by Talleyrand upon a case analogous to the present: he writes in a note, dated December 19, 1814.: "In order to recognize such an arrangement as legitimate, we must take for granted that the nations of Europe are bound together by no stronger links than those which unite them to the South-Sea Islanders; that their relations with one another remain, as it were, in a state of nature, and that what is called the public law of Europe does not exist; that, although all civil societies throughout the world are wholly or in part regulated by customs which are to them laws, still the customs which have grown up among the nations of Europe, and which they have universally and constantly observed among themselves for three centuries, are not binding on them; in short, *that everything is lawful to the strongest.*"

Let us now see how a publicist, as eminent as he was upright, Count Joseph de Maistre, defends the same right: "A king dethroned by a deliberation, a formal sentence of his colleagues! The idea is a thousand times more terrible than anything ever uttered from the tribunal of the Jacobins, for they were but playing their part; but when the most sacred principles are violated by their natural defenders, one begins to despair .... I should be sorry, indeed, if the most august of assemblies, a senate of kings, as we may call it, were to act like a lodge of Swedish Freemasons. It is idle to refer to kings who have been dethroned, to partitions, to expediency, or to draw a distinction between great and petty sovereigns. Sovereignty is neither *great* nor *small*; it is what it is" (October 26, 1814).

Or, in the profound words addressed by Pius VII. to Napoleon: "Great or small, sovereignties stand towards one another on a like footing of independence. Otherwise, *force is made to fill the place of reason.*"

However, it will be said, the population has pronounced: they have been twice consulted, and have twice voted for annexation. I have already spoken at length as to the first vote: the conclusive evidence of Lord Normanby, Mr. Scarlett, Mr. Bowyer, and others, has been officially corroborated by the Italian revolutionists themselves. We read in an official despatch addressed to the Dictator Cipriani, and printed *verbatim* in the papers of Upper and Central Italy: "In all the united provinces lists are to be drawn up, this task being intrusted to the good faith of honest and trustworthy friends, enjoining them to circumscribe their operations principally to the populous centres only" (*Per tutte le unite provincie, si diramarono le liste, raccomandandole alla fede di probi ed onesti amici, ingiungendo loro di circoscrivere principalmento l'azione ai soli centri popolosi*). So here are electoral lists, to be drawn up prudently by friends and brothers, who are directed to confine the elections almost entirely to populous centres only, that is, to centres where agitation is easiest, to the exclusion of the country population, that is, the great majority and the soundest part of the inhabitants.

What a barefaced deception! I appeal to every honest and conscientious man, if this is not a mockery and an outrage offered to that people, whose wishes are thus cared for, as well as to the principles upon which social order in Europe reposes.

But it is said the business has been begun afresh; and, if the first votes were objectionable, the second leave no room for doubt. For my part, I am far from thinking so. It is necessary here to guard against being dazzled, or carried away by one's feelings. The noble cause of true Italian independence evokes so much just sympathy, that nothing is easier than to forget here, through a sort of fascination, the principles of right and justice; but, indeed, a man must be very blind who applauds the farce that has been just played in Central Italy, or fancies that such a suffrage, under such circumstances, is to be viewed as the genuine manifestation of the will of a people, acting with perfect independence, according to the sole dictates of its convictions and its wisdom.

What, then, has lately occurred in Italy? And how were the notorious flaws of the previous vote redeemed by the new and noisy demonstrations which we have witnessed, by which Piedmont has hastened to profit, and of which such numerous populations have been the dupes or the victims?

I would ask, first of all, if the previous vote was confessedly defective, ought the same men who had organized it, who had governed the country despotically for eight months—in a word, ought the Piedmontese dictators, backed by the tyrannical pressure of a military occupation, to have received *full latitude* (the expression used by Count Cavour to M. Farini) to prepare and superintend a new suffrage? Was this an honest way of consulting a people? If Piedmontese influence had been carefully neutralized, if the Tuscans and the Romagnols had been *bonâ fide* left to themselves and to their own reflections—or even if the voting had been superintended by French authorities, whose honesty and impartiality no one would have suspected—then, indeed, it might have been regarded as a test of the people's genuine wishes; but does not the pressure of Piedmont throw as much suspicion on the second vote as on the first? It is not easy to convince us that Piedmont, present in arms, became all of a sudden passive and impartial, at the most critical moment of an affair so interesting to its policy and so enticing to its rapacity.

We ought to know something about popular votes. We learned, in February, 1848, how they may be biassed and moulded at will; how a people may be lured, deluded, and led blindfold. No, we have seen all this; others may be hoodwinked, but not we.[1]

---

[1] "France," says Mgr. Gerbet (bishop of Perpignan), "is a military nation, inured to political troubles. Still, at the com-

But enough of the details have reached us, though we have not heard all, to corroborate, by definite facts, what the very circumstances under which the voting took place were sufficient to render more than probable. Was the press free before the election? Had the inhabitants full liberty to vote against Piedmont? Doubtless these are two important questions.

And first, was the press free before the election? A letter from Florence, dated March 19, answers:—

"It is now a month since our dictators have refused to admit here any of the Piedmontese opposition papers. They have, at the same time, prohibited all the works published in France relating to the Pope—in short, every publication which might enlighten the Tuscans; they have also forbidden all the partisans of right to speak or express their opinions."

Another letter states:—

"At the same time, we were deluged with circulars from the revolutionary authorities, and also with a multitude of letters, signed and anonymous, printed and manuscript, all to the same effect, backing their advice by threats. There is not a single person of any property who has not received several; which also inform him that he will be held responsible for the votes even of his tenants and servants. While the good were forbidden to speak or publish anything, the provisional government forwarded unceasingly instructions to its subordinates to agitate and issue proclamations on the other side. A number of itinerant agents were despatched throughout all Tuscany to distribute money to all who would vote for Piedmont. To facilitate the voting, tickets were struck off and distributed gratuitously everywhere. But it was forbidden to print any against the annexation."

I am aware that the liberty of the press was apparently restored for a moment in Tuscany, by a decree of the dic-

mencement of the revolution of 1848, certain proconsuls, sent to the departments, succeeded in overawing a part of France. Imagine then the effect which must have been produced upon populations quite unused to resistance, by the dictators of a well-disciplined party, escorted by Sardinian bayonets, and with the veterans of Mazzini as a rear-guard."

tator Ricasoli, having been carefully suppressed at the very commencement of the revolution.

"But the decree, dated March 5, was only made public at Florence on the 7th, at 10 o'clock in the morning. In several provinces *it was only published on the very day of the voting.*"

What a mockery! But let us see what follows:—

"Although this edict appeared so late, still those hostile to the annexation attempted to take advantage of it, and print some documents at Florence. Impossible! all the printing-offices were monopolized, or rather confiscated to the use of the revolutionary government! The government had all the voting-tickets printed throughout all Tuscany, all, of course, for the annexation."

The following incident, related in the *Ami de la Religion*, enables us to estimate the value of this concession:—

"A writer named Alberi, having observed that this concession, granted three days before the opening of the ballot, was utterly futile, he was not allowed to publish his paper, under pretence that public order would be disturbed by it. But, on the very morning of the ballot, the official *Gazette* publishes the reflections of M. Alberi, accompanied by invectives, and threats of violence to any who might be of his opinion. Thus was received the only free opinion which was expressed."

Again, under this crushing oppression, this vast system of organized intimidation, it being literally impossible to utter an independent opinion, in what way was the question propounded? In a subtle and perplexing form, artfully leaving no alternative but one of a vague and suspicious nature.

"*Annexation to Piedmont, or a separate kingdom*, such was the alternative. What was to be understood by the two words, *regno separato?* Did they mean that we were to be Italian or Austrian? Did they mean government or anarchy, peace or war? The pretended alternative offered us left all this uncertain."

But let us examine the voting itself; if anything is unmistakable, it is the odious constraint and intimidation which were everywhere brought to bear upon it. To speak of the functionaries is unnecessary; their votes were already promised; for

"It is to be remarked that the military, the civic guard, those employed in all the public offices, the mayors and municipal councillors, the judges and magistrates of all sorts, all those employed in public instruction, the deputies—in short, all functionaries of whatever rank, all who had any part, direct or indirect, in the machinery of government, had long ago sworn allegiance to the king of Sardinia, in whose name the state had been administered for several months past: and the government did not even think of releasing them from their oath in order to give their vote a semblance of liberty."

I have before me a letter from the commander of the company of the national guard of Coriano to one of his lieutenants, dated March 8, 1860; it contains the following significant instructions:—

"The voting will take place here. If all the national guards cannot come on Sunday, they are to be invited for Monday, and *I enjoin you to have any arrested who do not appear, at least on that day, and brought to Coriano, to be dealt with by me.*"

A letter from Florence informs us that in an order of the day, addressed to all the national guards of the grand-duchy, every citizen is declared to be an *Austrian* who votes for a separate kingdom.

As to the troops, we find that, in the duchy of Modena,

"The decree which organizes the universal vote specifies that the officers, non-commissioned officers, and soldiers are to vote *under the superintendence of the officer highest in rank*, at the place where they are quartered."

Now it must be recollected that, as all the officers of the duke's troops had emigrated with their prince, these officers *highest in rank* were mostly foreigners from Piedmont.

"These *free citizens*, then, were marched to the vote as to a parade, and obliged, before the eyes of their officers, to place in the urn the open tickets which each had received on leaving the barracks, which of course all were for the annexation."

But perhaps the people at least were left free; we shall see :—

"The word was given, the very day that the decision as to the vote was come to, to force every one to wear a tricolour cockade, on the white of which was printed the word *annexation*. Some days later people had to add to this cockade a large square of paper, on which was likewise printed, but in larger letters, the whole form of annexation to the constitutional monarchy, &c., and those who dared to cross their threshold without this pledge to vote for Piedmont fastened to their hat, soon had reason to rue their folly. Insults, hisses, and violence taught them that they must not think for themselves."

Intimidation was carried so far, that

"Unfortunate peasants, threatened with eviction by their masters, and with imprisonment by the authorities, had to consent, to save their families from starvation, to place the ticket given them in the urn. As to those who were in a less dependent position, or whose masters were suspected of apathy or disaffection, the municipal authorities interfered directly. They had distributed, from house to house, the tickets of annexation, accompanied by a threatening injunction to carry them to the place of voting, and, above all, not to change them.[1]

---

[1] At Modena, during the two days of voting, the approaches to the town-hall were besieged by the clamorous populace, which always plays its part in times of anarchy; other like bands were stationed at the gates of the town, to watch the inhabitants of the suburbs. The latter were not allowed to come singly, they were assembled by sections, and so marched into town, conducted by a municipal agent, and escorted by a file of the national guard, the ticket of annexation in their hand, and the cockade and placard of annexation in their hat. The whole way from the gate to the townhall they were saluted by cries from the populace of "*the annexation for ever!*" and they had to cry the same, whether they liked it or no. And still under the same superintendence and the same pressure they defiled before the urn, where each threw in the fatal paper, on which often depended the fate of their families as well as their own security.

The bands ranged around the town-hall looked more particularly

" A good many functionaries, holding each several appointments, gave each several votes, in person or by proxy. One citizen, for instance, was professor at Modena, engineer in another *commune*, landholder in another, officer of the national guard, and member of the municipal council, in others—such pluralities are not uncommon—well, this good citizen gave, or had given in his name, votes in each of the communes where his name was on the register."

The following fact gives the finishing-stroke to these scenes, and reveals to us at the same time the impression produced by such doings even on the warmest partisans of Italian independence, who disapproved of dishonesty and unfairness. It took place at the Old Palace in Florence. The National Assembly, which had sat since the first days of the revolution, was convoked in order to vote a general approbation of the acts of the dictatorship, and to declare itself dissolved. Montanelli, the celebrated Italian patriot, rose and declared, with just indignation, that " such approbation was neither becoming nor genuine where freedom of parliamentary discussion and the liberty of the press were extinct; that the government might, indeed, go through the form of dissolving the Chamber; but that, in reality, he had long looked upon it as dead; *it had*

---

after the people of the town. The boldest citizen durst not approach or pass them without the cockade and the placard. No one was rash enough to refuse to cry hurrah for the annexation, and thus give the populace a pledge of the vote he was going to pronounce; and what vociferations, what hootings and menaces greeted those whose anti-Piedmontese sympathies were known! Had they even hesitated so far, they could not, once they entered the hall. The voting, which should have been secret, was completely public : it took place under the undisguised control and the minute inspection of Piedmontese agents. Such are some of the means by which a majority was secured for Piedmont.

"It is surely astonishing," says the bishop of Perpignan, "that the French papers which support the imperial government should use the same expression, *volonté nationale*, with regard to what took place in France (the universal suffrage for Napoleon III.) and the job perpetrated in the Romagna. Do they not see that such a way of speaking lowers one of the greatest demonstrations ever made of a nation's will to the level of a political juggle !"

died with Tuscany, and with the dearest hopes of her good citizens."

Let us recapitulate these details, and sum up, in a few words, the characteristic features of this vote.

The population of Tuscany is, in round numbers, 1,800,000 souls. Those over twenty-one years of age are more than a quarter of the whole, which gives 500,000. Such, then, should have been the number of electors. 360,000 voted; so that 140,000 kept aloof.

Now, those who voted did so under the most formidable intimidation, for the state functionaries and the peasants and farmers were threatened with dismissal or ejection if they did not vote for Piedmont.

The government had completely monopolized the press for ten months, and granted, three days before the vote, a liberty which was utterly nugatory, and which they even refused to those who proposed to take advantage of it.

The voters were, particularly in the country, conducted in ranks by the authorities, with music and banners, their tickets open, or in their hats, thus completely obviating any possibility of adverse votes or demonstrations.

The opponents of annexation were decried, traduced, and insulted, in all the journals, whether official or not, and represented as traitors in foreign pay.

The balloting urns remained for twenty-four hours in the hands of the mayors, who were creatures of the government, without any sort of supervision.

There was not the shadow of a check as to age of the voters, their identity, or registration; so that many, in fact, voted who were under twenty-one, and several voted twice, or oftener, in different places, and under borrowed names.

Such is the truth about this popular suffrage: no free discussion, intimidation, threats, manœuvres of all sorts, and finally, success. Nor is this surprising; it was but what might have been foretold, and one might safely predict a like success to any question submitted in a like manner to a popular vote.

We shall quote, as confirming our statements, the

follow letter from M. de Larochefoucault to the *Union* newspaper:—

"SIR,—A person above suspicion, whose candour and independence no one can question, has just arrived from Italy, having made some stay at Rome and Turin. He says, with just indignation, 'that it is impossible to conceive the intrigues, the jobbing, and even the coercion, resorted to by the revolutionary despotism to gain for Piedmont this mockery of a universal suffrage.' He adds that 'the great majority in Tuscany would be favourable to the return of the former sovereign, if the people were fairly consulted.' Woe to Europe if such culpable manœuvring to justify spoliation is allowed to pass without severe censure, and is not put down! Woe to Piedmont itself, for sooner or later it will be the victim of the revolutionary spirit with which it has allied itself, in obedience to a grasping and insatiable ambition! If such doings are allowed to pass, no sovereign for the future can sit unshaken on his throne, no nation will be proof against revolutions."

But enough of this unhappy triumph of Piedmont and its dictators. Let us turn our thoughts elsewhere, and judge, from the very confessions of our antagonists, what conclusions France and Europe ought to draw from these events.

This theory of annexation by vote has been condemned by those very persons who have imagined and put it in practice: and we cannot reflect more strongly upon the worthlessness and compulsory nature of the Italian suffrage, than the Piedmontese revolutionists themselves and Garibaldi, Lord John Russell, and England, the Swiss federal council and Russia. It is true that the wrath of our opponents is only directed against the votes of Savoy and Nice; but their strictures cut both ways, and apply inevitably, and far more effectively, to those of Central Italy; so that we need only combat our enemies with their own arguments.

In particular, how could England help seeing that, as the French Foreign Minister remarked, the events of Italy necessarily brought on the Savoy question? I fear that the real sympathy felt by England for the Italian cause was somewhat lukewarm, or served as a rather thin covering for her hatred of the Pope, and also her jealousy of France.

It could not have been disagreeable to her to see a powerful kingdom rise along our frontiers, promising to form a potent element in a coalition against us, when necessary, after having humbled the Pope and popery. Our claim of the French side of the mountains took her by surprise, and was a reproach to her usual perspicacity. Her eyes are opened, and having smiled upon all that was done in the Romagna, she begins to find fault with what took place in Savoy, though undeniably less objectionable. The more value we appear to set on Savoy, the more does it seem to our neighbours a precious, an inestimable jewel, and they are inconsolable to see it passing over to France. All of a sudden the British ministers perceive that "the settlement of affairs in Europe cannot be secure, nor peace reckoned upon, if Europe is to be exposed to continual violations of territory, and incessant fears of annexation and disannexation." (Reply of Lord John Russell to Mr. Horsman, March 26, 1860.) But how was it that England did not think of this before? How can she complain of what is, in Savoy and Nice, merely the sequel of what, in the Romagna, had her best wishes and congratulations? How is it that she is never scandalized at the maxims which now are current, except when they benefit France? Such are the inconsistencies and reproaches which one incurs, by sacrificing justice to one's interests or passions.

Lord John Russell further states, in a despatch to Lord Cowley (March 22, 1860), "that if a great military power like France may claim the territory of a neighbouring state, which it may judge, on its own theory, necessary to its geographical system of defence, it is obvious that no state can be safe from aggression on the part of a powerful neighbour; that force, and not right, must become the safeguard of territorial possessions, and that the integrity and independence of the *small states* of Europe would be continually imperilled."

Now, is not the English statesman's remonstrance quite as applicable to the case of Piedmont and the small Italian states, as to that of France and Savoy, with this distinction, that a coercion was used in the Piedmontese annexations, which was wanting in the French?

Lord John Russell acquiesces in the annexation of Tuscany. Why? Because, he says, first, the whole nation spoke; secondly, the throne was vacant. Well, we would ask, is the Romagna the whole Roman nation? Was the sovereign, Pius IX., not upon his throne? And, indeed, had he been at Gaeta, would that have altered his right?

Lord John Russell's respect for treaties will not allow him to approve of the separation of Savoy. Are there not treaties which guarantee the States of the Church? He fears that France may become too strong. Has the peace of Europe nothing to fear from Piedmont becoming also too strong? He reminds us that France had promised not to extend its territory. But had it not also promised to maintain the Pope's temporal power in its integrity? And did not England endeavour, by all the means in its power, to prevent that promise from being kept? He considers that the question of Nice and Savoy concerns, not the contracting parties only, but Europe also, inasmuch as it affects the balance of power on the continent. But is this less affected by the changes in Italy? He is incredulous as to the freedom of voting in Savoy and Nice, if France is to be present. In the Romagna, who held the urns? Piedmont. He appeals to the rights of the people, in the Romagna, against the Pope. Is their right less valid elsewhere?

The Swiss Federal Council wrote, in its turn, to Captain Harris, on the 27th of March, as follows:—" Any preliminary occupation of the territory, whether military or civil, would be a violation of the rights of Switzerland, and might, moreover, be considered as an obstacle to the free expression of the wishes of the people." But is not this just what the Pope said of Piedmont, with far more justice than Switzerland could say it of France?

Finally, Russia considers that the consent of the legitimate sovereign ratifies and justifies the cession of Savoy, but that it cannot supersede the rights of Europe. Therefore, the disapprobation of the legitimate sovereign is of some value, especially when it is confirmed by the law of Europe: and I might inquire why Switzerland and Russia kept back these opinions in the case of the Romagna?

By accepting at Bologna what she deprecates at Chambéry, England is caught in her own words, and others with her: the analogy is too palpable. But here we have something more than the inconsistencies of England and of European policy: it would really seem as if Providence had meant to give us, in Piedmont itself, a complete illustration of the truth of the inspired maxim, *Mentita est iniquitas sibi*. We find Garibaldi coming forward as the accuser of the vote of Central Italy, and in the novel character of defender of treaties, of the rights of sovereigns, and the law of nations. Every one has heard of the angry invectives uttered by him in the Piedmontese parliament, and of his energetic protest against the annexation of Nice to France, *as contrary to all international law; so much so, that the universal conscience of mankind exclaims at it:* yet he calls legitimate and necessary the annexation to Piedmont of the whole of Italy, Rome and Palermo included. Pitiful, but avenging self-contradictions! Garibaldi invokes against us a treaty of 1365, as Switzerland alleges one of 1564; and he slights a treaty of 1815, and twenty others! He cannot believe in the genuineness of the vote of Savoy and Nice, on account of the presence of the senators Pietri and Laity; but he is quite satisfied as to that of the vote of Bologna and Modena, taken under the armed pressure of Piedmont, and controlled by the dictators Farini, Pepoli, and the rest.

Indeed it is saddening and disheartening to listen to such incredible self-contradictions; and I do not allude to Garibaldi only—his inconsistencies go for little and do not surprise one—but to the statesmen of England and other countries.

It would seem really as if there were periods of general confusion for poor humanity, when the reason becomes bewildered, when truth seems put aside, and men's consciences utterly deranged. Everything is unsettled and unstable: principles become a dead letter; people invoke them when it serves their purpose, and trample them under foot when they are in their way: men wander at random without a compass and without a guide. Is there, then, no polestar in sight whereby to direct our steps during such storms, and do such earthquakes also hide the face of heaven? No; truth and justice will survive the passions of men, and sooner or later must be exalted. God grant that it may not be after appalling catastrophes.

The powers of Europe ought, at all events, to be convinced now, that the Italian revolution, such as it has shown itself, and as it is being followed out at this moment from one end of Italy to the other, is one of the most violent shocks that the law of nations has ever received in Europe. What parallel to it can be found in the annals of civilized nations? When has history seen a like alliance between sovereignty and revolution, leagued together for the overthrow of sovereigns? Where is the nation strong enough to resist such machinations, or the power skilful enough to disentangle itself from their grasp? No; the old sovereignties may still hold together for a time, longer or shorter, by their own weight; but their foundations have been undermined, and henceforth the first shock may overturn them: the Piedmontese monarchy as well as the rest, and perhaps sooner than they.

"I see in the air a shower of wretched republics and new disasters," said Silvio Pellico. "What is to be done?" added he. "Never despond. If I have little hope in men, I have much in God."

Like that honest and generous soul, I will yet hope. God always leaves to nations and sovereignties a principle of recovery. I believe in the power of right and justice. I believe in reason and good sense. I believe in the virtue of truth when set before men.

CHAPTER XXVI.

THE REFORMS DEMANDED FROM THE PAPAL GOVERNMENT. ARE THOSE SINCERE WHO DEMAND THEM?

Much noise has been made in France, as well as in the rest of Europe, about the question of reforms in the Papal States. It has been not indeed the cause of, but a pretext for all the threats and wrongs which have assailed the Holy See in our time.

I have therefore considered myself bound to study this question minutely and thoroughly. I have done my best to gain information, by every means within my reach. I have sought particularly to put aside any preconceived opinions, and to investigate the truth upon this question from the most authentic documents, from the most admitted facts, from things themselves; to distinguish what is true from what is false in the reports current on the subject; what can, or ought to be effected at Rome in the way of reforms, from what cannot, or ought not. Finally, I have endeavoured to arrive, not merely at a probable opinion, but at an imperative conviction, and I think I have succeeded.

To this end, I have questioned the most competent and most well-informed Frenchmen, including those who had, in 1849, treated themselves the question at Rome and Gaeta, in the name of France, whose representatives and plenipotentiaries they were. I have frequently conversed with men who have resided at Rome during the greater part of the last ten years, statesmen, ex-ministers, who have formed their opinions on the spot, and who were undeniably well qualified to observe facts with discernment, and to draw judicious conclusions. More than this, I have read the publications most hostile to the papal government; the answers of M. M—— to M. de Rayneval;

the most anti-Catholic journals, and the manifestoes of the different dictators. I have gone over the last work of M. d'Azeglio, and the long statement of Count Pepoli, of Bologna. I have even forced myself to read the work entitled *La Question Romaine*, whose author I need not here name. Finally, I am not personally a stranger to the question; I have sojourned long and frequently at Rome; I have seen with my own eyes.

Well, before going farther, I will candidly say that my impartial and thorough researches have had the effect of invalidating, in a remarkable degree, all the angry reproaches addressed to the Pontifical government, which had met with some credence even from myself. I saw that it was impossible not to admit the incredible injustice of which the Holy See has been the victim, or to fail to recognize here the agency of those implacable passions, which, misrepresenting or suppressing all facts that galled or condemned them, hurried on a separation which had ever been their real object, when a judicious conciliation might easily have re-established and preserved harmony and friendship between the subjects and their sovereign.

Accordingly, I had at first intended to conclude this volume by a thorough examination of the reforms demanded from the Pontifical government, entering fully into the minutest details. But it now occurs to me, would such an examination be opportune, considering what has been done and what is now doing in Italy? *Silent leges inter arma*, says the Roman orator. It is not reforms which are now demanded from the Pope by the revolutionists; the first spoliation has been accomplished, and imminent and utter ruin threatens him at the present hour. In such a state of things, a lengthened discussion of the practical details of reforms already granted, or to come, would seem out of place; besides, I am ready hereafter to undertake it, should better times permit.

However, it will be well, even now, to take at least a general view of the question; were it only to dissipate the vague and erroneous impressions which prevail, which have but too much misled public opinion, and secure too ready a hearing for sophisms and calumnies.

Such a general discussion is also a necessary preliminary to the consideration of details; and such a review of the heads of the subject will form an excellent introduction to the work which I may one day publish.

And, first of all, are improvements and reforms desirable in the Roman States? Are those sincere who call for them?

I.

ARE ANY IMPROVEMENTS OR REFORMS TO BE DESIRED IN THE GOVERNMENT OF THE PAPAL STATES?

Without entering into the question at all, one might answer; I cannot say for certain, but I should think there are. I think so, for I do not know of a state, a family, or a man upon earth, who does not stand in need of reforms.

I think so, for Pius IX. thought so himself, and, as we all know, led the way towards reforms among the princes of the Italian peninsula. Nor has his conviction altered; if revolutions had given him the time and the peace necessary to carry out, in calmness and wisdom, the reforms which he contemplated, Pius IX. would by this have finished his great work.

I think so, for I believe with Bossuet that men have necessarily human defects. I believe that no institution, confided to human hands, is clear of earthly imperfections.

I think so, not only as regards the temporal government of the earthly possessions which Providence has intrusted to the Church, but as regards the spiritual government of the Church, and that great divine institution itself; and that simply because it is confided to the hands of men. Men, not angels, have been placed by God over his Church; and if a divine promise insures the infallibility of Catholic teaching, as to dogmas, morality, and general discipline, that promise does not fetter human liberty; and that liberty, so noble, so meritorious, so fruitful, when well used, may also be employed with sad efficiency in the service of evil; and hence evil may at all times be expected to creep even into the Church. Hence, also, the Church is a society which is ever reforming itself; no society has laboured as much as she at its own reformation, and it is for this reason that she endures. The Christian Church is the most admirable of all societies, because she has within her a principle of continual self-reformation, which no other society possesses, a principle of regeneration which has never suffered any abuse to take root within her pale and to prevail against her.

During eighteen centuries, the Church has held eighteen œcumenical councils, and more than a thousand synods, in which reform of discipline and morals has at all times kept pace with dogmatic teaching and the condemnation of errors. Nor did the last general council, the Council of Trent, act differently from those which had preceded it. At the very time when the word *reformation* was convulsing Europe and separating whole nations from the Church, that immortal council, well knowing that true reformation in the Church can only be accomplished by herself, and can never mean schism or separation, boldly prefixed to its decrees the title DE REFORMATIONE, thus confounding the innovators by the spectacle of the only true and genuine reformation within the bosom of Catholic unity.

And we all, children of the Church, priests and faithful, profess, and are bound to profess, to be people who labour without ceasing to reform ourselves; we need continual reformation; and whenever, yielding to human weakness, we forget this, we are sure to suffer; for then Providence, which means us to reform ourselves unceasingly, because it calls us to perfection, makes a sign, and unexpected reformers appear; and the world, that world of which Tacitus has given the same definition as St. Paul, *corrumpere et corrumpi, sæculum vocatur*—the world and revolutions reform us by crimes, when we will not reform ourselves by virtues.

We make, then, no difficulty in accepting the word

reform, as applied to the Pope's temporal government, not however meaning by this to concede more than the unavoidable imperfections of all human things. We will even add, that if perfection might be looked for upon earth, it ought to be in the States of the Church. Yes, I have no objection to more being expected from the Pontifical government than from any other, and I look upon such requirements as an involuntary homage which does us honour, and of which we have no right to complain. Let people be severe upon the priest; they are right; it is but to assert what is true, that, being the minister of God, he ought, as such, to be the most striking personification of truth and justice upon earth.

We are not afraid, then, to attack the question of reforms: this much is certain. But I feel some suspicions as to the sincerity of those who call for them. I cannot, therefore, avoid putting the following question:—

II.

ARE THOSE SINCERE WHO CALL UPON THE PAPAL GOVERNMENT FOR REFORMS?

The Pontifical government has been bitterly censured, and a vast deal has been said about its need of reform; but, somehow, I cannot satisfy myself that those who call so loudly for reforms sincerely desire them; it even seems clear to me that what they wanted, and what they still want, is something quite different. The word *reform* played nearly the same part in the Italian revolution that it played in France in February 1848. It was used to rouse and agitate men's minds; the impetus once given, the clever conjurer's trick followed, alluded to by an adept in such matters, M. Ledru-Rollin, and then even the short-sighted saw that something else had been aimed at, and that behind reform was revolution.

Who can honestly believe that the party which was worsted at Rome in 1849 really wanted reforms in 1859, when they spurned them beforehand, and proclaimed in one of their organs which I have before cited, "Whatever Pope Pius IX. may do, the Roman people will not accept the new liberties which may be accorded to them; *they will only use them to overthrow the prince who resolved to grant them?*" Is it not clear that such men neither honestly suggest reforms, nor propose to use them for good? They cry out for them as a means to undermine the power they detest, as a *first step*, as *a stage*, upon the road they mean to travel; why, they tell us themselves they cannot stop short in *so grand a career*. Do we not see them already, after a moment's rest, taking up arms again? and has not Garibaldi, on starting for Sicily, told the Pope and all Europe distinctly enough what they have to expect?

Who can believe in his conscience that Piedmont ever sincerely wished for peaceful reforms, or tranquillity, in the Roman States? The ten years' history which we have gone over has sufficiently shown the contrary.

Or who imagines that Lord Palmerston would really be delighted never to have for the future anything but praises to bestow on the government of the Holy See?

We have seen M. Cavour, at the Paris congress, bitterly attacking the Pontifical government, in concert with the British plenipotentiaries, and denouncing it as *a permanent cause of disorder and anarchy;* but with what intention? To bring about reforms? It would be difficult to think so, as M. Cavour, at the same time that he declared the necessity of reforms, pronounced them absolutely *impossible*. Not only this, but to show clearly to the Italian revolutionists that the question was not meant to be seriously considered, that none of them need trouble themselves about it, and that it was a mere feint necessary to their tactics, M. Cavour declared that these reforms, without which the Papal sovereignty could not last, were reforms which the Pope not only *could not*, but *would not effect;* against which *he would struggle to the last;* to which he would lend himself only *apparently* and insincerely, his mind made up to do nothing honest or sincere, and resolved to render all the reforms *nugatory in practice*.

No; it is time to cease to trifle with our good faith. *Possible* reforms you do not ask for, and if they are granted you, you accept them only as instruments of destruction; *impossible* ones you call for loudly enough, certainly; but you proclaim, along with their radical *impossibility*, the absolute *impotence* and the incurable insincerity of the power which refuses them.

After such declarations, it is a mere mockery to talk about reform. It is but too clear that the real question at issue is the dismemberment, or rather the total confiscation, of the Papal States. Improvements, which you declare beforehand illusory and treacherous, cannot assuredly disarm or satisfy you.

In fact, so Count Cavour declared, in unambiguous terms. He proposed to begin by separating the Romagna; the Marches, Umbria, and Rome were shortly to follow; time alone was speedily to complete the ruin of the pontifical sovereignty. The pamphlet, *Le Pape et le Congrès*, as well as the Sardinian *Memorandum*, had no other object.

Well, follow up your object, but do not expect us to be your dupes as well as your victims; do not imagine that you can impose upon us by your affected lamentations for having failed to obtain reforms you did not wish for. It is clear to every one who has watched you, that what you want is revolution, and not reform. The Pope is ready enough to grant reforms; but you want to overturn his throne.

It is curious to see the pains you have taken to prove to the Pope that these reforms are beyond the reach of his power, and even inconsistent with his religion. And how, transcribing in the pamphlet the doctrines of the *Memorandum*, you there pretend that the Pope cannot reform his government without abrogating all the principles, the dogmas, and the laws of the Church. In vain it was shown to you that this was contrary to truth and common sense. It served your ends too well not to hear us.

If you were in earnest, what you should ask for is the reform of men, if they require it, and of abuses, if any exist; but no; you say *it is not men* who are to be secularized, *but principles*; it is not abuses which must be reformed, but dogmas. Abuses are invested with the same character as dogmas; they are even essential to, and absolutely inseparable from them. Could audacity and hypocrisy go further?

But I hear you answer, We only came to that after having asked everything else, at the proper time, without obtaining anything. Now it is too late; nothing will do now but separation. It is too late! But I answer that, in 1847, when many people thought it too soon, when the Pope, the present Pope—for we have the good fortune to be able to refer back to the same man—gave a signal of liberty and reform to Italy as well as to Rome, then great and solid reforms came to pass; soon to prove insufficient to satisfy those whom no reform will ever satisfy, unless one suppressing the Papacy as a sovereign and independent power.

How did you then act? You accepted these reforms, but used them only, first to coerce, and then to expel, their author.

In the present case, you have commenced by destroying, and insist upon a pretended refusal of reforms as a justication of your work of destruction; you have unblushingly advanced this pretext for a partial separation, which is but a step towards a total confiscation; for, as you say, the reasons for separating one province apply to all the others, and one day will be urged by them also.

As I have heard a great man say, if subversive or perilous reforms are suggested, they are good for no one, and would be even more fatal in the Legations than elsewhere, for there they must appear as a premium for past, and an encouragement to future revolts; but if the reforms sought be wise and fruitful, all the Roman states ought to benefit by them; no province should be excluded from the blessings of good, nor any be exposed to the evils of bad reforms.

Is it possible for the Pope to grant desirable reforms? That is, can he, while stopping short of concessions which would be a virtual abdication of his supreme authority, mould his government to the new needs of the times, and the legitimate desires of his people? Such is the real question. If, alleging the immutability of dogmas, it is to be decided in the negative, then reforms are out of the question; the Pontifical power must be abolished. If, however, it is answered in the affirmative, in the name of honesty and common sense, the question of reforms is raised indeed, but at the same time, the insurrection in the Romagna and the annexation to Piedmont are condemned. For if anything is clear, it is that what the insurgents in the Romagna sought was not liberty, but annexation. The aspiration of these generous patriots was to surrender themselves to Count Cavour.

That there are in the Papal States, as in other countries, questions undecided, works unfinished, and improvements checked, is what no one denies. But is this astonishing, and whose is the fault? Pius IX. has not been given one hour of peace, for the last ten years, to carry out the benefits he designed for his people. You continue to cry out for lay, instead of ecclesiastical government; you complain of delays; but, once more, who has delayed everything, if not they who murdered the lay prime minister of Pius IX., upon the threshold of a house of parliament, which was but inaugurating the reign of reform? And you cannot understand that, after such a lesson, statesmen should hesitate, or a sovereign pause to reflect!

Why, even in France, that powerful and prosperous country, no government—neither the first empire, nor the monarchy, nor the republic—has been able to realize every improvement which the people might justly desire; yet you cannot conceive why the States of the Church, hampered and embarrassed by extraneous influences, harassed without intermission by Piedmont and the revolution, could not, in spite of such obstacles, reform all present imperfections, and leave no future progress to be wished for; and you refuse the time and tranquillity which such task demands.

However, as I, like the Pope, am for improvements and reforms, though opposed to separation and revolution, let us examine what reforms you demand.

CHAPTER XXVII.

THE REFORMS DEMANDED FROM THE PAPAL GOVERNMENT.

It is stated that we are sorely puzzled by the question of reforms; but our opponents are far more so than we, when one turns and asks them flatly,—What reforms would you have?

Some talk vaguely of *liberty* and *emancipation*. *Apropos* of this, an English speaker wittily observed, " We have here an absolute sovereign explaining to another absolute sovereign what liberties it may be proper to introduce in states which belong to neither of them."[1] The most contradictory charges are brought against the Papal government. If one asks a Paris journalist what is wanting in the Roman government, he will most probably say, *liberty*. Ask a native of the Roman States the same question, he will answer, *security*. That government is too tyrannical, according to the former; too good-natured, according to the latter. Which is to be believed, he who sees things on the spot, or he who imagines them, at a distance? Without losing time in endeavouring to reconcile them, let us, if possible, single out one or two definite points from the torrent of declamation. All the *memorandums*

---

[1] Alluding to the article of the treaty of Zurich, whereby the emperor of the French and the emperor of Austria undertake to recommend reforms to the Pope.

of diplomacy, with all the polemical pamphlets and speeches on the subject, seem to insist, as if by concert, upon three words—to be found in a famous document, the letter to Colonel Ney, in 1849—*secularization, Code Napoléon, liberal government.* Let us consider them one by one.

I.

SECULARIZATION.

What is the precise meaning of this word? Is it the absolute separation of the spiritual from the temporal, which now are united at Rome in the same person? In fact, is the Pontiff to cease to be a prince? If so, do not talk of reforms; ask boldly for the destruction of the Pontifical power.

Does secularization mean the decentralization of the administration of public affairs, so that laymen in provinces and parishes may manage themselves their local interests? Well, in this respect, affairs are less centralized in the Roman states than in France; nowhere are the liberties of provinces and communes more ancient and more comprehensive.

Does it mean the administration of the Romagna by a lay viceroy? But why the Romagna only? Can a country have two laws, a nation two forms of government, or authority two heads? This would be absurd anywhere, but how much more in a little state of three millions of souls. And who was to have been the viceroy of the Romagna? The king of Piedmont? But could the Pope have been required to give himself up thus to his declared enemy?

Or is it meant absolutely to exclude all churchmen from the government of the States of the Church? But this is not to abolish a clerical privilege; it is unreasonably and unjustly to create a secular monopoly. "It is not enough," observes M. Saint-Marc Girardin, "to be a layman, to have a capacity for government; nor have history and experience shown that ecclesiastics are unfitted to conduct public affairs."

But no, it will be said; what we ask is, that laymen may have an extensive share in the administration of the country, and that they be eligible to all public functions; such a claim is but reasonable. Yes, but it has been fully attended to. We appeal to facts and figures: our former ambassador at Rome, M. de Rayneval, stated in 1856 :[1]—

"Outside Rome, how many ecclesiastics do people imagine the court of Rome employs, in all the eighteen provinces of the Papal States, the Legations, the Marches, Umbria, and the rest? Their number does not exceed fifteen, one for each province, except three, which do not reckon even one. They are delegates or prefects, as we should say. Under them, magistrates, councillors, functionaries of all descriptions, are laymen. There are in all 2,313 civil, and 620 judicial functionaries, giving a total of 2,933, or *but one ecclesiastical to 195 lay officials*. Can the most prejudiced mind object as a grievance to an ecclesiastical government so slender a proportion of men of its own cloth, employed as depositaries of its authority throughout all its provinces? Who can call this an intolerable abuse?"

In the city of Rome, the centre of government, the number of prelates, whether in priests' orders or no, employed in the administration, is necessarily more considerable than in the provinces. Still, the numerical superiority in favour of laymen is striking, and leads to the same conclusions.

"The Council of State numbers three ecclesiastics to ten laymen. The Home Office reckons seven ecclesiastics, besides fifteen prefects of provinces I have already mentioned: in all, 22 ecclesiastics to 1,411 laymen. Finance gives employment to 3 ecclesiastics and 2,017 laymen. Police to 2 ecclesiastics and 404 laymen. In the offices of war there is not a single ecclesiastic. As to judicial employments, reckoning the superior courts, which are of a mixed nature, there are 59 ecclesiastics to 927 laymen."

It is clear, then, that neither the evil nor the remedy

---

[1] His report has been published more than once, and recently in the *Recueil des Traités et Actes diplomatiques concernant l'Autriche et l'Italie.*—Amyot, Rue de la Paix, Paris.

lies here. The secularization pointed to as a remedy has long been a mere blind, employed to captivate foreign sympathy, and to pave the way for an attack on the very principle of the Pontifical government. The revolutionists did not presume to cry out, at first,—Down with the Pope! Such a cry would have excited alarm. They contented themselves with saying,—Down with priests!

And now, when they are answered, You called for lay officials; they have been appointed on all sides; they reply,—That is not what we wanted: "The Pope cannot accord a genuine secularization; for that does not consist in admitting *a few* laymen (*a few* laymen, 5,000 to 100 ecclesiastics!) to government offices, but in introducing the modern spirit into all the institutions of the country. That spirit is incompatible with the clerical government."—(*Bologna Memorandum*.)

Which means, in other words,—Down with the Pope! Well, but why could you not say so frankly at once? We knew well that was what you wanted, and you have more than once involuntarily allowed it to transpire. But cease, at least, to talk about a viceroy, or secularization, or reforms.

What is most painful throughout this controversy is the double-dealing one meets with at every step; but it is nowhere more striking or more odious than in this matter of secularization. And what is almost as bad, is the silly thoughtlessness of those well-meaning people who make themselves the mouthpieces of such deceit and hypocrisy: "Let those," justly observes M. Saint-Marc Girardin, "who desire the destruction of the great Catholic Pontificate, repeat, on all occasions, that the Roman administration must be secularized; I can understand them; but what I cannot understand is, that any who wish to maintain the Papal sovereignty can fancy it possible for the Pope to be the only priest in his government. If we are ever to see secularization carried out at Rome until the Pope remains the only ecclesiastic, the Papacy itself will have been secularized. The bishop must become a prince, and found an hereditary principality, if he is sufficiently powerful, or else Rome must fall into foreign hands, and the Pope become a mere parish priest."—(*Revue des Deux-Mondes*, May 15, 1860.) This is the language of honesty and good sense.

Assuredly Lord Palmerston himself did not agree with the opinions of M. Pepoli, when he said in the House of Commons, on the 15th of July, 1856, that it was difficult to conceive that a government like the Pope's, having at its head a man who had already given such proofs of his generous intentions and enlightened views, was incapable of so managing its affairs as to destroy any causes of discontent.

But let us go on to examine, notwithstanding the assertions of M. Pepoli, how and in what the Papal government can and ought to admit the *modern spirit*. We come, then, to the second point of the reforms, the *Code Napoléon*.

II.

THE CODE NAPOLEON.

Who first spoke of the Code Napoléon? I shall, perhaps, somewhat surprise those who reckon the Code Napoléon among those victories of the modern spirit with which, as they say, the Pope's temporal power is incompatible, by informing them that it was Pius IX. himself who first introduced the question of the Code Napoléon at the conferences at Gaeta, and that the representatives of Europe, for grave reasons, disapproved of such a reform: the diplomatists who were present at those conferences can testify to this.

I shall mention, in connection with this fact, another more generally known. When the author of the Code Napoléon, in whose person Italian genius and French good sense were united, founded the Court of Cassation, in order to give greater authority to the sentences of justice, and to insure the law being applied in its real sense, he called in the aid of Roman lawyers.[1]

---

[1] I may name M. Lasagni, and, if I recollect right, M. Zangiacomi, who is now so honourably represented among us by the heir to his name.

So that men would impose this code on the Pope, and yet he proposed it himself: it is to be granted as a boon to the Romans, yet its author was aided by Romans in its construction. I will add, that to substitute the Code Napoléon for the civil law of Rome would not even be so great a change as people fancy. What is the Code Napoléon? —a compound of Roman law, French customs, and ideas of equality borrowed from the Gospel. What is the law of modern Rome?—a compound of Roman law, Italian customs, and the rules of the Church, the guardian of the Gospel.

The old Roman law, of which it has been said that it was *written reason*, is the foundation of the present laws of Rome, as it is of ours, of which it forms more than half: not, indeed, the brutal law of the twelve tables, but Roman law as transformed by the Christian spirit, the law of Justinian, a law converted by the Gospel, and breathed upon by the heavenly justice and charity which descended among men eighteen hundred years ago.[1]

Thus the laws of Paris, as those of Rome, have sprung from the alliance of the Christian spirit with Roman law: they are of the same family.

It would not, by the way, be becoming in me, bishop of Orleans, to pass over the fact that the present French civil code was, in great part, dictated beforehand by a fervent Catholic of Orleans, our illustrious Pothier, who served or heard mass every morning in the cathedral of Sainte-

---

[1] See, on this great subject, the memoir by M. Troplong, "De l'Influence du Christianisme sur le Droit Civil des Romains." See, too, on the Roman law, Cujas, Domat, and Pothier, who have immortalized it among us.

The fact is, that the Roman law has governed for centuries the greater part of the civilized world, and is still the foundation of all European legislation. It is true that the Roman law has been modified at Rome in certain points by the canon law; but it must not be forgotten that that canon law is so far from contemptible that its study has kept pace, almost down to our own times, with that of the Roman law, in most of the universities of Europe; it is well-known, too, that all our modern codes have borrowed largely from it.

Croix, before retiring to his humble lodging to collate the Pandects.

I honour and share the attachment of the French nation to their civil laws; but I should be sorry to see it carried to the length of superstition, founded, like all superstition, on ignorance. What! people cry out against forcing even on a child the Gospel, a perfect work of a Divine Legislator; yet they are for forcing the French code upon a sovereign, under pain of deposal! • Are we, then, because we are French, to fancy ourselves the ideal, the *ne plus ultra*, of perfection in all things? And is that code perfect, which our opponents consider as the first reform to be introduced? How often has it not been reformed itself? Even now, contradictions, omissions, and imperfections are to be detected in it. Our good opinion of ourselves should not be carried so far as to prevent us admitting that there are laws, and good ones, at Rome; and not only a civil code, like the Code Napoléon, but others, which competent but impartial judges are far from despising.

Let us here, again, listen to one who speaks of what he saw: M. de Rayneval says, "I have carefully studied the different codes (of the Roman states), civil, criminal, and commercial; they are beyond the reach of criticism. The code of mortgages has been instanced to me as a model one by French lawyers who have examined it."

Where, again, is the study of law more fostered than at Rome, and in the seven Roman universities?

M. Pepoli speaks of the *modern spirit*, without troubling himself to tell us what he understands by the term: is the Code Napoléon synonymous with the modern spirit, so that the latter cannot exist where the Code Napoléon is not in force? The English, then, have not the modern spirit. A remark of M. Sainte-Marc Girardin, whom I must say I consider better qualified than M. Pepoli to define the modern spirit, is very apposite here: "To bring about great and general improvements in society, it is not advisable to substitute the spirit of our age for that of past ages."

The Code Napoléon: but which?—for, as I have said,

it has undergone frequent reforms and modifications. Is it the original unreformed one? or the new one, with the past reforms and modifications? And would you propose the future modifications also? The modern spirit, in 1792, introduced divorce into the civil code; in 1816, the modern spirit abolished it. The Christian spirit had always condemned it. And how many other serious modifications I could instance![1] And, in what remains, how much is there which morality and religion have to regret, and how much which jurisconsults and political economists condemn. I would here refer my readers to the able work just published by M. Sauzet, in defence of the Holy See; where will be found a minute and masterly comparison of the Roman with the French laws.[2]—(*Rome devant l'Europe.* Lecoffre, Paris, 1860.)

* * * * * *

Still, notwithstanding these serious defects in the French law, our codes might be consulted with advantage by Roman reformers; just as we ourselves would do well to adopt, in certain points, the Roman civil code: and I should be the first to desire such a useful interchange of laws, whereby, aided by the united experience and intelligence of various men and countries, we might hope ultimately to eliminate all injustice and imperfection from our laws. But no one at Rome objects to such an interchange. Nor is there any radical incompatibility between our laws and those of Rome. We would repeat, what men seem disposed to forget, that Rome is the country of the two sources of our laws, the Gospel and the Digest: to send our laws to Rome is to return them to the place which gave them

---

[1] The bishop here enumerates several changes made in the Code Napoléon; but as they are chiefly of a technical description, and possess but slight interest for the general, and particularly the foreign reader, I have thought it best to omit them.—*Translator*.

[2] Here follow details of several causes of complaint against the French laws, such as the non-recognition of the religious character of marriage, &c., which I have omitted for the same reasons.—*Idem*.

birth. But, as two brothers, in dividing an inheritance, may not display equal judgment in their choice, so Rome may have chosen the better part of the Christian spirit, while Paris, perhaps, has accepted, in its portion, certain articles of less sterling value. At all events, before deciding on substituting laws which perhaps are superior as to their precise and scientific arrangement for others which are probably at bottom more consonant with Christian morality, a careful comparative study is imperatively required, and each side should depute jurisconsults somewhat better qualified for such an examination than a French colonel or an English gentleman.

But I have also to ask, by what right are all the civil laws of one country to be forced upon another?—and why the French civil laws, not the English, Belgian, Spanish, Austrian, or Russian? Are not these nations civilized? Where do we find it written,—Outside the Code Napoléon there is no salvation? No; unfair advantage is taken of the weakness of the Holy Father. Such tyrannical conditions are only imposed upon him. To what other sovereign do people presume to say,—Accept a foreign code, or abdicate.

Again, as M. Sauzet most reasonably asks, Why does not Piedmont, for instance, which demands the acceptance of the Code Napoléon at Rome, adopt it at Turin? And why does it not endow Tuscany with it? M. Sauzet is convinced that Turin would obstinately resist, and that Florence would be still more tenacious of certain customs bound up with its very existence. It is not easy to conceive that Rome, too, may have a distinctive character of her own, and are we to lay down as a principle that all nations are to be moulded after the same model?

But is it not monstrous to see England proposing to force the Code Napoléon upon the Pope, she who has no code, neither that of Napoleon nor any other? England, with her partial legislation, so unjust, in some respects, as to the laws of inheritance; her inefficient and defective penitentiary system, her poor-rates, and her canker of pauperism—I do not mention the confusion and chaos presented by the laws of William the Conqueror, Elizabeth,

2 F

and Victoria, all huddled together. Bentham has said, speaking of the common law of England, its usages, and jurisprudence, so often clashing together, that it is a field set with snares, a disgrace and a curse to a civilised country.[1]

Not only, however, are the laws of Rome censured, but also the manner in which they are administered. The administration of justice at Rome has afforded a fertile theme for declamation and misrepresentation. For my part, I feel no difficulty in admitting that the French judicial system is perhaps preferable. But I cannot admit that we are right in so exclusively admiring the judicial forms of our country as to be unjust towards others. If we will but judge dispassionately, inquire into facts, and not be guided only by hearsay, we shall see that, in reality, in Rome every precaution is taken calculated to enlighten justice and to exclude any possibility of error. Such is even the distinguishing feature of the judicial institutions of the country; and it is well known that the decisions of the celebrated tribunal of the Rota have often called forth the universal approbation of Europe.

"In fact," says a high-minded and trustworthy authority, M. de Rayneval, "justice is impartially administered in the Roman states, making allowance for human and unavoidable errors. For my part, no decision has come to my knowledge of which the most renowned tribunal in Europe need have been ashamed. In criminal matters I may make the same assertion. I have followed some trials throughout all their details, and it was evident to me that all the precautions necessary as to the establishment of facts, all possible securities to insure the free

---

[1] The laws of all countries have their own usages. Should the queen of England be dethroned because the degrading punishment of flogging is permitted in her army? I am aware that it has been restricted by an order of the duke of Cambridge, dated the 9th of November last: but the new regulations still sanction its infliction upon men already found guilty of certain offences therein specified.

defence of the accused, including the publicity of the proceedings, were scrupulously observed."

Much is said about the rigour and cruelty of the Papal courts, of their sentences, their prisons, and their victims. These high-sounding words were made the most of by M. de Cavour at the Paris congress, and by Lord Palmerston in the British parliament. M. Pepoli has even presumed to say : "We doubt whether there is a country in Europe which, in proportion to its extent, numbers so many condemnations to death, to the galleys, and to exile, as the Romagna."—(Memorandum of October 3, 1859.) One does not know what name to give to such language. The fact is, on the contrary, that Pope Pius IX., on his return from Gaeta, granted the most generous and most comprehensive of amnesties; that no chastisement was inflicted on those who had overthrown the Pontifical government, and that not a drop of blood was shed. And if any general accusation can be brought against the Roman courts, I have always heard that it was rather an excess of clemency than an excess of rigour.

But, to descend to details, what is the exact meaning of these vague accusations? They cannot refer to the penalties inflicted for ordinary offences; murderers and thieves cannot be allowed to go unpunished, whether in the Romagna or elsewhere. It is only, then, political offences that can be alluded to. Well, these offences are put down in Rome as they are in England, in Russia, in France, and everywhere else, only with far greater indulgence. Are people serious in bringing such a charge? Since when have any states, whether monarchical or republican, been able to do without repressive measures? Is all punishment unnecessary, when it is public order that is attacked? Is there a government upon earth against which conspiracies are to be permitted, and which is to be forbidden to defend itself?

Look, not only at what Austria has done in Hungary, but at the conduct of Piedmont towards the insurgents of Genoa; what has England done in the Ionian Islands, and at home, against the Chartists? How did republican

France act after the 15th of May—after the bloody days of June, 1848, and imperial France after the 2nd of December? Is what is looked upon elsewhere as a matter of course, criminal at Rome? However, in fact, nothing of the kind has ever taken place in the Roman States. Enough has been now said upon laws and justice; let us pass on to another article of the reforms — *liberal government*.

CHAPTER XXVIII.

THE REFORMS DEMANDED FROM THE PAPAL GOVERNMENT, CONTINUED.

LIBERAL GOVERNMENT.

I.

THE great powers of Europe have, at different times, demanded from the Pope a more liberal government for his subjects. What is deficient in the Roman government in this respect? Is it a *liberal form* or a *liberal spirit*? Let us examine these two points successively.

1. *The form.*—But what do the different European powers understand by a liberal form of government? Is the same sense attached to these words at St. Petersburg and Paris, at London and at Vienna? To take France alone, what do we mean by them ourselves? Have they always been taken in the same sense at Paris—in 1830, in 1840, in 1850, and 1860? To which of these forms, liberal in so many different senses, is Rome to conform? It is clear that they who are the most pressing in their requirements on this head are neither consistent with themselves, nor in harmony with one another.

But to attack the question directly, I do not hesitate to affirm that free institutions, municipal and provincial liberties, equality before the law, an even distribution of taxes and public employments, the most large development of industry and commerce, as well as the progress of letters, arts, and sciences—in short, that *civil and political liberty and equality,* and all the great ideas contained in what is called a liberal and progressive government, are not disapproved by a single syllable of the Gospel, or a single definition of the Church; it is even notorious that it is the Gospel and the Church which have conferred them upon European society.

I know that these things are sadly abused; but what is not capable of abuse? I know that certain writers have pushed them to unwarrantable lengths, and I certainly do not mean to approve of all that men have understood by these terms; still, however, they are not empty sounds; they correspond to ideas which Catholics, as well as others, are free to accept and put in practice. The majority of minds in Europe now regard these ideas as true and salutary. I consider it, therefore, important that it should be understood that religion here presents no difficulty; any difficulty which exists is wholly political. What nations are able to bear these liberties, in what measure, and with what restrictions? Such is the only point to be cleared up.

But I must ask, can we, whose liberalism alters every ten years, at the breath of each revolution, pretend to impose upon Rome every new constitution conferred upon us by each successful outbreak, or each bold *coup d'état?* As to the liberty of the press, is it to be absolute and unlimited? Shall it be what we had in 1846 or 1849, or what we have now in 1860?[1] Again, whether shall it be

---

[1] Apropos of the press, it is worth remarking that the Holy See exposed as it is to the continual attacks and strictures of every newspaper and parliament in the world, is undoubtedly the most criticised government on earth. If the king of Denmark had thus at his heels all the pamphleteers, the orators, the diplomatists, and all the public prosecutors of mankind, he would not remain two years upon his throne.

that of England, Russia, or France? Is there to be free parliamentary discussion? Why, it is extinct among ourselves. Pius IX. had granted extensive parliamentary liberties; who suppressed them? The revolution. In 1849, when we had restored the Pope, and were discussing the measures advisable for him to adopt, the representatives of Europe were far from recommending him to re-establish the parliamentary *régime* which Rome had proved itself unfit for.

Still Pius IX., on his return, issued a *motu proprio* which satisfied Lord Palmerston himself,[1] as well as M. Thiers and republican France; though it did not re-establish the parliament, it must be admitted that it conferred extensive and precious liberties—municipal liberties, provincial liberties, and even political liberties—as to the regulation of taxes and finance. Yes, that barbarous country, which cannot be esteemed civilized, as M. Pepoli shamelessly asserted, enjoys all these liberties; Europe considered them sufficient; and the Pope not only freely and generously promised them, but has faithfully carried them into execution; in many respects he has even gone beyond what he had promised.

We have been told that the *motu proprio* remained a dead letter; but what do facts say? I find that

The municipal organization has been radically reformed. The ratepayers of the *commune*, along with those who have taken degrees in the different Roman universities, form an electoral body, who directly name the municipal councillors. The latter draw up, in their turn, a list of candidates, from which the government selects the members of the provincial council. These last present, in like manner, a list of names, among which the Holy Father chooses the members of the finance consulta of state.

Great latitude is given, both to the municipal and provincial councils, in the collection and allocation of funds. *It is not the representatives of the government who dispose*

---

[1] See his speech in the House of Commons, July 15, 1856.

of the funds of the commune or the province; this duty rests with an executive committee, elected by the council for which it acts, and which continues its sittings during the interval between the sessions. The delegates, or prefects, have only a right of supervision, *and take no direct part in the management of municipal or provincial affairs.*

Such are the municipal liberties in the Roman States; would Piedmont present them with better? Have we ourselves, in France, more extended municipal liberties? They have suffered with us, like all our other liberties, from our revolutions. Has not the government reserved to itself, and does it not use, the right of appointing municipal authorities in our towns, without consulting the councils elected by the citizens? Frequently, indeed, the elected councils are superseded by government commissioners. Nor do we make the remark in a spirit of censure; we know that allowance must be made for the necessities of the times; but it is very much to the point to show that it is not only in the Papal States that the spirit of revolution has retarded public liberties; and it seems to me but a poor compliment to France to pronounce Italy ripe for institutions which still require so many precautions among ourselves, and are subjected to such strict and jealous regulations.

Moreover, centralization is not the old Roman system: it is the offspring of the French revolution and the empire. The creation of the department of the Tiber destroyed many an ancient liberty, which it was found impossible to restore after fifteen years of French centralization; but municipal liberty is now as flourishing under Pius IX.— for all that M. Pepoli says—as in the most civilized countries in the world. That more still may be done, is possible; but to say that nothing has been done, is a calumny.

Let us now consider the Finance Consulta. This Finance Consulta is a supreme audit office, instituted to revise the expenditure of public money, and to give its opinion[1] as to the budgets, and, in general, as to all

---

[1] The opinion of the Consulta upon the budget is, in fact, decisive;

matters connected with taxation, income, and expenditure. It is a general financial council, whose members are taken from a list presented by the provincial councils, which themselves are appointed in the same manner by the municipal councils, *elected* in their turn by electors whose right of voting only depends upon certain qualifications.

It is sufficient to run one's eye over a Papal budget to become immediately sensible of the efficacious and salutary operation of the consulta. I have before me a summary of the amendments recommended by it, to the budgets from 1853 to 1859, and almost all of which were approved by the Holy Father; these amendments amount to 1,500. The budget of 1853 contained nearly 730 items; the Consulta amended nearly half.[1]

M. Pepoli asks, "How is it that the savings proposed by the Consulta have not been realized?" But if I glance at the tables placed at the head of each budget to indicate the general result of the amendments of the session, I find that the savings effected upon the two budgets of 1853 and 1854 amount to £130,320; that is, one-sixteenth of the expenditure. An equivalent saving upon the last French budget would amount, as has been remarked, to 112,000,000 francs.

Still, you say, the Papal finances are greatly embarrassed. Indeed, it is easy to conceive that they must be: you have done your best to render them so. One thing should not be forgotten when we hear the Pope's government impeached on the ground of its finances; namely, that its debts have solely been caused by revolution. As M. Sauzet observes, "one is struck, in the States of the Church, by a sort of rivalry between the revolution and

---

because the Pope's assent is almost always given as a matter of course.

[1] We abridge, preferring to refer to the laborious and able articles of M. de Corcelles in the *Correspondant* ("La Vérité sur le Gouvernement Pontifical"). He is an eye-witness, whose testimony is the more valuable on account of his great experience and high character.

the sovereigns; the one in destroying, the other in repairing the ravages of the former. Pius VIII. left his finances flourishing in 1830. The insurrection of 1831 imposed severe sacrifices on Gregory XVI., whose whole reign was occupied in doing away with the embarrassments they occasioned." But, not to go further back, look at the state in which the republic of 1848 left Pius IX.; a sum equivalent to £1,720,000 had been issued in paper money by Mazzini and Garibaldi; how did the Holy Father act? He made himself responsible for, and paid this £1,720,000. Notwithstanding this heavy sacrifice, and the increase of expenditure occasioned by the foreign occupations, and the necessary maintenance of a larger army than before, this decried financial administration had succeeded in establishing an equilibrium between income and expenditure in the budget of 1858, and that of 1859 presented a surplus in favour of the former, when M. Pepoli and Piedmont appeared, to derange all calculations, seized on the Romagna, and threatened the remainder of the Papal states. Yet it is M. Pepoli and Piedmont whom we now find accusing the Pontifical government!

The Pope has made three great concessions with regard to finance, which had not even been promised in the *motu proprio*.

1. He gave the Consulta a vote, in fact, as to the budgets brought forward, and a full control over the most delicate and complicated financial measures of his government.

2. For the information of his people, he had the votes of the Consulta published in juxtaposition with the financial measures proposed by the ministers; and with them the Pope's decisions, item by item; which decisions almost always confirmed the amendments of the Consulta.

3. He arranged that the Consulta should be represented during the recess by a permanent committee, in order that no financial measures might be taken without its co-operation.

And all this is as little taken account of, as if it never had been done.

In France, the Emperor Napoleon, when introducing certain restrictions,—serious ones, too, to our liberties, promised that one day these restrictions should end, and the fabric of the French constitution be completed. It is now ten years since that promise was made, and we have not yet seen the wished-for consummation. Should we revolt in order to obtain it?

Be, then, candid, and admit what has been done at Rome, in the face of such obstacles: and if much still remains to be done, whose is the fault, if not that of the eternal enemies of order in Europe? Pius IX., finding the great political liberties he had granted his people undone by the revolution, has again endowed them with such as were possible; and he is ready still to grant others on a greater scale. True, the Roman government, though in reality essentially liberal in its spirit and its institutions, is not of the same political form as the French government, which itself differs in form from the English. But surely we are not to be taught that there is but one orthodox liberal form, into which all the governments of the earth must be moulded.

2. *Liberal spirit.*—Enough has been said as to forms. They are but a means. What is really of importance is the spirit in which this means is used, and the end to which it tends. Now, is the spirit of the Roman government liberal? Or, in other words, does it tend to further the moral and material progress of its subjects? Let us examine this capital point.

M. Pepoli states that " the general rule of the Pontifical government is repression and not prevention. No improvements are introduced, either in education or administration; but punishment is ever on the increase." So nothing is done for education at Rome! Surely this is the most wanton calumny that could be uttered. M. Pepoli is perhaps the only man who is not aware that the popes have at all times encouraged letters, arts, and sciences, more than any sovereigns or parliaments. He has never heard that at Rome numerous institutions, chairs, and libraries bespeak the care which is taken of arts, sciences, and letters; and that, in particular, the education of the poor is so far from being neglected, that there is a schoolmaster in every commune, as there is a physician and a surgeon, who may be consulted gratuitously.[1]

Rome itself possesses more than four hundred elementary or grammar schools, and twice as many children as in Paris, in proportion, receive elementary instruction. As to higher studies, the difference is equally remarkable. In this little state of three millions of souls, there are seven universities with all their faculties complete, and frequented by more than 1,700 students:[2] that is, in proportion, *twice as many as in France*. Yet M. Pepoli dares to say that the Papal government has done nothing for the instruction of its people! No, in spite of these audacious calumnies, which unfortunately are too often acquiesced in, or at least not stigmatized by well-disposed people, Rome is, and ever will remain, the great metropolis of letters, arts, and sciences, as it is of faith and charity.

What is said of the ignorance of Rome is of a piece with what is said of its misery and oppression. The inhabitants of Rome ignorant, miserable, and oppressed! At all events, they do not seem aware of their unhappy lot, and to see them, on their holidays, so full of spirits and gaiety, one would set them down as one of the happiest of peoples, if enjoyment is a sign of happiness.

I must confess, for my part, that when, in the great manufacturing towns of England and Scotland, I saw a

---

[1] In one of our French departments, in which I am bishop, one of our prefects, M. Dubessey, whose memory will ever be dear to me, succeeded, with great difficulty, in establishing a physician and an apothecary, not in each commune, but in each canton; and for this he received encomiums from all parts of France.

[2] Of these, there are about 700 in law, and the same number in medicine. The numbers of the medical profession in the Roman States are about 7,000; the number of those occupied in the study and practice of law, exclusive of the magistrates, is 4,500.—*M. Sauzet.*

ragged, pale, and emaciated crowd issue from the mills; or when, in the public thoroughfares, I beheld those throngs of miserable beings, walking barefooted in the mud, half naked, alongside of those sumptuous equipages, the sight was far from convincing me that the condition of the masses in England was one greatly to be envied by the Romans.

My recollections of what I have seen are too lively to allow me to lend a ready ear to what is told us about the misery of that people. I have seen and observed them closely more than once; I have also seen and observed other peoples: I have seen the Romans on their holidays, in the midst of their favourite sports; I have seen, too, the amusements of other nations; but, at least for dignity, self-respect, and decorum, no less than for complete freedom from stiffness or constraint, no people can be compared to the Roman. Every Sunday in the month of October the whole population drive out to the country; not merely to the suburbs, as in certain great cities; they spend their holidays in the real country, amid the most lovely scenery on the hills of Frascati, Tivoli, and Albano. I have seen all this people assembled, on a Sunday afternoon in autumn, at the noble villa of Prince Borghese; I have been a spectator of their games, their chariot-races; it was most interesting to witness their high spirits, their joyous shouts, their eager applause; and impossible not to be struck by something noble and dignified in their demeanour. The carnival is particularly remarkable. I do not think one could conceive greater self-command and even politeness, combined with more unrestrained joyousness. Rarely has the police to interfere. Their whole heart is in their amusements, but their amusements are innocent: they enjoy, but do not forget themselves. Nothing is more curious or more picturesque. Moreover, the nobility, too, share these diversions; and the common mirth seems, as it were, to create a charming equality among all classes of society.

However, another topic is broached, and this people accused of indolence and sloth; they neglect, it is said, agriculture and industry. I do not pretend to say that the people of the south work like those of the north. The sun demands less assistance from the former than the latter. Still, in the Adriatic provinces, which people now want to take from the Pope, the crops are as fine as in any other country; it is true, that in other parts of the Pontifical states, pasturage—which is found indeed to pay well—prevails more extensively than tillage; but this is a very old habit, difficult to change, and which, as M. Sauzet proves, the Popes were far from encouraging. It is also a manifest injustice and exaggeration to complain of the state of industry at Rome. Every country has its own arts and manufactures. In some, Rome is even superior to many, if not all, other nations. The arts of the goldsmith and jeweller, painting, sculpture, engraving, mosaic, architecture, are perhaps more flourishing at Rome than anywhere else.

In fact, any dispassionate inquirer, who attentively compares the lot of the Pope's subjects, and more especially that of the poor, the labourers and artisans, with the condition of the corresponding classes in most other nations, needs some self-command not indignantly to retort their own accusations upon the traducers of the Pontifical government.

The necessaries of life are remarkably cheap and abundant in the Papal states; the bread of the poor is incomparably superior to what we have in France; the lowest classes have always been able to afford themselves wine, until several successive failures of the vines occurred; and, what is scarcely to be found elsewhere, all classes eat meat.

Extreme poverty is certainly unfavourable to the increase of the population; yet the population of the Pope's states has increased during the last ten years, much more, in proportion, than that of France. I find in M. Sauzet's work, that, from 1833 to 1853, the population of France has only increased seven per cent., while that of the States of the Church has increased fourteen per cent. in the same period.

Indigence undoubtedly exists at Rome; but such is the number of hackneyed falsehoods which have been reiterated on this topic, that I shall perhaps surprise many people by stating that indigence, at Rome and in the Roman States, is much less prevalent than elsewhere, and is more effectually relieved. Still this is but the truth. The numbers of poor at Rome and Paris have been compared, and have been found relatively less in the capital of the Catholic world. According to M. Sauzet, there is not at Rome, as there is at Paris, one indigent person to fifteen inhabitants, and he adds, that "London alone contains eight times as many as the whole of the States of the Church." There are poor at Rome as elsewhere, but we do not find there, as in England and other places, the hideous canker of *pauperism*. Public and private charity are so generously exercised, that there is no need of forced rates and taxes for the poor.

"The charitable resources of Rome are unrivalled. Her hospitals contain 4,500 beds for patients, to a population of 180,000 souls, while Paris has only 8,000 beds for a population of eight times the amount. London, with its 2,000,000 of souls, has only 6,000."—(M. Sauzet.) There are hospitals at Rome for all diseases, for men of all nations, whether from the east or north; asylums for every affliction, for the convalescent, orphans, and the aged; refuges, penitentiaries, shelters for exiles, succour for pilgrims. Another fact which may surprise, but is nevertheless beyond question, is, that the mortality is less in the Roman hospitals than in those of Paris, so admirably kept. M. Sauzet states that "it amounts to one-ninth in the Paris hospitals, and scarcely to one-twelfth in those of Rome."

M. Sauzet also says, "Everything at Rome is organized for the good of the people." Not only is this true, with regard to the relief provided for distress, but also in that no people in the world are burdened with fewer taxes. They do not pay one-half of what is exacted in France. We pay a multitude of taxes which are not even known at Rome,—such as the personal tax, the door and window tax, &c.: there are no duties on legacies to one's children, as with us; the duties on sales and exchanges are much lower than we pay; the duty on licenses, quite recently established, is not relatively the quarter of what it is in France.

The Pope's government is one which costs the country very little; it is a cheap government, in the true sense of the term. The pomp of the cardinals has been a theme for declamation; yet the stipend of a cardinal is far from equal to that of a senator in France; several members of the Sacred College lodge in monasteries, and owe it to the great simplicity of their life that they are able to keep up the appearance necessary to their rank. What is the outlay required for the stipends of the cardinals; the Pope's civil list; the ecclesiastical congregations; the keeping in repair of the churches, galleries, museums; for the nuncios, the whole foreign diplomatic corps, and even for the guards of the Holy Father? Hardly £120,000. The expenditure for the Pope's household, which is included in it, is not £4,000, and his personal expenses do not amount to a quarter of this sum. "The expenses of government, of the administration of justice, of public works, of public instruction, and those required to keep up the monuments of faith and the arts, scarcely come to £1,600,000, for a population of 3,200,000 souls."

Equality before the law is, doubtless, one of the principles of a liberal government. But it is unnecessary to introduce it at Rome. It is the universal principle of the Roman government. "Nothing can pretend to immunity from the empire of the law: equality before it is the soul of all institutions. The prince is subject to the same taxes as the artisan: everybody pays in proportion to his fortune, without overcharge or privilege. Entailed properties are subject to the land-tax as well as others. The lands of ecclesiastics pay it like those of laymen. Equality before the law, as well as equality of taxation, are, and have been from time immemorial, enjoyed at Rome. The nobility there possess only honours, and even-handed justice reigned over all the citizens, even in those times when Europe was still groaning under the burden of privileges and exclusions."—(*M. Sauzet*, "Rome devant l'Europe.")

I wish to conclude this chapter by some remarks upon a question which is entitled, from its importance, to a separate consideration,—I mean the liberty of conscience.

II.

The confusion of ideas upon this point is very great; many unjust accusations have been raised against the Church, through misconception of her principles. Without pretending to exhaust so wide a subject, I will endeavour to represent in its true colours the Roman doctrine on the subject. And, in the first place, if any imagine that there can be no liberty of conscience at Rome, and that, in fact, there is none, they are wrong. It is well known that the Jews have synagogues at Rome, and the Protestants a church. "Rome," says M. Sauzet, "has been at all times the refuge of the Jews, and they called it themselves their paradise, in the middle ages, when they were persecuted with ignorant barbarity all over Europe."[1]

Is it out of place to recall here that Pius IX. gave the marble for the statue of Washington, and sent alms to the Protestants of the Low Countries, during the inundations, and to the Mahometans ruined by the earthquake at Corinth, as well as to the Catholic Irish? As M. Sauzet remarks, "The heart of Pius IX. is not less paternal towards his strayed than his faithful children: it may be truly said that he relieves whatever is wretched, as he admires whatever is great."

But let us enter upon the essential matter of the ques-

---

[1] "The Jews have a quarter in Rome set apart for themselves, where they may compel the owners of houses to receive them; still they may remove from this quarter and live in other parts of the city, if they please."—*M. Sauzet.*

tion. If by liberty of conscience is meant the absurd principle of indifferentism, or the equality of all religions, then certainly it is in vain to ask the Pope's government to adopt it. It is a self-evident axiom that truth is different from error, as day is different from night. In this sense—that is, in a dogmatic sense—the true religion is, and ought to be, exclusive. Nay, more, in this sense every truth, even of the natural order, is exclusive and absolute, or else it is not a truth. I add, that the distinction between true and false, and the moral obligation to seek and adhere to truth, and to eschew falsehood, is precisely what constitutes the philosophical spirit and duty, as well as the religious spirit, and the duty religion imposes. The Church, therefore, cannot be asked to declare that error is something indifferent and morally irresponsible. No; and were she to do so, philosophy herself, and common sense, would exclaim. But while maintaining the rights and the royal majesty of truth, while elevating it above error, and proclaiming it the duty of the reason to search for, and to submit to it when found, ought we to go so far as to force it upon others? Should we impose the faith by force upon mankind?

I answer, first, that this is impossible. To force a person to believe is a thing we never can accomplish: so that constraint here can only lead to hypocrisy and subterfuge. I shall add, that such is not the doctrine of our masters in Christianity, to whom the eternal glory belongs of having founded and propagated the faith upon earth. Mahometanism was established by the sword; but Christianity by persuasion. St. Paul entertained the sublime ambition of reducing all minds, even the most stubborn, to the obedience of Jesus Christ,—*Redigentes omnem intellectum in obsequium Christi.* But how? By violence? No; by the divine virtue of preaching and of Jesus crucified. *Nos autem prædicamus Christum crucifixum.* The divine Founder of Christianity himself had not pointed out other methods to his apostles: *Euntes docete omnes gentes. Prædicate Evangelium omni creaturæ.*

"The truth is not preached," says St. Athanasius, "with swords or javelins, or by the force of armies, but by persuasion and advice. The nature of religion is not to constrain but to persuade."[1] Tertullian, that austere genius, says, "It is not the spirit of religion, to impose religion upon others; it ought to be willingly accepted, not suffered through violence; the victim of a willing heart is what is sought."[2] And the great convert, St. Augustin, addressing the heretics of his day, said, "Let those treat you harshly, who know not with what labour truth is found. But I, who have only been able to see the true light after having been long and severely tossed on the waves of error, cannot be severe towards you."[3] St. Hilary of Poitiers, in his own name and in that of his colleagues in the episcopate, wrote: "If such violence were to be used in the service of the true faith, the doctrine of the bishops would oppose it, and say, God does not desire a forced confession. He is to be sought with pure intention, and to be held fast by good will only."[4] Fénélon speaks the same language as these great bishops: "What is the object of the apostolic ministry? If you only seek to overawe men, and cause them to perform certain outward actions, raise the sword; all tremble, and you are obeyed. In this you have an efficient police, but not true religion. Men must be persuaded, and induced to love God freely, and independently

---

[1] Non enim gladiis aut telis, non militum manu, veritas prædicatur, sed suasione et consilio. Religionis proprium est non cogere, sed persuadere.—*S. Athan.* ad Solitarios.

[2] Non religionis est cogere religionem, quæ sponte suscipi debet, non vi, cum et hostiæ ab animo volenti expostulentur.

[3] Illi in vos sæviant qui nesciunt cum quo labore verum inveniatur. Ego autem, qui diu multumque jactatus tandem respicere potui, sævire in vos omnino non possum.—*S. August.* contra Manich.

[4] Si ad fidem veram istius modi vis adhiberetur, episcopalis doctrina obviam pergeret, diceretque: Deus non requirit coactam confessionem. Simplicitate quærendus est, voluntatis probitate retinendus.—*S. Hilar.* ad Const. i. 6.

of servile fear. Can force persuade men? Can it make them love what they do not love? No human power can force the impregnable intrenchment of the liberty of the heart." (" Discourse for the Coronation of the Elector of Cologne.")

Such is our doctrine, such our principles. If instances of a conduct opposed to them are on record,—if certain ages, countries, or sovereigns, have, since the origin of Christianity, preferred severity to liberty, in religion as well as other things, it is to be observed that this very diversity proves that the question is not one of principle, but simply what is called a political question, with regard to which the fluctuations of opinion, in different ages and nations, have suggested different lines of conduct.

What is certain is, on the one hand, that liberty of faith and conscience is not religious indifferentism; and, on the other, that in this liberty, which in no way affects moral obligation, there is nothing incompatible with the truth and integrity of Catholic doctrine.

I will say the same as to the civil liberty of different religions. To grant civil toleration to dissenting sects in no way implies assent to their doctrines, and does not contradict the dogmas of faith. As Fénélon said to the son of James II.: "Grant civil toleration to all, not approving of everything as indifferent, but patiently suffering what God suffers, and endeavour to bring men back to the truth by gentle persuasion." These principles are admitted at Rome as elsewhere.

But it must also be granted that the civil liberty of sects does not necessarily exclude a state religion, no more than a state religion is incompatible with the liberty of others. These things may co-exist in the same state.

Is it advisable that there should be a religion of state? What relations is it wisest to establish between the Church and the state? These are difficult questions, in which politics have a large share, and which have been differently resolved by us Catholics, as well as by those who differ from us. Are all religious persuasions on a footing of equality in free England? Has she not a state religion? How long is it since she, who now so loudly advocates toleration, granted it to the Irish? How long is it since she admitted the Jews, and the Catholics, into her parliament? A state religion always existed in France under the old monarchy; and was re-established under the Restoration, without excluding the widest liberty of all other creeds. A state religion still exists in almost every nation in Europe. Look at the map of Europe. Which are the countries which at present maintain a religion of the state? If I do not mistake, of schismatical nations, *all*; of Protestant, *the majority*; of Catholic, *a minority*. Why are schismatical and Protestant nations obliged to establish a state religion? Because, if they did not raise religion into a political institution, it would be a purely individual concern, acknowledging no authority, spiritual or temporal, and therefore must speedily come to nought. Why have Catholic countries more readily admitted absolute religious equality? Precisely because their religion has elsewhere an imperishable seat, because they possess a religious authority and hierarchy of divine institution.

The question, then, admits of no general, absolute solution, which will hold for all particular cases. Account must be taken of times, places, and circumstances. But, whatever may be done elsewhere, it is easy to see what must be the state religion at Rome, nor can it be a cause of offence to any one: on the contrary, a different arrangement would be incongruous and absurd. The Catholic religion evidently should be the religion of the state, where is the sovereign and essential seat of Catholicism, at the centre of the religion of all Catholic states.

I will add, that if ever not mere liberty of worship, but an indiscriminate equality between all religious persuasions were universally established, even in Catholic countries, from political considerations, which we have not to discuss here, it would be an honour and a great benefit to humanity that one spot at least should remain upon earth where, without prejudicing liberty or charity, a living protest might ever be raised against the determination of governments publicly to refuse to recognize any distinction between the truth of God and the errors of men, between Jesus Christ and Mahomet, between the Gospel and the Indian fables. We must either admit this, or conclude that truth is valueless and superfluous upon earth, and that Christian civilization can do no more for mankind than pagan idolatry.

As to the practical toleration which prevails at Rome, we can refer to evidence which is above suspicion. More than a century ago, in 1740, the President De Brosses, a man of learning and a wit, who did not spare the Church, wrote to a friend, "There prevails at Rome, at least, as great freedom of thought, and sometimes even of speech, as to religion, as in any city I know of. I have not heard of an instance of people brought before the Inquisition, or treated with rigour." All Protestant or schismatical travellers, English or Prussian, since the time of President De Brosses, speak the same language. Let us hear what Voltaire said, in one of his rare moments of impartiality: "The best answer to make to the detractors of the Holy See is the mildness and wisdom with which, at present, the bishops of Rome exercise their authority."—(Art. SAINT-PIERRE, *Diction. Philosophique*.)

We may recapitulate, then, what we have been examining, under three heads:—

1. As ministers of the Church, our duty is to teach publicly that the Gospel is the truth, the kingdom of heaven, and eternal salvation. Such is the duty, the right, the meaning, the end of a ministry to which our life, our faith, our whole being, are devoted. I will add, that the interests of mankind require this from us. Man needs a light in his darkness, a rule in his passions, a tranquillizing influence in his agitations, which are only to be found in consistent, unvarying, dogmatic teaching. As has been happily remarked, man does not require the aid of masters to doubt. In the maze of opinions which environs him, he looks to us for guidance, and our hearts and consciences alike impel us to enlighten his uncertainties, and point out to him, clearly and authoritatively, the

way of salvation. As far, then, as regards doctrine, we are and ought to be exclusive and uncompromising.

2. But what is the best means of inducing men to receive the truth? The answer to this question concerns not only the nature of truth, but also the nature of men, and the obstacles to their discerning and embracing what is for their good: for God has created the soul of man free. Sublime and divine design! God would not be served mechanically by man, as by an unreasoning slave, without liberty, merit, virtue, or glory. To bring back men to the truth, the best means is, then, loving zeal, free and charitable persuasion.

3. Again, what course is it wisest to adopt, when several modes of belief exist in a society? For my part—while I esteem that people the happiest who form but one heart and one soul, freely professing the same faith, the same hope, and the same love—when such happiness cannot be had, I confess that, though I know the dangers of controversy for weak minds, yet even for them I dread free discussion less than tyranny: because I believe truth and charity efficacious and beautiful enough to triumph in controversy, and tyranny odious enough to make even truth hated; and this is, in my mind, the worst of all evils. I am fully sensible of the difficulties which the question presents in practice at all times: still I take my stand with St. Athanasius and St. Hilary, and would repeat with them, "God desires not a forced confession: it is not by the sword that the truth is preached."

CHAPTER XXIX.

THE REFORMS DEMANDED FROM THE PAPAL GOVERNMENT. THE QUESTION OF RIGHT.

WHO has the right to require reforms at Rome?

I do not hesitate to answer, No one has a right, nor is any one called on, to constrain the Sovereign Pontiff in this respect, or to force his ideas upon him. The first thing required is the liberty of the sovereign. Reforms extorted by threats, improvements effected under compulsion, are neither meritorious nor well received, and consequently fail to pacify men's minds, or to re-establish order. Their only effect is to degrade the sovereign power, to coerce authority; and this can benefit neither party. The interests of the people themselves require the sovereign power to respect itself, and to impose respect upon others.

Pius IX., as I have often said already, is most willing to grant voluntary, practical, and fruitful reforms, but not compulsory, sterile, and chimerical ones; because he knows that the former alone honour the prince, and benefit the people, while the latter degrade the crown, and never content the people.

All questions of reform, then, ought to be treated of respectfully and without compulsion, with the legitimate sovereign, who is at the same time, in the present instance, the august head of the Church.

But no one has a right to intermeddle in the domestic affairs of any government, to exercise a control over its laws and administration, or to decide between its subjects and it. Such was the conclusion arrived at by the last congress of Paris. And even had the congress not told us so, the principle is assuredly essential to the dignity of nations and the peace of Europe, has been asserted by peoples with just pride, as well as by sovereigns, and is daily confirmed by examples. Now, when a feeble sovereign is in question, this principle of the law of nations becomes a law of honour as well as of justice. What! have the sacred words of right and honour no meaning when applied to Rome and the Holy See? Is what elsewhere would be called iniquity to be considered here a legitimate interposition? Are we to call that obstinacy in the present case which elsewhere would be the spirited language of a high-minded sovereign, repelling the affront offered to his nation and his person by a violent and unwarrantable foreign intervention?

But we are told that Rome is an exceptional state, and that it belongs to us all. This is an unanswerable argument in defence of the Holy See, which our opponents too easily forget when it is in their way; but who has a right to urge it as a reason for coercing the Pope, and imposing reforms upon him? Those who disbelieve Catholicism? Why, it cannot concern them. Those who believe in it? But not a word of reproach has fallen from them. Those who want to seize on the Papal states? They certainly have made bitter complaints; but, coming from them, were they honourable or graceful?

But, at least, has not France a special right to use her influence with the Pope, and even more than a right—a duty?

M. Thiers has already answered this question: " France, present at Rome in her army, could not commit the incongruity of herself coercing the Holy Father, whom she had delivered from the violence of a faction. Her duty was to restore to him his throne and his liberty, his full and unrestricted liberty, while offering him respectful advice, for this she had a right to do." Yes, it is rejoined; but, at least, we may withdraw our troops from Rome: no one can call that an act of violence. I answer, that before the war broke out in Italy, and occasioned the revolt in the Romagna, Pius IX. himself had proposed to the French government to evacuate the Pontifical territory: that government did not then think fit to do so: and now, after all that has occurred, the victories of the revolution, and the ebullition of such furious passions, it cannot be justifiable to recall the French army before Pius IX. again requests it. We have every reason to believe that he soon will do so: but till then honour forbids it; at least such are my feelings. If the revolutionists complain, they must know that we did not interfere in Italy to give them a triumph; if England grumbles, let her be told that France did not win the battles of Magenta and Solferino to obey her; if honest Italy, which seeks for wise liberties and just reforms, looks to us and implores our influence, she must acknowledge her error in looking to the revolution for what she can effectually obtain only from the parental authority and the noble heart of Pius IX.

But it will be said, if sovereigns have their rights, the people have theirs also. True; and we shall proceed to consider them.

I altogether deny the charge brought against us of habitually sacrificing, in all questions of the present description, the rights of the people to those of the sovereign. I fully admit the sacredness of both these rights, and would shrink from sacrificing either.

Have the people rights relatively to those who govern them, and ought their legitimate wishes to be consulted? I have not a doubt on this head. To give a negative answer would be to sanction all tyranny, oppression, and enslavement: this I should shudder to do. Bossuet has truly said, after St. Thomas, *The prince is not born for himself, he exists for others.* In other words, the power is for the people, not the people for the power. Bossuet says again, *The true part of the prince is to provide for the wants of the people. The prince who is useless to his people is culpable, as well as the cruel prince who oppresses them.* The essential object, then, of the supreme power is the good of the people. Bossuet adds: God's intention in establishing such great distinctions was not that some should be proud and the rest slaves. Our Sovereign Master has said that he came *not to be ministered unto, but to minister.* To serve, to sacrifice oneself to the good of those who are governed, is the end, the obligation, the sole reason of a social authority. And it is for this reason that it is entitled to the respect, the obedience, and even the gratitude of the people.

All this is indisputable: but Providence, which has established sovereign power for the good of the people, cannot have intended that there should exist in states an unceasing intestine war between the rights of the people and those of the sovereign: we might then expect, and there do exist, regular, peaceful, and efficacious means of arriving at just, useful, and necessary reforms. Ought not the people to prefer these to violent, subversive, and revolutionary remedies? And this is the true question in the present case. Are we to assume that the progress of the human race, that social improvements, are never possible without disorders, convulsions, and revolutions? The rights of the people! We assert them: but are they only to serve to hurl the people into revolt and anarchy, into war and disaster? The rights of the people! But are not those rights subject to the essential conditions of all other rights? Should they not be freely and honestly exercised, without injury to the rights of others? This is equally indisputable.

I confess that in the present controversy no tyranny seems to me more revolting than the tyranny of high-sounding words: all my sentiments of liberty, of honesty, and of justice are fired by the conduct of certain individuals, adroit enough so far to distort the sense of words, as to succeed, under their shadow, in crushing the very rights which they extol. How disheartening to hear the transparent sophisms, the solemn falsehoods, which these great words are made to countenance, which meet with so wide a credence, and not unfrequently decide the destinies of nations! How can any man of upright and noble heart patiently tolerate the injustice and calumnies of those who, under cover of hacknied and sonorous phrases, pretend to monopolize the credit and the profit which justly attach to all generous doctrines!

Thus it is that we are taunted with want of patriotism; with antiquated views; with seeking liberty to use it in the service of despotism; we are said to be strangers to national spirit, to carry on an underhand and implacable war against the progress of modern society, which we wish to convert into a miserable retrogression. I confess I cannot tolerate these odious accusations. Allow me, therefore, at the close of this volume, to offer some necessary explanations upon so grave a subject, which will, at the same time, carry with them the condemnation of the revolution which has seized upon the Pontifical states.

And, first of all, what is a revolution? I open a dictionary, and I find, as the sense which public opinion attaches to the word, *a sudden and violent change in the government of a nation.* The definition appears to me narrow and incomplete. Are we to conclude that sage and beneficial changes and reforms can never take place in a society without violence—prompted by a true philanthropy, and presided over by the discrimination and sagacity of genius? Are we to despair of ever finding in the hearts of men a love of justice and humanity sufficiently deep and pure to preclude the necessity of violence?

Surely Alfred the Great, Charlemagne, St. Louis, Louis le Gros have effected admirable reforms—revolutions in legislation and national institutions—and that without convulsions or disturbance. Again, when did the world see a reform, a revolution, more profound and wide-spread than that effected by the Gospel? The sword was used against it, but it did not resist with the sword. Without causing those to shed a tear whose principles it upset, whose traditions it superseded, its victory was the most decisive that history records.

Still, narrow and incomplete as is the above definition, it is sad to be forced to admit that it has been too often justified by the history of most revolutions which the world has witnessed.

Yet it is both true and consoling to assert, that happy and peaceful changes may take place in the lot of peoples: there may be mild and wise, as well as savage and violent revolutions; there may be honourable and glorious, as well as false and noxious reforms. Some revolutions proceed by sanguinary revolts, and even by pillage, scaffolds, and death; others by the commanding influence of superior genius and superior virtue. The Gospel did not counsel to slaves a sanguinary retaliation upon their masters; yet it disenthralled them more effectually than Spartacus. A true and genuine revolution is the victory of reason, not of force.

Two things are to be distinguished in a revolution—the *ideas* and the *facts;* that is to say, principles and events; and these are not always reprehensible. Thus, to take a celebrated example, in the French revolution, reasonable principles of equality and just liberty were asserted, indisputable rights were recognized, free institutions founded. But there were, and there are still among us, sons of the French revolution who set but little store by such things. What, in fact, they long for, are such social disorders as may give them individually a prospect of arriving at power and fortune, and a prominent part in public affairs.

In their principles and sentiments, Fénélon and the Duke of Burgundy, Massillon, Bourdaloue, and other illustrious Christians, and even Bossuet, in some degree, were not indeed revolutionists—the sinister associations, which have for ever dishonoured the name, forbid one to apply it to such men; but, if one considers only what there is of generous, of truly liberal, and of noble, at times, in similar great social transformations, I do not hesitate to say that, in the good sense of the term, these great men were *liberals:* and that in the seventeenth century, when liberalism was not fashionable—that is, partisans of those beneficial reforms, those wise and measured developments of liberty, which sages have at all epochs declared conducive to the welfare and dignity of nations.

I will subjoin some of the lessons given by Bossuet to the son of Louis XIV.; perhaps nobler or franker language never reached royal ears:—

" Under a just God, there can be no such thing as arbitrary power.

" Since absolute power has been established, there exists no barrier against it; it receives no homage which is not insincere; no sure bulwark protects chastity, nor is human life secure.

"Do not, then, fancy yourself of a different clay from your subjects; be to them what you wish them to be to you; be among them as one of them."

Bossuet added, indeed, "In reality nothing is less free than anarchy, which recognizes to men no legitimate right, and where force is the only law."

The lessons given, in his turn, by the great archbishop of Cambrai to the grandson of Louis XIV., were in harmony with the solemn teachings of Bossuet; and tended eventually to secure for France, by glorious and peaceful methods, the enjoyment of those just liberties we were destined to purchase so dearly, though we still possess them but imperfectly.

But a severer Providence had other lessons in store for us; we were not to be saved by wisdom and virtue. The disorders of the regency, the ignominious age of Louis XV., an eighteenth century of sophisms, falsehoods, and corrupt morals, sowed over the surface of our land the wind of impiety. We have reaped the whirlwind; it was but just. And now, sixty years of sufferings and anxieties authorize me in saying that the liberty of a great people is but ill nurtured under the breath of impiety, and amid the tempests of revolution.

Undoubtedly, Catholicism is eminently distinguished by the spirit of authority; but as eminently by the spirit of liberty.

Our apostles were the first to proclaim, in language strange to the world, the sacred and inviolable claims of every kind of just liberty, and to advocate the abolition of the varied forms of slavery which can oppress and lower the dignity of man.

St. Paul exclaimed one day, "I am a Roman citizen, *Civis Romanus sum:* I appeal to Cæsar." And Cæsar received his appeal. Yes, we may say to our adversaries, of liberty as well as philosophy, what J. J. Rousseau said to his contemporaries—"*All this was in the Gospel before it was in your books.*"

The measure, greater or less, of liberty—civil, political or religious—to be accorded to a people is always a question of justice; but always, too, a question of prudence. The wisdom of the ruling power, the father of the people, is shown in not withholding from a society which is worthy of them the liberties which are suited to its enlightenment, its tastes, and its real wants; in furthering those changes which are justly and naturally called for by the varying exigencies of a nation's life; for, by so doing, it lends itself to, it seconds the operation of Providence. Such changes may at times be seen to dawn upon the horizon of human affairs; genius descries them from afar. Happy the people, when wisdom prepares their way, and virtue hallows their peaceful triumph! Such revolutions are honourable and glorious, and history does not blush to record them.

The illustrious men whom I have named—Fénélon, the duke of Burgundy, the dukes of Beauvilliers and of Chevreuse, Massillon, Bossuet—had they lived in the nineteenth century, conforming to the new condition of society, would have approved whatever was noble and generous in its maxims; and like all the French bishops, ten years ago, would have, with the unanimous approbation of the Church, asked for those legitimate and necessary liberties, many of which are still wanting to us.

And the power which opposed their wishes would have been unwise: its resistance would have been ill-judged, and even culpable; for it is the duty, not less than the interest of the ruling power in a nation to satisfy its wants, and thereby dissipate the dangers of social order. To yield to legitimate demands redounds to the honour and strengthens the foundations of the supreme power, exactly in proportion to the degradation and weakening it is sure to incur, by giving way to unjust requirements. *To resist justice is blindness, not firmness,* says Bossuet: *such stiffness is fatal: what will not bend must break.*

And it is the part of the ruling power to do what is just and necessary in this respect; it alone can make changes beneficially; if it will not, others will make them, but in a noxious manner. Alternate displays of weakness and violence, of license and tyranny, must result: authority and liberty will alike be trodden under foot. Unhappy people! their woes will be unending; ages will scarcely restore peace among them: nay, human means can never do so; the influence of religion alone can seal, in peace and justice, the alliance of genuine and generous liberty with respected and efficient authority.

True, the crimes of the French revolution had so dishonoured the principles in the name of which they were committed, that many of the good long regarded all those principles with suspicion. But it now is time for the hacknied accusations against us to cease. We unreservedly accept, for ourselves, as for others, these liberties, so dear to those who taunt us with not loving them. We desire genuine toleration for all, free and generous discussion for all opinions. But, strange to say, all that we thus accept is at the present moment encroached upon and slighted by the leading organs of the party among us which takes the name of liberal, but which is, in truth, revolutionary and despotic. That party is ever revolving through a fatal cycle of mistakes and revolutionary excesses, while we, holding on our course, amidst the dust of revolutions, march straight for our end of true liberty, as it is understood and sanctioned by the Gospel.

I do not hesitate to say that all that is said by our opponents is injurious to liberty. Throughout all their doctrine, one can trace a sort of pantheism, an idolatry of the state, which threatens to ingulf all else: the individual, the child, the father, the mother, are nothing; the Church is nothing; the conscience, souls, are nothing: the state is everything, swallows up everything. Their warmest applause is reserved for the most complete absorptions of personal entity, the most inexorable overruling of individual liberty; they tell us that this is *the spirit of revolution* which they volunteer to defend and propagate.

Yes, but in their idea, the Revolution, then, is something opposed to liberty! It is not even that equality which the laws of nature and Christianity proclaim; it is not the triumph of the rights of conscience: no, it is tyranny and despotism, the despotism which befits only the first and the last childhood of nations; it is a social convulsion, turning men and things upside down, deranging the order and gradation of society, dethroning talent and virtue to elevate reckless and incompetent ambition to their place, —wafting to a tyrannic, though ephemeral supremacy, in contempt alike of the liberties of the people and the rights of sovereigns, the demagogues, the adventurers, or the *condottieri*, whom their good fortune or their audacity may befriend.

But enough of these general considerations, the gravity and deep interest of which have led me into this digression. Let us speak of Rome.

The Roman people have, like all others, an indisputable right to be well governed. And surely the Papacy would give proof of strange and unprecedented inconsistency, and would disavow all the traditions of its long history, if it were to slight, in the nineteenth century, the rights of the people, after having, for so many ages, been the sole asylum of the people against the tyranny of power; the only free voice which ever defended right in days when the sway of oppression and domineering force was undisputed.

But the Papacy has not altered. We know what Pius IX. has done for his people, with a perseverance which the tempests of revolution could not dishearten. If imperfections still exist in the Roman Government, if every possible reform has not yet been realized, we have seen what is the worth of this hacknied objection. People ask reforms from the Pope, which they do not desire. They ask for them, and they say that he *cannot* grant them; they declare them necessary, and at the same time impossible. Such as are impossible they cry out for, that he may refuse them; and then they taunt him with such refusal, which, in fact, is a reproach to themselves alone. Such as are possible they spurn, or only seek in order to overthrow the sovereign who accords them. They wish for forced, compulsory reforms, because, if meritorious or beneficial, they would not suit their purpose. And whatever he may do, whatever concessions he grant, they shut their eyes and will not see; they insist that he has done nothing. They cannot even define what it is they would exact. They declaim about a liberal government, but they do not venture to indicate to Pius IX. which he should adopt among the many which are in operation; they ask him for what they do not grant themselves.

Unfairness, inconsistencies, incongruities are multiplied: men speak as if, in condemning the Pope, they did not condemn themselves. They exact perfection from him, as if they were themselves perfect. Yet who among his accusers is without reproach? Who has a right to cast the first stone at Rome? Let England give redress to Ireland; let Sweden, Denmark, and Russia replace despotism by liberty; let France rid herself of her periodical revolutions; let Piedmont curb her insatiable rapacity, before any of them volunteer to judge or to instruct Rome.

Ah! you long for a liberal government at Rome; well, I wish for a government free to be liberal. Such freedom has long been wanting to the Pope: leave him free, and he will be liberal. Let us try to come to an arrangement; begin by removing hatred, and love will have liberty to act. Who does not know the magnanimity, the equity, the generosity of Pius IX.? He has now a right to say,— I intended to grant all the benefits you desired, and more; but I have not been permitted to do so: may God enlighten those who violently prevented me, and move them soon to lend me their co-operation, that we may together plan and carry out the great enterprise which my duty and inclination alike urge upon me! All, doubtless, has not been done at Rome; but what can the best of sovereigns effect without the confidence and the co-operation which is his due.

A change of laws cannot do everything. Naples possesses the French civil code and the French organization, yet you attack Naples. You must people Italy with French, if it is to be modelled in all respects after France; otherwise your reforms will be a failure.

I will admit, as to the army, that I believe it was but imperfectly organized; I will even add, that I was simple enough to be glad of it. I felt happy that there existed one government upon earth which, by its principles, could not make war, and which imposed neither a conscription nor a war budget upon its subjects. The Roman army was laughed at, and, for my part, I did not complain. The revolution has proved to me my error; and the brave General Lamoricière will perhaps cause admiration to succeed to contempt.

As to public works, I will admit that they, too, are behindhand; and that Rome has paid more attention to the fine arts than to railways, though indeed several are now in progress. I grant that the journey from Rome to Ancona ought not to require two days; or rather, I leave such matters to persons better qualified than I am. Still, there are two things which cannot be questioned; first, that we never can make Rome a great state, having a large revenue at its disposal; next, that the Papacy is not such a petty institution that it is to be weighed against questions of roads and engineering.

The Papacy! Ah! were I arguing with great and honest souls, if I might abandon myself to pleasing contemplations, and, borrowing the light of the philosophy of history, cast a prophetic glance upon the future—were I not continually recalled to vulgar and unwelcome prose, by the roll of drums, by the articles of journals, by the proclamations of Garibaldi—it would be my delight to anticipate and shadow forth a new transformation of the Papal sovereignty. In the political order, I might picture to myself a Papacy placed under the common guarantee of the European powers, secure in the love of Catholics, and the honour even of schismatical powers, who would at least respect it as a man of honour respects the wife of another; a Papacy unarmed, peaceful and secure; a bright example of peace to all nations, a standing protest against wars, invasions, and revolutions. I might contemplate the Romans as esteemed and honoured by all their brethren in the faith, receiving the homage of all Catholic lands, and having no reason to regret the narrow limits of their frontier; and all Catholics, on the other hand, citizens of Rome, eligible even to all functions there; and Rome, in this way, thoroughly Italian, and yet universal.

I will add yet another wish. There was once a great Pope, who conceived the idea of raising the sovereign Pontificate to the sublime office of universal arbitrator; his idea was frustrated by political considerations, but a great philosophical genius did not hesitate to say that it would have *brought back the golden age*, and no one can contest its unrivalled sublimity. Well, I imagine to myself, or rather I have before my eyes a Pope, whose generous ambition it was to render the states of the Church a model for other states, the most flourishing and free among the nations; where travellers might come from far to see for once a happy people, wise laws, tranquil liberty, the fruitful efficacy of the Gospel and of Catholic piety, and a solution of those social problems, which fatally perplex and consume the energies of modern nations: just as those who now are attracted to Rome by their admiration for the masterpieces of art, and their desire to form their genius. Is this a dream of mine? At all events, I am not the only one to whom it has occurred: there beats a noble heart whom this dream has enchanted also, and which still dwells upon it; and if the ineffable sweetness of that soul is tinged with bitterness, it is that it has failed to realize this desire. There lives a Pope who had one day hoped to render this ideal a reality. He can say with truth,—I was pacific, liberal, Italian, national: I am forced against my will to arm, to mistrust, to resist; evil has been returned to me for good, hatred for love. O my people, my people, what had I done to thee to be so requited?

Ah! the cause of this great and holy Pontiff would be already gained, did right and justice always triumph upon earth.

A vast conspiracy has been planned against him, and everything would seem to forebode the success of his enemies, if enduring success could ever be expected in the conflict against God and the Church. In spite of their increasing audacity, and the unhappy progress of their plans, a divine and invincible force sustains the weakness of the Papacy. God determines, in His unfathomable wisdom, the measure of the sufferings which He wills His Church to undergo, and will proportion the remedy to the evil.

The success of the wicked is often undone by their crimes, and their own agency suffices to baffle their designs. The most skilful and experienced fall into fatal mistakes, and the presumptuous prudence which had arrogated to itself infallibility, finds itself crushed by what it has done, and by what it has omitted to do.

No; the blindness of a people is not always incurable; and one day, when God's time comes, the cause of right will overcome; for "there is no wisdom, there is no prudence, there is no counsel against the Lord."—(*Prov.* xxi. 30.)

THE END.

www.ingramcontent.com/pod-product-compliance
Lightning Source LLC
Chambersburg PA
CBHW020832020526
44114CB00040B/592